Soft Target Hardening

The US government spends billions of dollars to secure strategic and tactical assets at home and abroad against enemy attack. However, as "hard targets" such as military installations and government buildings are further strengthened, vulnerable soft targets are increasingly in the crosshairs of terrorists and violent criminals. Attacks on crowded spaces such as churches, schools, malls, transportation hubs, and recreational venues result in more casualties and have a powerful effect on the psyche of the populace. *Soft Target Hardening: Protecting People from Attack, Second Edition*, continues the national dialogue started by the first edition by providing case studies, best practices, and methodologies for identifying soft target vulnerabilities and reducing risk in the United States and beyond.

Soft target attacks steadily climbed in number and scale of violence since the first edition of this book. New tactics emerged, as terrorists continually hit the "reset button" with each attack. In this volatile, ever-changing security environment, plans to protect people and property must be fluid and adaptable. Along with new hardening tactics, such as the use of tactical deception to disguise, conceal, and divert, the author has updated the text with new case studies to reflect and respond to the fast-moving transformation in methods from more complex and organized forms of terror to simpler, yet still-devastating approaches. This book is a must-read for those who secure, own, and operate soft target facilities, and for citizens who want to protect themselves and their families from attack.

Dr. Jennifer Hesterman is an academic author for Taylor and Francis; her book *Soft Target Hardening: Protecting People from Attack* was the ASIS Security Book of the Year for 2015. She also authored *Soft Target Crisis Management* (2016), *The Terrorist-Criminal Nexus* (2013), and more than thirty book chapters, journal essays, and magazine articles. She designs and teaches graduate-level security courses for the federal government and is a sought after public speaker for the FBI, DHS, ASIS, DoD, and state and local law enforcement agencies. She is also on the ASIS School Safety and Security and Women in Security councils. Dr. Hesterman can be reached at jennihesterman@gmail.com.

"Four years ago, Dr. Hesterman's book *Soft Target Hardening* started the dialogue about protecting civilian venues from attack. The second edition is updated with new content and case studies of recent attacks, new hardening tactics, and best practices garnered from the author's 32 years of experience in the security field."

—Jack Plaxe,
Founder/Managing Director,
Security Consulting Alliance

"Dr. Hesterman addresses the soft target hardening topic like no one else in the security industry. Attackers assess targets to see if they are inviting; the goal hardening is to stop the fight before it starts. This well-researched, superbly written book details the soft target hardening challenge from threat to vulnerability and mitigation."

—Lawrence J. Fennelly,
Security Expert and Author of over 35 books

"One fundamental problem in protecting free and open societies from terrorism is their virtually unlimited number of 'soft targets,' unprotected venues like churches, shopping malls, and dense public spaces. Dr. Hesterman's latest volume assesses the growing soft target threat and provides innovative hardening tactics to protect citizens from violent attacks."

—Daveed Gartenstein-Ross,
PhD, Senior Fellow, Foundation for Defense of Democracies;
and Chief Executive Officer, Valens Global

"Violent attacks against soft target locations are on the rise. This unique book assesses soft target vulnerability factors and provides best practices for handling an attack scene before responders arrive. Dr. Hesterman's background in counterterrorism and commanding emergency response in the military brings a practitioner's approach to this topic, a benefit to all readers."

—Joshua Sinai,
PhD, Counterterrorism Expert and
Senior Analyst at Kiernan Group Holdings

Soft Target Hardening

Protecting People from Attack

SECOND EDITION

Jennifer Hesterman

Routledge
Taylor & Francis Group

NEW YORK AND LONDON

First published 2019
by Routledge
52 Vanderbilt Avenue, New York, NY 10017

and by Routledge
2 Park Square, Milton Park, Abingdon, Oxon, OX14 4RN

Routledge is an imprint of the Taylor & Francis Group, an informa business

© 2019 Taylor & Francis

First edition published by CRC Press 2015

Library of Congress Cataloging-in-Publication Data
Names: Hesterman, Jennifer L., author.
Title: Soft target hardening : protecting people from attack / Jennifer Hesterman.
Description: 2 Edition. | New York : Routledge, 2019. | Revised edition of the author's
    Soft target hardening, [2015] | Includes index.
Identifiers: LCCN 2018035000 (print) | LCCN 2018038034 (ebook) |
    ISBN 9780429422966 (Ebook) | ISBN 9781138391086 (hardback) |
    ISBN 9781138391109 (pbk.) | ISBN 9781138391086 (ebk)
Subjects: LCSH: Terrorism--United States--Prevention.
Classification: LCC HV6431 (ebook) | LCC HV6431 .H475 2019 (print) |
    DDC 363.325/1720973--dc23
LC record available at https://lccn.loc.gov/2018035000

ISBN: 978-1-138-39108-6 (hbk)
ISBN: 978-1-138-39110-9 (pbk)
ISBN: 978-0-429-42296-6 (ebk)

Typeset in Sabon
by Apex CoVantage, LLC

Every day, there is a soft target attack in the world, carried out by the very same groups threatening us here at home. We must fight complacency, security fatigue and denial, wrapping our minds around the fact our citizens are now targets where they work, study, worship, and play. Consequently, they deserve to understand the threat and how to protect themselves and their families. Arming the public with this information will lessen, not increase, fear and make them force multipliers for resource-constrained law enforcement officers and first responders.

In the four years since the first edition of this book, I helped many organizations comprehend the threat, identify vulnerabilities and harden against attack. I discovered unique security methods while living in the Middle East for two years, many which can address our challenges. Prior military experiences securing installations and as an incident commander at airplane crashes, fires, hostage situations imparted the art and science of crisis leadership, readiness and response - skills every organization must now master.

In short, not preparing for a soft target attack is naive and reckless. Burying our heads in the sand because it feels more comfortable than confronting the rising terror and violent crime threat is something I am simply not willing to accept. For it is truly not a matter of "if" but "when."

Thank you for caring about this important issue and being a person of action.

Dr. Jennifer Hesterman
Colonel, US Air Force (retired)

Contents

Contents

Contents

Figures

Tables

Preface

I'm still at the Bataclan. 1st floor. Hurt bad! They are faster on the assault. There are survivors inside. They are cutting down all the world. One by one. 1st floor soon!!!!

—Benjamin Cazenovos, Facebook post, November 13, 2015

Hundreds of music lovers walked into the historic Bataclan concert hall in Paris on November 13, 2015, looking forward to an evening of fun and fellowship. As American rock band "The Eagles of Death Metal" played its first set, laughing and joking with the crowd, ISIS terrorists were circling behind the Bataclan, preparing for their violent assault. At 9:42 p.m., the gunmen sent a text to an unknown contact stating "We've left" and "We're starting." After throwing the mobile phone into a trash can, the group stormed the concert hall and began their assault with a barrage of AK-47 gunfire. People thought the action was part of the show, perhaps pyrotechnics or firecrackers, until the horrified band ran from the stage. What started as a night of fun in one of the world's most revered cities ended in tragedy, not only for those at the concert hall but also at a stadium and several outdoor cafés. ISIS successfully carried out its first coordinated soft target attack against a Western city, killing 130 people and injuring 350.

When I wrote the first edition of *Soft Target Hardening* in 2014, ISIS was growing in size and lethality, but it was contained in Iraq and Syria. They defied the predictions of counterterrorism experts who underestimated their sophistication and reach. When some overzealous officials were declaring early victory against ISIS, the group was fielding unmanned aerial vehicles on the battlefield and leveraging the Internet to spread radical ideology and to recruit Westerners. Within months, ISIS rapidly expanded operations, directing or inspiring horrific attacks throughout the world. Just two months after the Paris attack, they delivered on threats to strike inside the United States with an ISIS-inspired attack in San Bernardino, California. While ISIS was carrying out a particularly brutal and sadistic campaign on the battlefield, its tentacles of terror spread to Brussels, Orlando, Nice, Berlin, London, Stockholm,

Manchester, and Barcelona. Innocent citizens going about their daily activities were not just caught in the crossfire but purposely and heinously targeted.

We spend time preparing our homes and families for an unexpected natural disaster or other crisis, stockpiling food, water, money, gas, and other necessities to live. Security systems and firearms protect our property and the ones we love from those who may do us harm. Yet we must leave the safety of our homes daily, whether going to work, school, church, traveling, or for shopping and recreation. Unfortunately, while we're out living our lives, you and I, and our friends and families are now in the direct crosshairs of not only terrorists but also violent criminals and people irrationally acting out on their anger. Vulnerable, unprotected, high-density public spaces and their occupants are easy targets.

THE PERFECT STORM

A major theme in this edition of the book is the emergent challenges contributing to both threat and vulnerability, creating the perfect storm for the expansion and escalation of soft target attacks. The first factor is terrorism. The rise of ISIS; the re-escalation of al-Qaeda and its splinters; and unrelenting, 40-year-old terror groups like Hezbollah and Hamas present a massive challenge to counterterrorism, intelligence, and law enforcement officials. Despite their best efforts, every single day there is a terrorist attack somewhere in the world targeting innocent men, women, and children. Terrorists use bloodshed and fear to break a citizen's will, turn them against their government, compel them to assist the enemy, or relinquish their territory by fleeing.

We must remember these attacks are perpetrated by the very same groups threatening us here at home. We should expect copycat operations and replication of successful tactics. Consider the Westminster Bridge truck-into-crowd attack (March 2017) and the deadlier London Bridge assault (June 2017), copycat operations mere blocks from each other. In New York City, months later, a truck driven by an ISIS-inspired immigrant mounted a bike path and killed eight riders. We should expect the replication of successful attacks abroad on our own soil. Further complicating the picture: we cannot only worry about foreign terrorists who enter our country wishing to do harm. In the last four years, we've experienced a sharp increase in US citizens who radicalize and attempt to carry out violent attacks. Their ability to stay off law enforcement's radar and their intuitive cultural understanding and knowledge makes homegrown radical terror plots potentially deadlier.

The second factor is crime. Criminal activity at every type of public location is on the rise—in schools, churches, hospitals, malls, businesses, recreational venues, and on the street. There is a steady rise in violent crimes in our country, not just in the sheer number of criminal acts but in the scope of violence unleashed during an assault. The number of mass shootings, where four or more people are shot and/or killed in a single event, are rising. Contributing factors are epidemic-level illegal drug use, rising mental health issues, and access to semiautomatic weapons and accessories like bump-fire stocks, which allow semiautomatic weapons to simulate automatic fire, increasing casualty counts.

Of the thirty deadliest shootings in the US dating back to 1949, nineteen happened in the last ten years—five of those in just the last two years. In June 2016, the Pulse Nightclub attack was the worst mass shooting in US history (forty-nine killed, fifty injured). In October 2017, the Las Vegas massacre took over the top spot (fifty-eight killed, eight hundred injured). Just a month after the Las Vegas attack, the Sutherland Springs church shooting in Texas (twenty-seven killed, twenty injured) became the fifth deadliest massacre in US history. 2018 got off to a horrific start with school massacres at Marjorie Stoneman Douglas High School (seventeen dead, seventeen wounded) and Santa Fe High School (ten dead, thirteen wounded).

The data proves these are terribly violent times. Psychologists are discussing how the public is becoming numb to these horrific events as they "normalize" in our culture. Losing the will to fight will merely embolden bad actors and failing to properly secure facilities enables their success. We compartmentalize and quickly move forward, failing to take the time needed to "marinate" in our security failures, learn, and improve. We forget that history isn't a series of events; it is the same event over and over.

The third aggravating factor is rising anger in society, and worse, the propensity to violently act on those impulses. Jilted lovers go to college campuses and department stores to exact their revenge, killing complete strangers. A 14-year-old boy in a rural South Carolina town kills his father, then goes to a grade school and shoots innocent children in a schoolyard. An angry ex-spouse goes to his former mother-in-law's church and in an act of vengeance, slaughters her fellow worshipers. And when confronted by law enforcement, criminals now step up and challenge officers, instead of running away.

Finally, the average citizen is generally not prepared for emergencies and crisis situations. They don't believe they are a target, and if caught up in a violent situation, will typically respond poorly. There is a tendency to over rely on resource-constrained law enforcement and first responders instead of taking lifesaving and preserving actions. Often, victims chose to spend their last minutes taking video and texting, instead of improvising weapons and making a plan to fight the attacker. For my work, it is important to be as close to the scene as possible to analyze the attack, response, and aftermath. I've spent hundreds of hours reading unfiltered eyewitness accounts and viewing graphic video and photos. Shoppers at the Westgate Mall in Kenya did all of the wrong things during the terrorist attack, for example, choosing to hide instead of run when they had the chance, wrongly guessing the shooting would only last a few minutes when the event lasted days. The military and police activity outside the mall was uncoordinated and chaotic, and responders even mistakenly fired on each other during hostage rescues. In footage from terrorist attacks at airports abroad, people are seen pushing heavy luggage carts while "fleeing" from the attackers, instead of dropping everything and running for their lives. In one attack, a man was oblivious and on his phone while the shooter was closing in behind him, guns drawn.

People also forget training during crisis. There is video from an airplane accident in 2017 when passengers didn't exit immediately, but instead opened the overhead bins, grabbing their carry-on luggage and attempting to jump onto the escape chutes with the bags. Even in the miraculous Hudson River landing, with the airplane clearly floating in the water, the investigation found only ten passengers took their life vests from under their seats before stepping out onto the wing, and most had them on incorrectly. When an engine blew on a Southwest Airlines flight in 2018 resulting in depressurization of the cabin, most passengers had their oxygen masks on incorrectly, forgetting to cover both their noses and mouths. These examples illustrate how videos and demonstration alone won't guarantee people will properly respond in crisis.

WE ARE NOT HELPLESS!

If you take one thing away from this book, understand we are not helpless in these uncertain times. There are best practices, lessons learned, and creative thinking about how to address these asymmetric challenges. Understanding the threat, assessing vulnerability, and taking measures to lower risk is the pathway to deterrence and mitigation, and this book provides the necessary tools.

My work is predicated on the idea that if citizens are aware of the threat and educated to respond, they are less afraid. They become force multipliers for law enforcement and first responders. This book does not present a rosy picture about the terror and crime threat; it is realistic and based on fact.

There are many approaches to the soft targeting topic; the tactician will ask how the bad actor attacked, and the social psychologist will ask why. I discovered both are equally important to understanding the soft targeting phenomenon, thus both are covered in this book. In the soft targeting realm, there are two types of actors: the opportunist who is triggered and acting out of rage, randomly chooses a target and attacks, and the planner who methodically prepares. The good news? Soft target hardening will repel and mitigate all types of actors, from criminals to insiders. It will also make your building occupants and customers feel safer and empowered, allowing them to have a more enriching experience whether at school, church, medical appointments, shopping, or relaxing at a sporting or recreational event. This book harnesses hundreds of sources with case studies, best practices, and methodologies for identifying vulnerabilities and mitigating risk. My thirty-two years of experience protecting and defending military installations, working in the counterterrorism and security fields, and living in the Middle East gives a unique perspective on vulnerability, threat, and response.

I know from consulting with owners and managers of soft target venues how the topic of terror and violent crime feels overwhelming and efforts appear fruitless at times. As with all change, there is resistance, especially when we feel that altering our way of life is conceding victory to adversaries. But the world has changed, and so must we.

Thank you for all you do to help keep people and facilities safe in this increasingly violent world. You may never know the attacks you've prevented and lives you've saved.

About the Author

Dr. Jennifer Hesterman, US Air Force (retired), served three Pentagon tours, commanded both logistics support and mission support squadrons, and served as a base commander in the months following the attacks of 9/11. Her last assignment was vice commander, 316th Wing, at Andrews Air Force Base in Maryland, the home of Air Force One. In this role, she was responsible for installation security, force support, and the 1st Helicopter Squadron, and regularly escorted the President and other heads of state on the ramp. Her decorations include the Legion of Merit, the Meritorious Service Medal with five oak leaf clusters, and the Global War on Terrorism medal.

Dr. Hesterman has a doctoral degree from Benedictine University, master of science degrees from Johns Hopkins University and Air University, and a bachelor of science from Penn State University. In 2003, she was a national defense fellow at the Center for Strategic and International Studies in Washington, DC, where she immersed herself in a year-long study of the nexus between organized crime and international terrorism. The resulting book won the 2004 Air Force research prize and was published by AU Press. She is also a 2006 alumnus of the Harvard Senior Executive Fellows Program.

After her retirement from the military in 2007, Dr. Hesterman worked as a private contractor in Washington, DC, studying international and domestic terrorist organizations, transnational threats, organized crime, and terrorist and criminal exploitation of the Internet. This unique background, combined with experience protecting and defending military installations and two years living in the Middle East, led to her work in soft target hardening. Dr. Hesterman provides training and security assessments for Fortune 500 companies, Major League Baseball, universities, K–12 schools, churches, malls, hospitals, hotels, and airports. She is vice president for Business Resiliency and Education Services for Watermark Risk Management International, a member of the board of directors for the International Foundation for Protection Officers, and advises the Homeland Security Training Institute at the College of DuPage. She previously was a senior fellow at the Center for Cyber and Homeland Security at George Washington University, serving on the Homeland Security and Emergent Threats panel.

An academic author for Taylor and Francis, her book *Soft Target Hardening: Protecting People from Attack* was the ASIS Security Book of the Year for 2015. She also authored *Soft Target Crisis Management* (2016), *The Terrorist-Criminal Nexus* (2013), and more than thirty book chapters, journal essays, and magazine articles. She designs and teaches graduate-level security courses for the federal government and is a sought after public speaker for the FBI, DHS, ASIS, DoD, and state and local law enforcement agencies. She is also on the ASIS School Safety and Security and Women in Security councils. Dr. Hesterman can be reached at jennihesterman@gmail.com. She would like to thank family, friends, and colleagues for their continued support of her work.

CHAPTER **1**

Soft Targets

Because you have to tell America to stop bombing Syria and Iraq. They are killing a lot of innocent people. What am I to do here when my people are getting killed over there. You get what I'm saying? You see, now you feel, now you feel how it is, now you feel how it is.

—Omar Mateen, Pulse Nightclub Shooter in his call to 911

INTRODUCTION

Omar Mir Seddique, also known as Omar Mateen, killed forty-nine people and wounded fifty-three others in a mass shooting at the Pulse gay nightclub in Orlando, Florida, on June 12, 2016. During calls with negotiators, Mateen pledged his allegiance to Abū Bakr al-Baghdadi, the leader of the radical Islamist terrorist group ISIS. Mateen was born in New Hyde Park, New York, had an associates degree in criminal justice technology, and worked for nine years as a security guard—on the surface, an unlikely terrorist. However, as the case study in Chapter 5 discusses, Mateen was unraveling through the years, culminating with his mass shooting at Pulse. In his calls with police negotiators, Mateen pledged his allegiance to ISIS and said the shooting was "triggered" by an airstrike six weeks earlier in Iraq that killed Abu Wahib, an ISIS commander (Orlando Sentinel 2016). Mateen's target selection methodology came to light during the FBI's questions of his wife; he was looking for a lightly protected venue, packed with unsuspecting people (CBS News 2018). After surveilling a Disney park and another nightclub, both with armed law enforcement at the entrance, he chose Pulse.

In the post-9/11 world, the United States made great strides to further reinforce already hardened targets such as military installations, government buildings, and transportation systems. Those facilities now employ concentric rings of security, more cameras, and a robust security workforce, serving to repel would-be terrorists and violent criminals. However, as these hard targets are further reinforced with new technology and tactics, soft civilian-centric targets such as the

Pulse nightclub are of increasing interest to terrorists. But this concept is not new; although lost in the news at the time, evidence collected following the 9/11 attack proved the aircraft hijackers also accomplished preliminary planning against soft targets, surveying and sketching at least five sites, including Walt Disney World, Disneyland, the Mall of America, the Sears Tower, and unspecified sports facilities (Merzer, Savino, and Murphy 2001). Despite horrific terrorist operations against civilians, such as the 2002 Beslan school massacre, the 2005 Moscow theater siege, the 2008 Mumbai attacks, the 2013 Nairobi shopping mall assault, and the 2015 Paris attack, few resources are applied toward hardening similar soft targets in the United States. A very small portion of our national security budget and effort is spent protecting civilian venues. Responsibility for security is often passed on to owners and operators, who have no training and few resources. In military terms, we are leaving our flank exposed.

The problem is far more complex than a simple lack of funding; the challenges are also psychological and tactical. First of all, contemporary terrorism has no moral boundaries. Who could have predicted, even ten years ago, that schools, churches, and hospitals would be considered routine, legitimate targets for terrorist groups? Outrage and outcry at the beginning of this soft targeting era has given way to acceptance. Psychologically, it is more comfortable to pretend there is no threat here in the homeland, and these heinous attacks will always happen "somewhere else." Americans also have a very short memory — a blessing when it comes to resiliency and bouncing back from events like devastating civil and world wars, the Great Depression, and 9/11. However, in terms of security, this short-term memory can be our Achilles heel when faced with a determined, patient enemy. In fact, we almost have a revisionist history, downplaying and explaining away previous attacks as individual acts of violence by groups of madmen, not seeing the larger trends.

Some facility owners and managers choose to roll the dice, sacrificing a robust security posture to provide a more pleasant experience for students, worshippers, shoppers, or sporting or recreational event fans. In a clear example of how we fail to learn from violent massacres and change, take the case of the Valentine's Day massacre on 2018 at Marjory Stoneman Douglas High School in Parkland, Florida. The building had the exact same doors that doomed Sandy Hook six years earlier—locking from the outside with a key, and glass window panes in the doors to allow the attacker to see students and shoot inside the room. We are a change-resistant culture fighting several emotional traps that, frankly, keep getting innocent people killed.

We must remember the choice of target for terrorists is not random, particularly for radical religious groups seeking elevated body counts, press coverage, and a fearful populace in order to further their goals.

Hardened targets repel bad actors, and, as the case studies in this book illustrate, unprotected soft targets invite.

Attacks against soft targets have a powerful effect on the psyche of the populace. Modern terrorist groups and actors redrew the battlefield lines, and places where civilians once felt secure were pulled into the war zone. Persistent, lethal attacks by al-Qaeda-affiliated terrorists against churches, hospitals, and schools in the Middle East and Africa have even successfully shifted the center of gravity in major conflicts. When places formerly considered "safe" become targets, frightened civilians lose the will to fight. They may flee and surrender the territory to the aggressor or be compelled to assist their efforts. Alternatively, as seen with Boko Haram in Nigeria, the suffering population may rise up en masse, compelling the government to militarily engage or make concessions to insurgents to stop the brutality against noncombatants.

Due to our country's adherence to the Geneva Conventions, we will not attack soft targets with no military necessity, even if the enemy takes shelter among citizens. In our eyes, civilians are not treated as combatants and therefore are not targets. Injured civilians are protected, not fired upon. Places of worship are never purposely hit. Schoolyards filled with children are not a target. We are intellectually unwilling to imagine an enemy who does not share what we believe to be universally accepted moral codes; therefore, have a severe blind spot and are wholly unprepared to protect soft targets in our country.

Our enemies see a busload of children and a church full of people as legitimate targets. Terrorists do not care about "collateral damage," a phrase Timothy McVeigh unremorsefully used to describe the daycare children killed in his attack at the Alfred Murrah building. We also tend to forget domestic terrorists, our fellow citizens, routinely attack soft targets in our country, from arson to shootings and bombings. Hate groups and crimes are also on the rise; no matter your gender, race, religion, or sexual preference, there is a group in the United States actively or passively targeting you. Therefore, in light of this complex threat from a variety of bad actors, we must prepare both psychologically and tactically to harden our soft targets and lessen their vulnerability.

Protecting soft targets presents unique challenges for law enforcement since the buildings are usually privately owned and responsibility rests on the owners to secure the property and its occupants. Therefore, collaboration is critical: educating the owners on the threat, assisting with vulnerability assessments, and helping to harden the venue or establishment. However, when I speak with college presidents, high school principals, clergy, or owners of soft target venues about the possibility of a terrorist attack on their property, they may convey a feeling of hopelessness (there is not much we can do to prevent or mitigate the threat), infallibility (it will never happen here), or inescapability (it is destiny or unavoidable, so why even try). Those who frequent soft target facilities—employees and patrons alike—typically believe "It can't happen to me." They have a sense of invulnerability. Even worse, others may believe "If it is going to happen, there is nothing I can do about it anyway," expressing inevitability. People with these mindsets are a detriment not only in security efforts before an attack but also in emergency situations, with no awareness of the threat, mental preparation, or sense of determination to engage during the situation. In an emergency, those without a plan or resolve may wait for first responders and law enforcement to arrive and rescue them before taking steps to save their lives and those of others. The Sandy Hook shooting event was over in six minutes, with twenty-six dead: there is no time to wait for help when the attacker is determined and brings heavy firepower to the fight. You are the first responder.

Most experts agree that, with our newly robust intelligence capabilities, another coordinated mass casualty event in multiple locations on the scale of the 9/11 attacks is unlikely. However, a Paris or Mumbai-styled event in a city with multiple avenues of approach, or a mass casualty bombing at a soft target location is more probable, and will still have an associated shock factor.

There is a general hesitation for the government to share specific threat information with the public, and perhaps officials do not want to cause panic; however, education is the best way to lower fear, as people will feel they can protect themselves and their loved ones. As witnessed in several natural disaster events in our country since 9/11, citizens are overly reliant on the government, lacking supplies at home as simple as flashlights, radios, batteries, nonperishable food, and water. Unfortunately, many police departments and hospitals took large funding cuts due to our country's budgetary crisis and have been slow to rebound. Meaning response time may be slower than anticipated. During mass casualty events such as shootings or a fire, victims routinely are unable to locate emergency exits and they have no plan to defend themselves and others. Furthermore, most people do not understand what it means to "shelter in place" or how to follow other orders given during a serious emergency. The combination of lack of education about the threat, a feeling of invulnerability regarding soft target attacks, over-reliance on the government for help, and lack of first-response resources is potentially disastrous. We must educate citizens on the threat and response, so they become valuable force multipliers, instead of adding to challenges at the scene.

Security training and resources are typically the first to go during budget-cutting drills. When faced with a budgeting dilemma, leaders should ask: "What is the cost for not protecting our people?" Certainly, most schools, churches, and hospitals are not flush with cash and find it difficult to spend valuable dollars on security. Often, they make arbitrary decisions instead of using a system to assess vulnerability and threat, and then obtain the right mitigation tools to lower risk and protect their unique venue. With regard to profit-making soft targets such as malls and sporting and recreational venues, there is a desire for balance between security and convenience, minimizing impact to the customer. Business owners see customer backlash when other facilities like airports add layers of active, hands-on security and it likely discourages them from pursuing similar activities. For example, the addition of backscatter technology at airports drew the ire and scrutiny of millions of people, many of whom did not even fly on a regular basis. Even news of the almost-catastrophes in flight with shoe and underwear bombs did little to persuade the public for the necessity for these systems. Security may not be popular, and security decisions should not be made by consent.

If businesses are concerned about their reputation for long security lines and visitor frustration, owners should consider the damage to their reputation should a mass casualty terrorist or violent criminal attack happen on their property. For instance, the movie industry as a whole was impacted by the shootings at the Cinemark Theater in Aurora, Colorado, on July 20, 2012, at the premiere of the movie *The Dark Knight Rises*. In response to the violent attack, the film's producer, Warner Brothers Studios, pulled the movie and all of its violent movies from theaters. As attendance dropped dramatically worldwide in light of the shooting, theater owners paid extra for increased security to reassure their customers. Cinemark not only paid the burial expenses of the twelve victims but also gave each family $220,000 and covered their legal bills. The company avoided paying millions of dollars of hospital bills for the seventy injured theatergoers, as they were forgiven and funded by the state. However, despite these actions, Cinemark was still sued by the families for not preventing the event, with some decisions still pending.

Another example—the lavish Westgate Mall, portrayed as a symbol of Kenya's future and costing hundreds of millions of dollars to build, had high-end stores and affluent customers who generated millions of dollars in revenue weekly. The mall was completely destroyed in the four-day siege with al-Shabaab terrorists, and only half of the store owners had terrorism insurance (Vogt 2014). Stores were looted during and after the event by corrupt soldiers, adding to the financial ruin of shop owners. Rebuilding the mall was necessary to show resilience and national pride; however, the cost, approximately $17 million, was exorbitant for the country and insurers. Also, the inability of mall personnel to detect the planning stages of the attack, the ineffective response by armed mall security to put down the offensive, and the lack of communication with shoppers and store owners inside the mall about the unfolding events were widely criticized. The downplaying of the severity of the situation by the government and its sluggish, uncoordinated response cast doubt on its ability to handle violent events in the country. The tourism industry, critical to Kenya's fragile economy, was hit hard, with 20 percent fewer visitors in the months following the attack and hopes for hosting future Olympic games and World Cup soccer events dashed. Lax security at one mall sent devastating ripples through an entire national economy and harmed future prospects for development.

Although international terror remains a viable threat to our country, domestic terrorism from right-wing, left-wing, and single-issue groups is perhaps a greater daily concern for our law enforcement agencies. The growing propensity of these organizations and their members to "act out" on soft targets and to step up and engage law enforcement is alarming. The radicalization of Americans continues, with several successful attacks by homegrown jihadists and more than one hundred more thwarted since 9/11 (Crenshaw, Dahl, and Wilson 2017). Exacerbating the threat, the lack of a rehabilitation program means there is no way of ensuring those who serve their prison sentence and return to society will not go back to their old terroristic ways . . . with a vengeance. Furthermore, the threat of lone actors, already embedded in society and isolated, with unyielding determination, is extremely worrisome. Factor in an unprecedented increase in hate groups and gangs in our country, and the domestic terrorism picture becomes quite grim, with resource-constrained law enforcement agencies struggling to juggle myriad challenges. Finally, brutal Mexican drug trafficking organizations are now operating in the United States; cartels are using gangs to move product and corrupting border patrol officers who open lanes, permitting people and drugs (and potentially worse) into our nation. They are in most every state and are now exploiting rural areas. Cartels use brutal tactics against soft targets in an effort to influence the political process and instill fear in the populace—factors elevating them beyond mere criminal groups. We should expect the same type of horrific violence south of the border to eventually end up on our streets.

This book remains the first of its kind to explore the topic of soft targeting. The work studies the psychology of soft target attacks, our blind spots and vulnerabilities, and attributes making civilian-centric venues appealing to bad actors. Next, looking through the lens of past, current, and emergent activities, the research yields an estimate of the motivations and capabilities of international and domestic terrorist groups, as well as drug trafficking organizations (arguably terrorists), to hit soft targets in our country. A current assessment of soft target attacks worldwide will give insight to trends and operational tactics and security failures. Studying the activities of terrorist groups, such as ISIS, successfully and repeatedly striking soft targets reveals security vulnerabilities and how poor government engagement and response can intensify the number of casualties. The book explores new tactics and challenges, and the human as the "best weapon system" in this battle. Finally, training and tactics for psychological and infrastructure hardening, as well as planning and exercising strategies, provide a road map for those who own, operate, protect, and use soft target locations.

THE DIFFERENCE IN THREAT, VULNERABILITY, AND RISK

A few working definitions will help frame the discussion of soft targeting. The concepts of threat, vulnerability, and risk are routinely intermingled and exchanged; the graphic in Figure 1.1 helps explain the concepts and their relationship.

Examining and understanding our vulnerabilities is the first step. We must address cultural and personal limitations keeping us from fully comprehending and addressing soft target threats. Your ability to deter attack is amplified by understanding the threat, and Chapters 3 and 4 analyze the groups and actors mostly likely to strike soft targets. Case studies presented in the book about successful or attempted soft target attacks give insight on how future attackers may emulate or change tactics to increase their likelihood of success.

Typically, after a successful or failed terrorist attack, much of the focus is placed on the "how" of the operation—methodology and tactics

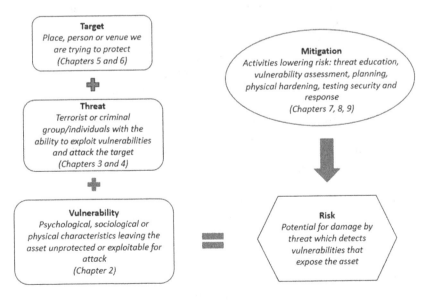

FIGURE 1.1   Threat, Vulnerability, and Risk Model

used by the perpetrators. Certainly, the data helps us harden targets against copycats or other would-be terrorists and discussed in this book. However, to harden psychologically, soft targeting science demands time spent on "why"—why do bad actors strike a soft target? The book addressed this to enhance understanding of how soft targeting evolved and how we might deter, discourage, and disincentivize actors from striking.

Chapters 5 and 6 assess the targets themselves and their unique venues, users, and environs to provide insight into hardening challenges (and advantages). The chapters provide case studies and analysis of fifteen major soft target terrorist attacks since 2014, as well as the Las Vegas, Nevada, and Sutherland Springs, Texas, mass shootings. Chapter 7 is new for this edition, a "what's next" section exploring new soft targeting tactics and emergent threats, such use of drones. Chapter 8 is also new; it explores the human aspect of soft target hardening. The use of imagination and intuition is critical when addressing soft target threats. Perhaps the most powerful statement in the 9/11 Commission report comes from its Chapter 11, "Foresight—and Hindsight." The investigators cite a lack of imagination as a root cause of the two worst attacks in our country's history: Pearl Harbor and 9/11. The final chapters educate on how soft targets are hardened overseas, basic principles, and specific hardening activities, tools, and checklists. This work introduces the concept of effects-based hardening (EBH) as a systematic methodology to effectively apply resources to lessen vulnerability. Using this process, you can assess venue-specific risk, develop effective mitigation efforts, and implement tailored solutions to better protect your soft targets and their innocent users from attack.

This book encourages critical thinking about soft targeting; and those entrusted with protecting venues should actively run "what if" scenarios through their minds while reading. Questions might include "Is it possible my building and its users might be targeted in this manner? What is the one most vulnerable feature; is it access? Location? The users themselves? Our mission?" In addition to this type of brainstorming and soft targeting education, training, and planning activities, I also recommend in Chapter 9 that facility owners accomplish military-style red teaming activities, as well as both tabletop and live exercises. Testing your security and response is the only way to reveal deficiencies in both planning and infrastructure and will build confidence in your ability to handle an attack. New in this edition is a soft target hardening curriculum in Appendix J to help organizations further explore and discuss the threat and assist law enforcement and other types of training.

We must also examine mass attacks that are not terrorism related to glean tactics, target selection, and other methodology. The United States Secret Service released an important report in March 2018 entitled "Mass Attacks in Public Spaces." Between January and December 2017, there were twenty-eight incidents of mass attacks in public places (three or more harmed), with 147 killed and 700 injured. Half were motivated by a personal grievance, half had histories of criminal charges, mental health symptoms, and/or illicit substance use or abuse. All of the attackers had at least one significant stressor within the last five years and over half had indications of financial instability in the same time frame. Over three-quarters made concerning communications and/or elicited concern from others prior to carrying out their attacks. The twenty-eight incidents were carried out at thirty-one different sites, thirteen at businesses, nine in open spaces, four in schools, three at transportation hubs, and two in churches. In twenty-three cases, a firearm was the weapon of choice; vehicles were used in three cases and knives in two. Half of the devastating attacks were over in five minutes or less (USSS 2018). The rise of mass attacks further complicates our security efforts.

This book is a broad brushstroke regarding the phenomenon of soft targeting and is meant to stimulate thought about vulnerability, threat, and response. It is not merely focused on response to an attack, but the critical front work of detection, prevention, deterrence, and mitigation. By reading this work, you are participating in mental hardening, making you a force multiplier, whether a citizen, community leader, principal, clergy, hospital administrator, sports or recreational venue or shopping mall operator, law enforcement, intelligence analyst, or first responder.

We must stand together to confront and repel this imminent threat to our nation.

REFERENCES

CBS News Online. "Pulse Nightclub Shooter Intended to Attack Disney, Prosecutors Say." March 28, 2018. www.cbsnews.com/news/orlando-pulse-nightclub-shooter-omar-mateen-intended-to-attack-disney-shopping-complex-prosecutors-say/

Crenshaw, Martha, Erik Dahl, and Margaret Wilson. "Jihadist Terrorist Plots in the United States." START, University of Maryland, College Park, MD, December 2017.

Merzer, Martin, Lenny Savino, and Kevin Murphy. "Terrorists Reportedly Cased Other Sites: Sports Facilities, Disney World, Disneyland and the Sears Tower Were Surveyed." Philadelphia Inquirer, October 13, 2001.

Orlando Sentinel. "Transcripts: Pulse Shooter Omar Mateen Conversations with Police." www.orlandosentinel.com/news/pulse-orlando-nightclub-shooting/os-transcripts-pulse-shooter-omar-mateen-police-20160923-htmlstory.html (September 23, 2016).

United States Secret Service. "Mass Attacks in Public Places." United
     States Secret Service National Threat Assessment Center, Washing-
     ton, DC. March, 2018.
Vogt, Heidi. "Shaken Kenya Aims to Rebuild Mall and Its Confidence."
     Wall Street Journal, February 28, 2014.

CHAPTER 2

The Psychology of Soft Targeting and Our Unique Vulnerability

First time ever being in Florida, first time ever being in Orlando, first time even being at Pulse Nightclub . . . We went from having the time of our lives to the worst night of our lives in a matter of minutes.

—Patience Carter, Pulse Nightclub Massacre Survivor
(WSB-TV 2016)

INTRODUCTION

Patience Carter, a 20-year-old college student and intern for Fox 29 news in Philadelphia, was visiting Orlando on June 12, 2016, with her two best friends, cousins Tiara Parker and Akyra Murray, and Akyra's parents. Based on glowing reviews on the Internet, the friends decided to go to Pulse nightclub for the evening. Her friend's parents dropped them off around 11:30 p.m. and they entered the club. After having fun dancing and listening to music, they booked an Uber for a ride back to their hotel before 2 a.m. Getting ready to leave, they heard the first gunshots.

Unfortunately, ISIS-inspired Omar Mateen was also doing Internet searches for Orlando nightclubs that evening. After surveilling a Disney property and another nightclub and determining there was too much security, he drove up to Pulse at 1:30 a.m. Just after 2 a.m. he approached and began his shooting rampage. The event dragged on for hours. Patience and her two friends were injured but made it into a handicap bathroom stall packed with other clubgoers. Mateen shot through the door of the bathroom and down into the stall, into the pile of screaming, pleading club patrons. He paused his massacre to call 911. Those in the bathroom heard him pledge allegiance to ISIS and realized he wasn't going to stop shooting until they were all dead. As police closed in on

Mateen, he escalated the bathroom killing spree, shooting down the row of bodies on the floor. When he came Patience, already shot in the both legs, Jason Josaphat, a stranger, threw his body over her, as a shield from the gunfire. He gave his life for hers. Tiara was also shot several times but survived. Sadly, their friend, Akyra, died from her injuries. The Pulse Nightclub attack was the deadliest terrorist attack since 9/11, and at the time, the worst massacre in United States history.

What Is Terrorism?

The word "terror" comes from the Latin word *terrorem*, meaning "great fear." A terrorist uses violence (or threat of violence) to kill, cause fear, intimidate, coerce. A terrorist act translates intentions to action. The first use of the word terror as related to violent acts comes from the French Revolution or the *regime de la terreur* (reign of terror) that prevailed in France from 1793 to 1794. The Revolution leader, Maximillian Robespierre, set out to rid France of the enemies of the Revolution and killed large numbers of Frenchmen. According to Robespierre, "Terror is nothing other than justice, prompt, severe, inflexible; and is therefore an emanation of virtue; it is not so much a special principle as it is a consequence of the general principle of democracy applied to our country's most urgent needs" (Halsall 1997). Robespierre believed the "ends justified the means," including the execution of 40,000 of his fellow citizens. This mentality is prevalent among terrorists today.

The US Code of Federal Regulations defines terrorism in the United States as "the unlawful use of force and violence against persons or property to intimidate or coerce a government, the civilian population, or any segment thereof, in furtherance of political or social objectives" (28 C.F.R.). We struggle with the definition of the words "terrorism" and "terrorist" due to political and social aspects of the government definition. Weren't the concertgoers in Las Vegas terrorized by mass shooting? How about the churchgoers in Sutherland Springs? Even after Omar Mateen pledged allegiance to ISIS, officials tripped over the word "terrorist" in their official briefings. Same with white supremacist Dylann Roof's massacre at the AME church in Charleston and the San Bernardino Christmas Party ISIS attack. We still struggle because we are in deep denial. Perhaps the definition doesn't matter whether an act is criminal or terrorist, since clarification won't bring back the dead or heal the injured. However, it does make a difference in terms of our hardening against the terror threat.

Terrorism is different from other crimes. Through acts of extreme violence, most terrorists seek to advance an agenda, be it political change or religious domination. Terrorism is a crime but does not lend itself to the same disincentives as normal offenses. The threat of prison or even death does not deter. We also must be careful in our approach to terrorists due to a dangerous paradox: the more brutal and oppressive we are, the more we make them martyrs to be emulated by others (Dershowitz 2002).

Also, terrorism is a complex phenomenon. There is no one root cause fueling terrorist activity; if so, we could simply fix the issue by addressing the aggravator and dissuade new group formation. Although the "hearts and minds" strategy is important to pursue, focusing solely on factors such as poverty and illiteracy fails to explain why groups with far greater grievances do not resort to terrorism (Dershowitz 2002). The approach also fails to explain why upper-class, educated individuals answer the jihadist call. Of course, we should continue to address perceived root causes of terrorism, but we must continue to study the ambiguity and myriad factors involved in the terrorism phenomenon.

WHO BECOMES A TERRORIST?

The terrorist believes his or her goals are just and actions taken to further the cause are justifiable. A very black-and-white picture is painted of the "enemy" or those who stand in the way of goal attainment. In the quest for social, religious, or political change, the terrorist lashes out directly either at the perceived opponent or at another target with the intent of bringing attention to the cause.

However, after intense study of modern terrorist activity and the psychology of terrorism, I believe terrorists are very rational actors. There is no conclusive evidence that terrorists are abnormal, psychotic, or have personality disorders. Consider how, in the last decades, foiled terror plots included rational actors who were educated, middle or upper class, and dedicated to their jobs and families. Statements from those closest to the terrorist suspect are usually very telling, and they typically indicate no suspicion the person they knew and loved for years would load a Jeep with explosives and park it in Times Square or fly to an unfamiliar country and detonate a suicide vest. We routinely underestimate the terrorist's intelligence and sophistication—another blind spot. They continue to learn and improve with every attack or unraveled plot. And they use the same tools we do—drones, the Internet, smartphones, and communication and fund-raising apps hiding their identity, such as Telegram and WhatsApp.

TERRORIST MOTIVATIONS

What motivates an individual to join a terrorist group? Jessica Stern, noted Harvard professor and terrorism expert, interviewed numerous members of terrorist groups. When discussing al-Qaeda, Stern (2003) notes:

> Militants have told me terrorism can become a career as much as a passion. Leaders harness humiliation and anomie and turn them into weapons. Jihad becomes addictive, militants report, and with some individuals or groups—the "professional" terrorists—grievances can evolve into greed: for money, political power, status, or attention.

Therefore, the initial powerful "hook" for joining the jihadist movement may give way to other incentives over time. Consider ISIS, which now consists of a few religious zealots, but mostly murderers, rapists, land grabbers, and bored people seeking adventure like the "ISIS brides." Those who were rescued from or escaped ISIS tell stories of seeing no Korans and no call to prayer. An American woman held captive by ISIS for three years states: "All I saw was a bunch of drug-using thugs who had no place. They created their own state here and called it in the name of God" (Walsh and Abdelaziz 2018). Recent recruits actually have a poor understanding of Islamic faith. Turns out, those with a firm grasp on the Koran's teachings and Sharia law are less prone to radicalization. So the group preys on potential recruits with little knowledge of Islam. According to ISIS documents, at the height of ISIS's recruitment of foot soldiers in 2013 and 2014,

> typical recruits included the group of Frenchmen who went bar-hopping with their recruiter back home, the recent European convert who now hesitantly describes himself as gay, and two Britons who ordered "The Koran for Dummies" and "Islam for Dummies" from Amazon to prepare for jihad abroad.
>
> (Batrawy, Dodds, and Hinnant 2016)

ISIS imams indoctrinated them upon arrival in the war zone, according to court testimony, papers and interviews of former ISIS foot soldiers by the Associated Press.

The area of terrorist motivation is ripe for further exploration. Before taking up the cause, the terrorist group member is profoundly influenced. What trigger flipped the switch from "off" to "on" and turned a father, mother, son, daughter, student, or professional into a jihadist? What compelled them to leave comfortable homes and lives for a battlefield faraway, or to turn against their own country? By exploring these central questions, we may develop a type of preemptive deprogramming operation preventing the spread of the radical Islamist ideology or supplanting a counternarrative, pushing the continuum toward our goals. There are three general schools of thought on what motivates an individual toward group membership, regardless of the type of organization:

1. Instinct theory: Group membership behavior is a function of a person's instinct rather than activities that are conscious, purposeful, and rational.
2. Reinforcement theory: The decision to be part of the group is strongly affected by knowledge of rewards from its past behaviors.
3. Cognitive theory: Belonging to the group is influenced more by a person's belief and expectations for future rewards, not possible consequences.

Understanding the motivation to join a terrorist group is important for providing the counternarrative to recruiting efforts and to offering alternatives for those susceptible to the message of violence and hate. Looking at a mature group/corporation such as Hezbollah in total can be overwhelming when it comes to engagement and disruption. However, excavating the group down to the individual members and their motivations could be significant in developing deradicalization tools and dissecting the group from within. In postmodern society, micro-level changes are proving to be much more powerful than those taken at the macro-level.

TERRORIST BEHAVIOR

Individuals are drawn to certain groups, feeling a unique connection at some level. Perhaps there is a demographic similarity among members such as religious belief or shared collective experience. Chapter 4 delves further into this issue in the discussion regarding homegrown radicalization and terror. Individual behavior and traits imprint on the entire group, so with the admission of a new member, the group changes in subtle but perhaps important ways. Group members bring their biographic background (including any "baggage"), abilities, intelligence, expectations, and personality into the organization. In terms of structure and culture, the group has norms, roles for members, and a level of cohesion. Size plays a role in a group's behavior, as well as its composition. In terms of performance, there are several possible outcomes; members are either satisfied or there could be turnover and even desertion.

We tend to act helpless when it comes to terrorist groups; however, they are quite easy to understand when viewed through the lens of general group theory, and we could take significant action to alter their course. For example, we may provide a counternarrative to group members and inject game changers. My work illustrates how we can target every variable and dynamic in a terrorist group to change its overall behavior and course (Hesterman 2017). Viewing a terrorist group through a construct made popular by organizational behavior experts Szilagyi and Wallace is extremely valuable. If we adhere to the theory that terrorist groups have normative behaviors, despite their goals, adapting standard organizational behavior theory from Szilagyi and Wallace (1990) to terrorist behavior yields a new set of truths:

1. Behavior in terrorist groups is caused.
2. Behavior in terrorist groups is purposive and goal directed.
3. Behavior of the terrorist group is learned.
4. Individuals differ, but a terrorist group will have a shared set of values and characteristics.

Therefore, understanding individual and group dynamics could yield new solution sets for protection against soft target attack.

TERRORISM'S EFFECTIVENESS

Everything making democracies great also makes them vulnerable to this enemy. Terrorism is much more effective against democracies than closed societies such as North Korea and China. For instance, consider the free press. Terrorism is an elaborate marketing campaign, and publicity adds to the legitimacy of the group and furthers its goals of creating fear. Democracies believe in freedom of information, providing the perfect tool for group member motivation, recruitment, and garnering public sympathy. Technology also plays a role, inasmuch as unfiltered news is often generated and distributed within seconds of an event taking place through Twitter, Facebook, and other social media outlets, in addition to traditional news channels. A closed society controlling the press and its "message" would not provide the terrorist organization this type of advantage.

For instance, how could a fundamental change in Western media's reporting of events impact the power of a terrorist group? Very much so, since fear as a desired outcome of attacks. Consider social psychologist Kurt Lewin's "force field analysis," a system for predicting the motivated behavior of an individual in his or her "life space." Lewin (1943) defined the life space as an individual's perceived reality based on the many factors at play, real and imagined. In terms of the threat of terrorism, it is important to emphasize the word "perceived" for this analysis. For instance, if a man believes he is being followed down a dark alley, this is his perceived reality and whether a pursuer actually exists is irrelevant. The man will suffer physiological changes associated with fear and panic, and his "fight or flight" instinct will involuntarily take over. Factors such as press coverage feed our perceived reality of the threat of terrorism; panic is induced by the quick spread of false information through social media; and, if the terrorists are savvy enough, a psy ops (psychological operations) campaign may make us believe something false—for instance, more attacks are imminent, they belong to a large cell, or possess and used a WMD agent.

Also, closed societies do not exercise restraint when retaliating against terrorist groups and their members, taking swift, brutal countermeasures to suppress their activity. In a democracy, we believe a person is innocent until proven guilty in a court of law. We provide due process and legal representation to even the most heinous bad actors in society and give them a chance to present their case to a jury of peers for decision. For conviction, the law requires proof beyond reasonable doubt—something difficult to obtain when it comes to the arrest of sleeper cell members and would-be terrorists; they may receive light sentences and return to society quickly and without any type of rehabilitation.

Consider the case of Jose Padilla, former member of the Latin Kings street gang, al-Qaeda member, and so-called dirty bomber. Federal agents arrested Padilla in 2002, but it took five years for his case to go to trial and another year for sentencing. In non-Democratic countries, a decision would be rendered quickly with immediate and severe punishment. When a terrorist is identified and detained in our country, innocent family members are not a target for retaliation; however, in other societies, they are arrested as accomplices, their homes may be razed, and they are punished and sometimes killed. Finally, the ease of moving about a democracy undetected is attractive to terrorists. Our country lacks internal checkpoints and is heterogeneous, with a broad demographic base. This allows bad actors to move more easily across our borders and then just disappear into society. In short, our democracy provides fertile ground for terrorists.

Alan Dershowitz, author of *Why Terrorism Works* (2002), proposes that amoral societies would engage in several (arguably successful) ways to stop the terrorist threat. For example, they would

Completely control the media's reporting on terror incidents and, simultaneously, use the media for disinformation operations.

Monitor all citizen communications.

Criminalize "advocacy" of the terrorist group through inciting speech.

Restrict movement within the country with layered identification checkpoints and even segregation of certain demographics within the country.

Carry out collective punishment with family members and even entire neighborhoods to compel others to engage would-be terrorists, dissuading future activities.

Initiate preemptive attacks against the group. Get on the offensive.

Naturally, this does not sound like a course of action likely taken by the United States due to our protections under the Constitution and our innate sense of justice. However, consider the impact any of these activities, taken alone, partially, or in total, would have in our fight against terror. Is there a gray area? The events of 9/11 led to enhanced law enforcement activity, such as more extensive surveillance and wiretapping powers under the USA PATRIOT Act. The resulting skepticism was warranted, as we certainly must safeguard our constitutional protections and closely monitor any erosion of our civil liberties because this is a "slippery slope." However, in the asymmetric fight against an unpredictable, dangerous, and adaptable enemy, we may not be able to have it both ways when dealing with modern terrorist groups. We clearly need a corresponding modern and flexible solution set. To summarize, terrorist groups exploit and leverage the very ideals constituting a democracy—a primary reason we are struggling to contain the threat.

There are many persistent disagreements regarding the rise of modern terrorism, such as those revolving around democracy, capitalism, and Christianity, all of which may make the United States a target . . . or hegemon and invader. The specific characterization of terrorism is also very difficult to define: criminal act, holy obligation, reaction to oppression, or freedom fighting? Each government agency has its own definition and interpretation, but we intuitively know, whatever the reason or definition, one thing is clear: terrorism is a threat to our national security. Investigating the terrorism phenomenon through a scientific lens eliminates both individual and institutional biases and removes emotions such as fear and anger. This approach also helps organizations move beyond sunk cost, "groupthink," and other unproductive and dangerous decision-making behaviors thwarting our efforts to eliminate terrorist groups.

SCIENCE VS. EMOTION

A scientific approach to the phenomenon of terrorism is perhaps the purest way of viewing the topic. The very root of the word terrorism—"terror"—naturally provokes an emotional and personal response. Many Americans lost loved ones in acts of extreme violence perpetrated on 9/11 and the two major combat engagements fought in its aftermath. We also remember the horrific scenes broadcast live on the then-new CNN network of marines being pulled out of the embassy rubble in Lebanon in 1983, and in 1985, we saw Navy diver Robert Stethem's lifeless body thrown from his aircraft onto the tarmac of the Beirut airport by Hezbollah hijackers. The bombing of the World Trade Center in 1993 and the Oklahoma City attack in 1995 again brought the horror of terrorism, foreign and domestic, into our homes, minds, and hearts. Recent large-scale attacks in Nice, Paris, London, Orlando, and San Bernardino keeps fear alive. Peeling it back and looking at the odds of being in a terrorist attack is helpful to put things into context.

For instance, the CATO Institute studied terrorist attacks perpetrated in the US by foreign-born actors, *including* the 9/11 attack. They found from 2001 through 2017, the chance of an American being murdered by a foreign-born terrorist was 1 in 1,602,021 (Nowrasteh 2017). On the other hand, one's odds of dying from a car accident is 1 in 102; assault by firearm, 1 in 285; accidental drowning, 1 in 1,086; exposure to smoke or fire, 1 in 1,506; cataclysmic storm, 1 in 62,288; lightning, 1 in 114,195; earthquake, 1 in 148,756; flood, 1 in 175,803; and aircraft accident, 1 in 205,552 (National Safety Council 2018).

In raw numbers, using the Global Terrorism Database, we find from 2006 to 2015, the average number of Americans killed annually by foreign jihadist-inspired terror attack was 2.6; by US born jihadist-inspired attacks, 2.4; and by right-wing domestic terrorists, five. Despite these incredibly low numbers of deaths due to terrorism, we spend billions of dollars to counter possible attacks and experience some amount of angst, fear, or even panic about the threat.

Jenny Anderson (2017) explores the interesting phenomenon of why Americans are so afraid of something they are many times less likely to experience in their lifetime than a lightning strike. Jihadists killed ninety-four people inside the United States between 2005 and 2015. During that same time period, 301,797 people in the US were shot dead. Yet terrorism frightens Americans more than guns, even though guns are 3,210 times more likely to kill them. Before the rise of modern terrorism, discussed in Chapter 3, risk perception was an analytical equation: multiply the probability of an event by the potential damage of its outcome. However, fear caused by terrorism threw that entire equation off kilter. Anderson (2017) uncovered a study by Dr. Paul Slovic, a professor of psychology at the University of Oregon, which noted the many factors now affect our perception of risk. For instance, whether you trust the person you are dealing with; control vs. lack of control, with lack of control inflating risk perception; is it catastrophic or chronic, with catastrophic inflating risk perceptions; does it incite dread or anger, with dread inflating risk perceptions; and uncertainty, lack of knowledge about something inflates risk perceptions. Her essay also quotes Mark Egan, an associate advisor at the Behavioral Insights Group in London: "Most people do not distinguish well between a one-in-a-thousand risk and a one-in-a-million risk." Media saturation as well as politicians overstating the risk are two likely culprits for the increased fear of terror attack. The data shows we are very unlikely to be part of a terror attack in our lifetime— but that does not mean we should not prepare, as that would allow a permissive environment, contributing to its proliferation.

TERRORISM'S TARGET

Unlike many criminal activities, terrorist attacks are not typically indiscriminate, as we explore in later chapters through case studies and analysis. Targets are carefully chosen to ensure the advancement of political or religiously motivated objectives. In soft targeting, the most vulnerable place will be selected as a way to maximize casualties—often venues where people will not be armed and will be paralyzed by the element of surprise. Perhaps it is helpful to think of terrorist targets in four categories: symbolic, functional, logistic, and expressive (Drake 1998).

Terrorists attack symbolic targets to elicit a psychological reaction, whether the assassination of a key political figure or the physical penetration or destruction of a government building or monument. Functional targets are obstacles to the success of the terrorist or group, such as the military, security officers, or opposing groups. Logistical targets are hit for financial profit, to obtain money or goods such as weapons, fuel, or food. Kidnapping is a lucrative business for criminals and terrorists, and wealthy executives and their family members are logistical targets. Expressive targets are those hit as a response to emotion, for example, an attack on a lone American working for a nongovernmental agency in rural areas. Expressive targets are not part of an overarching strategy and will not result in any political gain to the terrorist group. Usually, the victim is simply in the wrong place at the wrong time. Soft targets are a new addition to the playbook, complementing all of the preceding activities.

SOFT TARGET VIOLENCE: A COLLECTIVE TWENTY-FIRST-CENTURY BLACK SWAN

The black swan theory is a metaphor describing a surprising event with major impact thought to be impossible, but then rationalized by observers in hindsight. The combination of low predictability and significant impact of black swan events is central to this book's narrative concerning the asymmetric tactic of soft targeting.

In the first century AD, a Roman poet, Juvenal, called something presumed not to exist or deemed impossible a "black swan." Interestingly, Dutch explorer Willem de Vlamingh spotted a black swan in Australia in the 1600s while traveling through the area. The discovery of this creature, thought to be nonexistent, was deemed the "black swan problem" and introduced the concept of "falsifiability" to the scientific world. Scientists soon realized what they thought was unequivocally true might be proven otherwise. Modern black swan events were characterized by Nassim Nicholas Taleb in his 2010 book *The Black Swan: The Impact of the Highly Improbable*. Taleb regards almost all exceptional scientific discoveries, historical events, and artistic accomplishments as black swans, or undirected and unpredicted occurrences. The rise of Adolph Hitler, the personal computer, the Internet, and the September 11 attacks are Taleb's examples of black swans. Taleb's comments in a *New York Times* article are important to frame our discussion regarding the social networking phenomenon:

> What we call here a Black Swan (and capitalize it) is an event with the following three attributes. First, it is an outlier, as it lies outside the realm of regular expectations, because nothing in the past can convincingly point to its possibility. Second, it carries an extreme impact. Third, in spite of its outlier status, human nature makes us concoct explanations for its occurrence after the fact, making it explainable and predictable.
>
> I stop and summarize the triplet: rarity, extreme impact, and retrospective (though not prospective) predictability. A small number of Black Swans explains almost everything in our world, from the success of ideas and religions, to the dynamics of historical events, to elements of our own personal lives.

Major axioms of the black swan theory include:

1. The disproportionate role of high-impact, hard-to-predict, and rare events beyond the realm of normal expectations in history, science, finance, and technology
2. The noncomputability of the probability of the consequential rare events using scientific methods (owing to the very nature of small probabilities)
3. The psychological biases making people individually and collectively blind to uncertainty and unaware of the massive role of the rare event in historical affairs

The theory refers only to unexpected events of large magnitude and consequence and their dominant role in history. Such events, considered extreme outliers, collectively play vastly larger roles than regular, predictable occurrences. In short, these are game changers, such as the rise of modern terrorist groups, cartels, and transnational organized crime groups. The advent of the domestic terrorist, a citizen who turns on his or her own government and kills innocent civilians to further his or her cause, might be considered a black swan.

Black swan logic makes what you do not know far more relevant than what you do know. Therefore, in the counterterrorism business, we should be exploring "anti-knowledge" or what we do not know and what we do not expect from the enemy. In the security realm, we typically use specific data to make strategic decisions, instead of stepping back and viewing the entire issue with all of its complexities and changing environmental factors. We expect groups to engage in a similar manner as they have in the past, and we harden facilities and screen people accordingly. Unfortunately, we expend an inordinate amount of resources to prevent history from repeating itself, while the groups and individuals with a violent ideology work to hit us from an unexpected or asymmetric angle. As we discuss in Chapter 3, this resource drain and diversion of focus, effort, and resources is exactly what enemies hope to elicit, and we often play right into their hands.

The story of the Maginot Line shows how we are conditioned in this manner. After World War I, the French built a wall along the previous German invasion route to prevent re-invasion. However, Hitler simply went around the wall and marched into France. Over-reliance on past events as a predictor of future action, underestimating the creativity of the enemy, and the inability to think "outside the box" clearly leave us vulnerable. In black swan vernacular as related to terrorist events, history does not crawl, it jumps.

THE INTERNET AS A TOOL

Similarly, with the black swans of rapid technological and communication advances, we were wholly unprepared for how social networking would change our society, the definition of "community," and the manner in which people communicate. The Internet is a virtual world where people can be compelled (even unconsciously) to change their opinions, join movements, and even take up arms for a new, captivating cause. These new members are not forced to join; they are volunteers, who always make the best recruits in both licit and illicit groups. Sitting in their comfortable middle-class homes or at the local Wi-Fi–enabled coffee house, they do not have to be suffering, hungry, or uneducated to join in the dialogue. The impact of the Internet in the crime and terror realm was unforeseen and perhaps marginalized with the excitement of rapid growth, social networking sites, and virtual banking and commerce. Every piece of technology we enjoy—every application making our life easier or helps us communicate—is exploited by bad actors. Later in the book, we'll discuss the 6,000 pieces of propaganda ISIS put on the Internet in 2017 and how this impacts our war on terror.

The main product of the terrorism marketing campaign is fear; however, by-products include recruitment, empathy seeking, and fundraising. As with all marketing operations, terrorism is meant to shift the public center of gravity through use of symbolism or themes, and these techniques can be overt or covert. We must also remember that, for many groups, this is a long crusade; the enemy is patient and thinks in terms of millennia, not years. Our children's children may indeed be challenged by the same terrorism and transnational crime issues with which we struggle today, and a quick fix is simply not possible.

Every day I scan numerous websites in an open-source intelligence collection activity supporting research, lecture, and writing efforts. In the spirit of "know thy enemy," an axiom of the great war strategist Sun Tzu, I also access current web caches of various jihadi sites and the pages of domestic and single interest terror groups. Often it is just the same day-to-day rhetoric; however, I have sensed a shift from outright violent threats to a more subtle, understated threat. For instance, Facebook pages appearing friendly and inviting will pull in the curious and then redirect them elsewhere for further discussion on edgier topics. Of course, many groups do not sugarcoat the message or their hate for the United States and also use the open forums to blatantly spread false information and propaganda. With the Internet, they are literally "hiding in plain sight" and, indeed, why should groups go underground when their Internet activities are perfectly legal? For a more in-depth examination of the exploitation of the Internet for recruiting, clandestine communication, and funding, please see my previous work on the terrorist–criminal nexus (Hesterman 2013).

The perpetrators of recent shooting events signaled their intentions in advance on social networking websites, or in the case of Omar Mateen, posted during their rampage. On the night before he killed fifteen students and teachers at his former high school in Germany, Tim Kretschmer blatantly chatted on the Internet about his intention to commit mass murder. He wrote (Davies and Pidd 2009):

> I've had enough. Everybody's laughing at me. No one sees my potential. I'm serious. I have weapons and I will go to my former school in the morning and have a proper barbecue. Maybe I'll get away. Listen out. You will hear of me tomorrow. Remember the place's name: Winnenden.

Website administrators and users could become force multipliers if trained on what to look for, how to engage, and how, what, and where to report provocative comments such as Kretschmer's. Fortunately, private citizens are taking things into their own hands and reporting violent posts on social media. In 2018, several school shootings were prevented in this manner.

SOFT TARGETING MOTIVATIONS

We need to understand a group's or individual's motives to attack a soft target and what gains may be reaped from the event. The case studies in the book discuss specific operations; however, there are similar motivations and goals crossing all brands of terrorist and criminal groups:

Easier, cheaper, and short planning cycle. Consider the Kenya Westgate Mall attack planning cycle was just one year and executed with a small team of shooters with basic weaponry, whereas it took seven to eight years to plan the complex attacks of 9/11. The scope of the events differed, of course, with the events of 9/11 killing thousands and drawing the United States and its allies into protracted, expensive, and deadly wars in Afghanistan, Iraq, and elsewhere. However, even small attacks tear at the fabric of a nation, sowing seeds of fear and forcing expensive security measures.

Increased likelihood of success. The probability of a successful attack against an unprotected soft target is higher than against fortified hard targets.

Credibility. A successful attack garners instant status for the group or cause.

Recruiting value. Sympathizers are more likely to join the cause of a "winner."

Flexing muscle. In the past ten years, US government officials have repeatedly stated al-Qaeda (AQ) was diminished and dying. Many thought the splintering was a sign of decline, yet the AQ 1.0 and 2.0 groups are successfully attacking and inspiring attacks. Al-Qaeda is resurgent and poses a significant threat to the US. Even small soft target attacks show the group is thriving and viable.

Compensating for weakness. If a group does not have the resources to hit a hard target, or ongoing planning is moving too slowly, they can quickly hit a soft target.

As a last gasp. If a group is declining, an easier soft target attack could be the last hope to recruit and gain credibility.

Backed into a corner. When a group is trapped, the situation becomes extraordinarily dangerous. Consider the Liberation Tigers of Tamil Eelam (LTTE) terrorist group case study in Chapter 7: when the government corralled the group and boxed them into one area of Sri Lanka, LTTE took 100,000 civilians hostage on a beach and used them as human shields. This scenario is especially worrisome if dealing with a desperate religious group with apocalyptic intentions; its members may field their best weapon, possibly a WMD (weapon of mass destruction).

Test a new strategy, tactic, or weapon. Hitting a soft target could be a dry run for a group honing an operation. It also could be used to assess emergency response and crowd evacuation procedures and to gather points for a later, larger attack including secondary or tertiary devices and possibly chemical, biological, or radiation agents.

Fund-raising. Soft target attacks may result in kidnapping and hostage taking for ransom or in selling humans into slavery, such as the tragic case of hundreds of schoolgirls taken from their dormitory in Nigeria by Boko Haram. Piracy of a cruise ship or ferry could also quickly raise tens of millions of dollars.

Quickly damage a market. As witnessed with the airline industry after 9/11, the movie theater industry after the shootings in Aurora, Colorado, and attacks against resorts and hotel chains in Egypt, a soft target attack will immediately cause fear and avoidance of similar venues.

Delegitimize a government. A successful soft target attack immediately casts doubt on the government's ability to protect its people, who will scrutinize intelligence operations, law enforcement, and first-response efforts. We already have a conspiracy theory-fueled public, with tens of thousands of "truthers" who not only distrust officials but also believe events such as 9/11 and the Boston Marathon bombing were government "false flag" operations to cause fear and maintain tight control on citizens.

Cause political instability. If properly timed, a soft target attack could change the course of an election and history. The group could get a candidate more favorable to its cause into office or repel voters from polling places. This type of political pressure routinely happens in Mexico with the drug cartels, which violently engage prior to and during elections to shape outcomes by killing mayors, police chiefs, and political candidates.

Make a country look weak internationally. A soft target attack such as the Pulse nightclub bombing makes the country appear weak and unable to protect its citizens. Terrorists appear to be able to attack at will and plan under the radar. Even worse is the "known wolf" that had prior contact with law enforcement. The ability for a country under attack to project power in the world is diminished; a country unable to protect its own people has difficulty convincing it can protect others.

To attain global media coverage. A soft target attack will receive coverage in the 24/7 news cycle, such as the live television coverage of the Beslan massacre, the Mumbai attacks, and the events of 9/11. If the group wants immortality, press coverage is the best course of action, as the images of destruction and suffering are shown over and over. Many groups will broadcast on social media, even using Twitter during an event to air their grievances and inject more fear with threats of further attacks. Al-Shabaab terrorists were using Twitter throughout the attack on the Westgate Mall. Omar Mateen posted live on Facebook from his massacre at Pulse.

A **target-rich environment.** Soft targets abound, and groups can quickly bring a city to its knees, for example, the Mumbai attack where a hospital, hotels, trains, and a train station were simultaneously targeted. In the Paris and Brussels attacks, terrorists struck targets in a staggered manner instead of simultaneously, to add the element of surprise, instill massive fear in the public, and thwart first-response operations. Even in a small town, terrorists could hit a school, church, and mall all at once, or hit one and then the next in a campaign of terror. If the objective were to seize land and property, or even an entire small town, this type of timed multi-target operation may work in the United States as it has for the drug cartels in Mexico.

Psychological fear. A successful soft target attack wreaks havoc on the psyche of citizens. Perhaps nothing is worse than fear for the safety of your family, especially children. Specifically targeting children in soft target attacks fuels the terror multiplier effect (TME). Some experts believe Post Traumatic Stress Syndrome affects people far removed from the attack location, as they can access videos taken from the scene and experience dread and fear. The constant news cycle feeds this type of stress.

Make a domestic issue international. Hitting a soft target is a way to vault local or regional issues to the national scene, a hope of special-interest domestic terrorists such as those belonging to animal and ecorights groups. For instance, the Dakota Access pipeline protests gained international attention, as did the right-wing rally in Charlottesville that turned violent.

So, why hit soft targets? After considering the potential benefits, the answer is obvious: why not?

OUR UNIQUE VULNERABILITY

Perhaps the softest, most vulnerable target is you—the human being. Due to our culture and history, Americans tend to cast a psychological blind eye toward soft targets. In the aftermath of World War II, which saw the mass slaughter of innocent civilians during combat operations by adversaries, the US government helped establish the 1949 Geneva Conventions, which protect noncombatants and civilians in and around the war zone. Therefore, our military doctrine is never to hit a soft target, even if the "most wanted" terrorist in the world is attending a religious service, visiting his child at school, or having a medical treatment. Instead, we will patiently wait for another opportunity to minimize collateral civilian casualties. We see the world through this lens and believe (or hope) others will employ the same restraint.

Unfortunately, our enemies, foreign and domestic, do not play by the same rules. The new battlefields are in neighborhoods and communities, and civilians are the target. Terrorists have made this very clear in the United States with asymmetric attacks planned against civilian-rich, non-military/nongovernment environments such as the Boston Marathon and the San Bernardino Christmas party attacks. We routinely underestimate the sophistication of terrorists and criminals as they constantly exploit our vulnerabilities and naiveties to increase the chances of operational success. Also, for bad actors, there is no such thing as a "failed attack": every event is a learning experience. The free press typically overshares information about why the operation was successful or unsuccessful, and would-be attackers worldwide adjust their tactics. Professionals who fail to understand these emergent factors are at a disadvantage when protecting soft target venues, as we have transitioned to an entirely new security environment and paradigm in the last few years.

Hard targets including government buildings, military installations, and buildings with symbolic significance such as monuments were further hardened over the years. Bad actors know hitting them not only will be more difficult but also likely result in less shock factor to the American public. For instance, mass shootings on military installations such as the Navy Yard in Washington, DC, in 2013, and Fort Hood, Texas, in 2009, usually garner less public sympathy and outcry than those committed in schools, restaurants, and churches. Perhaps the occupants of government facilities are considered legitimate targets due to their profession. This type of soft target rationalization pushes the would-be terrorist to strike elsewhere, to areas where the shock, outrage, and fear factors will be higher.

WHAT DO WE MOST FEAR?

Although typically avoided, we need to "go there" and desensitize when it comes to soft targets. What do we most fear? It seems the generations before us were much more adept at facing their collective fears and taking steps to educate the populace, including children. The employment of the atom bomb in 1945 and the Soviet Union's attainment of nuclear capability in 1949 transformed the meaning of civil defense in the United States. During the early days of the Cold War, the government produced a video teaching children self-protection from a nuclear attack; the children practiced "duck and cover" exercises and were prepared to take care of themselves during attack if adults were not around (Mauer 1951). New York City issued 2.5 million identification bracelets, or dog tags, for students to wear at all times, with the unspoken purpose to help identify children who were lost or killed in a nuclear explosion. Over time and with the fall of Communism, the fear of nuclear attack waned along with civil defense exercises and preparation for WMD events. For decades, the government was quiet about threat and individual response.

After the attacks on 9/11, the Department of Homeland Security (DHS) attempted to re-engage in this realm and educate members of the public on how to protect themselves. For instance, on February 10, 2003, in response to intelligence information indicating terrorists were planning a WMD attack in the United States, DHS issued an advisory directing Americans to prepare for a biological, chemical, or radiological terrorist attack by assembling a disaster supply kit. Shelves were cleared of duct tape and plastic to seal homes and offices against nuclear, chemical, and biological contaminants. The DHS eventually faced ridicule and the advisory was jokingly referred to by comedians as "duct and cover." Certainly, this type of response by the public should be factored into future advisories.

What types of trauma are experienced after an attack like those perpetrated on 9/11? Typically, there are changes of behavior; for instance, a community or nation may pull together during a mass casualty situation, putting differences aside for the greater good. However, an attack may cause ruptures in relationships and lead to suspicions and poor treatment of ethnic or religious minority groups, similar to what Japanese Americans experienced during World War II after the Pearl Harbor attacks and what the American Muslim community suffers today. In Kenya, following the Westgate Mall attacks by the Somali-driven al-Shabaab, many Somali citizens were rounded up in the country and deported. It makes no sense that we are fighting in multiple countries to protect Muslims from radical Islamists, yet we marginalize them in our country. This behavior and rhetoric divides us, and feeds bin Laden's dream for our "death by 1,000 cuts."

When a domestic terrorist attacks fellow citizens, a sense of denial typically sets in and we search for some type of foreign influence to explain the behavior. This reaction could hinder the investigative process, as it did immediately following the Oklahoma City bombing in 1995. The World Trade Center bombing executed by al-Qaeda was just two years before, so the immediate assessment was the Murrah Federal Building had undergone a jihadist attack. I was working at the Pentagon at the time and vividly recall the discussions and assumptions being made by military planners. Naturally, they were influenced, as were all Americans, by the press, which fueled the fire with inflammatory baseless statements:

"The betting here is on Middle East terrorists," stated CBS News's Jim Stewart just hours after the blast.

"The fact that it was such a powerful bomb in Oklahoma City immediately drew investigators to consider deadly parallels that all have roots in the Middle East," piled on ABC's John McWethy.

"Knowing that the car bomb indicates Middle Eastern terrorists at work, it's safe to assume that their goal is to promote free-floating fear and a measure of anarchy, thereby disrupting American life," the New York Post editorialized on April 20. "In due course, we'll learn which particular faction the terrorists identified with—Hamas? Hezbollah? the Islamic Jihad?—and whether or not the perpetrators leveled specific demands."

"It has every single earmark of the Islamic car-bombers of the Middle East," wrote syndicated columnist Georgie Anne Geyer in the Chicago Tribune on April 21.

Also on April 21, according to the New York Times's A. M. Rosenthal, "Whatever we are doing to destroy Mideast terrorism, the chief terrorist threat against Americans, has not been working."

Even after the FBI released sketches of the suspects on April 24, the news media still would not let go of their assumptions. Thankfully, investigators found the VIN number from the vehicle used in the bombing at the scene and led to former soldier McVeigh, pulled over for speeding in a remarkable coincidence. Otherwise, the attack could have led us down the wrong path diplomatically and, possibly, militarily.

HOW SHOULD WE RESPOND?

A measured response to a terror event would be the best approach, although this is nearly impossible due to the proliferation of the Internet and 24/7 news broadcasts. As analysts and investigators, we need to avoid the "light pollution" obscuring the true threat as people gravitate and cluster around groundless theories, as they did immediately following the Murrah Building explosion. Fighting this clustering activity and being a skeptical empiricist is critical, as well as valuing and encouraging out-of-the-box thinkers who may identify and prevent a looming black swan event that will hit the "reset" button in history. With regard to data analysis, any statistician will caution the tendency towards confirmation and distortion bias when looking at a terrorist attack situation. We also should not adopt a revisionist history of past attacks. Taleb calls this tendency the "triplet of opacity" and points out how three factors can affect our understanding of history: the illusion of understanding, retrospective of distortion, and the over-evaluation of facts.

Security fatigue is another dangerous and exploitable phenomenon. Americans are weary of long airport security lines and, now, a loss of communications privacy. Security is often inconvenient and especially trying for those unaccustomed to being targets. Therefore, we must find the right balance in our world and our places of work, education, worship, and play between living vigilantly and normally. In the end, however, personal security is a personal choice: if citizens choose not to face the threat and their fears, play out a potentially horrific scenario in their minds and planning, they will likely respond poorly during a soft target attack.

After we prepare mentally to engage the soft target threat, understanding the motivations and emergent tactics of those who might strike is key to planning efforts. The next two chapters introduce international and domestic terror groups and the rise of soft targeting.

REFERENCES

Anderson, Jenny. "The Psychology of Why 94 Deaths from Terrorism Are Scarier Than 301,797 Deaths from Guns." *Quartz, LLC*, January 31, 2017.

Batrawy, Aya, Paisley Dodds, and Lori Hinnant. "Leaked ISIS Documents Reveal Recruits Have Poor Grasp of Islamic Faith." *The Independent*, August 16, 2016.

Davies, Lizzy and Helen Pidd. "Germany School Killer Gave Warning in Chatroom." *The Guardian*, March 12, 2009.

Dershowitz, Alan M. *Why Terrorism Works*. New Haven: Yale University Press, 2002.

Drake, C. J. M. *Terrorists' Target Selection*. New York: St. Martin's Press, 1998.

"The Geneva Conventions of 1949 and Their Additional Protocols." International Committee of the Red Cross. www.icrc.org/eng/war-and-law/treaties-customary-law/geneva-conventions/ (October 27, 2018).

Halsall, Paul. "Maximilien Robespierre: Justification of the Use of Terror." *Modern History Sourcebook*. https://sourcebooks.fordham.edu/mod/robespierre-terror.asp (August 1997).

Hesterman, Jennifer. "Reverse Use of Organizational Development Theory: A Unique Methodology for Analyzing and Disrupting Terrorist Organizations." In *Theory & Practice of Terrorism: Alternative Paths of Inquiry*. New York, NY: Nova Science Publishers Inc, 2017.

———. *The Terrorist-Criminal Nexus: An Alliance of International Drug Cartels, Organized Crime, and Terror Groups*. Boca Raton, FL: CRC Press, 2013.

Lewin, Kurt. "Defining the Field at a Given Time." *Psychological Review* 50 (1943): 292–310.

Mauer, Raymond J. "Duck and Cover: Bert the Turtle Civil Defense Film, 1951." www.youtube.com/watch?v=IKqXu-5jw60

National Safety Council. "Odds of Dying." http://injuryfacts.nsc.org/all-injuries/preventable-death-overview/odds-of-dying/ (2018).

Nowrasteh, Alex. *Fatalities and the Annual Chance of Being Murdered in a European Terrorist Attack*. Washington, DC: CATO Institute, September 13, 2017. www.cato.org/blog/european-terrorism-fatalities-annual-chance-being-murdered

Stern, Jessica. "The Protean Enemy." *Foreign Affairs*, July/August 2003.

Szilagyi, Marc J. and Andrew D. Wallace. *Organizational Behavior and Performance*. Glenview, IL: Scott, Foresman/Little, Brown Higher Education, 1990.

Taleb, Nassim N. *The Black Swan: The Impact of the Highly Improbable*. New York: Random House, 2010.

Walsh, Nick Paton and Salma Abdelaziz. "Beaten, Tortured, Sexually Abused: An American ISIS Widow Looks for a Way Home." *CNN*, April 19, 2018.

WSB-TV Atlanta, Georgia. "Raw Video: Patience Carter Recalls Orlando Shooting Massacre." www.youtube.com/watch?v=i6TiFu6ubSo (2016).

CHAPTER 3

International Terror Groups

Propensity and Ability to Mount Soft Target Attacks

> Russian soldiers are killing our children in Chechnya, so we are here to kill yours.
>
> —Chechen fighter at the Beslan school massacre (Steele 2004)

INTRODUCTION

After understanding the psychology of soft targeting and our vulnerabilities to the threat, it is important to comprehend the phenomena of postmodern terrorism: first we must understand how we arrived at this violent juncture in our history.

MODERN TERRORISM'S ROOTS

The era of modern terrorism, delivering us to the Beslan massacre and others, began on July 22, 1968, with the hijacking of an airliner traveling from Rome to Tel Aviv by the Popular Front for the Liberation of Palestine, or the PFLP. The group, whose goal is the establishment of a Palestinian state, is still in business after forty-six years. For five weeks, terrorists held twenty-one passengers and eleven crew members in Algiers as the world helplessly watched and learned about the PFLP cause. Eventually, the terrorists released the hostages, in exchange for sixteen Arab prisoners held in Israeli jails. This was not the first hijacking of an airliner; however, the PFLP's brazen use of the tactic to draw attention to its political cause, as well as concessions given by Israel to the hijackers, ignited the phenomenon of modern terrorism as we know it today (Hoffman 2006).

The State Department started designating foreign terrorist organizations (FTOs) in 1997. Sixty-seven FTOs are on the current list, actively engaged in some type of terrorist activity threatening our national security. This list has steadily grown throughout the last decade roughly at a rate of one new group per year. With the geographical expansion of ISIS, four new groups, ISIS-Bangladesh, ISIS-Philippines, ISIS-West Africa, and ISIS-Greater Sahara were added in early 2018. A scan of the FTO list (Appendix A) illustrates the variety of worldwide terrorist threats, from dormant groups, such as the religious cult Aum Shinryko/Aleph in Japan, to the resurgent Abu Sayaaf group in the Philippines. Eighteen of the original FTOs designated in 1997 are still on the list, illustrating the staying power of more "corporate" groups, and the persistent political and/or religious ideology. Most, if not all, FTOs target civilians to further their goals. Missing from the list but providing an equally vexing and emergent national security threat are the fear-inducing global organized crime syndicates like the mafia and Mexican cartel groups, which exhibit brutal tactics and are equipped like small armies.

Figure 3.1 depicts the successful rise of radical groups and modern terrorism. Early social and psychological science theorists had a substantial

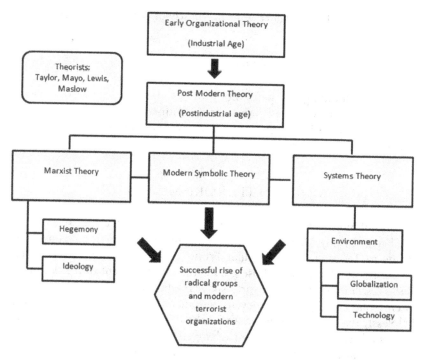

FIGURE 3.1   Organizational Theories and the Rise of Modern Terrorist Organizations (Hesterman 2013)

impact on the way we presently view and interact with organizations and their members. Postmodern theories and the associated thinking process build on this foundation and provide a remarkable means for understanding and diagnosing the emergence of revolutionary and terrorist organizations in the latter twentieth century. The discussion of the rise of postmodern terrorist groups is deeply rooted in the soft sciences; a fusion of psychology, sociology, and organizational development and behavioral theory allows insight into many of the vexing "whys" about the terrorism phenomenon. Understanding how our actions and the environment contributed to the rise of terrorism is key to better decision making with respect to response to terrorist threats and activity. For a detailed explanation of this original model, please refer to *The Terrorist–Criminal Nexus: An Alliance of International Drug Cartels, Organized Crime, and Terror Groups*, Chapter 2, "Postmodern Terrorist Groups" (Hesterman 2013).

AQ AND AFFILIATES

> Al-Qaeda's resurrection: With the demise of the Islamic State, a revived al-Qaeda and its affiliates should now be considered the world's top terrorist threat.
>
> —Bruce Hoffman, terrorism expert (2018)

The most vexing and persistent threat to our national security is al-Qaeda (AQ), which morphed from a centralized group to a high-performing, decentralized, leaderless organization. Although US forces killed Osama bin Laden in 2011 for inspiring and directing crimes against humanity, his death did not result in the dissolution of al-Qaeda; the radical ideology persists and serves as the glue holding this organization and its myriad affiliates together. After we destroyed much of their home base in Afghanistan, AQ splintered and franchised, with global cells that train, equip, and fundraise independently. These cells also do not require the "permission" of a leader to carry out a mission; the original fatwas remain in force, and the target is the Western world and Islamic countries deemed too Westernized. An expert on modern terror networks, Marc Sageman (2003), calls this the "bunch of guys" theory: members reinforce their group identities through the adherence to an ideological orientation and a strong bond of mutual commitment.

Like many emergent postmodern organizations, al-Qaeda and its offshoots are leaderless yet high performing. In the book *The Starfish and the Spider: The Unstoppable Power of Leaderless Organizations* (Brafman and Beckstrom 2006), the authors assert the reason al-Qaeda originally grew in power and persists is because bin Laden never assumed a traditional leadership role of the organization. The book uses a very applicable illustration, discussing how the Apache Indians managed to hold off the Spanish army for more than 200 years. They had no chief with positional power; they consistently chose and followed a nant'an, a spiritual and cultural leader who led by example and had no coercive power. The Apaches followed him because they wanted to, not because they had to. If a nant'an died, another would quickly step up and fill the void. Geronimo was a nant'an, and although never in an official leadership position, he had power and many wanted to take up arms and fight with him or on his behalf after his death. The Spanish army also failed to defeat the Apaches due to their loose organizational structure; power and operations were both decentralized. Raids on Spanish settlements were planned, organized, and executed in three separate places simultaneously. Attacks by the Spanish over time made the Apaches even stronger; they learned, adapted, and became even more dispersed and decentralized to frustrate their enemy. Interestingly, the operation to find and neutralize bin Laden was dubbed "Geronimo"—perhaps a nod to his mystique. The Apaches prevailed after the death of Geronimo, and al-Qaeda lives on after bin Laden.

The Ideology

Much is written and discussed about the operational tactics of al-Qaeda. However, as the group morphs and persists, a lesser-studied and potentially more valuable topic is its glue and fuel: the radical ideology. We start with Sayyid Qutb, born in Egypt and moved to the United States to attend college in the late 1940s and early 1950s. His experiences as a college student in Colorado led to a hatred of the Western way of life; he believed the society was amoral and women were promiscuous and too independent and outspoken. Upon graduation and return to Egypt, he joined the Muslim Brotherhood and quickly became a respected leader.

In 1952, a group called the Free Officers Movement, led by Gamal Abdel Nasser, overthrew Egypt's pro-Western government. Nasser initially appeared to court Qutb and the Brotherhood, although he was secretly plotting its demise. Once Qutb realized Nasser's intentions, he became an outspoken, forceful, and violent opponent of the ruling government, inciting the Muslim Brotherhood to action. The Nasser government cracked down on the dissidents, and, in 1954, arrested, jailed, and tortured Qutb. Eventually, he was left alone in prison and allowed some freedoms, including the ability to write. A prolific and powerful writer who masterfully used imagery and poetry to make his point, Qutb created his two most important works during this period: Fi Zilal al-Qur'an (In the Shade of the Qur'an), and a manifesto of his view of

Islam, Ma'alim fi-l-Tariq (Milestones). Both of these essays are widely read and revered and help us understand the seeds of radicalism. Qutb was the first and most vocal proponent of an Islamic world order, or caliphate. He foresaw inevitable ideological conflict between Islam and the West, and he believed Islam's political and cultural influence would end the advance of westernization and modernization. The Egyptian government released Qutb from prison in 1964 by request of the Iraqi government; he immediately reconnected with the Muslim Brotherhood to plan the assassination of the Egyptian prime minister and overthrow the ruling government. The government re-arrested and executed Qutb in August 1966.

However, the damage was done: Qutb's timeless writings were his legacy, inspiring a school of thought called "Qutbism." Following Qutb's death, his brother, Muhammad, conducted lectures at King Abdulaziz University in Jeddah, Saudi Arabia—events regularly attended by Osama bin Laden. Qutb mentored Ayman al-Zawahiri, who went on to become a member of the Egyptian Islamic Jihad, mentor to bin Laden, and de facto leader of al-Qaeda after bin Laden's death. Qutb's writings inspired the latest generation of radical Islamists; while imprisoned in Yemen, Anwar al-Awlaki would read hundreds of pages a day of Qutb's works, stating that he was "so immersed with the author I would feel Sayyid was with me in my cell speaking to me directly" (Jones 2012). Later, al-Awlaki himself would inspire domestic terror attacks in the United States, such as the Fort Hood shooting and Christmas Day "underwear bomber," Umar Farouk Abdulmutallab. ISIS leaders Abu Musab al-Zarqawi (killed by the US-led coalition in 2006) and his replacements, Abu Omar al-Baghdadi (killed by the coalition in 2010) and Abu Bakr al-Baghdadi (present leader) purposefully carried on Qutb's vision.

Rise of Bin Laden and al-Qaeda

As a student of this subject, you likely have a basic knowledge of the history of al-Qaeda. To fully grasp how bin Laden and his group emerged as arguably the most dangerous and successful terrorist group in history, I strongly recommend the award-winning books Age of Sacred Terror by Daniel Benjamin and Steven Simon (2002) and The Looming Tower by Lawrence Wright (2007). Both are extremely well written and should provide the basis for all academic discussions regarding al-Qaeda.

In the 1980s, inspired by his mentors, bin Laden left a lucrative engineering career and a young family to volunteer in Afghanistan and assist the mujahedin-led and US-supported fight against the Soviet Union's infiltration of what was considered holy and sacred Muslim land. As the Soviets withdrew in the late 1980s, Abdullah al Azzam, the architect of the successful war and his protégé, bin Laden, were left with a network of at least 10,000 Islamists. Azzam and bin Laden formulated a plan to use these forces to form a new group called al-Qaeda, meaning "the base," and take their cause to other countries, not specifically to the West. However, any goodwill toward the West for its help in Afghanistan evaporated in 1990 when the United States postured for Operation Desert Storm, in support of Iraqi-invaded Kuwait. Bin Laden, who returned to Saudi Arabia in early 1990 as a hero for his efforts in Afghanistan, met with King Fayd and pleaded with him not to accept Western help with repelling Iraq from Kuwait and protecting the kingdom. He was rebuffed and went underground, plotting his revenge against the West while military operations were underway in the region. His first attack was the simultaneous bombing of two hotels in Aden, Yemen, on December 29, 1992, where US troops were thought to be residing. A few months later, on February 26, 1993, Ramzi Yousef, nephew of Khalid Sheikh Mohammed (KSM), carried out the first attack on the World Trade Center. KSM was at the helm of operational planning for the basement bombing, meant to topple the North tower into the South tower. Although six people died and more than 1,000 were injured in the massive explosion and resulting smoke, they were not satisfied. Yousef and KSM then planned the 1994 "Bojinka" plot to destroy US-flagged airliners in the Pacific, but their plan unraveled when a practice bombing by Yousef failed to bring down the plane, and a subsequent investigation uncovered the plot. The 1998 simultaneous embassy bombings in Africa and the 2000 bombing of the USS Cole further raised al-Qaeda's profile and strength. But the catastrophic attacks on 9/11 would be bin Laden's greatest accomplishment, just nine years after his first attack against the West. The attack itself killed 2,975 and injured more than 6,000. Another 1,000 plus first responders and those who worked at Ground Zero and the Pentagon sites have succumbed to 9/11-related diseases. US spending on post-9/11 wars reached $5.6 trillion in FY2018 (Crawford 2017). Add that to the hundreds of billions spent on insurance payouts and medical care; impact to the airline industry, tourism, and the stock market; and money spent to clean up the damage and reconstruct.

Emergent al-Qaeda

Al-Qaeda made its initial appearance on the State Department's foreign terrorist organization (FTO) list in 1999, in light of the embassy bombings the previous year. Over half of the current sixty-two FTOs are radical Islamist al-Qaeda offshoots or affiliates (Appendix A).

AQAP

The most deadly AQ splinter is Al-Qaeda in the Arabian Peninsula (AQAP). After the 9/11 attacks and our subsequent military operations to destroy its base in Afghanistan, al-Qaeda scattered to safe havens in the Middle East, including Yemen, the ancestral homeland of the bin Laden family. AQAP quickly formed and grew in strength. The group was founded by Said Ali Al Shihri and Ibrahim Suleiman Al Rubaysh, both former Guantanamo Bay detainees whom the United States released to the Saudi deradicalization program. Unfortunately, both these terrorists left the Saudi program, made their way to Yemen, and joined two other terrorists, Nasir Al Wuhayshi and Qassim Al Raimi, who had escaped from Yemeni prisons. Together, the four built AQAP into a formidable transnational enterprise. Al Shihri was killed by a drone attack in Yemen on September 10, 2012. Al Wuhayshi rose to become AQAP's leader, and was seen in a video on April 16, 2014, addressing a large group of AQAP fighters in public in Yemen, threatening to eliminate the United States. He was killed in a US airstrike in June, 2015, and Zawahiri named al-Raymi as the new "Emir" of AQAP. Saudi citizen Ibrahim al-Asiri is the expert bomb maker for AQAP and the mastermind of several attempts against the United States, such as the failed bombing of an airliner over Detroit on Christmas Day 2009. He also built the bombs found on cargo planes in May 2010 as a result of intelligence received from Saudi Arabia's security chief. The aircraft left Yemen for the United States, and were stopped at their stop-overs, the East Midlands Airport in the UK and Dubai in the United Arab Emirates. One week later, AQAP took responsibility for the plot, and for the crash of UPS Airlines Flight 6. He was last seen in 2016 on a video threatening the US.

AQAP attracted supporters such as Anwar al-Awlaki, a US citizen and radical Islamist. Al-Awlaki was born in the United States and obtained a BS degree (civil engineering) from Colorado State University, an MA (education leadership) from San Diego State University, and worked toward a PhD at George Washington University. Inspired by the writing of Qutb, al-Awlaki met with and encouraged the 9/11 hijackers at the Dar al-Hijrah mosque in northern Virginia and persuaded and supported Nidal Hassan's plan to kill soldiers at Fort Hood through eighteen emails sent from abroad. He met Christmas Day airline terrorist Umar Farouk Abdulmutallab at an al-Qaeda training camp in Yemen and inspired and encouraged Faisal Shahzad to bomb Times Square. Due to his terrorist activities, al-Awlaki was placed on a CIA kill list by President Barack Obama in April, 2010. In a somewhat controversial move, the US government targeted and killed al-Awlaki in a drone attack in Yemen in 2011. Also killed in the vehicle was the first editor of *Inspire*, al-Qaeda's online magazine used for recruitment and rhetoric, and to educate followers on bomb building and terrorist tactics. The killing of al-Awlaki rekindled a long-standing debate about the definition of a "terrorist," since he was not a trigger puller but rather the inspiration behind attacks. The United States was sending a clear and unequivocal message: if you provide logistical support or, in this case, the ideological fuel fanning the flames of radicalism, you are a terrorist and a legitimate target. Although not the target, al-Awlaki's 16-year-old, US-born son was killed in a US drone strike in Yemen on October 14, 2011. Al-Awlaki's 8-year-old daughter was killed in a raid by US special operations personnel in Yemen on January 29, 2017.

By utilizing Internet archive services, it is possible to read al-Awlaki's writings and interaction with his followers (http://wayback.archive.org/web/20110707150524*/www.anwar-alawlaki.com/). Through his words, we can better understand his psychological and sociological construction, how he radicalized, and his initially quiet ascendance to power as a spiritual leader of a religious terrorist group. The comments of hundreds of followers posted on his blog give great insight to hatred against the West, and there are repeated calls by all for the destruction of the United States. Of course, the permanent cache of his writings and tapes also continue to inspire would-be terrorists.

In September 2014, a Shia paramilitary force, the Houthis, overran the Yemeni capital of Sana'a, forced out the president and took control of the city. The resulting civil war between the new government of Yemen, supported by Saudi Arabia, and the Houthis has raged for almost four years. The country is basically lawless and in a mass humanitarian crisis. AQAP is exploiting the opportunity to recruit disenchanted Yemenis, and now the group numbers between two and three thousand.

ISIS and Other AQ Splinter Groups

In the years following the 9/11 attack, al-Qaeda affiliates grew worldwide in at least fifteen countries. These "al-Qaeda 1.0" groups have also now splintered into "al-Qaeda 2.0" groups, with ISIS as the most formidable. The following is a list of AQ splinter groups of the greatest threat to the United States.

Al-Qaeda in Iraq (AQI), now known as the Islamic State of Iraq and the Levant (ISIL or ISIS): ISIL originated in Iraq as Jama'at al-Tawhid wal-Jihad in 1999, pledging allegiance to al-Qaeda. The group participated in the Iraqi insurgency following the 2003 invasion of Iraq and capture of Sadaam Hussein by the US-led coalition. In October, 2004, the group was known as al-Qaeda Iraq, or the Zarqawi Network. They proclaimed themselves a worldwide caliphate and started calling themselves the Islamic State in June 2014, following the ouster and death of Sadaam Hussein. The original goal of AQI was to force the withdrawal of coalition forces from Iraq, and they were responsible for horrific attacks against coalition forces, mosques, and the country's new leadership. ISIS tactics were brutal and cruel, including video-taped executions of hostages and Iraqi citizens by beheading, fire, and drowning. Lured by Syria's civil war, AQI fighters entered the northern part of the country and began recruiting members, possibly up to 2,000, and it challenged the Jabat al Nusra al-Qaeda splinter group for control. In 2014, AQI began hitting targets inside Lebanon and Turkey, pushing violence across the Syrian border and into neighboring countries. In January 2014, ISIS seized Fallujah from the Iraqi government, declaring it an Islamic state and its home base. The recapturing of Fallujah by the insurgents was a major victory against coalition forces that had fought long and hard for control of the city. The first ISIS attack in Europe happened in May 2014, when an ISIS-trained Frenchman who had traveled to Syria, Mehdi Nemmouche, killed three tourists at the Jewish Museum in Brussels. He escaped from the scene but was caught during a routine customs check on Friday as he arrived by bus in Marseille from Brussels. Nemmouche was the first European trained by an al-Qaeda affil-iate to carry out an attack in Europe. Back in Iraq, the group was growing in strength and gaining territory. ISIS was the perpetra-tor of a genocide of Yazidis, a Kurdish-speaking Iraqi minority with a unique religion, thought by ISIS to be devil worship. In August, 2014, ISIS forced 200,000 people out of Sinjar, the Yazi-dis' ancestral land in Northern Iraq. Over 40,000 Yazidis, with no food or water, took refuge on Mt. Sinjar, a rocky 4,000-foot hill. The United Nations reported that more than 5,000 Yazidis were murdered by ISIS during this offensive, and 5,000 to 7,000 women and children abducted. The young girls were kidnapped and used as sex slaves and brides. Lured by Syria's civil war, AQI fighters entered the northern part of the country and began recruiting members, possibly up to 2,000, and it challenged the Jabat al Nusra al-Qaeda splinter group for control. In mid-2014, AQI began hitting targets inside Lebanon and Turkey, pushing violence across the Syrian border and into neighboring coun-tries. By September 2014, ISIS commandeered a wide swath of Syria and Iraq, claiming a caliphate. The group's plan to spread throughout the Middle East, as well as into Europe, India, and Indonesia was revealed on USBs and computers seized during military operations in Syria and Iraq. The group also planned WMD attacks, including Y pestis, or bubonic plague. ISIS has specifically threatened the United States, posting pictures of their operatives standing in front of key targets such as the White House, a mall in Charlotte, North Carolina, and landmarks in Chicago. The terrorist group released a specific message for

Americans via Twitter, stating "We are in your state; we are in your cities; we are in your streets." ISIS 2014 attacks included the attacks of the Parliament in Canada, a hatchet attack in Queens, New York, and a fatal police stabbing in France. ISIS attacks escalated in 2015 in Iraq, Syria, Europe, and the US, killing at least 1,020. Targets were museums, hotels, mosques, trains, and restaurants. The most notable attack was in Paris in November 2015, with 130 killed and 368 injured. In December, the US had its first ISIS attack in San Bernardino, California, when an ISIS inspired attack killed fourteen and wounded twenty-four. ISIS was now the deadliest terrorist group in the world. Unfortunately, 2016 was an even deadlier year with ISIS attacks in fifteen countries, most notable in Brussels (airport and train), Incirlik (airport), Nice (Bastille Day), Orlando (Pulse nightclub), Ohio State University (vehicle and stabbing), and Berlin (Christmas Market). In 2017, ISIS again stepped up their attacks, striking pedestrians on bridges in London and on city streets in New York City, Stockholm, and Barcelona, and attacking the Ariana Grande concert in Manchester, UK, targeted young girls. ISIS attacks appear to be on the decline; in early 2018, there were just five attacks. The group's influence in Iraq is greatly diminished with the loss of Fallujah, Raqqa, and Mosul. They were also expelled from Palmyra and Deir ez-Zor. In Syria, US-led coalition forces were, at one time, killing at least 1,000 ISIS soldiers a month. Splinter ISIL-Khorasan (ISIL-K) was designated as an FTO in January 2016. Despite their demise in the Middle East, the group stepped up recruiting in an unstable region, and the State Department designated three new groups on February 27, 2018: ISIS-Bangladesh, ISIS-Philippines, and ISIS-West Africa. Finally, Afghanistan increasingly presents a breeding ground for ISIS. As the Taliban is trying to re-assert its influence in the country following the removal of most coalition forces, ISIS is also trying to gain ground and is escalating their violent attacks. In early 2018, ISIS carried out several bombings in Kabul, including one killing nine reporters and a mosque attack killing fourteen.

Tehrik-e-Taliban Pakistan (TTP): TTP is a loose alliance of militant groups in Pakistan, affiliated with the Afghani Taliban and the force behind the failed Times Square bombing attempt in May 2010. TTP provided training and logistics to American Faisal Shahzad, subsequently landing on the State Department's FTO list within days of the event. The group attacked the Army Public School in Peshawar, Pakistan, on December 16, 2016, killing 149 people including 132 schoolchildren. They continued to attack schools throughout 2017.

Harakat al-Shabaab Mujahideen (al-Shabaab): Al-Shabaab (meaning "the youth") operations in Somalia exploited the country's continued descent into lawlessness, exacting proceeds from pirating operations in the Gulf to fuel its growth. The group's goal is to establish a caliphate in Somalia. An American commander in al-Shabaab, Abu Mansur al-Amriki, grew up in Alabama as Omar Shafik Hammami; he radicalized and fled to Somalia in 2006 to join the effort, quickly rising through the ranks to become its leader. Al-Amriki was surprisingly killed by al-Shabaab in 2013, after a falling-out with the group over videos he posted on YouTube deemed narcissistic. Amriki's hypnotic, rap-styled music enticed Americans to join al-Shabaab in Somalia. His "First Stop Addis" has disappeared and reappeared many times on YouTube, but a simple keyword search will pull up the latest version. The music is almost mesmerizing and the message clear and compelling; Amriki himself sings the lyrics. As we continue to study how the radicalizing switch gets turned from "off" to "on" in the human brain, these videos provide insight into how jihadist recruiters tap into certain messages and themes to persuade, encode, and then distribute through the Internet. One of al-Shabaab's most fertile recruiting grounds is Minnesota, home to the largest Somali population in the United States. Shirwa Ahmed and Farah Mohamad Beledi, the first two confirmed US suicide bombers, traveled from Minneapolis to Somalia to receive al-Shabaab training. Other Somali American recruits came from Ohio, California, Virginia, New Jersey, and New York, according to a list compiled by the Anti-Defamation League (Council on Foreign Relations 2013). In 2012, US Army veteran and intelligence specialist Craig Baxam was arrested in Kenya, boarding a bus to Somalia with the intent to join al-Shabaab. Several recruits successfully traveled to Somalia and died in suicide bombings; others were arrested in the United States as they prepared to leave the country. It is estimated that more than forty Americans traveled to Somalia to fight for al-Shabaab, a trend the FBI has describes as a top domestic terrorist threat (CNN 2013). The concern is that they will return home with tactics and training and carry out attacks inside the United States. Al-Shabaab controls the southern part of Somalia and has started recruiting heavily from neighboring Kenya, which engaged through the 2011 Operation Linda Nchi, targeting al-Shabaab's training camps with aerial bombing campaigns. Although the group declared its loyalty to al-Qaeda in 2008, the relationship was formally cemented in 2012 with a proclamation from Ayman al-Zawahiri welcoming the al-Shabaab and its members to al-Qaeda. Following the announcement of formal ties with al-Qaeda, at least 500 al-Shabaab fighters traveled to Yemen in 2012 to join AQAP. Al-Shabaab was responsible for the expertly planned and executed operation against the Westgate Mall in Nairobi in September 2013, killing sixty-seven people and injuring 175; this attack is covered in depth in Chapter 5. On April 2, 2015, al-Shabab militants killed 148 people at Garissa University College. In late 2015, ISIS asked al-Shabaab to renounce its loyalty to al-Qaeda and become part of ISIS. Al-Shabaab split, with part of the leadership joining ISIS. In October 2017, al-Shabaab, which left the city six years prior, announced their return with a truck bomb at the newly refurbished market in Mogadishu, killing more than 500 people in the worst terrorist attack since 9/11. Two weeks later, they attacked a hotel in the city, killing twenty-nine, including government officials and police officers. In November, a US airstrike killed 100 al-Shabaab militants. The group is resurgent, although in need of cash and plundering villages. They recently started recruiting from nearby Kenya.

Al-Qa'ida in the Islamic Maghreb (AQIM): AQIM is centered in Algeria, where it has launched an insurgent campaign to turn the country into an Islamist state. AQIM arose from Salafist Group for Preaching and Combat, GSPC, and the group mainly engages in hostage-taking and ambushes against government leaders and law enforcement. After standing up the Boko Haram group in Nigeria in 2009, the AQIM was quiet until the kidnapping of several European tourists from the Timbuktu, Mali, UNESCO World Heritage site in 2011 and their execution in 2013. Also, AQIM took responsibility for a September 2013 car bombing in Timbuktu killing two civilians. A major battle at Timbuktu that saw the destruction of ancient buildings and artifacts was likely initiated and fueled by AQIM. In 2013, an AQIM splinter faction seized control of an oil field in Algeria to protest France's involvement in neighboring Mali. Using helicopters and assault weapons, the terrorists took over the facility, randomly killing workers and taking six hostages, including Americans. Unfortunately, all were killed in a botched rescue attempt by the Algerian government. In 2015, AQIM began recruiting sub-Saharan African men to fill its ranks, and began attacking military targets, including a base in Gao, killing seventy-seven. AQIM raised at least $50 million through high profile kidnappings over the last ten years and partnered in 2016 with militant group al-Murabitoun, known for their hostage-taking tactics. AQIM is the epitome of the terror–crime nexus, an asymmetric group working both ends of the equation to meet their financial, logistical, and operational goals. Splinter Ansar al-Dine, a front group for AQIM, is also a designated FTO.

Boko Haram (AQIM splinter): Boko Haram, meaning "Western education is sin" in the local Hausa language, is a jihadist militia with ties to AQIM that has attacked churches and government buildings in an attempt to establish Sharia law. The group has carried out at least 500 brutal attacks in Nigeria, Chad, Cameroon, and Niger since its formation in 2011, killing at least 20,000 and displacing two million (Wilson 2018). In the period from January 2014 to March 2014, Boko Haram was responsible for the brutal killings of almost 1,800 civilians. Strict Islamists, members of Boko Haram are responsible for horrific soft target attacks against Christians in Nigeria, with many fleeing the country in fear after their villages and churches were razed and burned to the ground. In 2014, the group escalated its campaign against churches, striking at least one per week. Boko Haram has singled out women and girls in its campaign of fear; the group was responsible for the kidnapping of 275 girls from a boarding school in April 2014. The group's leader, Abubakar Shekau, stated: "There is a market for selling humans. Allah says I should sell. He commands me to sell. I will sell women. I sell women" (Shekau and Levs 2014). However, not all Nigerians are against the presence of Boko Haram, with one stating: "If I was attacked by Boko Haram, it's like being attacked by God. It's God's wish and I have no problem with that" (Raghavan 2012). Boko Haram pledged allegiance to ISIS in March 2015 and carried out 127 attacks in 2016. In 2017, the group mounted 150 attacks, killing 967 people. In both years the highest number of attacks were in January, just after Nigeria's president claimed the group was defunct. The Nigerian military has been unable to engage or disarm Boko Haram, and the country seems to be resolving itself to its brand of ruthless violence. Boko Haram militants took a page from the Hezbollah playbook and now are embedded in villages amongst civilians. Instability in Nigeria is also being exploited by Iran, which is creating a "Nigerian Hezbollah," known as Islamic Movement of Nigeria (IMN). The group's leader, Sheikh Ibrahim Zakzaky, draws inspiration from Hezbollah leader Nasrallah, whose picture is carried at IMN demonstrations. The group's website, www.islamicmovement. org/, is a treasure trove of information about Iran's attempt to influence events in Nigeria.

Chechen separatists: The Islamist Chechen separatists fighting Russia have ties to al-Qaeda dating back to 1999, when their

leaders visited bin Laden in Khandahar, Afghanistan. Following the hostage-taking at Moscow's Dubrovka Theater in 2003,
the State Department designated three Chechen groups as terror
organizations: the Islamic International Brigade, the Special Purpose Islamic Regiment, and the Riyadus-Salikhin Reconnaissance
and Sabotage Battalion of Chechen Martyrs. Chechen terrorists prefer to hit soft targets such as theaters, schools (Beslan
attack of 2004), train stations, and trains. The Chechen "black
widows" are ruthless female terrorists who typically carry out
suicide bombings against targets; the original group consisted
of vengeance-seeking women widowed by Chechen operations.
The Boston Marathon bombers, the Tsarnaev brothers, were
of Chechen descent and were at the very least influenced by
Chechen radical Islamist ideology. Chechens, or *shishani* in
Arabic, were fighting alongside ISIS in Iraq, notably in Mosul.
Tarkhan Batirashvili, known as Abu Omar al-Shishani or Omar
al-Shishani, was a former sergeant in the Georgian army who
became a Chechen jihadist. He rose to ISIS highest military position In Syria and commanded their operations in the country
before his death in Iraq via US airstrike in July 2016.

Although the al-Qaeda affiliates may struggle in the face of stepped-
up US and regional engagement, they remain a formidable and flexible
force, moving to and operating in areas of conflict and lawlessness, preying on the vulnerable populace.

Bin Laden Speaks

On May 2, 2011, a US-led military team entered a compound in Abbottabad, Pakistan, and killed Osama bin Laden. Special Operations
personnel removed a treasure trove of sensitive site exploitation (SSE)
material from the compound for analysis, with seventeen documents
released to the public. The 2012 study "Letters from Abbottabad" (US
Military Academy 2012) analyzes the seventeen declassified documents
gathered during the SSE operation at the compound, providing outstanding insight and analysis of bin Laden's unyielding role in shaping
al-Qaeda and the affiliates, as well as activities assisting other terrorist
groups). Bin Laden opined about conducting a mass attack on communications systems, targeting railroad infrastructure, and striking smaller US
cities. He also pondered ways to use the media in his favor and to induce
political dissent in our system. Despite being in exile from the group, the
documents revealed he had a hand in nearly all of the major terrorist
attacks since 9/11, including the siege in Mumbai.

AQ's Morphing Goals and Tactics

According to terrorism expert Dr. Bruce Hoffman, al-Qaeda's goals changed in the decade after 9/11, impacting how they now target us (2010). His key points include:

1. Al-Qaeda is increasingly focused on overwhelming, distracting, exhausting us.
2. In the wake of the global financial crisis, al-Qaeda s stepped up a strategy of economic warfare.
3. Al-Qaeda is still trying to create divisions in alliances by targeting our partners.
4. Al-Qaeda is aggressively seeking out, destabilizing, and exploiting failed states and other areas of lawlessness.
5. Al-Qaeda is actively seeking recruits from non-Muslim countries who can be easily deployed for attacks in the West.

Often called the "death by a thousand cuts" strategy, AQ's strategy is to exhaust and overwhelm our government and people. The FBI often reminds us that, in a 2004 video, bin Laden stated he "bled Russia for 10 years until it went bankrupt and was forced to withdraw in defeat . . . We are continuing in the same policy to make America bleed profusely to the point of bankruptcy." Of course, the low cost to execute the 9/11 attacks and the resulting devastation to our economy from extensive military engagement overseas have not gone unnoticed by groups wishing to do us harm. Dragging us into a "long slog" is not just a hope but an operational tactic.

In March 2018, Zawahiri issued a statement entitled "France Has Returned Oh Descendants of the Lions," a call to arms for the Islamic Magreb. He talks about the Arab Spring as "earthquake that shook the world mightily" and speaks to the "descendants of the lions," or the children of the men who died fighting for Sharia and the Caliphate. Then he asks "So where are you? Where is your Islamic zeal? Where is your eagerness? Where is your settlement of your duties for the inheritance of your fathers?" (Joscelyn 2018).

In light of Zawahiri's message and the resurgent al Qaeda, Dr. Hoffman provided his updated assessment, stating: "With the demise of the Islamic State, a revived al-Qaeda and its affiliates should now be considered the world's top terrorist threat" (Hoffman 2018). With the US, coalition allies and the Middle East focus on eliminating ISIS from Iraq and Syria, al-Qaeda quietly continued their rebuilding effort starting before, and emboldened by, the Arab Spring uprisings of 2011. As previously stated, the military method of decimation, or eliminating the top 10 percent tier of a group, will not lead to its demise.

Al-Qaeda is global and growing; in Syria, they have more than 20,000 fighters, and tens of thousands throughout the African continent.

A new and dangerous extremist group spawned from al-Qaeda is quietly consolidating power in northwestern Syria, taking advantage of the US's focus elsewhere in the country. Hayat Tahrir al-Sham is extending control across the Idlib province, under leader Abu Mohammad al-Julani, a former al-Qaeda fighter. Al-Julani is vowing to conquer Damascus and impose Islamic rule across Syria. In January 2018, he asked followers to engage in "a war of ideas, a war of minds, a war of wills, a war of perseverance" (Rasmussen 2018). The new terror group is enforcing their version of Sharia and raising funds by taxing flows of people and goods through its territory.

Although ISIS did execute, direct, and inspire spectacular attacks in Europe and the United States, al-Qaeda is the terrorist group with the resources, capability, and reach to execute an even more destructive agenda.

HEZBOLLAH

American terrorism is the source of every terrorism in the world.

—Hassan Nasrallah, Hezbollah leader

We must remember that, prior to 9/11, Hezbollah was responsible for the deaths of more Americans than any other terrorist group. The group had a hand in the 1983 bombing of the Marine barracks in Beirut (241 US military dead, sixty wounded); the 1985 hijacking of TWA flight 847, during which US Navy diver Robert Stethem was murdered; the kidnapping and murder of US officials in Lebanon; and the 1996 Khobar Towers bombing in Saudi Arabia (nineteen US military dead, 372 wounded). When tensions escalate between the United States and Iran or Syria, Hezbollah inevitably starts a campaign of saber rattling and threats of strikes against our country. Perhaps no group is better positioned to strike within the United States, as Hezbollah has a strong presence north and south of our border, as well as internally with fundraising cells and sympathizers. We cannot overlook the potential for an undetected sleeper cell to lash out upon direction from one of its sponsors, Iran or Syria.

Hezbollah has been in operation for thirty-six years and designated as an FTO by the State Department in 1997. Formed in 1982 following the Israeli invasion of Lebanon, the Lebanon-based radical Shia group takes its ideological inspiration from the Iranian revolution and the teachings of the late Ayatollah Khomeini. The group generally follows the religious guidance of the Iranian Supreme Leader. Hezbollah is closely aligned with Iran, but also provides technical and operational support to Syria, and more than 7,000 of its fighters are embedded with Assad's army. The group is complex in nature with several "arms," including military, political, and community support. This complexity makes engagement extremely difficult. For example, due to the comingling of activities, sanctioning one of its "charities" often means taking money away from the needy as well as militants. The group is now global, with a presence in Central and South America, Africa, and Europe, operating in the same "space" as other major terror groups such as al-Qaeda and ISIS. The liaison of Hezbollah with these groups, sharing tactics, trafficking routes, etc., is of great concern. The group vigorously raises funds in the United States through charities and intellectual property crime, especially through selling knock-off designer purses, DVDs, baby formula, and high-demand pharmaceuticals such as Viagra (Hesterman 2013).

Despite decades of overt and covert attempts to dismantle the group, it is still one of the world's most effective terrorist organizations. A review of Hezbollah reveals an organization leveraging unique sources of power to wield influence in the Middle East and globally.

Methodology and Objectives

Hezbollah has a history of suicide bombing attacks; however, this tactic has fallen out of favor in the past twenty years. More recently, the group relies on physical attacks of government employees, facilities, and tourists. They utilize kidnapping as a way to engage in prisoner exchange and also field a unique weapon: the group is very adept at leveraging the world audience through press campaigns, political activity, and humanitarian engagement.

Primary Area of Operations

Hezbollah operates in the formerly Syrian-controlled Bekaa Valley, the southern suburbs of Beirut, and southern Lebanon. The State Department's "Country Reports on Terrorism" most recent report (2017) gives a glimpse into its global reach, stating that Hezbollah has established cells in Europe, Africa, South America, North America, and Asia. The group's training bases are mostly in the Bekaa Valley, with headquarters and offices in southern Beirut. Hezbollah is now a "state within a state," similar to how the Palestinian Liberation Organization used to operate in Lebanon.

Tactical Proficiency

According to the US State Department (2010) and the FBI, Hezbollah is the most technically capable terrorist group in the world. The Israeli National Security Council (NSC) is concerned about Hezbollah interface with Russia in the Syria conflict, which may help the terror group evolve to a more adaptable "learning organization" (Opall-Rome 2016). The report, by Dima Adamsky warned their interaction could lead to improvements in Hezbollah's cyber-warfare and special forces capabilities, allowing them to carry out more sophisticate missions, including possible incursions into Israel.

Active and Deadly

The following is a timeline of major Hezbollah activity in the last twelve years.

2018: Hezbollah steps up activity in Syria in support of Assad's civil war. Rhetoric and border skirmishes with Israel continue, as Israel tries to thwart increased Iranian presence and activity in neighboring Syria. US estimates Iran provides Hezbollah at least $700 million annually and sanctions eight people and seven companies associated with Hezbollah activity in Africa and other countries. DoJ creates a special task force to investigate narco-terrorism by Hezbollah in Central and South America, as well as in Africa.

2016: In June 2016, Hezbollah detonates a bomb outside the BLOM Bank in Beirut. The bank has started closing Hezbollah-related accounts in support of Lebanon's new Hezbollah International Financing Prevention Act.

2015: Cypriot authorities arrested Hezballah members and Lebanese-Canadian national Hussein Bassam Abdallah after finding 8.2 tons of liquid ammonium nitrate in the basement of a residence in Larnaca.

2014: An Ontario judge ordered the seizure of more than $7 million in bank accounts and property in Canada belonging to Iran. Hezbollah is heavily engaged in the Syrian conflict, working with the Assad loyalist militia known as al-Jaysh al-Sha'bi, which was created and is maintained by Hezbollah and Iran's Islamic Revolutionary Guard Corps-Qods Force. Hezbollah pushed Syrian conflict violence across the border into Lebanon and Turkey.

2012: On July 18, Hezbollah attacked Israeli tourists boarding a bus at Bulgaria's Burgas airport. Five Israeli citizens, a Bulgarian bus driver, and the bomber were killed. A similar attack was planned in Cyprus.

2011: Hezbollah was reportedly behind a bombing in Istanbul in May 2011, wounding eight Turkish civilians in a possible assassination attempt on the Israeli consul to Turkey.

2009: When Israel engaged HAMAS in Gaza, Hezbollah did not intervene militarily (possibly at the behest of Syria), but influenced the battlefield in a variety of ways. Prior to the conflict, Hezbollah's leadership invited Arab nations to join it in protesting Israel's embargo of goods entering Gaza. Their tactic contributed to the propaganda associated with the conflict and also demonstrated Hezbollah's ability to engage from afar via psychological operations.

2008: After three days of bloodshed, heavily armed Hezbollah fighters seized West Beirut. This was the first use of Hezbollah's military arsenal against its host nation to increase territory and span of control. The conflict began when the government attempted to shut down Hezbollah's vast telecommunications network.

2006: Hezbollah militants kidnapped two Israeli soldiers in northern Israel, sparking the month-long "Lebanon war," which devastated the country's infrastructure. During the conflict, Israel bombed Lebanon and deployed troops and tanks and Hezbollah fired 4,000 rockets across the border into Israel. In all, more than 1,000 Lebanese (mostly civilians) were killed, and 120 Israeli soldiers and forty-three Israeli civilians lost their lives.

Operations in the Western Hemisphere

Hezbollah continues to expand its sphere of influence methodically around the world while receiving weapons and training support from Iran, Syria, and now possibly Russia with their joint operation in the Syrian civil war.

South America

Hezbollah's activity in the Western Hemisphere is of great concern. For instance, the group has a stronghold in South America, especially in the triborder area (TBA), where Paraguay, Brazil, and Argentina intersect. Approximately 25,000 immigrants from Lebanon came to the area in two waves: after the 1948 Arab/Israeli war and, in 1985, after the civil war in Lebanon. Hezbollah has garnered support from these communities and is heavily engaged in charitable fund-raising, DVD piracy, tax evasion, and money laundering schemes, as well as other money-making ventures. With an estimated $12 billion a year in illegal commerce, the TBA is the center of the largest underground economy in the Western Hemisphere (House Report 2012).

In 1992, Islamists attacked the Israeli embassy in Buenos Aires, Argentina, with a car bomb, killing twenty-nine people and injuring more than 250 others. The Islamic Jihad organization, directly linked to Hezbollah, claimed responsibility. In 1994, Hezbollah used a truck bomb to attack a Jewish community center in Buenos Aires, killing eighty-seven people and injuring hundreds. Investigators linked the plot directly back to Iran, which also executed copycat bombings, just eight days later, attacking the Israeli embassy and a Jewish community center in London.

The TBA is not the only Hezbollah stronghold in the region. In 2009, the SOUTHCOM commander testified that a Hezbollah presence was detected in Colombia, and the group is heavily involved in the drug trade (Senate Armed Services Committee 2009). A final concern, Hezbollah's liaison with al-Qaeda in Latin America, was documented as far back as November of 2002. At that time, intelligence agencies reported a "summit" meeting took place in Ciudad del Este between Hezbollah leaders and other radical Islamist terrorist groups, including al-Qaeda (Boettcher 2002).

Venezuela's long-term, established liaison with Hezbollah is also worrisome. In 2006, following the end of hostilities in Lebanon with Israel, Hezbollah's leader, Hassan Nasrallah, called the now deceased Hugo Chavez his "brother," and signs reading "Gracias, Chavez" were hung to thank him publicly for his support. In response to the Israeli engagement in Gaza in 2009, President Chavez ejected the Israeli ambassador and staff from his country. Chavez openly invited Hezbollah members to live in Venezuela, and his embassies in the Middle East were used to launder Hezbollah money, according to investigation by the United States. Chavez's replacement, President Nicolas Maduro, continues to court Hezbollah and asked for the group's assistance during student uprisings in 2014. State Department-sanctioned Hezbollah terrorist Ghazi Atef Nassereddine is now living in Venezuela and gives updates in Spanish via his Twitter account (@GhaziAtef).

Hezbollah and Iran are finding new strength in South America. The commander of the US Southern Command told Congress in 2015 testimony that "our limited intelligence capabilities make it difficult to fully assess the amount of terrorist financing generated in Latin America, or understand the scope of possible criminal-terrorist collaboration" (Ottolenghi 2017). Many sanctions the US put into place in past years are not enforced or updated, and legislation passed by Congress in 2015 is just now used to interdict Hezbollah's financing of operations in the Middle East from South America. Officials in Paraguay may be succumbing to Hezbollah's attempts to corrupt their government, as the State Department pointed to a $1.2 billion money laundering investigation with evidence. Other countries in the region are also failing to step up and confront the Hezbollah threat: to date, no Latin American country lists Hezbollah as a terror organization. Therefore, they cannot arrest or prosecute any citizens providing material or other support to the group and lack certain investigative and prosecutory powers. The confluence of inability to collect intelligence, lack of enforcement of sanctions, and corruption of government officials in the tri-border area means Iran and Hezbollah will continue to operate at will and gain influence.

Canada

Undeniably, Hezbollah has a very strong presence in Canada. In 2012, the United States uncovered a Hezbollah-related scheme to launder the proceeds of narcotic trafficking and other crimes through Lebanese financial institutions, with amounts totaling more than $480 million. Proceeds were moved through West Africa, and the buying and selling of used cars was the primary method of moving the dirty money. One bank of interest connected to the laundering was a Lebanese-Canadian institution that forfeited $150 million of proceeds from the scheme. In a chapter from his book *Hezbollah: The Global Footprint of Lebanon's Party of God*, terrorism expert Matthew Levitt (2015) reveals Hezbollah activated suspected "sleeper cells" in Canada to carry out an attack to avenge the targeted killing of Imad Mughniyeh. According the annual *Public Report on the Terrorist Threat to Canada*, the number of Canadians abroad with a nexus to terror is steadily rising, from 130 in 2015 to 180 in 2016 and 190 in 2017. Terrorist financing is the most pressing concern.

At the Mexican Border

The number of Hezbollah operatives operating in Mexico has increased in recent years. In 2009, former Syrian military officer Jamal Yousef was arrested in New York City on narco-terror charges for his involvement in a weapons-for-cocaine scheme between Hezbollah and FARC, using Mexico as a safe haven. According to the indictment, a weapons cache of 200 rifles, 2,500 hand grenades, C4 explosives, and antitank munitions was stolen from Iraq by Yousef's cousin, a member of Hezbollah, and moved to the home of family members in Mexico, also affiliated with the terrorist group. Yousef planned to deliver the weapons to FARC in Colombia, in return for 2,000 pounds of cocaine, but the Drug Enforcement Agency (DEA) intervened. Yousef pled guilty and received a twelve-year prison sentence (US District Court, Southern District of New York 2009).

   Although he is widely believed to be a lone operator, Jameel Nasr was an international Hezbollah operative, taking direction from Lebanon to establish a Hezbollah network in Mexico and throughout South America. Nasr traveled regularly between Lebanon, Venezuela, and Tijuana, Mexico, and, in 2010, Mexican authorities arrested him upon return from one of these trips. Mexican authorities said Nasr had been "entrusted with forming a base in South America and the United States to carry out operations against Israeli and Western targets" (Investigative Project on Terrorism 2010).

In late 2011, prosecutors in Virginia charged a Lebanese man, Ayman Joumaa, with smuggling at least "tens of thousands of kilos" of Colombian cocaine into the United States, with 85,000 kilos sold to the Los Zetas cartel. Joumaa and his associates laundered more than $250 million in proceeds through Spain, West Africa, Lebanon, Venezuela, and Colombia (US District Court for the Eastern District of Virginia 2011). According to the US Treasury Department, Hezbollah derived financial support from the criminal activities of Joumaa's network through the sanctioned Lebanese-Canadian National Bank of Beirut (Rotella 2011). In 2011, a former undercover law enforcement officer discussed the Hezbollah interface with drug trafficking organizations (DTOs), saying the group received cartel cash and protection in exchange for giving its expertise on subjects ranging from "money laundering to firearms training and explosives training." He also discussed his discovery of Hezbollah safe houses in Tijuana and Durango (KGTV News, San Diego 2011).

In 2012, a US House of Representatives Homeland Security Committee Subcommittee on Oversight, Investigations and Management tied Middle East terror organizations to Mexican drug cartels. The report, "A Line in the Sand: Countering Crime, Violence and Terror at the Southwest Border" stated that the "Southwest border has now become the greatest threat of terrorist infiltration into the United States." It specifically cites a "growing influence" from Iranian and Hezbollah terror forces in Latin America and concluded that "Iran and Hezbollah pose a threat to the entire Western Hemisphere including the United States and our Southwest border."

Tunnels   Hezbollah constructed a network of tunnels in Lebanon used to secure the group from Israeli airstrikes and permit covert maneuvering of forces. The tunnels have medical facilities, dormitories, lighting, heating and cooling systems, and even digitally controlled surveillance and weapon systems. Recent reports from Beirut indicate how, with the help of Iran, Hezbollah has tunneled mountains in the Bekaa region and into Syria (Yaghi 2012). HAMAS has also constructed a network of 400 main and 1,000 feeder tunnels between the Gaza Strip and Egypt, many of which can accommodate vehicles. Their tunnels are used to smuggle weapons, personnel, medicine, construction material, fuel, and other goods embargoed due to the ongoing Israel–Palestine conflict (Zaboun 2012).

Tunnels built by Mexican drug trafficking organizations to cross clandestinely from Mexico into the United States have grown increasingly sophisticated. Law enforcement agents have discovered more than 150 tunnels since 1990, most crude and incomplete, but a few operational with tracks to move carts loaded with contraband across the border. In July 2012, DEA and Immigration and Customs Enforcement (ICE) agents discovered, under a strip mall in San Luis, Arizona, an expertly constructed 240-yard, $1.5 million tunnel with 6-foot ceilings and wood walls and equipped with ventilation, lighting, hydraulic systems, and other high-tech components. This was not the common dirt tunnel through a sewer system previously found. DEA agents believed the tunnel was the work of experienced engineers (Spagat and Billeaud 2012). If Mexican cartels want better tunnels, they will recruit the expertise they require. A former US law enforcement agent with extensive experience working undercover in Mexico believes the expertise and construction features seen in the latest cartel tunneling efforts point to Hezbollah's involvement (KGTV News, San Diego, 2011). The longest tunnel ever found under the US-Mexico border was equivalent to the length of eight football fields.

Bombs   A new weapon in the cartel's battle for control was imported directly from Middle Eastern terror groups and debuted in July 2010 with the successful detonation of a vehicle-borne improvised explosive device (VBIED) in the border city of Juárez. The Juárez cartel deliberately targeted first responders by placing a bound, wounded man in a police uniform at the scene, luring law enforcement and medical personnel to the area. A nearby vehicle, inconspicuously laden with 22 pounds of Tovex, exploded moments later, killing three people and wounding twenty. Tovex is a water gel explosive widely used as a substitute for dynamite for industrial and mining purposes. Theft of Tovex in Mexico is a common occurrence; in February 2009, masked gunmen stole 900 cartridges of the substance from a US firm in Durango, Mexico (Caldwell and Castillo 2010).

In July and August 2012, a wave of car bombings in northeast Mexico targeting a city hall and the homes of security officials were detonated by Zeta and Gulf cartels as part of their campaign to influence local elections. Two of the bombs were sophisticated and detonated by use of a cell phone. VBIEDs are widely used by insurgents in Iraq and Afghanistan and terrorist groups such as Hezbollah and al-Qaeda. Richard Schwein, the former FBI special agent in charge of the El Paso office, stated, "It certainly seems like they've taken a page out of the Middle East [book]" (Bracamontes 2010). The cartels' use of these tactics presents an evolutionary change in Mexico's war and calls for increased vigilance on the US side of the border as the violence pushes north.

United States

> We in the Intelligence Community do, in fact, see continued activity on behalf of Hizballah here inside the homeland. We are watching very closely for additional signs of that activity here in the homeland.
>
> **—Nick Rasmussen, Director of the National**
> **Counterterrorism Center, October 2017**

Within the United States, there were more than forty arrests of Hezbollah activists in the past ten years based on Joint Terrorism Task Force investigations in Philadelphia, New York, Detroit, Michigan, and San Antonio. From an operational standpoint, the organization's footprint in the United States is growing in size and tactical power; Hezbollah cells attempted to obtain Stinger missiles, M-4 rifles, and night vision equipment in the United States (US Senate Committee on Homeland Security and Governmental Affairs 2012). Hezbollah is heavily engaged in intellectual property theft, mortgage fraud, and other financial schemes in the United States and also has US citizen sympathizers willing to do some of its leg work.

In 2010, seven Florida men who owned an export business in Miami were arrested for falsifying paperwork and invoices and illegally shipping electronics such as Sony PlayStations and digital cameras to a shopping center in Paraguay for resale. The men falsified wire transactions, moving and hiding money illegally (FBI 2010). The managers of the mall gave a certain percentage of their earnings to Hezbollah, estimated in the tens of millions of dollars annually. And, in 2013, a former leader of a Hezbollah militia group, Wissam Allouche, attempted to secure a job and security clearance from the Department of Defense. Allouche is a Lebanese man who married a US Army officer in Germany and moved to San Antonio, Texas, in 2002. The marriage dissolved, yet he became a US citizen in 2009, became a contractor for the L3 Corporation, and worked in the Middle East as a linguist. He came up on the FBI's radar when applying for a sensitive government job. As the FBI investigated, he completed security clearance paperwork in which he lied about his previous connections to Hezbollah and the dissolution of his marriage. He also falsely claimed to be a US Special Forces officer during visits to Joint Base San Antonio-Fort Sam Houston and tried to date women from the post, possibly to gain access to sensitive information. Prosecutors used pictures of Allouche from his Hezbollah days in court, and revealed his Arabic name, given by the terrorist group and meaning "god of death" (US District Court, San Antonio 2014).

As it proves increasingly difficult to plant their members in society, all terrorist groups are using a new technique: recruiting US citizens. In August 2012, the State Department specially designated Hezbollah for its financial support of the Syrian regime. After decades of support from

Syria, officials say Hezbollah is now "repaying its debt to Assad by providing training, advice, and extensive logistical support to the Government of Syria" (www.state.gov/r/pa/prs/ps/2012/08/196335.htm). Hezbollah has stepped up efforts to elicit sympathizers to leave the United States and join the government's army in Syria, similar to the group's successful efforts to lure thousands of Eastern European Muslims into the fight. Americans recruited to support the regime, al-Qaeda extremist rebel groups, and ISIS have fought against fellow Americans in Syria. The FBI is worried the Americans fighting in Syria will return to the United States with their newfound skills to carry out terrorist attacks on behalf of Hezbollah or al-Qaeda (Washington Post 2014). These new techniques by Hezbollah and al-Qaeda, either to plant agents in the United States or to recruit from the US populace, are very worrying.

Hezbollah activity in the United States increased in 2017. In February, Fadi Yassine, was arrested in Cedar Rapids, Idaho, and charged with arranging to send weapons to a Hezbollah member in Lebanon. In June, Ali Kourani, 32, New York, and Samer el Debek, 37, Michigan, were arrested and charged with providing material support to Hezbollah's Islamic Jihad Organization, the IJO. Kourani was casing John F. Kennedy airport in New York City for a potential Hezbollah attack. The men lived double lives, told to "maintain ostensibly normal lives but could be activated and tasked with conducting IJO operation" according to Kourani (Kaufman 2017). Around this same time, Samer El Debek of Dearborn, Michigan, was arrested and charged with traveling to Panama to conduct surveillance against Israeli targets and the Panama Canal.

HAMAS

HAMAS is an acronym for the group's name in Arabic: Harakat Al Muqawama Al Islamiyya (Islamic Resistance Movement); HAMAS is also a word in itself meaning "zeal" or "enthusiasm." HAMAS originated in 1987 as an arm of Egypt's radical Muslim Brotherhood. The group's home base is in Gaza City, in the Palestinian Gaza Strip. HAMAS has historically received support from Iran and from private donors, especially in Saudi Arabia and the Arabian Gulf region. It has also received funds from Palestinian expatriates in the United States and other countries. Many funds used to find their way to HAMAS through Islamic charity organizations, but this funding has slowed since crackdowns on terrorist financing following 9/11. HAMAS hopes to establish an Islamic state in the West Bank and the Gaza Strip and its charter states: "HAMAS regards nationalism as part and parcel of the religious faith. Nothing is loftier or deeper in nationalism than waging jihad against the enemy and

confronting him when he sets foot on the land of the Muslims" (www.
thoughtco.com/what-is-hamas-2353468). Historically, HAMAS has called
for the destruction of the state of Israel and refuses to recognize it.

HAMAS routinely aims for soft targets in Israel. However, the group
is not above using its own citizens as pawns in the battle. Independent
reports give detailed evidence of HAMAS using hospitals, schools, homes,
and mosques to hide weapons and soldiers during the Gaza War, an Israeli
military initiative from December 2008 through January 2009. At twenty-
five miles long and six miles wide, with a population of 1.5 million, Gaza
is the sixth most densely populated place on earth, providing a very
complex battleground situation. The UN report on the war mentions
the possible use of children, women, and the elderly as human shields by
HAMAS. Malam, an Israeli intelligence think tank, produced a report
using declassified material such as videotapes, maps, and operational
plans recovered on the ground by Israeli Defense Forces (IDF) troops.
The information indicates HAMAS hid IEDs in and around civilian
homes and hospitals and a screenshot from a video taken from a helicopter appears to show the use of children and the elderly as human shields
for soldiers engaged in operations. Of the 1,444 Palestinians killed in the
offensive, approximately 340 were children. On July 8, 2014, in response
to the death of three Israeli teenagers in the West Bank presumed at the
hands of HAMAS, the IDF launched Operation Protective Edge. In addition to massive missile strikes on the West Bank and in Gaza, the IDF
conducted a ground operation to find and destroy HAMAS tunnels. A
ceasefire commenced on August 27, with the death toll standing at more
than 2,000 Palestinians and eighty Israelis killed. The intense bombing
of houses and apartment buildings left approximately 30 percent of the
Palestinian population homeless. The UN investigated human rights violations on both sides of the conflict. Certainly, the collocation of HAMAS
with civilians has brought suffering to the Palestinian people and, as with
previous engagements, approximately 90 percent of the deaths were civilian noncombatants, and 20 percent children.

HAMAS may be moving to a new chapter in its thirty-one-year exis-
tence. In 2016, HAMAS worked with Egypt to root out and eliminate
Islamic terrorist organizations in the Sinai, in return for economic aid. In
May 2017, HAMAS surprised many with the unveiling of a new charter.
They are no longer calling for Israel's destruction but for liberation of
Palestine and to "confront the Zionist project." The charter stated accep-
tance of the 1967 borders as the basis for establishing a Palestinian state,
and stated HAMAS is not an offshoot of the Muslim Brotherhood. In
October 2017, Fatah and HAMAS signed another reconciliation agree-
ment, this one addressing civil and administrative matters involving Gaza
and the West Bank. In November 2017, national elections, reform of the
Palestine Liberation Organization (PLO) and possible demilitarization of

HAMAS were discussed by all parties. HAMAS is clearly attempting to moderate its image, a move in the right direction.

Worrisome is the partnering of Hezbollah and HAMAS operating in the same "space" in terms of benefactors such as Iran and Syria and financing activities in the TBA area of South America. Although the ideologies differ, the two groups are forming an increasingly strong partnership in the Middle East. For instance, during the December 2008 to January 2009 Gaza War, HAMAS and Hezbollah maintained continuous communication in all phases of the conflict. During the battle, Hezbollah's influence on HAMAS's tactics was apparent, with the group relying more on rocket attacks and less on suicide operations. Iranian sources report Hezbollah trained HAMAS in military tactics used to attack Merkava tanks, the main battle tank employed by the IDF. A Hezbollah parliamentary official confirmed the tactical exchange (Berti 2009).

Relations between Iran and HAMAS grew stronger towards the end of 2017. An outstanding essay entitled "The Iran-HAMAS-Hezbollah Connection" (2017) by Khaled Abu Toameh from the Gatestone Institute helps paint the picture of how and why these relationships are growing and impact in the Middle East. In September, a senior HAMAS delegation visited Tehran to brief Iranian leaders on the reconciliation agreement between HAMAS and the Palestinian Authority. It was the first time senior HAMAS officials visited Iran since 2011 when the relations became strained over the group's refusal to support Assad's actions in Syria. A few weeks later, another senior HAMAS delegation traveled to Tehran for the funeral of a senior Iranian security official's father. In November, a senior HAMAS official, Musa Abu Marzouk, said "relations between HAMAS and Hezbollah were never cut off," and the groups were working to strengthen the relationship.

> We have ongoing contacts and understandings. But we preferred to keep them away from the spotlight. HAMAS and Hezbollah are in one line in the fight against Israel, and we coordinate our positions regarding the Palestinian cause. HAMAS will continue to cooperate with resistance groups that support the Palestinian resistance.

This renewed relationship is setting off alarms, particularly in Israel since, with the help of Hezbollah, Iran has control of large portions of Syria and Lebanon. Gaza may be next.

HAMAS in the Western Hemisphere

HAMAS sympathizers also raise funds in the United States through false charities. Holy Land Foundation for Relief and Development, of

Richardson, Texas, had offices in three states and raised $13 million in 2000 alone. The foundation was the largest Muslim charity in the United States and, although claiming donations went to aid Palestinians, it was singled out for support of HAMAS, mainly to the families of suicide bombers (US General Accounting Office 2003). In Canada, the International Relief Fund for the Afflicted and Needy Canada was designated as a fund-raising charity for HAMAS in 2011, sending the group more than $14 million dollars in a four-year period. Finally, the American organization CAIR, the Council on American–Islamic Relations, is thought to be a HAMAS sympathizer. CAIR-Canada changed its name in 2013 to National Council of Canadian Muslims (NCCM).

As HAMAS continues to "rebrand" itself, some countries and organizations like the UN and EU may start soften their hardline approach. We should support their demilitarization and de-escalation. However, in light of growing relationship with Hezbollah and Iran, we must stay engaged to detect any impact to our national security interests.

SUMMARY OF THREAT

After discussing the international terrorist groups most likely to strike the United States, it is possible to assess the threat they pose to our soft targets as summarized in Table 3.1. The next chapter explores the rising threat of domestic terror, another vexing security challenge.

TABLE 3.1   Summary of International Threat Against Soft Targets

International terrorist group	Past and/or propensity for hitting soft targets?	With intent to kill?	Reach into US?	Capability?
Al-Qaeda, affiliates	Yes	Yes	Yes, both from foreign nationals and US citizens	Yes
ISIS	Yes	Yes	Yes, both from foreign nationals and US citizens	Yes
Hezbollah	Yes	Yes	Yes, operational cells and US sympathizers	Yes
HAMAS	Yes	Possibly	Possibly, through US sympathizers	Maybe

REFERENCES

Benjamin, Daniel and Steven Simon. *Age of Sacred Terror*. New York: Random House, 2002.

Berti, Benedetta. "Assessing the Role of Hezbollah in the Gaza War and Its Regional Impact." *Terrorism Monitor* 7, no. 4 (2009).

Boettcher, Mike. "South America's 'Tri-Border' Back on Terrorism Radar." *CNN*, 2002.

Bracamontes, Ramon. "Experts: Car Bomb in Juárez Mimics Middle East Terrorist Tactics." *El Paso Times*, July 17, 2010.

Brafman, Ori and Rod A. Beckstrom. *The Starfish and the Spider: The Unstoppable Power of Leaderless Organizations*. New York: Portfolio Publishers, 2006.

Caldwell, Alicia A. and E. Eduardo Castillo. "Car Bomb in Mexico Drug War Changes the Ground Rules." *The Independent*, London, England, July 17, 2010.

CNN. "Al-Shabaab Backed by Money for US." September 29, 2013.

Council on Foreign Relations. "Al-Shabab." www.cfr.org/somalia/al-shabab/p18650 (September 29, 2013).

Crawford, Neta. *US Budgetary Costs of Post-9/11 Wars through FY2018: $5.6 Trillion*. Providence, RI: Brown University, 2017.

FBI. "Seven Charged with Illegal Export of Electronics to U.S.-Designated Terrorist Entity in Paraguay." *News Release*, February 19, 2010.

Hesterman, Jennifer. *The Terrorist-Criminal Nexus: An Alliance of International Drug Cartels, Organized Crime, and Terror Groups*. Boca Raton, FL: CRC Press, 2013.

Hoffman, Bruce. "Al-Qaeda Has a New Strategy." *The Washington Post*, 2010.

———. "Al-Qaeda's Resurrection." *Council on Foreign Relations*, March 6, 2018.

———. *Inside Terrorism*. New York: Columbia University Press, 2006.

House of Representatives. "A Line in the Sand: Confronting the Threat at the Southwest Border." Committee on Homeland Security, Subcommittee on Investigations, Washington, DC, November, 2012.

Investigative Project on Terrorism. "Mexican Arrest Indicates Hizballah Seeking Foothold." www.investigativeproject.org/2046/mexican-arrest-indicates-hizballah-seeking (July 7, 2010).

Jones, Seth G. *Hunting in the Shadows: The Pursuit of Al Qa'ida since 9/11*. New York: W. W. Norton & Company, 2012.

Joscelyn, Thomas. "Zawahiri Incites Followers in the Maghreb." *The Long War Journal*, March 6, 2018.

Kaufman, Ellie. "2 Americans Led Double Lives as Hezbollah Agents, Officials Say." *CNN*, June 9, 2017.

KGTV News, San Diego. "House Homeland Security Chairman Tells Team 10 'Hezbollah in U.S.'" May 4, 2011. www.10news.com/news/terrorist-group-setting-up-operations-near-border

Levitt, Matthew. *Hezbollah: The Global Footprint of Lebanon Party of God.* Washington, DC: Georgetown University Press, April 9, 2015.

Opall-Rome, Barbara. "Russian Influence on Hezbollah Raises Red Flag in Israel." *Defense News*, November 6, 2016.

Ottolenghi, Emanuele. "Hezbollah in Latin America is a Threat the US Cannot Ignore." *The Hill*, June 11, 2017.

Raghavan, Sudarsan. "Niger Struggles against Islamist Militants." *The Washington Post*, August 17, 2012.

Rasmussen, Sune Engel. "As Islamic State Fades in Syria, Another Militant Group Takes Root." *The Wall Street Journal*, April 18, 2018.

Rotella, Sebastian. "Government Says Hezbollah Profits from U.S. Cocaine Market Via Link to Mexican Cartel." www.propublica.org/article/government-says-hezbollah-profits-from-us-cocaine-market-via-link-to-mexica (2011).

Sageman, Marc. *Understanding Terror Networks.* Philadelphia, PA: University of Pennsylvania Press, 2003.

Senate Armed Services Committee. "Posture Statement, Commander, U.S. Southern Command." United States Senate, Washington, DC, March 17, 2009.

Shekau, Abubakar and Josh Levs. "'I Will Sell Them,' Boko Haram Leader Says of Kidnapped Nigerian Girls." *CNN*, May 5, 2014.

Spagat, Elliot and Jacques Billeaud. "Drug Tunnels Discovered between U.S.–Mexico Border Contained Railcar System, Tons of Pot." *AP*, July 13, 2012.

Steele, Jonathan. "Bombers' Justification: Russians Are Killing Our Children, So We Are Here to Kill Yours." *The Guardian*, UK, September 6, 2004.

Toameh, Khaled Abu. *The Iran-HAMAS-Hezbollah Connection.* New York, NY: The Gatestone Institute, November 8, 2017.

US Department of State. "Assessing the Strength of Hizballah." Washington, DC, 2010.

———. Country Reports on Terrorism, 2017. www.state.gov/j/ct/rls/crt/2017/index.htm

US District Court for the Eastern District of Virginia. "Sealed Indictment: Ayman Joumaa." www.investigativeproject.org/documents/case_docs/1856.pdf (2011).

US District Court, San Antonio, Texas. "Sealed Indictment against Wissam 'Sam' Allouche." https://caselaw.findlaw.com/us-5th-circuit/1867790.html (2014).

US District Court, Southern District of New York. "Sealed Indictment: Jamal Yousef." www.justice.gov/archive/usao/nys/pressreleases/May12/yousef/yousefjamals4indictment.pdf (2009).

US General Accounting Office. "Terrorist Financing: U.S. Agencies Should Systematically Assess Terrorists' Use of Alternative Financing Mechanisms." Washington, DC, November 2003.

US Military Academy. "Letters from Abbottabad: Bin Laden." West Point, NY, 2012.

US Senate Committee on Homeland Security & Governmental Affairs. "The Future of Homeland Security: Evolving and Emerging Threats." Washington, DC, July 11, 2012.

Washington Post. "FBI Director: Number of Americans Traveling to Fight in Syria Increasing." May 2, 2014.

Wilson, Mark. "Nigeria's Boko Haram Attacks in Numbers: As Lethal as Ever." *BBC News*, January 25, 2018.

Wright, Lawrence. *Looming Tower*. New York: Knopf, 2007.

Yaghi, Sobhi M. "Israel Is Preparing for War Tunnels and Hezbollah Elements in the Southern Syrian Border." www.aljoumhouria.com/news/index/15409 (July 2, 2012).

Zaboun, Kifah. "Gaza Tunnel Trade: Matter of Life and Death for HAMAS." *Asharq Al-Awsat Newspaper*, August 31, 2012.

CHAPTER 4

Domestic Terrorism and the Homegrown Threat

Collateral damage.

—Timothy McVeigh,
regarding the nineteen children killed in his attack

INTRODUCTION

Perhaps nothing is as hard to comprehend and explain as domestic terrorism. What motivates individuals to kill fellow citizens unremorsefully and target the very institutions providing for their safety and prosperity? Many of the drivers are the same as those found in international terrorism, such as an extreme religious or political ideology and the ability to find inspiration, encouragement, tactical techniques, training, and resources anonymously through the Internet. With domestic terror, lone actors are of particular concern, as they are already embedded in society and their clandestine activities are more difficult to detect. These factors make the neutralization of the domestic threat extremely difficult for law enforcement agencies. Psychology is a factor, as well; the inherent disbelief in the phenomenon of domestic terrorism may result in a blind spot for investigators and first responders, a vulnerability best mitigated through education and training on the threat.

As a nation, we seem more transfixed by the threat of international terrorist groups striking on our soil, yet the number of domestic terror attacks has historically far outpaced international attacks on our soil.

Since 9/11, our engagement in the Middle East resulted in thousands of US and coalition casualties, invoking the wrath of terrorist groups. All the while, we continue to fight domestic extremism at home, interrupting at least 100 radical terror plots on our soil (Inserra 2017). Clearly, securing our populace from the terror threat has evolved into an exhausting and complex situation for resource-constrained organizations. We cannot merely prioritize and address threats accordingly; each is significant and could be catastrophic to our country and its citizens. Terror groups can prey on this complex situation by fronting threats that may not exist (such as al-Qaeda's suitcase nuclear bombs), which incites fear in the populace and forces us to spend billions of dollars on countermeasures. A low-cost domestic scenario might be to set off a rudimentary improvised explosive device (IED) and claim it was a dirty bomb. Panic would ensue, and even if the government assured there was no radioactive material, it is likely that in the current environment of skepticism and a conspiracy-minded public, a sizeable portion of the population would not believe the statement. Playing on our fears can cause as much psychological damage as a larger-scale attack.

The definition of domestic terrorism morphed since the events of 9/11 and subsequent attacks. Under current US law, set forth in the USA PATRIOT Act, acts of domestic terrorism are those which:

Involve acts dangerous to human life that violate federal or state law;
    Appear intended (i) to intimidate or coerce a civilian population; (ii) to influence the policy of a government by intimidation or coercion; or (iii) to affect the conduct of a government by mass destruction, assassination. or kidnapping; and
    Occur primarily within the territorial jurisdiction of the U.S.

Some legal experts point to the broad nature of these definitions, which could lead to the monitoring of innocent civilians and the erosion of freedoms such as free speech and the right to protest. Certainly, the balance between constitutional rights and security is delicate and must be at the forefront of every discussion regarding the investigation and prosecution of all criminal activities. As the dangers and complexities associated with domestic terrorism continue to grow, so must our corresponding detection and mitigation activities to fully protect citizens.

HISTORY OF DOMESTIC TERRORISM IN THE UNITED STATES

There is an extensive list of domestic terrorist attacks in the United States, which some believe date back to the Boston Tea Party, fueling the debate that "one man's terrorist is another man's freedom fighter." On December 16, 1773, a group of colonists called the Sons of Liberty disguised themselves as Native Americans, boarded British ships, and dumped cases of tea into the harbor as a sign of rebellion against the ruling government and its taxation laws. The attack prompted the passing of the Coercive Acts by the British, meant to contain and suppress rebellion among the colonists; however, they caused outrage and sparked the war for independence. Was the Tea Party freedom fighting or an attack against the state?

To support the discussion of the persistence and lethality of modern domestic terrorism, we start in 1865 with the emergence of the Klu Klux Klan (KKK) at the end of the Civil War, marking the beginning of a new era of violence and unrest in our country. A secret vigilante group with extreme methods, the KKK violently murdered and intimidated African Americans and the white legislators who fought for their freedom from slavery and full integration into our society. The group routinely burned homes and bombed churches and schools with dynamite, in a campaign of killing and terrorizing. The KKK's attempts to keep black Americans from exercising their constitutional rights such as voting led to the passing of the Civil Rights Act of 1871. The act banned the use of terror, force, or bribery by the KKK to prevent people from voting and made these and other terroristic activities federal offenses. The Klan continues to be an underlying current of hate in our country, with other white supremacists expanding the racist agenda to include anti-Semitism, such as Christian Identity offshoot Aryan Nations, which formed in the 1970s. Terrorism expert Bruce Hoffman (1988) considers the Aryan Nations the first "truly nationwide terrorist network in the U.S."

Violent anarchism has existed in the United States for almost 100 years. In April 1919, an anarchist group, the Galleanists, mailed thirty-six dynamite bombs to high-ranking officials, including the attorney general of the United States. The delivery was meant for May 1, when Americans celebrate the international labor movement; however, several bombs exploded early, and their unique packaging led to the discovery and neutralization of the other devices. Not content with this operation, the group struck again on the evening of June 2, 1919, when large dynamite and metal slug bombs simultaneously exploded in eight US cities. The group was targeting government officials and judges who endorsed anti-sedition laws and sentenced anarchists to prison. On September 16, 1920, a horse-drawn wagon bomb exploded on Wall Street in front of the J. P. Morgan bank, killing thirty-eight people. The device consisted of 100 pounds of dynamite and 500 pounds of cast iron weights to amplify the casualties. No one person or group was ever officially charged with the crime. Continuing labor struggles and anti-capitalist sentiment led by anarchist groups such as the violent Galleanists were likely at the root of this bombing. Anarchists are still very active around the world, protesting and resorting to violent tactics as needed. They are especially known for a blatant disregard for law and for their willful destruction of property.

Bath, Michigan, was the scene of a "lone wolf" soft target, anti-government attack on May 18, 1927. Andrew Kehoe, upset with policies and tax law he believed led to his farm foreclosure, murdered his wife, and then detonated three dynamite bombs at the Bath Consolidated School, where he worked as the treasurer. Kehoe spent months planting explosive material throughout the building in a premeditated act that stunned the country. When confronted at the scene by law enforcement, he detonated a vehicle bomb, killing himself and the school superintendent.

The 1960s and 1970s saw the rise of far-left violent antiestablishment groups such as the Weather Underground, a group formed at the University of Michigan, Ann Arbor, campus in 1969. The group held Marxist views of the elite ruling the middle class and bombed both the Pentagon and the State Department, as well as corporations. The Symbionese Liberation Army, which started as a black revolutionary group and grew into a violent guerilla-type organization, carried out robberies, bombings, and murders, once using hollow-point bullets packed with cyanide to kill a school superintendent and his deputy. The militant Black Panthers began with a socialist agenda but soon morphed into an anti-establishment group routinely targeting law enforcement. Spurred by anti-Arab and anti-Muslim ideology, the Jewish Defense League (JDL) launched twenty-seven attacks against organizations it perceived to be anti-Semitic, including universities and academics. Black September, the Palestinian group responsible for killing eleven Israeli athletes at the 1972 Munich Olympics, was quite active in the United States, plotting to kill Prime Minister Golda Meir during a visit to New York City in 1973 with three pre-positioned car bombs, which failed to detonate. Political ideology fueled the Puerto Rican paramilitary group, the Fuerzas Armadas de Liberación Nacional (FALN), which was particularly brutal in its tactics and executed 120 bombings in the United States between 1974 and 1983, with targets including restaurants and a theater. The FALN was a Marxist-Leninist group wanting the United States out of Puerto Rico both militarily and politically.

Moving forward to 1978, the country was transfixed by attacks perpetrated by Theodore Kaczynski, a Harvard University graduate and former mathematics professor. Kaczynski was a self-professed "neo-Luddite," or one opposing modern technology who destroys private property as a means of protest. He lived in a wood shack in the forest, forgoing water or electricity; Kaczynski became enraged when developers moved into the area, destroying trees and displacing animals. Over the course of the next seventeen years, Kaczynski sent sixteen letter bombs to academics and others working in technological fields, killing three people and injuring twenty-three. Labeled the University and Airline Bomber (UNABOM) by the FBI, his lengthy manifesto was published in 1996 in the *New York Times* and the *Washington Post*, under the threat of more attacks. Kaczynski's campaign of terror against soft targets ended with capture when his brother recognized his work and called authorities.

On April 19, 1995, in the deadliest act of domestic terror in our country's history, Timothy McVeigh detonated a truck bomb in Oklahoma City, killing 168 people and injuring 680 others. Victims included children in a childcare center located within this government facility. McVeigh and co-conspirator Terry Nichols met in the army, becoming anti-government survivalists who supported the militia movement. McVeigh was likely aligned with the Christian Identity group and Nichols with the sovereign citizen movement. McVeigh was enraged with the government's handling of the 1992 Ruby Ridge, Idaho, standoff, as well as the 1993 Waco, Texas, standoff with the Branch Davidian religious sect. McVeigh visited Waco during the siege and after its tragic ending, when the compound caught on fire, killing seventy-five occupants including children. McVeigh stated the Oklahoma City bombing was retribution against the government for Waco. Prior to his death by lethal injection in 2001, McVeigh was housed in the same Supermax wing, known as "bomber's block," with Ted Kaczynski and al-Qaeda mastermind Ramzi Yousef. After the deadly Oklahoma City bombing, then-Attorney General Janet Reno formed a special task force to coordinate the country's response to the threat of domestic terrorism. The task force was scheduled to hold one of its monthly meetings on September 11, 2001, but did not due to the attack. In fact, because the threat of jihadist terrorism has taken so much of the government's attention since 9/11, the special task force has never met again.

Eric Robert Rudolph, also an army veteran, was responsible for a series of deadly bombings between 1996 and 1998, killing two people and injuring more than 100. His targets included Centennial Park at the Olympic Games in Atlanta, two abortion clinics, and a gay bar. Rudolph was a member of the Christian Identity movement, a white nationalist sect believing God's chosen people are white and all others are condemned to hell. Although Rudolph claimed religious motivation and his antiabortion, antigay agenda for his attacks, he stated his actions were not racially motivated. He was on the run until 2003, when caught in a small North Carolina mountain town, rummaging through a dumpster for food. After pleading guilty and apologizing to family members of those he killed and injured in the Atlanta attack (only), Rudolph avoided the death penalty and is serving a life sentence at the Supermax facility, just down the hall from Kaczynski and Yousef.

In 2009, an act of domestic terror occurred on a military installation at Fort Hood, Texas. Former Major/Dr. Nidal Malik Hasan, a man who took not only the oath to protect and defend our country but also the Hippocratic oath to prevent harm to humans, stunned our country when he ambushed and killed thirteen of his fellow soldiers as they processed for deployment. Inspired to carry out his plan by radical Islamist Anwar al-Awlaki through a series of emails, Hasan voiced his extremist views and opposition to his upcoming deployment to Afghanistan to his chain of command prior to the shooting but no action was taken. Federal law enforcement agencies were aware of the communication between Awlaki and Hasan, yet the information was not passed to the base. On August 28, 2013, Hasan was found guilty of thirteen counts of premeditated murder and thirty-two counts of attempted murder and was sentenced to death. Being on death row has not changed Hasan's propensities; in August 29, 2014, he wrote a letter to the leaders of ISIS asking for "admittance" to the Islamic State.

On February 18, 2010, software engineer Joseph Stack set his house on fire and then flew a small aircraft into the Internal Revenue Service building in Austin, Texas, which housed three hundred workers. Stack was furious about his tax problems and angry with collection agencies. His February 18, 2010, suicide note stated:

> Violence not only is the answer, it is the only answer and I saw it written once that the definition of insanity is repeating the same process over and over and expecting the outcome to suddenly be different. I am finally ready to stop this insanity. Well, Mr. Big Brother IRS man, let's try something different; take my pound of flesh and sleep well. The communist creed: From each according to his ability, to each according to his need. The capitalist creed: From each according to his gullibility, to each according to his greed.

(CBS News 2010)

Stack's attack killed an IRS manager, seriously injured fifteen other workers, and cost the IRS $38 million to replace the building and its operation.

These are just a few examples of acts of domestic terror attacks in the United States to show the breadth and depth of the challenges facing law enforcement.

THE TWENTY-FIRST CENTURY AND THE RISING TIDE OF DOMESTIC EXTREMISM

Before delving into the topic of domestic terrorism, we should first have a basic understanding of associated terms. Extremism is advocacy of extreme measures or views, radicalism. Radicalism, which we will discuss later in the chapter, is favoring extreme changes in existing views, habits, conditions, or institutions.

Note that not all extremists are violent. Some people have extreme views on religion, political issues, social issues, and single-interest issues like the environment or animals—but they never cross the line into violence. Also, there are distinct kinds of extremism. There is nonviolent "pen/tongue" extremism, where essays, speeches, and "think tanks" may incite others to violence. Although peaceful in orientation, if the views do not further peace and harmony in society, then a line is crossed. Also, pen/tongue extremism activity may serve to inspire, incite, recruit, boost morale, and fundraise. At times in our democratic society, we may leave these pen/tongue activities alone, believing they provide a "vent," giving groups a way to engage peacefully and ultimately preventing violence. However, these groups and thinkers may not actually pull the trigger but could be putting the gun in someone else's hands. In February 2018, the Canadian Security Intelligence Service released research findings on mobilization to violence and noted not all violent extremists progress from words to deeds; many espouse violent extremist ideas, but never undertake violent extremist activities. Intelligence and law enforcement agencies continue to grapple with the issue of how to determine whether a person has both intent and capability to physically transition from thought to action—or to mobilize to violence.

"Gun/bullet" extremism ends in physical violence. Violent extremism, which fuels terror, is defined by the FBI as "beliefs and actions of people who support or use violence to achieve radical ideological goals." Violent extremists have a distorted, divergent interpretation, beliefs, and values. They also think their beliefs or way of life are under attack. In terms of extremism in the US, we find it in every kind of terrorism explored in this book: right-wing, left-wing, single-interest, and religious.

Unfortunately, unlike foreign terror organizations, there is no open-source government repository for information regarding the number and scope of domestic terror groups in the United States. Other groups stepped into the void: the Heritage Center with its tracking of radical Islamist domestic plots; the George Washington University's Center Project on Extremism tracking ISIS in America; the Combatting Terrorism Center at West Point with analysis; the START program's compilation of terrorist attacks, and the Southern Poverty Law Center (SPLC), cataloguing hate groups and activity. This chapter uses data from all four to paint a holistic picture of the domestic terror threat.

Postmodern domestic terror is similar to international terror because groups are often loose coalitions and franchises, held together by ideology, rather than a strong and charismatic leader. According to radicalization expert Daveed Gartenstein-Ross, the most frequently cited work on the concept of "leaderless resistance" was published by white supremacist Louis Beam in his "Inter-Klan Newsletter & Survival Alert," in 1983, and again in his journal, *The Seditionist*, in 1992. Beam believed the traditional hierarchical methods of organizing the white separatist left it vulnerable to destruction by the government; therefore, at some point, white separatists would not have the option of belonging to a group. He proposed a "leaderless resistance" structure, modeled after "committees of correspondence that existed throughout the thirteen colonies during the American Revolution." Beam postulated that each committee receive information from the government, but be a secret cell, operating independently, acting on a local level. He also proposed organization around "very small or even one-man cells of resistance" and advocated staying away from pyramidal organizations that are "an easy kill" for the government in light of federal informants and intelligence-gathering capabilities. "The last thing [f]ederal snoops" want, according to Beam, are "a thousand different small phantom cells opposing them" (Gartenstein-Ross and Gruen 2010).

Leaderless resistance, or the "phantom cell," has moved from the white supremacist realm into all other areas of domestic terrorism. By leveraging the Internet, groups can give tactical direction, guidance, inspiration, and money to followers, who then conduct operations independently. The anarchist magazine *Do or Die* explains:

> The North American ELF [Earth Liberation Front] has no central authority, no membership, no public meetings and no mailing lists. People from all walks of life are taking action as ELF activists, and this loose structure has created a network that is effective and very hard for state and industry forces to infiltrate and destroy.
>
> (Cecil-Cockwell 2008)

The leaderless resistance methodology also culls lone actors from society and encourages and enables them to act. Therefore, an engagement strategy might be more effective if the ideology itself is countered rather than attempting to confront individuals or dismantle groups.

Further complicating the challenges: according to the National Consortium for the Study of Terrorism and Responses to Terrorism (START), a DHS Center of Excellence led by the University of Maryland, terrorist attacks in the United States between 2010 and 2016 were typically carried out by individual perpetrators only loosely linked to a specific organization or ideological movement (Rivinius 2017).

DOMESTIC TERRORISM: PERSISTENT AND LETHAL

We can break domestic terrorism down into three categories, the first being active domestic terrorism, which is cyclical with violent clashes such as anarchists, environmental activists, and peaceful protests that turn violent. Second is dormant domestic terrorism, which exists but is latent and inactive, for example antiabortion and black extremism. Third is persistent domestic terrorism, which is always present, namely white supremacist groups—the number one domestic terror concern for DHS. Unlike in the international terror realm, there is no comprehensive list of domestic terror groups.

For a general overview of the domestic terror landscape, data compiled from 2010 to 2016, collected and analyzed by START, indicates the proportion of terrorist attacks by religious and right-wing extremists is on the rise in the US (Rivinius 2017).

> In the 2010s, compared to the 2000s, there was a sharp decline in the proportion of terrorist attacks carried out by left-wing, environmentalist extremists during the first seven years of the 2010s (from 64% to 12%). At the same time, there was a sharp increase in the proportion of attacks carried out by right-wing extremists (from 6% to 35%) and religious extremists (from 9% to 53%) in the United States.
>
> (START 2018)

Other agencies are also sounding an alarm about the rise in white supremacist violence. According to a May 2017 intelligence bulletin by the FBI and DHS, white supremacist extremism poses a persistent threat of lethal violence and was responsible for forty-nine homicides in twenty-six attacks from 2000 to 2016—more than any other domestic extremist movement (Winter 2017). The Anti-Defamation League's Center on Extremism report, "Murder and Extremism in the United States in 2017" shows that extremists killed thirty-four people last year. Twenty of those victims, or 59 percent, were killed by right-wing extremists, a 157 percent increase over the seven people killed by white supremacists in 2016. Also double the number of people killed by domestic Islamic extremists in 2017 (ADL 2017).

In addition to political and religious extremism, hate fuels terror. The SPLC is a nonprofit civil rights organization dedicated to fighting hate and bigotry and seeking justice for the most vulnerable members of society. Founded in 1971, the organization successfully prosecutes cases against white supremacist groups and other extremist organizations on behalf of its clients. Part of the SPLC mission is to "track the activities of hate groups and domestic terrorists across America," and many federal agencies are the benefactors of its vast repository of information. The groups tracked by SPLC include anti-government, radical religious, neo-Nazi, Klu Klux Klan, Aryan Nations, black separatist, antigay, anti-immigrant, and the newest category, anti-Muslim groups. Some question the SPLC's methodology for labeling a group as "extremist" but its database is extremely valuable for tracking trends, tactics, and ideology.

In 2001, the SPLC reported 676 domestic hate and extremist groups; this number steadily climbed to 954 in 2017, with the high of 1,018 groups in 2011. Hate crimes are motivated by bias, targeting victims or institutions because of certain characteristics. As a result of the emotions involved, hate crimes can be more violent than traditional crimes.

The FBI hate crime database, populated from the Uniform Crime Reporting (UCR) system, is a good starting point for analyzing hate crime trends in the US, https://ucr.fbi.gov/hate-crime. In 2016, 57.5 percent of hate crimes were motivated by a race/ethnicity/ancestry bias; 21.0 percent by religious bias; 17.7 percent from sexual-orientation bias; 2.0 percent by gender-identity bias; 1.2 percent by disability bias and 0.5 percent by a gender bias. In 2016, more than 2,000 of the hate crimes resulted in physical assault.

Domestic terror groups and incidents are often categorized as right-wing, left-wing, "single-issue," or radical Islamist, or in this case, "homegrown." Although it is impossible to cover all groups in one mere chapter, most either have a history of attacking soft targets or the will to do so to further their goals.

RIGHT-WING EXTREMISM

Right-wing groups often adhere to the principles of racial supremacy and embrace anti-government, anti-regulatory beliefs. Right-wing terrorism is typically associated with those espousing neo-Nazi and racist ideologies, as well as opposition to foreigners and immigration. According to the FBI, in the late 1990s, right-wing extremism overtook left-wing terrorism to become the most dangerous domestic terrorist threat to the country. A joint 2013 report by the National Counterterrorism Center, the National Consortium for the Study of Terrorism and Responses to Terrorism, and the Southern Poverty Law Center found right-wing extremists are responsible for 56 percent of domestic terrorist attacks and plots since the 1995 Oklahoma City bombing (Sofer and Bernstein 2012). The Ruby Ridge confrontation and the Waco Siege cemented the right-wing faction and ideology in our country. Hot-button issues such as immigration, gun control, abortion, and anti-Muslim sentiment, along with an increase of government conspiracy theories present unique drivers for right-wing radicalization and recruitment. *Challengers from the Sidelines: Understanding America's Violent Far-Right* (Perlinger 2012) is an outstanding report from the Combatting Terrorism Center at West Point. The study delves into the dramatic rise in the number of attacks and violent plots originating from individuals and groups who self-identify with the far right of American politics. It provides a conceptual foundation and empirical analysis of right-wing violence, as well as naming its characteristics and drivers.

White Supremacists

White supremacists believe white people are superior to those of all other races, especially the black race, and should therefore dominate society.

Due to its lengthy history and staying power, the most well-known white supremacist group is the KKK, covered earlier in this chapter. Black Americans are the Klan's primary target, but it also attacks Jews, immigrants, gays, and lesbians. According to the SPLC website, there are approximately seventy-two KKK chapters in twenty states. A recent case involved a former Klan leader. On April 13, 2014, Frazier Glenn Miller (aka Frazier Glenn Cross), 73, opened fire at a Jewish community center in Overland Park, Kansas, killing three people, including a 14-year-old Eagle Scout and his grandfather. Miller, a retired Army veteran and Green Beret, was the founder and former leader of the Carolina Knights of the Ku Klux Klan and the White Patriot Party.

Adherents of white nationalist groups, numbering around 100 in the US, believe that white identity should be the organizing principle of the countries that make up Western civilization. The Alternative Right, Stormfront, the American Freedom Party, Identity Evropa, and Right Stuff are the most widespread groups. The Alt-Right movement has grown since 2010, when white supremacist Richard Spencer used the term to describe a group of white nationalists. The group basically formed on the Internet through 4chan and other forums. SLPC reports that more than 100 people were killed and injured in thirteen attacks by alt-right-influenced perpetrators since 2014 (Hankes and Amend 2018). From August 11 to 12, 2017, the Unite the Right rally was held in Charlottesville, Virginia, with the stated goal to oppose the removal of a statue of Robert E. Lee from Emancipation Park. Another organizer, Nathan Damigo, said the rally was intended to unify the white nationalist movement in the United States. Protestors included white supremacists, white nationalists, neo-Confederates, Klansmen, neo-Nazis, and various militias. Some marchers chanted racist and anti-Semitic slogans, carried semiautomatic rifles, swastikas, Confederate battle flags, and anti-Muslim and anti-Semitic banners. By the second day of the rally, counterprotestors arrived and tempers flared. Law enforcement was overwhelmed and unprepared to deal with the size of the crowd and violence erupted. DeAndre Harris, a black man, was beaten by six white men in a parking garage right next to police headquarters. Fourteen protestors were injured in street brawls. The violence culminated at 1:45 p.m. on the second day of the protests, when James Alex Fields, Jr., age 20, a Nazi sympathizer, accelerated up a street filled with counterprotestors and deliberately drove his vehicle into the crowd, killing one and injuring nineteen. Before his name was revealed, there was a massive disinformation campaign online by the AltRight regarding the identity of the driver. Later, conspiracy theorists picked apart video of the attack, stating that no one died and those injured were crisis actors.

In August 2017, the FBI expressed concern over what it labels Black Identity Extremism (BIE), a violent extremism that grew from the Black

Lives Matter (BLM) movement. BLM started in 2013 after the acquittal of George Zimmerman, who shot and killed black teenager Trayvon Martin in Florida. Although starting as a peaceful movement indorsed by celebrities and lawmakers, some BLM protests turned violent when counterprotestors engaged the crowd, and the events also became targets of opportunity for white supremacist violence. On November 24, 2015, in a premeditated act, four Minnesota men shot and wounded five BLM protestors in Minneapolis. The men initially connected online in racist web forums, and they launched a plan to disrupt the demonstration. One shooter appeared in a racially tinged video a few days before the protest and said he was planning to livestream the protest to "rile things up." Violence from the BLM protestors only threw fuel on the fire. On July 7, 2016, a BLM protest in Dallas, Texas, was peaceful and wrapping up. Twenty-five-year-old Army vet Micah Xavier Johnson opened fire in an ambush, killing five police officers and wounding seven others and two civilians.

BIE perceptions of police brutality against African Americans spurred an increase in premeditated, retaliatory lethal violence against law enforcement. Police killing increased following the August 9, 2014, shooting of Michael Brown in Ferguson, Missouri, and the grand jury's decision not to charge any police officers. Some of the philosophical and ideological underpinnings of BIE are reflective of the "Moorish" sovereign citizens, and several of those arrest in cases of police attack are affiliated. Moorish sovereign citizens emerged in the mid-1990s on the East Coast with the merging of sovereign citizen ideas with some of the beliefs of the exclusively black Moorish Science Temple of America, a religious sect dating back to 1913, founded by Noble Drew Ali. The Nation of Islam arose from the Moorish Science Temple movement after the death of Noble Drew Ali, which splintered the organization. Some BIE members claim they are part of the "Washitaw Nation," a leaderless "virtual" group originating in Louisiana.

There were other right-wing violence cases in 2016 and 2017, such as the Charleston AME church massacre committed by white supremacist Dylann Roof (covered in Chapter 5); the racially motivated killing of three Indian men in a bar in Olathe, Kansas, by a man who thought they were Middle Easterners; and the slaying of a black man on a New York City street by an attacker with a sword, saying it was a "dry run." Racial unrest and violence continues to plague American society and fuel domestic terror.

Militias

By definition, a militia is a military force of ordinary citizens who seek to provide defense and law enforcement to society without pay. According to the Michigan Militia Corps, "A well-armed citizenry is the best form of Homeland Security and can better deter crime, invasion, terrorism, and tyranny" (mmcw.org, 2018). The original militias were force multipliers during the Revolutionary War, protecting towns and citizens from the British army. However, modern militias are right-wing groups with paramilitary training stockpiling weapons and explosives, espousing a conspiracy-oriented ideology. The modern militia movement arose after the Waco and Ruby Ridge events, as members disagreed with the government's actions. Timothy McVeigh was aligned with the Michigan militia, which has the most active members in the country. Lee Miracle, a postal worker who goes by the moniker "Weapon M" has his own webpage and participated in an interview with a major news network showing his young daughter expertly handling a shotgun. Although Miracle is a moderate in the militia realm, advocating for his troops to stockpile and prepare for a homeland defense mission, most militia websites are replete with paranoid, anti-government rhetoric and warnings about a dark future filled with disasters, calamity, and FEMA "concentration camps" that are currently under construction. Also, a member of the Michigan Militia, Mark Koernke served a three-year prison sentence for assaulting a police officer and resisting arrest. Upon return to society, he started the Liberty Tree Radio station and a series of webcasts. Programs like Koernke's and videos on the Internet, both protected by the First Amendment as free speech, further spread conspiracies about forthcoming martial law and a crackdown by the "new world order." The Michigan Militia Corps Wolverines are a very active militia with an extensive website, http://mmcw.org/. A very "progressive" group, the website states:

> Everyone is welcome, regardless of race, creed, color, religion or political affiliation, provided you do not wish to bring harm to our country or people. If you are a United States citizen (or have declared your intent to become such), who is capable of bearing arms, or supports the right to do so, then YOU ARE the MILITIA!

There are almost 100 militia groups in the United States with an overarching, harmless sounding motto to "protect the Constitution against all enemies, foreign and domestic." However, their definition of a "domestic enemy" is worrisome and can include government leaders they believe are sapping rights and freedoms. For instance, many militias see healthcare reform and any type of gun control as unconstitutional. There is a lengthy list of orders they refuse to follow, many of which could bring them weapon-to-weapon with law enforcement and our military during states of emergency. The Oathkeepers, a group formed in 2009, was linked to the militia movement. A prominent Oathkeeper site (www.lincolncountywatch.org/links.html) states openly: "The greatest threat we face today is not terrorists; it is our federal government"—a declaration becoming a mantra for members of right-wing extremist groups. Militias are not opposed to carrying out violent acts against soft targets to further their goals. For example, the Hutaree, a Michigan militia also part of the Christian Patriot movement, prepared for what they believed would be an apocalyptic battle with the Antichrist, who would be supported and defended by law enforcement. Their plan was to kill a law enforcement officer in March 2010 and then stage an attack on the officer's funeral procession and kill many others (US Department of Justice 2010). Despite hundreds of hours of video showing training and exposing the group's ideology and plans, seven of the nine convictions were overturned in court with the judge stating the prosecution failed to make its case. Two group members served two years on weapons charges.

Sovereign Citizens

The sovereign citizen group is unusual in its tactics, ranging from white-collar crime to impersonating and killing law enforcement officers. Experts believe the group has more than 100,000 core and 200,000 fringe members and has operated in the United States for at least twenty years (McNabb 2010). A spinoff of the defunct, violent Posse Comitatus, a white supremacist, anti-Semitic group from the 1980s, the group's most famous member is Terry Nichols, who conspired with Timothy McVeigh to destroy the Murrah Building. The sovereigns' ideology has changed through the years, first believing "God gave America to the white man" and espousing conspiracy theories regarding Jewish control of the government. The group has moved away from this ideology, now believing it can operate outside any government authority. Therefore, its members do not adhere to laws or pay taxes. The group also believes in the "redemption theory," certain that the US government went bankrupt when it abandoned the gold standard basis for currency in 1933 and began using citizens as collateral in trade agreements with foreign governments. This notion fuels the sovereigns' belief that the government does not act in the best interests of its citizens and gives permission to steal from the US Treasury rightfully to secure money with the people. Sovereigns also create and sell fraudulent documents such as driver's licenses, diplomatic and law enforcement credentials, and concealed firearms permits. The sovereign citizen Declaration of Independence states (grammatical errors included):

> We the People inhabiting the North American continent, free men and women convened under God, having been granted by the Creator dominion over all the earth, to restore the blessings of liberty for

ourselves and the posterity, do hereby invoke our sacred right to alter or abolish destructive government as memorialized in The unanimous Declaration of the thirteen united States of America, c. 1776 by declaring herewith this solemn declaration to the people of the earth and all governments and nations derived there from.

Any confrontation with law enforcement is likely to end in violence. Since 2000, group members have killed eight law enforcement officers, wounding several others. In 2010, two Arkansas police officers stopped sovereign citizen extremists Jerry Kane and his 16-year-old son during a routine traffic stop on Interstate 40. Joseph Kane immediately jumped out of the vehicle and opened fire with an AK-47 assault rifle, instantly killing both officers. In 2011, sovereign citizen James Michael Tesi shot a police officer in Texas on a traffic stop; the officer survived. In 2012, Sheriff's Deputies Brandon Nielson and Jeremy Triche were ambushed and killed at a trailer park in La Place, Louisiana, while investigating an earlier shooting in which two deputies were shot and wounded working a traffic detail. A SWAT team entered the trailer park and apprehended the group—four men and three women, some with ties to the sovereign citizens and others with criminal records. The group was under surveillance in Tennessee and then De Soto Parish, Louisiana, after brushes with the law including weapons charges, high-speed chases, and having sovereign citizen's paraphernalia. Unfortunately, the group left law enforcement radar just a few weeks prior to the shooting, moving to La Place (Galofaro 2012). Although an official investigation report was never released, information was likely not shared between federal and local law enforcement, creating an ambush situation for the officers.

Sovereigns have also engaged in elaborate planning to kill law enforcement and government officials, as well as their families. For example, in 2011, five people, including popular activist Schaeffer Cox, were arrested in Fairbanks, Alaska, for conspiring to kill multiple Alaska state troopers and a federal judge, his children, and grandchildren in what is labeled the "241" murder conspiracy case. The group stockpiled grenades and weapons with silencers and conducted surveillance on the homes of their targets. The five faced several state charges, including conspiracy to commit murder, to commit kidnapping, to commit arson, and tampering with evidence, according to troopers. All pled guilty and were convicted, with Cox receiving a twenty-six-year sentence (Burke 2012).

Cox, who unsuccessfully ran for Congress in 2008, was on law enforcement's radar since 2009 as the leader of the Alaska Peacemakers Militia and the Second Amendment Task Force. He organized multiple gun-rights and personal freedoms rallies and was a member of a "Liberty Bell network," which sends out mass notifications to assemble a crowd of witnesses when a member believes his or her rights are being violated by the police. Cox's video repository can still be viewed online, and it serves as a great education tool for the mindset of a sovereign citizen, the conspiratorial nature of this ideology, and the willingness to use violence to "kill in the name of liberty" (The Solution: Schaeffer Cox Speaks on the Future of the Liberty Movement 2012).

Although most sovereign citizen-related crime in the last four years was tax fraud or filing false claims, a few violent events kept the group on law enforcement's radar. On June 6, 2014, Dennis Marx, a member of the sovereign citizens movement, opened fire in a Forsyth County, Georgia, courthouse, injuring one deputy before being shot and killed. In 2015, 40-year-old E-Yage Bowens was sentenced to 485 years in prison for repeatedly raping a 16-year-old girl and forcing her to cut herself; Bowens claimed that as a sovereign citizen he was immune from US laws. On December 13, 2016, Markeith Loyd, a self-proclaimed sovereign, killed his girlfriend and was on the run until spotted at a Walmart in Orlando. As police officer Debra Clayton approached, Loyd shot and killed her. Finally, in April 2017, sovereign Steven Thomas Boehle was arrested in Austin, Texas, and police seized three guns and more than 1,000 rounds of ammunition. Boehle was planning a mass shooting attack to celebrate his 50th birthday.

According to the FBI, sovereigns may be identified through the following behaviors:

Using the terminology "freeing money from the strawman," a reference to the redemption theory and the US Treasury.

Names spelled in all capital letters or with colons (e.g., JOHN SMITH or Smith: John).

Signatures followed by the words "under duress," "Sovereign Living Soul" (SLS), or a copyright symbol (©).

Signing in red crayon or personal seals, stamps, or thumb prints in red ink.

The words "accepted for value."

Presenting false identification, especially driver's licenses.

Sovereigns not only have an inherent distrust of law enforcement but also step up and engage, and then videotape, analyze, and share the officers' response. Sovereign Cop Watch, which has a branch specializing in "undercover and reverse sting police conduct investigations," has a strong presence on the Internet. YouTube channels includes a series of videos instructing members on how to resist arrest and manipulate law enforcement situations in order to win in court. The group has an active Reddit page, and is a strong voice on the Facebook page "Police the Police" with more than one million members.

Sovereign citizens present a complex and dangerous challenge for law enforcement and society. Training and recognition of the groups' culture and tactics, as well as information sharing between agencies and states, is critical to engaging and mitigating the threat.

LEFT-WING EXTREMISM

Left-wing groups typically possess a revolutionary socialist doctrine, viewing themselves as the protectors of the people from capitalism and imperialism; however, they are willing to attack soft targets and kill citizens to further goals. Left-wing activism in the United States was spurred by anti-Vietnam sentiment, the perception law enforcement was spying on citizens, and events such as the shooting of students at Kent State by National Guard personnel in the 1970s. These events caused government distrust, which led to protest and violent clashes. Leftist extremists were responsible for a preponderance of the domestic violence in the 1960s and 1970s and for three-fourths of the officially designated acts of terrorism in America in the 1980s. The United States was not the only country facing a strong threat from the left; internationally, of the 13,858 people who died between 1988 and 1998 in attacks, 74 percent were killed by leftist organizations. The threat from the left in the United States diminished in the 1980s and 1990s, as a result of the arrest of many group leaders and the loss of support from nations formerly affiliated with, or part of, the Soviet Union. As the START data shows, the proportion of domestic terrorist attacks carried out by left-wing extremists from 2010 to 2017 is 12 percent (START 2018). However, we should not sideline the danger from the left-wing extremists, especially from anarchist and single-issue activists.

Anarchists

Anarchism is a political philosophy viewing the State as undesirable, unnecessary, and harmful. Anarchists instead promote a stateless society, or anarchy. An anarchist is an individual who furthers his or her political and/or social goals through force or violence and violation of law. They may typically espouse anti-capitalist, anti-globalization, communist, Marxist, and socialist philosophies. There are branches of the movement with specific agendas such as left, green, free market, and people of color. Anarchists promote a system called agorism, or revolutionary market anarchism. In a market anarchist society, law and security would be provided by market actors instead of political institutions.

Anarchists are now present at nearly every international gathering and they escalate fear among attendees, residents, and business owners, driving up security costs. For instance, Canada spent $900 million to secure Toronto for the G-20 summit in 2010, but it was not enough to keep anarchists from wreaking havoc on the streets, burning police cars, smashing storefronts, and terrorizing citizens. Those arrested were not just Canadians; anarchists from the United States and European countries traveled to the summit location to participate in the violence. Anarchist groups continue to use the black bloc technique, which originated in German riots in the 1970s in which protestors wore black hoods, balaclavas, and helmets as a show of solidarity and as disguise. After the violent acts are perpetrated, the clothing can be stripped off so the anarchist will blend in with other citizens and escape.

Anarchists are now moving beyond protests at events to actively planning attacks. In 2011, the FBI arrested an anarchist group for a plot to blow up a bridge in Cleveland, Ohio, using C-4 explosives. The attack was meant to bring down financial institution signage on the bridge, not necessarily the bridge. This event served as a good reminder about target selection not always being what it appears; had the bridge fallen due to the attack, the investigatory process may have leaned toward a homegrown terror theory and away from the true perpetrators and their rationale.

The anarchists regularly use Twitter to give real-time directions about where to rally, what to wear, and how to engage law enforcement, and they also extensively use websites and chat rooms to communicate, educate, and coordinate protests. When Los Angeles transit police officer Johannes Mehserle shot and killed Oscar Grant early New Year's Day, 2009, the anarchist community vigorously protested. Their activity escalated on July 8, 2010, when Mehserle's court case ended with a verdict and sentence. While monitoring anarchist websites and Twitter, I captured the following communiqué:

> To everyone coming out to 14th and Broadway on Verdict Day: Some of us will be with you at 14th and Broadway on the day of the verdict. We know that the pigs will be looking to cause trouble, but we're not going to give them an excuse. We want everyone in Oakland to come out to 14th and Broadway. We'll leave it to the will of the people assembled to decide what goes down there. Also, we just heard that Alameda County dropped at least $675,000 on an LRAD 300X sonic weapon system, so bring earplugs.

The communiqué indicates the very essence of leaderless resistance and the ability of the group to gather inside information and adapt operations based on law enforcement's posture.

The establishment of the Center for a Stateless Society (CSS), an anarchist think tank, has brought a group of academic elites to the table. CSS has a staff and advisory panel of experts, including professors from large universities, and also collects donations for its cause. The website includes a 106-question quiz to identify social and political "philosophy," and there is a large repository of well-written articles on anarchy (http://c4ss.org). The lesson CSS teaches is that we should not envision anarchists as mere thugs, storefront smashers, and "occupiers." Some of our academic elite believe in a stateless society and are in a position to compel others. A new organization, the Students for a Stateless Society, recently launched its webpage with ideas for events from bake sales to protests; seven universities currently have chapters (http://s4ss.org/).

After 9/11, some American anarchists joined the ranks of the "truthers," who developed conspiracy theories about the attacks, believing the World Trade Center contained bombs, the Pentagon was hit with a missile, Israel was behind the attacks, or the event was an inside job done by the CIA so the US would go to war in the Middle East. The Boston Marathon attack was dissected frame by frame on the Internet by truthers who believe it was a false flag event staged by the government with actors, moulage, and props. Some even believe the attack at Sandy Hook elementary was a government-staged false flag operation. Just minutes after the horrific Las Vegas massacre, conspiracy theorists took to social media discussing a second shooter, crisis actors, fake blood at the scene and so forth. Naturally this type of rhetoric is painful to family members of the deceased and those injured in the attack. One student injured in a mass shooting, who was hounded and threated by people who accused her of being a crisis actor, is taking legal action against a conspiracy-fueled radio show. Wild speculation regarding the Sutherland Springs church massacre turned violent; two conspiracy theorists engaged in a violent and cruel act against the pastor whose daughter was killed in the incident.

In terms of the larger threats to our country, it is interesting that American anarchists give little or no thought to 9/11, actively attempting to devalue the event and its impact on our country and world. The only significance they see is in how follow-on laws such as the PATRIOT Act impacted their cause. For instance, consider the following quotes from a recent document entitled "Ten Years after 9/11: An Anarchist Evaluation" (Anarchist Developments 2011):

> Anarchists, I argue, were among the few radicals whose analysis of history and power was not transformed, directly or indirectly, by the events of 9/11.
> A host of obvious questions accompany an attempt to encapsulate an event such as 9/11 and the ten years that followed, foremost among them: Why situate 9/11 as a date of exceptional importance? Does a reflection of this kind merely contribute to, for example, neoconservative attempts to enshrine 9/11 as a propagandistic tool? The response of the US government (and capitalist states worldwide) to 9/11 diminished the capacity of anarchist social movements through a barrage of

draconian laws, militarization of police forces, and repressive new forms of technological surveillance.

In a discussion about the "We Will Never Forget" slogan, the counterproposal is "The Forgetful Memory of 9/11."

While accomplishing research for an article on anarchism, I participated in an online chat anonymously with self-professed anarchists. We were discussing terrorist threats from al-Qaeda and other groups, and most participants did not perceive any kind of danger at all, believing the government has overblown the situation to justify military activities abroad and additional policing activities in the United States. I mentioned the overarching goal of extremists who want to turn the United States into an Islamic republic under Sharia law. One of the participants stated he would "rather see the flag of any group or country flying over our Capitol than the flag of the US," and several others piled on with their concurrence. I found this discussion extremely shocking and worrisome, but not because these opinions are provocative or different from the mainstream. The concern arose from the perspective of anarchists being hyperfocused on an ideology to the point where they do not perceive outside threats and exclude the possibility they may exist, or they, as Americans, are in the crosshairs. Furthermore, in terms of liaising with international or domestic terror groups, although this is not a goal of anarchists, the groups do all share a common enemy: the government—any government.

Anarchism and the Military

The increasing number of ex-military members posting on anarchist blogs is also something of interest; they typically receive a warm welcome and of course bring a host of expertise to the table for the movement (Figure 4.1).

The case of US Army PFC Michael Burnett and his three accomplices allows insight into a case of anarchism and dissension within the active military ranks. Their domestic terrorism plot was revealed during the investigation of the murder of PFC Michael Roark and his

anon - Mon, 2012-08-27 15:15

Look at this   troll.

Signed, a US army combat veteran, who does support the overthrow of the state, but also knows what anarchy is.

FIGURE 4.1   Post From a Popular Anarchist Forum

girlfriend, who were executed by the group on December 4, 2011, as "loose ends" who knew about their plans and were going to warn authorities. On August 27, 2012, Burnett testified about the plot to overthrow the government as part of a US military anarchist/militia group called FEAR: Forever Enduring Always Ready. FEAR spent almost $100,000 on equipment, firearms, and property—money taken from the life insurance policy of the deceased pregnant wife of one of the group's members (her death is now under investigation as a possible murder). FEAR plotted to take over its home station, Fort Stewart, Georgia, and then bomb targets in Savannah, Georgia, including the Forsyth Park fountain. They also wanted to destroy a dam in Washington state and poison the apple supply. Group members had matching tattoos resembling an anarchy symbol. The ultimate goal of FEAR was to assassinate President Obama and "give the government back to the people" (Bynum 2012). The group members are serving prison terms ranging from thirty years to life without parole.

Anti-Fascism (Antifa)

The Antifa movement consists of many autonomous, self-styled anti-fascist militant groups in the United States. Their stated goal is opposition to fascism through the use of direct action. The group has lashed out in militant protests, resulting in property damage and physical violence. They are anti-capitalist, far-left, and militant left and include anarchists, communists, and socialists. Their stated focus is on fighting far-right and white supremacist ideologies directly, rather than politically. Anti-facism is not new; in the US, this ideology first came forth in the 1920s, when militant leftists engaged pro-Nazi organizations such as the Friends of New Germany. In the 1970s and 1980s, anti-fascism moved back to the mainstream with punk rock music, where the group Anti-Racist Action (ARA) would peacefully engage or counter skinhead recruitment activities at concerts. As the white supremacist movement grew in 2016, so did the countering anti-facist movement. In 2017, law enforcement began using the term "Antifa" to describe the growing movement. Although short of being labeled a domestic terror group, Antifa was on DHS radar and labeled a faction of "anarchist extremism." Like most protest groups, there are violent and nonviolent undertones to Antifa. One member punched white supremacist Richard Spencer in the face on air, yet others helped with lodging for those displaced by Hurricane Harvey. By the end of 2017 and beginning of 2018, the movement started to lose momentum. However, this type of activity is persistent and cyclic, and could easily regroup and rise again to meet its ideological enemies.

SINGLE-ISSUE OR SPECIAL-INTEREST TERRORISM

Single-issue or special-interest terrorism is a brand of extremism different from right- and left-wing terrorism, as groups try to influence specific issues, rather than to affect political change. Actors are on the extreme fringes of animal rights, environmental protection, pro-life, and antinuclear movements, attempting to sway public opinion in their favor. Thirty percent of all domestic terror attacks since 1995 were related to special-interest terrorist groups (Sofer and Bernstein 2012). A difficult extremism to comprehend, group members often believe it is justifiable to kill a human being in the name of saving an animal, a tree, or an unborn child. Groups typically operate underground, with no hierarchy. They are basically leaderless with small cells around the world, and the ideology (as well as the Internet) serves as the glue for the cause. Thousands of acts of violence and property damage in the last ten years are attributed to special-interest terrorism. Leslie Pickering, a spokesperson for ELF, explains how acts of violence help draw attention to a cause: "The whole time I was protesting, nobody cared. The whole time I was writing letters, nobody cared. The whole time I was doing civil disobedience, nobody cared except for the media. But all of a sudden, when buildings were blowing up, a lot of people cared" (Cecil-Cockwell 2008).

The Earth Liberation Front

According to its press office, ELF uses "economic sabotage and guerrilla warfare to stop the exploitation and destruction of the environment." This activity is also known as "ecotage." Originating in the United Kingdom in 1992, ELF's first activity in the United States occurred in 1996, when the group spray-painted buildings and used glue to damage locks on McDonald's restaurants in Oregon. Their activities quickly escalated; in March 2001, the FBI classified ELF as the top domestic threat due to a string of arsons destroying a ranger station, large houses, and a Land Rover dealership, as well as the firebombing of a lab at Michigan State University. The group was active throughout the next decade, destroying a 206-unit condominium complex in San Diego in 2003, and four multimillion-dollar homes on Seattle's "Street of Dreams" in 2008. Oddly enough, the Street of Dreams homes were "green" and the emissions from the ELF fire did far more environmental damage than the homes would have in 100 years. The group seems to be diminishing over time; their website is archived, and there are no documented activities in recent years.

Animal Liberation Front

Members of the Animal Liberation Front (ALF) see themselves as the liberators and rescuers of animals. Also, a primary goal is to inflict economic damage on those who profit from the misery and exploitation of animals. ALF's roots are in the United Kingdom, dating as far back as 1976; it appeared in the United States in 1982. Early ALF activities identified illegal animal research and resulted in legal action against the perpetrators of the crimes; however, ALF abroad became violent in the 1980s, sending letter bombs to government leaders. The group then began to engage in elaborate hoaxes, claiming to have poisoned food products and cosmetics and costing companies millions of dollars in recalls, product destruction, and lost customers. Fur companies were firebombed, and devices were planted on executives' vehicles and at their doorsteps. This brand of violence moved to the United States in the 1990s and grew in intensity, with a string of incidents leading to injuries to innocent bystanders and millions of dollars in property damage.

On January 20, 2006, as part of Operation Backfire, the US Department of Justice announced charges against nine American and two Canadian activists calling themselves "The Family." At least nine of the eleven pleaded guilty to conspiracy and arson for their role in a string of twenty fires from 1996 through 2001; damage totaled $40 million. The Department of Justice called their activity domestic terrorism, with incidents including arson attacks against meat-processing plants, lumber companies, a high-tension power line, and a ski center in Vail (US Department of Justice 2006). Environmental and animal rights activists have referred to the legal action by the government as the "green scare," and the roundup does not seem to have deterred the groups. ELF has been somewhat quieted, but ALF has stepped up its efforts, breaking into farms and liberating exotic animals, hacking websites, sabotaging race tracks, and burning meat trucks. Its press office website, which has a section with pictures of federal agents who investigate the group, as well as "snitches and informants," instructs followers:

> Talking to law enforcement will always hurt you and others. The Feds or the local police are not your friends no matter how much they ensure [sic] you that they are trying to help you. Law enforcement will always resort to fear and intimidation and we must resist such divisional tactics.
>
> (NAALPO n.d.)

A favorite quote among left-wing groups is, "Snitches get stitches, and end up in ditches."

The ALF website still exists, and the press office issues commentary on current events (https://animalliberationpressoffice.org/NAALPO/). The group seems more focused now on anti-fur protest, targeting stray animal "kill" shelters, and liberating domesticated animals. In terms of future operations, ALF ideology could certainly be in line with attacks against the meat supply in our country. Many experts believe they would easily liaise with other terror groups to further each other's goals and bring attention to their disparate causes.

Climate Activists

In the last few years, we've seen the rise of a new group of climate activists emerge, separate from ELF. A recent case involves the new $3.78 billion Dakota Access Pipeline project, which is working to install a 1,172-mile-long underground oil pipeline from northwest North Dakota, through South Dakota and Iowa, to the oil tank farm in Illinois, which then connects to an underground pipeline to Texas. Activists opposed the Dakota pipeline since it passes through Native American burial grounds and other archeological sites and could contaminate underground water sources in the event of a spill. The Standing Rock Reservation, located on top of the projected pipeline, was the site of a months-long protest receiving worldwide attention and support.

The new wave of environmental protestors are primarily focused on delaying projects, mostly in peaceful ways, but with sporadic violent engagement such as arson or sabotage of drilling equipment. They are also involved in targeting private sector entities involved with the projects, such as banks, construction companies, and freight trains. The goal is to stop or at least delay projects and drive the cost upwards. A DHS source confirmed to me that any claims of radical extremism related to the Dakota pipeline protests were investigated and not substantiated. A new project, the Atlantic Coast Pipeline, is moving forward, and is set to run 600 miles between West Virginia and eastern North Carolina—again infringing on Native American territory. The front and flashpoint for protest will likely be Pocahontas County, West Virginia.

HOMEGROWN TERROR

Our long-held belief that homegrown terrorism couldn't happen here has created a situation where we are today, stumbling blindly through the legal, operational, and organizational minefield of countering terrorist radicalization and recruitment occurring in the U.S.

—Bipartisan Policy Center (2010)

There have been at least 100 domestic terror plots, either successful or mitigated since the tragic events of 9/11. Some are more memorable than others: Richard Reid, the shoe bomber; Jose Padilla, the dirty bomber; the Lackawanna Six; the Fort Dix plot; the LA Airport "Doomsday" plot; the Raleigh jihad group; Najibullah Zazi's backpack plot against the NYC subway; Shahzad, the Times Square bomber; and Abdulmutallab, the underwear bomber. Other homegrown plots since 9/11 include the planned or attempted bombing of buildings, bridges, and landmarks, and the targeting of malls, railroads, and subways. In June, 2018, US citizen Demetrius Pitts, also known as Abdur Raheem Rahfeeq, was arrested in Cleveland, Ohio, for a plot to bomb the crowd on the fourth of July. Pitts, who pledged allegiance to al-Qaeda, conducted reconnaissance at various targets. Pitts discussed giving remote control cars packed with shrapnel to children of military members. When asked by the undercover FBI agent if he was worried about injuring children, Pitts said, "I don't care and I have no regrets" (Fedschun 2018).

The Henry Jackson Society think tank in the United Kingdom spent years analyzing US challenges regarding al-Qaeda and issued a 700-page report entitled "Al-Qaeda in the United States: A Complete Analysis of Terrorism Offenses," by Robin Simcox and Emily Dyer (2013). General Mike Hayden, former director of the CIA, wrote the preface. I attended the book unveiling in Washington, DC, in 2013, which was moderated by General Hayden, and was stunned to hear the statistics compiled by the researchers. The publication provides a comprehensive analysis of 171 al-Qaeda and al-Qaeda-inspired terror convictions in the United States between 1997 and 2011. Profiles of those who committed these al-Qaeda-related offenses (AQROs) are included, and the report contains a statistical breakdown and analysis of key trends, including nationality, age, occupation, percentage of religious converts, education levels, type of charge, the role of each individual offender, connections to terrorist networks, whether terrorist training was undertaken, place of residence, and whether the individual had combat experience.

Major report findings include (Simcox and Dyer 2013):

Demographics

95 percent of offenders were men.
Age at the time of the charge was from 19 to 63.
Almost a third were between the ages of 20 and 24.
36 percent were born in the United States, citizens; 18 percent were naturalized citizens. 46 percent were in the country on visas or expired visas.
82 percent of offenders were living in the United States.

Religion

23 percent were religious converts to Islam; all of those born in the United States were converts and all were converts from Christianity.

95 percent of all convert offenders were US citizens.

Employment and Schooling

44 percent were employed; 20 percent in blue collar jobs.

52 percent were college educated.

23 percent had either graduate or doctoral degrees.

13 percent were students.

Plot Type and Training

Of the 171 offenders, sixty-three were active participants plotting operationally large-scale attacks against the United States; forty-three were aspirants; thirty-six were facilitators taking care of administrative and logistics support; twenty-six were trained aspirants; and three were ideologues.

57 percent of individuals were linked to a designated foreign terrorist organization (FTO); 38 percent were linked to al-Qaeda or an al-Qaeda-inspired group such as Lashkar-e-Taiba or al-Shabaab.

There were thirty-six mass casualty operatives (MCOs) planning ten attacks in the United States to cause mass loss of life.

47 percent of all individuals had received terrorist training. Afghanistan and Pakistan were the main countries where this took place; of US citizens, one-third had received training.

11 percent of individuals had received no training at all.

47 percent of offenders had received training in formal terrorist camps in the United States.

18 percent of offenders had combat experience.

87 percent of combat trained offenders were directly linked to an FTO

50 of the cases were cracked during an undercover investigation; however, these were mostly aspirants, not active plotters.

Often the plots by US citizens against their own country are elaborate, well-constructed, and close to execution when detected. I unknowingly stood in the very spot in East Potomac Park where Rezwan Ferdaus, a US citizen from Ashland, Massachusetts, with a degree in physics, planned to launch a remote-controlled aircraft packed with 25 pounds of C-4 plastic explosives to attack the Pentagon in 2011. Following the initial strike, Ferdaus hoped to use six people, pre-positioned in the Pentagon parking lots and armed with AK-47s, to shoot into the crowd of panicked building evacuees. He acquired one of the aircraft through a PayPal account under a false name—a 6-foot-long drone, capable of flying up to 100 miles per hour. While planning this attack, Ferdaus also rigged IED detonators and gave them to FBI agents he believed were al-Qaeda operatives who would deliver them downrange for field testing. He was pleased to learn from agents that his first detonator "killed" American soldiers. After Ferdaus's arrest, scientists tore the plot apart, detailing for the press exactly why it would not have worked based on his selected radio frequencies and the weight of the C-4 load. They corrected the specifications, feeding the data to future plotters, no doubt. Also, there was so much rhetoric about the improbability of such an attack that the very essence of the operation was lost: it was creative, asymmetric, and plotted by a fellow citizen. Ferdaus was determined to kill Americans and attack what he called the "great Satan," his own country of birth.

I was fortunate to serve as a senior fellow for two years at the George Washington University's Center for Cyber and Homeland Security from 2014 to 2016 and become acquainted with the Project on Extremism (POE). The POE started collecting data on ISIS in America, the first look at who, how, and where. Their December 2015 report "From Retweets to Raqqa," examined cases of all US citizens arrested, indicted, or convicted in the US for Islamic State-related activities. Using legal documents as empirical evidence, they were able to extract demographic factors related to those arrested. They also examined Americans who engaged in Islamic State (IS)-inspired behavior but were not in the legal system. IS-related mobilization in America was also a topic and they learned the 160 individuals studied in the report did not produce a profile of the typical "American IS supporter."

Researchers looked at individual motivations, the role of social media and the Internet, in the recruitment and radicalization process, whether radicalization occurred alone or in a group, and the degree of tangible links to ISIS. ISIS has a very specific online recruitment strategy; first they seek out new recruits, then isolate them, and finally, encourage them to take action. To consider the speed of radicalization, take the case of Abdul Razak Ali Artan, who was inspired by ISIS to attack fellow students at Ohio State University, Artan was born in Kenya after his family fled Somalia; they then went to Pakistan and legally immigrated with a large family to the US. Artan graduated with an Associate of Arts degree from Columbus State in the spring of 2016 and then took a non-credit class for summer 2016. He had no record of behavioral or disciplinary issues during his time at Columbus State and graduated with honors. He was a student at Ohio State pursuing a bachelor's degree, and doing well in his classes. From Home Depot fellow employee: "He was very sweet and kind, he used to write me bravos all the time, he'd get a lot of them. He was employee of the month," Convenience store owner: "He used to stop in every day," "He didn't smoke, didn't drink. He was very respectful, very educated." Neighbor described Artan as very friendly. "He always asked me how my day was going. He always said, 'Hello, let me help you,'" she said, adding that he didn't seem capable of such an attack. "I don't even understand why he did it." On November 28, 2016, the morning of his attack, Artan went to his Home Depot and purchased a knife. He posted a rant on a Facebook page before the attack in which he expressed anger about the treatment of Muslims around the world, talked about ISIS, and praised Anwar Awlaki. He called in a fire alarm to the chemistry building, waited until people poured out, then drove his car into the crowd, got out and started stabbing shocked students. In all, he injured thirteen with his car and a knife. We'll never know exactly how Artan was radicalized, as he was shot and killed by the first responding campus police officer. His friends said he "loved America."

Americans targeted for radicalization vary in demographics. Some cases are shocking and show the futility of profiling activities. Consider the son of a Boston police captain who plead guilty in May 2018 to his ISIS-inspired bomb plot to detonate a pressure cooker in a college cafeteria. Twenty-five-year-old Alexander Ciccolo obtained guns and began to make homemade bombs in 2015. Fortunately, Ciccolo's father alerted the FBI, which conducted an undercover investigation and unveiled the attack plan. Ciccolo had pro-ISIS postings on his Facebook page, including a photo of a dead American soldier that said "Thank you Islamic State!" and was building bombs in his home.

GWUPOE produces a monthly "ISIS in America" report. As of October 2018, the number of individuals charged in the United States on offenses related to the Islamic State stands at 166. According to their latest analysis: The average age of charged individuals was 28; arrests occurred in twenty-eight states and the District of Columbia; the average prison sentence was 13.5 years; 42 percent were accused of traveling or attempting to travel abroad; 33 percent were accused of plotting domestic terror attacks; 56 percent were arrested in an operation involving an informant and/or an undercover agent; and 115 individuals have pleaded or were found guilty. The average prison sentence upon conviction is 13 years. Although the FBI continues to work more than 1,000 open ISIS cases, the group's recruitment in the US may be waning; from February to May 2018, the Justice Department did not charge anyone associated with the Islamic State. Analysts believe ISIS's reach is declining in the US. Another trend: the ages of those charged is climbing, indicating ISIS's attraction to younger people in the US is fading. The website https://extremism.gwu.edu/isis-america provides regular updates on the status of ISIS in America.

We also can't forget the "travelers"—Americans who left the country to join ISIS on the battlefield. An October 2017 study by the Soufan Center and the Global Strategy Network tracked 5,600 foreign fighters who have returned to their home countries. They found that 250 Americans attempted to join ISIS in Iraq and Syria, with 129 traveling to join the fight. As of August 2017, the US charged 135 people with terrorism-related offenses for interactions with ISIS, with seventy-seven convictions (Barrett 2017). However, per GWUPOE data, most terrorist plots in the US have been the schemes of terrorists who did not go abroad. They are more likely to conduct attacks than are returning travelers.

The number of disrupted plots in our country is on the rise, meaning either we're getting better at detection, or there are potentially many other undetected would-be terrorists or terrorist cells operating off the grid. Radicalized Americans are usually educated, like Ferdaus. Leveraging the Internet, they move quickly along the continuum from contemplation to planning to execution. They are creative and highly adaptable, learning from failed operations. For example, when the Times Square bomber Faisal Shahzad ran away from his vehicle, leaving a smoking dud for a bomb, he was chastised by his handlers for failing to stay and work on the device until it exploded, and internal al-Qaeda correspondence indicated this doomed scenario would never happen again. Many experts came forward to explain why the vehicle didn't explode. The enemy is watching and learning; there is no such thing as a failure, only a stumbling block on the path to perfection. Unfortunately, our culture is hyperfocused on the last attack or attempt and fails to look forward, but terrorists continue to progress in methodology and target selection. They go on surveillance missions and measure the number of people and cars passing by and the distance from weapon to target. They probe and accomplish dry runs, perfecting the plan. Our very public "celebration" over a disrupted plot should be tempered by the thought the next bomber is likely an American sitting in his or her home, watching the same newscast, devising new and improved ways to kill us and destroy our way of life.

Not much time is spent contemplating what happens after the domestic terrorist is arrested. Few, if any, receive the life sentences given to Reid, Padilla, and Zazi. Most sentences are between three and twenty years, and the lengthy periods of time spent in jail awaiting the court case are typically awarded as time served and deducted from the length of the sentence. As a result, many domestic terrorists and conspirators convicted since 9/11 have already served their prison sentences and were quietly released back to society. Those released include members of the Lackawanna Six and Portland Seven terror groups who traveled to Afghanistan for training with the Taliban and met bin Laden. Many other Americans convicted on terrorism charges are set to come out of prison in this year and the next, yet we have no plan for their rehabilitation and reintegration into our neighborhoods. Re-radicalization is possible, perhaps with a renewed fervor due to anger projected toward the government. With the spread of al-Qaeda affiliates around the world and an increasingly disenfranchised population, the radicalized homegrown threat will, at the very least, remain constant, but is likely to rise.

Rehabilitation and the Domestic Terrorist

A terrorist is only temporarily neutralized by imprisonment.

—Dennis Pluchinsky (2008)

The editors of The Counter Terrorist Magazine approached me to write an article on jihadist recidivism—those who leave prison and return to a life of terror—for the April/May 2010 issue (Hesterman 2010). I found an extraordinarily small body of research on the topic, despite the pressing nature of the problem. The list of former Guantanamo Bay detainees who are assuming leadership positions in al-Qaeda, its offshoots, and ISIS continues to grow, and jihadist recidivism is a persistent and growing feeder of manpower to international and domestic terror groups and operations. Also, recidivism provides a valuable resource to terrorist groups: experienced jihadists who have gained firsthand insight into enemy counterterrorism practices and agents through their arrest, sentencing, and detainment.

Capturing a terrorist is a resource-intensive event and taking an enemy combatant off the battlefield and out of our neighborhoods is clearly a victory. However, the process must not end with the arrest, or even conviction; apprehension is merely the tip of the iceberg. Perhaps an even greater investment must be made on activities occurring during a prisoner's incarceration, rehabilitation, and release to ensure the jihadist remains permanently out of the fight. Unfortunately, our homegrown terrorists are not rehabilitated; they merely walk out of prison back to society. Resource-constrained law enforcement agencies couldn't possibly open a new case and monitor the individuals, ensuring they remain law-abiding citizens. While in prison, the jihadists can recruit and radicalize others and naturally cross paths with terrorists, gang members, and criminals. In November 2017, a convicted felon who was radicalized in prison and expressed support for the Islamic State has pleaded guilty to acquiring a gun after he was released from a Virginia prison. Casey Charles Spain spent more than seven years in prison after being convicted of abduction with intent to defile. Federal prosecutors said that while incarcerated, Spain expressed a desire to commit violence, swore a pledge of loyalty to the leader of ISIS and obtained a tattoo of the ISIS flag. Several weeks after he was released in August, Spain was arrested after he received an inoperable semiautomatic gun during an FBI sting operation.

Recognizing the growing threat of radicalization of our citizens, in 2014, then-US Attorney General Eric H. Holder, Jr., announced the creation of a task force within the Justice Department to combat an "escalating danger" from "homegrown" terrorists within the United States. Called the Domestic Terrorism Executive Committee (DTEC), the interagency task force is a re-creation of one formed after the 1995 Oklahoma City bombing to focus in on right-wing domestic terrorists like Timothy McVeigh. DTEC efforts are aimed at US citizens or visitors radicalized via the Internet. In November 2017, US Senator Dick Durbin introduced legislation, called the Domestic Terrorism Prevention Act, to address the growing threat of white supremacist groups and other violent domestic extremists. The legislation will enhance the federal government's efforts to assess threats and provide training and resources to assist state, local, and tribal law enforcement in addressing the dangers. Also, the bill will formalize the DTEC, as an appropriate organization to respond to emerging extremist movements so we can get on the offensive.

The most important element of domestic terror challenge is the person who is radicalized, yet the soft sciences still are not part of the solution set. Why do we have "the travelers" who leave comfortable lives for a battlefield in a faraway country? Why would three high school girls in the UK leave their upper middle-class homes to become the brides of ISIS terrorists in the middle of a war-torn country? Calling themselves "lionesses of Allah," there may now be more than 600 Western women with ISIS, having their children—"cubs of the caliphate." Shannon Maureen Conley, a 19-year-old nurse's aide from Denver was one of the first US female ISIS recruits, and stopped before boarding her flight out of the country. She was sentenced to four years in prison. Two young, successful college students in Mississippi, Jaelyn Young and boyfriend (now husband) Muhammad Dakhlalla, went down the path of online radicalization and were arrested just before boarding a flight to Turkey. Fortunately, they were detected and offroaded by FBI agents. Jaelyn was sentenced to twelve years in jail, and Muhammad received an eight-year sentence. The *Atlantic Magazine* article, "How Two Mississippi College Students Fell in Love and Decided to Join a Terrorist Group" (Green 2017) provides fascinating insight into how two kind, smart teenagers would make such a drastic decision to join ISIS. We must protect all citizens, especially youth, from heeding the call of Jihad, as the court system will have no mercy. Understanding why people radicalize should be the first step in addressing this complex, human issue.

Emergent Issue

Countering Violent Extremism: Why People Radicalize

In March 2016, I was part of an all day, live webinar *Countering Violent Extremism*, broadcast from the Homeland Security Training Institute at the College of DuPage in Illinois. My segment focused on why people radicalize—what flips the switch from "off" to "on" in the brain of a rational, sane person? How are they indoctrinated, even brainwashed by the radical ideology, to the point where they are prepared to kill and die for it? We certainly need to wrap our minds around this phenomena before considering the best courses of action to engage.

First, we need to understand the definition of ideolog as a systematic body of concepts about human life or culture and the manner or the content of thinking that is characteristic of an individual, group, or culture. There is also a sociopolitical context to the assertions, theories and aims of an ideology. An ideology can be a very powerful force. Consider this quote by Karl Marx, the father of Marxism: "*They do not know it, but they are doing it.*" Marx used ideology as the production of images of social reality; a person is thinking consciously and rationally, it is true, but with a false consciousness because of the ideas implanted. The real motive forces impelling him remain unknown to him. This process could also be thought reform. Typically, there is a process to implant an ideology—first, demoralization—telling people they are miserable. Over time, even content individuals will become restless. Next, a period of destabilization where the current system is rocked and destabilized, perhaps over a timeframe of 2–5 years. Next, the introduction of a crisis (false or real). Then normalization with the new system, and weary citizens see it as their savior from a bad situation. History is replete with examples of this type of social engineering. We even see it today with the radical Islamist ideology.

Ideology is "Something absolutely vast and powerful . . . beyond all perception and objective intelligibility" and "in you more than yourself" (Žižek 1989). Something bigger consumes you. Your purpose becomes to "feed the beast." Those who implant ideology can take a healthy brain and subtly (or not so subtly) retrain it. Ideology is a powerful force that can quickly change society. Think of Hitler, a homeless artist who turned into one of history's most murderous dictators. He preyed on the German population; demoralized after a crushing loss in WWI. Hitler stepped into the leaderless void, expertly crafted an ideology and used propaganda to motivate citizens towards ethnic cleansing and another war.

What drives a rational person towards radical ideologies/groups? We have to understand this process in order to deconstruct. First of all, understand that most terrorists are rational actors. They were once operating normally in society and something happened to transition from the "light" to the "grey" area and then "black." Ideology driving reframing their reality. Instinct theory defines behavior as a function of a person's instinct rather than conscious, purposeful and rational activities. Merriam Webster defines instinct as: The tendency to make a complex and specific response to environmental stimuli without involving reason. Behavior mediated by reactions below the conscious level. Think of when we condition a pet using the "click" method. We tell a pet to sit and use a clicker and give a treat. Over time, the dog will sit on command merely for the reward of the click. Pavlov's dogs would hear the whistle, and start to salivate, knowing food was on the way. Also at play is cognitive theory; an individual's behavior is not as much a function of consequences, as it is a person's future belief and expectations. Delayed gratification is something appealing to jihadists; resisting a smaller but more immediate reward in order to receive a larger or more enduring reward later.

The need for affiliation drives all humans towards groups. As portrayed in Maslow's Hierarchy of Needs, once basic needs of food and shelter are met, a person seeks to affiliate, they need to feel a sense of involvement and "belonging" within a social group. This is very similar to the way we reach out via alumni groups, fan clubs, political groups or support groups for people with similar medical afflictions. Anxiety and stress feed need for affiliation. Think about people who undergo something together, for instance the passengers of the flight that landed on the Hudson—they are linked forever. No one else understands what they went through. In fact, two are now married. The problem with terrorist and some criminal groups is the affiliation turns into domination ad the group begins to impose its will on the member; leaving is not an option.

Of course, ideology doesn't provide the entire explanation for the behavior—there's no one-size-fits all reason a rational person acts irrational. Maybe the violent actor has a superficial attachment to ideology, but has a gripe and seeks revenge against an organization. Or they may be coerced, paid, manipulated, or shamed into participating. Violent extremism may even become a career, as discussed in Chapter 3.

Groups are complex animals, which is why a quick, easy solution to deradicalization of its members is complicated. Think about your own workplace—everyone has the same goal, but different reasons for being there. They are motivated differently and seek different outcomes; some work only for the money, others for prestige and some because they are just bored. Therefore, targeting one "type" of motivation does not address the entire problem. Consider ISIS which is now comprised of a complex group of members from thrill seekers to murderers and rapists. Some former ISIS captives report never seeing a Koran in camp, no adherence to Muslim traditions such as Call to Prayer. This perfectly illustrates how motivations also change over time.

Online Propaganda—There Forever

Al Qaeda and ISIS have a large volume of material on the Internet to recruit, inspire, train and equip their followers—and it will be out there forever, despite our efforts. In April 2018, Europol released information on an international operation to destroy Internet propaganda of the Islamic State group. Cyber specialists from Europe, Canada and the US targeted online sites including ISIS's main broadcasting site, Amaq News. Data will help police identify administrators and those connecting with the website (BBC 2018). International operations have targeted Amaq web systems previously, but it always comes back online.

Naturally these operations help, but even if we are able to shut down websites and social media accounts, the material is still out there for access by interested parties. ISIS even produces its material in different languages to appeal to a broad recruitment audience. Total media produced and posted online by ISIS in 2016 was 6,300 publications. This is why we should put equal, if not more, effort to counter the radical ideology itself. Not only is the cache of al Qaeda and ISIS material readily available with a quick Internet search, but the dark web now is a new repositories, with back issues of magazines, guides for how to build bombs, newsletters, et al. Perhaps this development is even more worrisome since the reader can also move on to make a purchase, whether credit card numbers, beans for making ricin, weapons with serial numbers scratched off or even passports (Figure 4.2).

services > Documents

GENUINE British passports

Price	357.32333 BTC
	$ 3,125.40 £ 2,000.00
€ 2,541.60	
Ship from	UK
Ship to	World wide
Stock	998
Created in	2012-01-19 09:12 UTC
Last update	2012-05-10 13:30 UTC

More images:

Your balance isn't enough to buy this item! Please deposit the needed funds before.

Description

I have used a stock photograph to illustrate the listing, I am NOT claiming it to be one of my passports.

I can source GENUINE British passports, issued in whatever name you want with your picture from the UK Passport Agency. Don't ask how, just drop me an email at (

FIGURE 4.2   British Passports for Sale on the Dark Web

Final Thoughts

Ideology is extremely hard to dislodge, as it is truly a battle of ideas—whether political, economic, single issue like global warming, or the strongest ideology of all, religious. Think of deconstruction as swimming upstream against a very strong current; challenging thinking and paradigms. Jean-Francois Lyotard, a 20th-century a French philosopher, described deconstruction as "collapse of grand narratives." If we tell someone the most important principle they believe is false, we can expect them to strongly resist and question us. One of Lyotard's classic statements requires some thought, but certainly applies in this world of many unknowns: "What I say is true because I prove that it is—but what proof is there my proof is true?" Finally, a deconstructed ideology must be replaced with something else, a "vacuum" is not an option. Therefore we must ask—do we really want to deconstruct this "undesirable" social structure or ideology? And replace it with what reality? Is containment a better strategy, as, over time, people naturally lose interest and what was once a compelling, life-or-death impulse is no longer of concern. (For more information on the psychology of terrorists and terror groups, as well as unique methodology to dismantle ideology, see the book *The Theory and Practice of Terrorism: Alternate Paths of Inquiry*, Chapter 7 [Hesterman 2016].)

JIHADIST DEFINED

A jihadist can be defined as a Muslim who believes Islam is under attack by the West with the objective of destroying Islam, perceives the United States as the primary enemy of Islam, believes it is Islam's manifest destiny to the rule the world, and believes the only proper response to this threat to Islam and the Muslim Ummah (members of the Islamic community) is militant jihad.

Jihadists differ from terrorists who are not religiously motivated. The call to jihad (which means "struggle" in Arabic) is powerful and typically comes in response to a fatwa, a binding religious decree. Jihadists are also revered as martyrs for the cause, which means carefully selecting operational tactics so as not to amplify their deaths. Former Secretary of Defense Donald Rumsfeld once remarked that for every jihadist we kill, we recruit three more. Islamic scholar and journalist M. J. Akbar (2002) provides great insight into jihad, describing it thus: "The power of jihad pervades the mind and soul of Islam. The mind is where the current battle will be fought, and this is why it will be a long war."

Recidivism

A recidivist is defined as one who, after release from custody for commission of a crime, is not rehabilitated (Pluchinsky 2008). Although the term is now applied in the counterterror realm, recidivism is closely tracked in the US prison system and the statistics are startling; according to the Department of Justice, an estimated two-thirds (68 percent) of 405,000 prisoners released in thirty states in 2005 were arrested for a new crime within three years of release from prison, and three-quarters (77 percent) were arrested within five years. More than a third (37 percent) of prisoners who were arrested within five years of release were arrested within the first six months after release, with more than half (57 percent) arrested by the end of the first year. Three in four former prisoners in thirty states were arrested within five years of release (Bureau of Justice 2014). Recidivism substantially increased from the previous decade, in spite of extensive education and job training efforts, as well as life skills and re-adjustment counseling provided to convicts during incarceration. Recidivism by convicted criminals clearly illustrates how arrest, confinement, and rehabilitation alone do not preclude further nefarious activities. The same is true for jihadists, for whom the stakes of returning to the fight are much higher for our country.

Counter-Radicalization Efforts

Jihad is a powerful call and dislodging (or neutralizing) the radical ideology is not an easy task, not even for lifelong Muslims. Many countries have established jihadist rehabilitation and engagement programs, including Algeria, Egypt, Jordan, Singapore, Indonesia, and Malaysia. Notably, Yemen's program is now defunct and there is no curriculum or facility in place today to process returning Yemeni nationals from Guantanamo. Many have returned to their career in terrorism.

When releasing detainees from the Guantanamo facility, the US government has heavily relied on the "Saudi program." The program was established after the 2003 bombings in Riyadh and is a "soft" counterterrorism program, meant to combat violent extremism and mitigate the ideological and intellectual justifications of jihad. The program is not punitive, but rather a benevolent, second-chance program with a large social welfare component. Although the exact numbers are questionable, the Saudis claim an overall 80 to 90 percent success rate for the program. They have processed approximately 3,000 individuals and 1,400 have reportedly renounced their former ways and were released. Of the group, there are thirty-five acknowledged recidivists. The rest of the extremists will remain in the program until deemed ready for release. Of 120 Saudi citizens sent to the rehabilitation program from the Guantanamo facility, ten remain in the program and six were re-arrested by officials. Of the 110 released, many re-radicalized and became "most wanted" men in Saudi Arabia (Kohlmann 2009).

Inside the Saudi Program

Christopher Boucek is a Middle East specialist who has studied the Saudi approach to recidivism since its inception. His 2008 paper, entitled "Saudi Arabia's 'Soft' Counterterrorism Strategy: Prevention, Rehabilitation, and Aftercare," gives an inside look at this secretive program.

The Saudi program relies on several primary tenets:

Violent radical Islamic extremism cannot be defeated by traditional security means alone.

Violent ideology is based on corrupted and deviant interpretations of Islam.

Obedience and loyalty to the state and its leadership are key.

Extremists lack the authority and understanding of religious doctrine.

These principles are enforced through a program of co-optation and persuasion by a system called PRAC, which consists of three interconnected phases:

Prevention: The prevention phase fosters cooperation between the state and the public, highlights the damage done by terrorism and extremism, and ends public support and tolerance for extremist beliefs. Hundreds of programs are aimed at youth in and out of school; there are also massive public information campaigns, and highway billboards decrying terrorism as part of this phase.

Rehabilitation: The focal point of the rehabilitation phase is counseling by clerics and academics to re-educate and rehabilitate jihadists. It begins with the assumption that these individuals were misled by extremists who follow a corrupted form of Islam and misinterpret the Koran.

Post-release care: Most Guantanamo returnees entered the program at this point since they were not tried and convicted of crimes in Saudi Arabia. During this phase, residents live in a "halfway house," the Care Rehabilitation Center. The center has guards and fences, but the prisoners are not confined or restrained in any way. The post release phase focuses on reintegration into Saudi society; the Guantanamo returnees receive additional psychological counseling and participate in activities designed to help them adjust to freedom.

Once an individual has satisfactorily renounced his or her extremist beliefs, job placement services are provided along with other benefits, including a government stipend, a car, and an apartment. The added social support is intended to deter the rehabilitated terrorist from returning to his or her former lifestyle. The Saudi program was subjected to scrutiny; after several former Guantanamo detainees returned to al-Qaeda, DHS sent a team of FBI officials and terrorism specialists to the center for a firsthand look. Although a formal report to the public was not released, one of the team members spoke to the press about his experience. Dr. John Horgan, director of the International Center for the Study of Terrorism at Pennsylvania State University stated, "when I asked Saudi officers how they knew these people were safe to release, all they could say was they got a feeling." He also opined that prisoners are not being deradicalized and their fundamental views have not changed. Another criticism was the lack of any reliable risk assessment to decide whether an individual should be allowed back into society. "Sex offenders have to meet all sorts of criteria before they are released," Dr. Horgan said. "Why shouldn't it be the same for terrorists?" (Lamb 2010).

Germany is taking steps towards a deradicalization program. In 2010, Daniel Koehler, a Fulbright scholar who studied religion and economics at Princeton, was in Germany to start his master's degree in peace studies from the University of Hamburg. Exit-Germany, a program tailored to far-right extremists who wanted to reinvent themselves hired Daniel. In 2014, he founded the German Institute on Radicalization and Deradicalization Studies (http://girds.org/) and the peer-reviewed *Journal for Deradicalization*. Both are outstanding sources of current thought on deradicalization, particularly since the US and Germany face similar international and domestic terror threats.

In February 2018, France announced a new program to combat radicalization to deal with violent extremists within prisons and reintegrating former radicals into society. A total of 512 people are currently serving prison time in France for terrorism offenses, and another 1,139 prisoners were flagged as radicalized to violence. Authorities look to create 1,500 places in separate prison wings "especially for radicalized inmates." Philippe also announced plans for three new centers that will attempt to reintegrate "radicals" (www.france24. com/en/20180223-france-deradicalisation-programme-jihad-islamist-extremists-prisons-centres-philippe).

The same month, Spain introduced deradicalization efforts in their prisons. They plan to define the "risk of radicalism" through the monitoring of prisoners in European prisons convicted of terrorism, or those with a profile that could turn them into "recruiters" for violent jihad. Over 270 prisoners have been imprisoned for crimes related to terrorism in Spain. They will also work with prisoners with violent profiles who may be susceptible to recruitment by violent jihadist circles, because of certain traits (Lázaro 2018).

Possible Solutions in the United States

In addition to using portions of PRAC domestically, a potential model for a domestic rehabilitation program comes from the US military, which successfully delved into the rehabilitation realm in Iraq through the decommissioned Task Force 134 and its "House of Wisdom" program. Through this operation, vetted Iraqi clerics encouraged debate with detainees for the purpose of refuting and mitigating extremist arguments (Azarva 2009). Also, scientific study shows disengagement of radical ideology is best done through support of an individual's social network (Boucek 2009); therefore, including the American public in the dialogue is a necessity. Avoiding the issue and simply sending the terrorist back to society and our neighborhoods without a support structure is unwise. Finally, the government previously announced intentions to acquire the Thomson Correctional Center, a large, vacant state prison in northwestern Illinois, to house detainees transferred from the Guantanamo facility. Because this plan never came to fruition, perhaps the facility could be used to rehabilitate American jihadists before returning them to society.

In Minnesota, a state plagued by al Shabaab and ISIS recruiting its young Somali population, officials are trying a controversial deradicalization program. Enter Daniel Koehler of the German deradicalization program. After Minneapolis law enforcement officials visited with Koehler in Germany, he agreed to come to the state and help start the US's first government program. When the Terrorism Disengagement and Deradicalization Program was announced in March 2016, the mission statement was a wake-up call: "Untreated radicalized individuals will infect communities and continue to seek opportunities to harm others and martyr themselves." Koehler believes that a person heading towards radicalization, sees all of their problems and solutions whittled down to one; he calls this "depluralization." The one problem is persecution based on race or religion and the solitary solution is violence. For radicalized youth, such as the five he worked with in Minnesota, Koehler sees little point in starting moral or theological arguments, but, advocates "repluralization": the careful reintroduction of problems and solutions (Koerner 2017). Koehler's program also seems to focus on offroading and re-routing of the energy and passion found in young people wanting to make a difference. The FBI online effort "Don't Be a Puppet: Pull Back the Curtain on Violent Extremism," https://cve.fbi.gov/, is a good start, but we need to do more.

Counterterrorism and homeland security experts are perhaps not the best researchers for this complex issue. Similar to the analysis of the other terrorism-related issues, the answer may instead lie in the "soft" sciences: psychology, sociology, organizational theory, and theology—disciplines providing a multifaceted understanding and approach to the problem.

Professionals in these fields could best answer the following questions:

Do religious terrorists have a higher recidivism rate than terrorists without the radical religious ideology? If so, why? What are the implications in the United States?

Can we draw any parallels between terrorist rehabilitation and cult deprogramming or the successful neo-Nazi and leftist guerilla rehabilitation programs?

How can we better use psy ops and the Internet to introduce a deliberate theological counter ideology to jihad and prevent reradicalization? How can we detect, subtly engage, and offroad those searching the Internet for information on radical movements and thought?

Are there any aspects of the Saudi program we can apply to would-be domestic terrorists in the United States if they eventually return from detention to our communities?

Recidivism is just one source of manpower for al-Qaeda, ISIS, and other radical groups seeking to harm the United States and its allies. The ability to tap a US citizen for a mission in his or her home country is something foreign terror groups continue to pursue and have made easy through the Internet. Understanding how the switch is flipped from "off" to "on" is critical for prevention, and knowing how to turn it "off" again is fundamental to the domestic deradicalization process. Recidivism is undesirable, but likely unavoidable. There is no such thing as a perfect criminal justice system: the question must be in which direction we want to deflect the likelihood of error.

THE LONE WOLF

According to the FBI, a lone wolf draws ideological inspiration from formal terrorist organizations but operates on the fringe. Despite their ad hoc nature and generally limited resources, lone wolves can mount high-profile, extremely destructive attacks, and their operational planning is often difficult to detect. The FBI considers the lone wolf a significant domestic terrorism threat, since detection and mitigation are hampered by relative anonymity. A lone wolf does not necessarily mean one person working alone; Timothy McVeigh's bombing of the Murrah Federal Building in Oklahoma City is a good example. The ideology of a group influenced McVeigh and his accomplice, yet they worked clandestinely on the fringe to develop an undetectable plan for mass destruction. Other notable lone wolves include Ted Kaczynski, Eric Robert Rudolph, the perpetrator of the Tylenol poisoning event in 1981, the mailer of anthrax letters just after 9/11, and Joseph Stack, who flew his aircraft into the IRS building. Stephen Paddock, the perpetrator of the worse mass shooting in US history appears to have solely planned and executed his attack in Las Vegas. Many of the domestic terror attacks and plots since 9/11 were planned by a lone individual.

Other countries have also experienced horrific lone wolf events against soft targets. Anders Behring Breivik, 32, was a Norwegian lone wolf who planned his operation for nine years and committed two stunning attacks on July 22, 2011. First, Breivik detonated a vehicle-borne improvised explosive device (VBIED) in Oslo outside the prime minister's office, killing eight people. The device was constructed with fertilizer and explosive primer. Breivik then traveled to Utøya Island by boat, infiltrating a Norwegian Labor Party camp for children. Dressed as a police officer to garner unimpeded access and trust from children, he opened fire, killing sixty-nine children and counselors before law enforcement arrived. Breivik surrendered without a fight. With a right-wing extremist ideology and racist, anti-Muslim viewpoints, Breivik believed killing the children was justified. In his estimation, he eliminated the next generation of Marxists who were going to turn Europe into what he calls "Eurabia." Convicted in August 2012, Breivik received the maximum sentence given in Norway to convicted killers: twenty-one years; after serving the sentence, the courts will consider his release. Breivik published his manifesto on the Internet just prior to executing the attacks, a long missive entitled "2083: A European Declaration of Independence," and he also posted a video urging conservatives to "embrace martyrdom" and showing himself dressed in a uniform and pointing a Ruger Mini-14 (Berwick/Breivik 2011). A self-professed Freemason and Knight Templar officer, Breivik continues to espouse his right-wing ideology and has started the "Conservative Revolutionary Movement" of activists across Europe from his prison cell. Profiling Breivik would be helpful to understanding the motivation and activities of lone wolves against soft targets, particularly vulnerable citizens such as children.

As these cases amply illustrate, the human behavior and motivations of a lone wolf are broad, complex, and somewhat unpredictable; in this case, the criminal may not be completely motivated by ideology, and many psychological factors, such as anger and paranoia, can be at play. The radicalized homegrown lone wolf is the most dangerous, fueled by religious ideology and a duty to answer a divine call. Perhaps a new perspective on this type of violence is necessary and the threat continues to morph and adapt to the ever-changing landscape of violence, ideology, and extremism.

Emergent Issue

Lone Actor Terror (LAT)

In November 2017, I was part of an all day, live webinar called *Domestic Terrorism: The Lone Wolf Threat*, broadcast from the Homeland Security Training Institute at the College of DuPage in Illinois. My segment focused the definition and motivations of the so-called Lone Wolf. I believe the "Lone Wolf" moniker is sensationalistic and, alone, causes fear. Thinking of an individual, hidden in society and planning a mass attack is scary. The word "wolf" itself conjures a stalking, stealthy, hungry predator moving about society, acting at will. There is a rush to use the phrase "lone wolf." If one person is involved in an operation, one "trigger puller," there's a tendency to immediately say it was a lone wolf attack. Possibly because it makes everyone feel better to think there's no larger cell. Naturally, law enforcement starts quickly digging to gather evidence, and prevent possible future attacks.

Let's shift the paradigm and rename this type of activity as Lone Actor Terror (LAT). LAT is undertaken by individuals who plan, prepare for, and execute violence without external assistance. They are isolated. For instance, studies show that 90 percent of lone actors plan at home, not elsewhere. Only 13 percent raise funds.

LAT actors draw ideological inspiration from formal terrorist organizations but operate on fringes of movements. We must understand even these margins can be enough to trigger someone and despite the ad hoc nature and limited resources of a lone actor, he or she can mount high-profile, extremely destructive attacks. A group, any group, vocalizing that violence is necessary and acceptable influences would-be violent actors. Certainly, if you hear over and over how violence is the solution, it normalizes the idea of killing in the name of an ideology.

There are two types of lone actors. Some are well adapted to society, and mentally fit. They make a tactical choice to engage alone, and leave society to go underground and plan. The second type of lone actor is not well adapted to society, perhaps suffering mental health issues or is in some type of psychological distress. In this case, society leaves them. In either case, social isolation is a key variable.

The International Centre for Counter-Terrorism (ICCT 2018) at the Hague, Netherlands, is working on a groundbreaking project. Countering Lone Actor Terrorism, ICCT's Countering Lone Actor Terrorism (CLAT) project seeks to improve understanding of lone actor terrorists, their behavior, and their activities in the period leading up to their intended attack. The database is now assisting governments and front-line law enforcement and intelligence analysts to counter the threat. For instance, their research shows lone actors select targets early in the planning process, as there's typically a specific grievance, person, group, industry at the root of their operation. In the last thirty years, only 11 percent of lone actor terror cases are targets selected spontaneously, unlike more traditional terror planning. Also, 38 percent of lone actors conducted surveillance of the target. Around 62 percent choose firearms, the rest other methods, usually an IED. However only 35 percent of those who select firearms have extensive training, most have just basic, recently acquired knowledge. Data from another outstanding source, *The Age of Lone Wolf Terrorism* (Hamm and Spaaiij 2017) shows that 49 percent of lone actors had contact with law enforcement at some time prior to attack—these would be the "known wolves."

Lone actors not only don't want help but they see people as a threat since they may talk them out of the attack or, even worse, report their activities. For instance, the Las Vegas shooter Steven Paddock sent his girlfriend out of the country. Lone actors want to act at will, at the time and place of their choosing, so they eliminate anyone and anything in the environment that might change the plan. In a group you need consensus, there's a leader and group dynamics. So it is preferable to work alone.

What is an "Inspired Wolf?" An inspired wolf is not a true lone wolf. From 1978 to 2011, there were fifty-five cases of what we would call lone wolf attacks. In those cases, 62 percent of the actors had contact with extremist. These so-called virtual entrepreneurs engage online, drawing inspiration. The ability to quickly access material and the sensitive nature of that information are two major concerns regarding indoctrination and radicalization through the Internet. Lone actors don't need to connect with a human, they can remotely view material like videos, how-to manuals, and propaganda. They can query, study, and learn tactics. By digging into a treasure trove of information about successful (and not so successful) attacks, they can plan an improved-upon copycat mission. Sometimes lone actors get sloppy; slip up and don't use a virtual private network, maybe engage in spurious financial transactions, ask questions in forums patrolled by the good guys, and gather materials through mail order. These amateur behaviors provide leakage and a footprint, so an opportunity for detection, tracking, and possibly providing an "off ramp."

Final Thoughts

Lone Actor Terror is a complex issue requiring a complex solution set. As this is a human problem, the soft sciences are critical in this fight, and must complement law enforcement efforts. We're not helpless; there is growing body of research and case studies on lone actor phenomena. There's a trigger or a cognitive opening and they often engage in leakage behavior or sloppy preparations. But we have to know what to look for and connect the dots to stop these potentially deadly attacks.

MEXICAN CARTELS CROSS THE BORDER

Just south of our border, Mexican forces are fighting an insurgency against multiple drug trafficking organizations (DTOs) threatening their country's economy and security. In 2009, the previous director of the CIA, General Michael Hayden, surprised many when he stated: "Escalating violence along the US–Mexico border will pose the second greatest threat to US security this year, second only to al-Qaeda" (Hayden 2009). In 2011, the Justice Department (2011b) said Mexican DTOs represented the greatest organized crime threat to the United States. In 2014, our government responded in part by placing thousands of National Guard troops on the border as part of "Operation Jump Start," assisting US Customs and Border Protection. Also, hundreds of federal agents were pulled from other duties and sent to robust DEA (Drug Enforcement Administration), ATF (Alcohol, Tobacco, and Firearms), and FBI offices in major cities in border states. And despite economic woes, the United States aided Mexico's fight against the DTOs under the provisions of the Merida Initiative, a multiyear $1.5 billion anti-narcotics package to robust law enforcement cooperation, intelligence sharing training, and equipment. When Merida expired in FY 2015, the US started giving Mexico approximately $320 million a year. Finally, the $6 billion "virtual fence" project, SBInet, and deployment of expensive aerial drones to monitor the border certainly indicate the government's concern regarding border issues. The players, tactics, alliances, and leaders of the DTOs morph, but the threat to our country persists . . . and is growing.

The illicit drug trade is a shared problem. DHS estimates $19 to $29 billion per year flows from the United States to the Mexican traffickers, and that is just in cash and excludes the money sent by wire transfers, prepaid cards and other illicit methods.

Ideology: Money

Prior to US engagement in the so-called drug war beginning in the 1980s, the primary drug trafficking route into the United States was from Colombia, through the Caribbean and into Florida. As we closed off these avenues but failed to lower user demand in our country, Mexico became the primary conduit for the drug pipeline. As criminal elements exacted their "fee" for moving the product through the country, we witnessed the rise of alliances, or cartels. In addition to moving Colombian drugs, cartels now oversee the cultivation of marijuana and large labs producing methamphetamines. The money at stake is exorbitant; a Justice Department report estimates Mexican and Colombian DTOs generate, remove, and launder between $18 and $39 billion in wholesale drug proceeds annually.

Consider this important fact, which serves to frame the discussion of drugs and the existing or potential nexus with other nefarious groups:

dealers and users in the United States do not care who supplies their drugs. It could be a cartel or al-Qaeda; all that matters is the product and getting it into the hands of the 27 million users in our country, many of whom will give their last dollar or possession to get high. In a recent case in Tennessee, a woman actually tried to sell her 5-month-old baby on Craigslist for money, and said she sold a child before. Drug use in the US has skyrocketed in the last twenty years and there are now more than 14,000 addiction centers, serving hundreds of thousands in recovery. Total drug overdoses in 2017 were 63,632, double the number from 2006. More than 600,000 people have a heroin addiction, with another 300,000 using recreationally. Cocaine demand is up, with CBP seizing almost triple the amount at the border in FY 17 than FY 16. More than 118 million Americans have used marijuana in their lifetime and thirty-eight million have used cocaine. In 2017, more people died from opioid use than breast cancer; more than 42,000 deaths were attributed to heroin, fentanyl, or other opioids (Kounang 2017).

The DTOs have responded to the demand and, with crackdowns at the border, they have moved inside the United States and now oversee the planting of marijuana fields in US national parks. Although surprising, the National Park Service (NPS) reports people have cultivated marijuana on our public lands for more than twenty-five years. In 2010 and 2011, its internal reports documented the vast amount of marijuana eradicated on NPS land during the period. Between standing plants, or plants harvested and packaged for distribution at the time of interdiction, the NPS estimated a total street value of more than $405 million. Nearly all these cases of marijuana grown in national parks were identified as transnational organized crime-related operations (Martin 2012). Law enforcement officials think many trespass grows are set up by Mexican drug cartels, which prefer to ship marijuana from state to state rather than smuggle it over the international border. Not only do the plants choke out the natural vegetation, insecticides, rat poison, and other chemicals used by the cultivators kills fish and wildlife.

Tactic: Brutal Violence Against Soft Targets

Protecting this vast drug enterprise is critical for the DTOs. In Mexico, the areas of operation for the cartels are called plazas. Plazas allow safe passage for pipelines, or supply corridors into, through, and out of Mexico. The cartels have the upper hand in these plaza through bribery or intimidation of officials and citizens. Some of these formerly vibrant areas have turned into ghost towns due to the persistent escalating violence unleashed by the DTOs to maintain control of the plazas, most of which are at the US/Mexico border.

DTO violence is like none before and is a form of criminal terrorism, terrorist acts used to facilitate crime and criminal profits. The perpetrators have no respect for the rule of law and employ no moral restraint, willfully (and exuberantly) killing innocent people every day. Kidnapping, rape, human trafficking, extortion, larceny, arson, and weapons offenses—nothing is off the table for DTOs in the name of making money, widening their sphere of influence, and controlling plazas and pipelines. DTOs are transnational organizations; the US National Drug Intelligence Center reports that not only are they operating in the United States and nineteen Latin American countries, but they are also present in unexpected regions, such as Australia. This indicates their global reach and ability to transport their products worldwide.

Prior to December 2006, DTO violence was sporadic and contained by the government. During the election that year, Mexican president Felipe de Jesús Calderón Hinojosa stated his primary goal was to grow his country's economy by creating jobs and reducing poverty. However, once in office in late 2006, President Calderon opened a strategic front against the DTOs, declaring "war" against the cartels. Interestingly, this action was not unilaterally supported by the citizens of the country, whose small towns benefit financially from the movement of drugs through the area. Also, as they feared, innocent civilians inadvertently ended up on the frontlines of the battle. At least 200,000 people were killed in the violence between the start of President Calderon's offensive and June 2014, or about two every hour. Soaring levels of drug-related violence made 2017 Mexico's most murderous year on record, according to their government statistics. There were 25,339 homicides in Mexico, a 23 percent jump from 2016 and the highest number since 1997, when they began tracking the data (Gillespie 2018). The 2014 arrest of Joaquin "El Chapo" Guzman, the boss of one of Mexico's most powerful drug trafficking operations, the Sinaloa cartel, actually caused a spike in violence during a battle for control of the group. The homicide numbers do not include the 27,300 kidnapped and missing citizens, called "disappeareds" by the Mexican government (Molloy 2013). They are suspected to have suffered brutal deaths at the hands of the cartels, with their bodies unceremoniously dumped in the desert. Mass graves are often discovered in the desert, like one with 250 skulls discovered last year in Veracruz.

In 2017, cartel violence came to the streets of tourist hot spots of Cancun and Cozumel, claiming the lives of 205. The 2018 outlook is grim; an explosion on a ferry in Playa del Carmen injured more than twenty people, including five American tourists. News of this explosion, followed by the discovery of explosives on a different ferry near Cozumel, triggered a US Embassy alert warning of a "security threat" in the area. In April, 14 people were killed in a 36-hour period. In mid-April, two cartel gunmen opened fire on the Cancun beach area from jet skis, targeting a merchant. Fortunately, there were no injuries.

The battle between cartels for control has led to the preponderance of these mainly civilian deaths. The cartels target the government, with bombs regularly exploding in front of police stations and at city halls. However, soft target attacks are a more compelling way for cartels to push their agendas. Shootouts in the street happen daily, as thousands of videos taken by civilians and posted on the Internet attest. Innocent men, women, and children caught in the crossfire are seen by DTOs as collateral damage and are now the very targets of the rampant violence by groups sending "messages" to towns and each other. Many murders, such as beheadings, death by gasoline-induced fire, dismemberment, and acid baths, are premeditated and gruesome. Politicians and police officers are often hung in effigy from bridges in major cities with signs threatening those who are battling the cartels to back off. In January 2010, 36-year-old Hugo Hernandez was kidnapped in the state of Sonora by Sinaloa cartel members, who carved his body into seven pieces, dropping them at separate locations. Finally, his face was sliced off and stitched to a football, which was delivered to city hall with a warning to the Juárez cartel (Rodriguez 2010). Cartel violence often begets violence; a few days later, masked gunmen attacked teenagers in the border city of Juárez—children who were enjoying a combination birthday and high school soccer victory party—leaving sixteen dead and fourteen wounded. The very same evening in Torreon, in the border state of Coahuila, shooters ambushed students in a college bar: ten were left dead and eleven wounded. In the case of the children and college student massacres, the shootings were simply meant to send a message to rival cartels, law enforcement, and government leadership, with a by-product of terrorizing the public (Jasper 2010).

Many of these activities are carried out by the "enforcement arms" of the cartels, which are paramilitary groups possessing the training, knowledge, and sophisticated equipment of small armies. Street gang spinoffs of the main organization will also accomplish some of this dirty work, so if they are apprehended by authorities, the main leadership of the cartel and its business activity remain unaffected.

Goals: Money, Power, Control

The primary goal of cartels is to gain power, territory, and control so they can move drugs, money, guns, and human cargo unopposed. Cartels seek to create a void in leadership and rule of law in cities so they can step in and take control. Corruption of police, military, and government leadership is a tool used to create instability, ruin the government's reputation with citizens, and cause citizens to turn to others for protection. Instilling fear in the populace is a primary goal, compelling citizens to assist the DTOs or, at the very least, not resist their land grabs and activity in the community. Anything and anyone standing in the way of the cartels' progress is seen as a threat that must be eliminated. Conversely, anything and anyone helping attain their goals is an ally.

MAJOR DTOS IMPACTING THE UNITED STATES

For an in-depth look at the history and growth of individual cartels, please see my previous work in Chapter 5 in *The Terrorist-Criminal Nexus: An Alliance of International Drug Cartels, Organized Crime, and Terror Groups* (Hesterman 2013). For purposes of the discussion regarding soft targets, it is important to know all of the major DTOs now have a presence in the United States.

According to a report by General McCaffrey and Dr. Robert Scales (2011), "Drug cartels exploit porous borders using all the traditional elements of a military force, including command and control, logistics, intelligence, information operations and the application of increasingly deadly firepower." Indeed, the DTOs have slipped past the border and into our heartland, and nearly every state in our country is experiencing Mexican DTO activity. The cartels are using multiple points of entry at the border via plazas or tunnels, leveraging contact with gangs inside the United States to move drugs, and recruiting. In 2008, DTOs were present in 230 cities in the United States; startlingly, this number rose to more than a thousand US cities by 2010. According to the US Justice Department's National Drug Threat Assessment for 2017, these six Mexican DTOs hold the greatest drug trafficking impact on the US: Sinaloa Cartel (main hub Phoenix, AZ), Jalisco New Generation Cartel (hubs in Los Angeles and San Jose, CA), Juarez Cartel (hubs in New Mexico and East Texas), Gulf Cartel (hubs in Rio Grande Valley to Houston, TX), Los Zetas Cartel (hubs in Laredo, Dallas, New Orleans, and Atlanta), and Beltran-Leyva Organization (hubs in Phoenix, Los Angeles, Chicago, and Atlanta). DTOs expanded their US footprint in 2017, expanding into the New England area with heroin and meth.

Cartel violence is emerging in our major cities. Phoenix, a city of 1.6 million has not enjoyed the same decrease in murders as other cities, such as New York City, which only had 290 murders last year, an all-time low for a city of 8.5 million. After a historic low of 116 murders in 2015, Phoenix homicides leaped by 25 percent to 146 in 2016; then again by another 10 percent to 161 in 2017. About one-third of the murders go unsolved, with 166 open cases from 2016 to 2017. The problem is getting witnesses to cooperate, most likely because they have been threatened by cartels or gangs and are afraid. The state is also starting to experience the cartel's brand of brutal violence. The first beheading by a DTO in the United States occurred in an apartment in Phoenix in 2010, carried out by a member of the Sinaloa cartel (Associated Press 2013). DTO-related home invasions in the Phoenix area are also on the rise; in June 2008, several men wearing Phoenix Police Department uniforms forced their way into a Phoenix home, killing an occupant and spraying the home with fifty to one hundred bullets. In addition to violent home invasions, kidnappings in Phoenix are also prevalent. They are not alone; other US cities, such St Louis, Chicago, Baltimore, and Detroit, blame their escalating violent crime on cartel-related violence.

The cartels routinely issue a "green light," authorizing the killing of police and military. According to the Department of Homeland Security, in 2010 the Barrio Azteca issued a green light authorizing the murder of law enforcement officers in El Paso (DHS 2010). The Barrio Azteca gang formed in Texas prisons in the 1980s and is affiliated with a Mexican gang, the Aztecas, who carry out hits for the Juárez cartel's La Linea enforcers (US Department of Justice 2011a). Shortly after the green light was given, the Aztecas targeted and killed pregnant US consulate employee Leslie Ann Enriquez Catton and her husband at the border in Ciudad Juárez. The husband of another consulate employee, Jorge Salcido, was also killed in the attack. Miraculously, the Catton's young child, strapped in a car seat, was unharmed (US Department of Justice 2010). High-profile murders of US law enforcement agents by DTOs include ICE Special Agent Jaime Zapata and Border Patrol Agent Brian Terry. In a country where the killing of police officers is on the rise and respect for law enforcement on the decline, we must be concerned about an escalation of the deliberate targeting of police by cartels and gangs.

Special Concern: Los Zetas

Imagine, for a moment, that one of America's elite special operations units goes "rogue" and starts using its specialized skills, equipment, and training against the US government. The members of the unit participate in illegal activities such as drug trafficking, gun running, and human smuggling. They also serve as hit squads, willing to murder innocent victims in return for cash. The unit does not fear, hide, or run from law enforcement; rather, it engages.

Meet the Los Zetas organization. The fastest growing DTO in Mexico, this is the first to use the Internet, the first to savagely behead innocent civilians to send "warnings," and the first to drop propaganda leaflets from aircraft. With an estimated membership of 2,000, the core of the Zetas is composed of former members of the Grupo Aeromóvil de Fuerzas Especiales, or the GAFE. The GAFE is the Special Forces arm of the Mexican army; its members receive specialized training in jungle, amphibious, urban, and high-mountain operations from the best counterterrorism and counterinsurgency units in the world. They are also trained to deploy forward into hostile foreign territory and to blend in and operate undetected. In recent years, the GAFE's primary mission morphed from providing protection to key officials and buildings to one of assisting the country in dismantling drug cartels. Along with their counterintelligence, disguise, and insurgency training, the Zetas are a complex and lethal force. Although other paramilitary or "enforcement groups" are present in every cartel, such as the CJNG (Knights Templar), the DEA labels the Zetas as "the most technologically advanced, sophisticated, and violent" (DEA 2008). Alejandro Trevino-Morales, one of Mexico's most wanted men and Los Zetas leader, also known as "42" or "Omar," was captured and arrested in Nuevo Leon, Mexico, in March 2015. His replacement, Guizar Valencia, US citizen known by his Zetas code name Z-43, was captured in Mexico in February 2018. Both were on the US's most wanted list with a $5 million reward for their capture.

Zetas Tactics

Zetas should not be viewed as a criminal enterprise, but as a lethal, complex army. They have specialized training in navigating and operating in all terrains; they have river swimmers, divers, jungle experts, and training in urban warfare. Money from their drug trade and other nefarious activity enables Zetas to buy top-of-the line equipment; they have tanks, surface-to-air missiles, rocket-propelled grenades (RPGs), night-vision equipment, boats, helicopters, and aircraft. They often operate in small fire teams and use snipers and countersnipers.

Their executions are savage; they often set their targets on fire, decapitate them, or saturate their bodies with bullets. The scope of violence is escalating; in May 2012, Lazcano gave orders for the massacre and dismemberment of forty-nine innocent civilians in the so-called Mother's Day Massacre. They also engage law enforcement and the military, using ambush tactics and the element of surprise to kill officers before they can react.

We should not underestimate the sophistication of the Zetas; undetected, they plan and practice for operations, performing surveillance and patiently waiting for the right time to strike. The brazen daytime attack on a casino in Monterrey, Mexico, in August 2011, which left at least fifty-two people dead, is an example of the escalation and calculation of Zeta violence. Twelve gunmen entered the casino and started shooting into the crowd; other attackers simultaneously doused exits with gasoline and threw grenades into the building to start multiple fires. Such attacks are less about the target (in this case, a casino) and more about the message. Clearly, the Zetas are not merely a criminal element; they use terroristic tactics to further their goals.

The Zetas are also known for their sicarios, or assassins. Take the case of Rosalio Reta, a US citizen born and raised in Laredo, Texas. At 13 years of age, Reta was kidnapped by Zeta members and taken to Mexico, where he became a Zetita, or "little Zeta," attending tactical training camps. His initiation came shortly thereafter, when he was directed to shoot a man in the head at a bar in Nuevo Laredo. He returned to live in Laredo at the age of 15, where he was used by the Zetas to kill several men and young boys throughout Texas. Reta's assassinations and apprehension are detailed in the 2012 book, *The Executioner's Men*, by George W. Grayson and Samuel Logan, the most comprehensive book available on the Zetas.

Increasing Reach in the United States

In addition to sicarios, the Zetas have clearly operated in the border region for many years; however, the stunning 2011 arrest of fifteen Zetas in Chicago perfectly illustrated the reach of the group within our borders. The case detailed the movement of drugs from Nuevo Laredo, Mexico, through Texas and into Chicago, via a US fugitive working for the Zetas. The street value of this cell was staggering: feds seized 12 million US dollars in cash and 250 kilograms of cocaine (DEA 2012). According to the FBI, in addition to all of the border states, Zeta cells are believed to be present in Tennessee, Oklahoma, South Carolina, and Georgia (FBI 2008).

A battle is also raging for control of Interstate 35, a highly desired route for drug traffickers. I-35 begins at the border in Laredo and traverses major cities like Dallas, where, according to a Justice Department memo, Zetas have been active since 2003 as part of the Gulf cartel. Following the shooting death of Dallas Police Officer Mark Nix in 2007, law enforcement agents are still looking for Maximo Garcia Carrillo, a suspected Zeta and the triggerman in the shooting who owned a house in the Oak Cliff suburb of the city. On the other side of Dallas, I-35 has intermittent empty stretches of highway, but eventually passes through Oklahoma City, Kansas City, and Minneapolis. The interstate ends in Duluth, Minnesota, at the Canadian border. The importance of this corridor to the cartels is significant; as the former head of the DEA's El Paso Intelligence Center once stated, "Drug traffickers kill for I-35." More recently, the Zetas have also become involved in the human smuggling business, charging a 10 percent commission for use of their border plazas, pipelines, and the Interstate 35 corridor. It seems incredible that Zetas charge smugglers to operate on US real estate, and it is even more egregious they would buy property and live illegally in our cities, right under the nose of law enforcement (Hesterman 2009). For instance, Zeta assassin Marciano "Chano" Millan Vasquez actually moved to San Antonio, Texas, with his family. US officials found him, and he was arrested and sentenced in 2017 to seven life terms for his role in eighteen horrific deaths, in which he sawed the limbs off of a 6-year-old girl while she was alive, in front of her parents. He then killed them and fifteen other hostages in the same manner. He also participated in a rampage in which more than 300 people were slaughtered.

The Zetas also have some amount of control over US gangs such as MS-13, the Mexican Mafia, and the Texas Syndicate. The FBI's gang assessment indicates a number of alarming trends, including that street gangs in the United States are growing in size, operating at the border, and forming ties with DTOs (US Department of Justice 2017). The imitation of tactics typically indicates some type of liaison at the training or operational levels; gang members in our country are now engaging in nontraditional crimes such as human trafficking and alien smuggling. They are acquiring high-powered weaponry and showing new sophistication in terms of recruitment and communication. These attributes make them attractive to cartels to work their street-level issues, launder money, and move product. Law enforcement believes the Zetas may have already used MS-13 in several operations in the United States, providing training and weaponry.

The Zetas may be on the decline due to battle losses with the other cartels, like the emergent Jalisco Cartel New Generation (CJNG), as well as the persistent capture or killing of their leaders. The US continues to put massive bounties on the heads of DTO leaders, compelling people to call with tips and information. The Old School (Zetas Vieja Escuela) and the Northeast Cartel are now the most important factions of the Zetas. Overall, the Zetas may still receive between $15 and $20 million a month from cocaine to the American Midwest, and have a large cash reserve in Mexico, possibly between $30 and $50 million.

SUMMARY OF DOMESTIC TERRORIST THREATS AGAINST SOFT TARGETS

As the chapter illustrated, the domestic terror threat is vast and growing. New groups arise, mature groups splinter and very few organizations will dissolve. An extremist ideology persists and has staying power. Grassroots and lone actor attacks can be devastating; planning for mass casualty attacks doesn't have to be sophisticated, or overly ambitious.

TABLE 4.1   Summary of Domestic Threat Against Soft Targets

Domestic Terror Group	History/propensity for hitting soft targets?	With intent to kill?	Reach?	Capability?
Right-Wing Religious	Yes	Likely	Yes	Yes
Right-Wing Militia	Possibly	Possibly	Maybe	Maybe
Right-Wing Sovereign	Yes	Yes	Yes	Maybe
Left-Wing Anarchist	Yes	Unlikely	Yes	Maybe
Left-Wing Single Interest (Animal, Eco, Etc.)	Yes	Unlikely	Yes	Maybe
Homegrown Jihadist	Yes	Yes	Yes	Likely, training outside the US or through online propaganda
Lone Wolf of Any Ideology	Yes	Yes	Yes	Maybe
Drug Trafficking Organizations (Cartels)	Yes	Yes	Yes	Maybe, through street gangs

Soft targets are vulnerable and abound. The good news is there is a growing body of academic thought on violent extremism and soft sciences are finally factoring into the solution set.

Many groups already targeted innocent civilians to further their political or religious goals and have a propensity, reach, and/or capability to hit soft targets in the United States; Table 4.1 provides a fresh assessment.

Now that we understand the international and domestic threats to our country and its citizens, we next take an in-depth look at their potential targets and our vulnerabilities.

REFERENCES

Akbar, M. J. *The Shade of Swords: Jihad and the Conflict between Islam and Christianity.* London: Routledge, 2002.

Anti-Defamation League. "Murder and Extremism in the United States in 2017." *ADL*, 2017.

Associated Press. "Crisantos Moroyoqui-Yocupicio Gets 14 Years in Cartel Beheading in Arizona." May 8, 2013.

Azarva, Jeffrey. "Is U.S. Detention Policy in Iraq Working?" *Middle East Quarterly*, Winter (2009): 5–14.

Barrett, Richard. "Beyond the Caliphate: Foreign Fighters and the Threat of Returnees." *The Soufan Group*, October 2017.

BBC. "IS Web Media Targeted in EU-Led Attack." *BBC News*, London, England, April 27, 2018.

Boucek, Christopher. "Clearing a Path for Guantanamo Returnees: Rehabilitation and Risk-Assessment." *Carnegie Endowment for International Peace.* www.carnegieendowment.org/2009/01/28/clearing-path-for-guantanamo-returnees-rehabilitation-and-risk-assessment/ 341 (2009).

———. "Saudi Arabia's 'Soft' Counterterrorism Strategy: Prevention, Rehabilitation, and Aftercare." *Carnegie Papers*, 2008.

Breivik, Anders Behring. "2083: A European Declaration of Independence." www.youtube.com/watch?v=KjCy90NVLQM (2011).

Bureau of Justice. "Recidivism of State Prisoners Released in 2005." Bureau of Justice, Washington, DC, 2014.

Burke, Jill. "Guide to Alaska Sovereign Citizens Trial: Patriots, Militias and Going to Extremes." www.alaskadispatch.com/content/guide-alaska-sovereign-citizens-trial-patriots-militias-and-going-extremes (May 20, 2012).

Bynum, Russ. "Prosecutor: Army Soldiers Planned Terror Plot." *Northwest Herald*, 2012.

"C4ss: Center for a Stateless Society." http://c4ss.org

CBS News Online. "Man Angry at IRS Crashes Plane into Office." www.cbsnews.com/news/man-angry-at-irs-crashes-plane-into-office/ (February 19, 2010).

Cecil-Cockwell, Malcolm. "The Earth Liberation Front: Sabotaging a Way of Life." *Epoch Journal* 2, no. 3 (2008).

DEA (Drug Enforcement Administration). "National Drug Assessment." Drug Enforcement Administration, Washington, DC, 2008.

———. "Twenty Charged in Chicago with Various Drug Trafficking Offenses, Including Five Allegedly Tied to the Mexican 'Zetas' Cartel." Drug Enforcement Administration, Washington, DC, 2012.

DHS (Department of Homeland Security). "Officer Safety Alert." Department of Homeland Security, Washington, DC, 2010.

FBI (Federal Bureau of Investigation). "Los Zetas Expanding Reach into Southeast and Midwest United States." Federal Bureau of Investigation, Washington, DC, 2008.

———. "Sovereign Citizens: A Growing Domestic Threat to Law Enforcement." Federal Bureau of Investigation, Washington, DC, *Counterterrorism Analysis Section*, 2011.

Fedschun, Travis. "July 4 Terror Plot Thwarted in Cleveland, Suspect Pledged Allegiance to Al Qaeda, FBI Says." Cleveland, OH: Fox News, www.foxnews.com/us/july-4-terror-plot-thwarted-in-cleveland-suspect-pledged-allegiance-to-al-qaeda-fbi-says (July 2, 2018).

France 24. "French Prime Minister Unveils New Deradicalisation Programme." www.france24.com/en/20180223-france-deradicalisation-programme-jihad-islamist-extremists-prisons-centres-philippe (February 23, 2018).

Galofaro, Claire. "7 Suspects in St. John Deputy Shootings Are Tied to Violent Anti-Government Group." *The Times Picayune*, August 17, 2012.

Gartenstein-Ross, Daveed and Madeleine Gruen. "Leadership vs. Leaderless Resistance: The Militant White Separatist Movement's Operating Model." *Foundation for Defense of Democracies*, February 18, 2010.

Gillespie, Patrick. "Mexico Reports Highest Murder Rate on Record." *CNN*, January 22, 2018.

Grayson, George W. and Samuel Logan. *The Executioner's Men: Los Zetas, Rogue Soldiers, Criminal Entrepreneurs, and the Shadow State They Created.* New Brunswick: Transaction Publishers, 2012.

Green, Emma. "How Two Mississippi College Students Fell in Love and Decided to Join a Terrorist Group." *The Atlantic*, May 1, 2017.

Hamm, Mark S. and Ramon Spaaiij. *The Age of Lone Wolf Terrorism.* New York, NY: Columbia University Press, 2017.

Hankes, Keegan and Alex Amend. "The Alt-Right is Killing People." *Southern Poverty Law Center*, February 5, 2018.

Hayden, Michael. "Armed Services Committee CIA Director Testimony." United States Congress, May 12, 2009.

Hesterman, Jennifer. "Catch and Release: Jihadist Recidivism." *The Counter Terrorist Magazine*, April/May 2010.

———. "The Mexican Drug War Spills Over the Border." *The Counter Terrorist* (2009): 26–38.

———. *The Terrorist-Criminal Nexus: An Alliance of International Drug Cartels, Organized Crime, and Terror Groups.* Boca Raton, FL: CRC Press, 2013.

———.Chapter 7, "Reverse Use of Organizational Development Theory: A Unique Methodology for Analyzing and Disrupting Terrorist Organizations." In *The Theory and Practice of Terrorism: Alternate Paths of Inquiry.* Hauppauge, NY: Nova Science Publishers, 2016.

Hoffman, Bruce. "Sources of Concern and Future Prospects." In *Recent Trends and Future Prospects of Terrorism in the United States.* Santa Monica, CA: RAND Corporation, 1988.

Inserra, David. "New York City Truck Attack Is 100th Terror Plot on US Soil Since 9/11." *The Heritage Foundation*, November 1, 2017.

International Centre for Counter-Terrorism (ICCT). *Countering Lone Actor Terrorism Project*. The Hague, Netherlands. https://icct.nl/topic/lone-actors-terrorist-groups/ (2018).

Jasper, William F. "Escalating Chaos on Our Border." *The New American* (2010): 17.

Koerner, Brendan I. "A Controversial New Program Aims to Reform Homegrown ISIS Recruits Back into Normal Young Americans." *Wired Magazine*, January 24, 2017.

Kohlmann, Evan F. "'The Eleven': Saudi Guantanamo Veterans Returning to the Fight." http://counterterrorismblog.org/2009/02/nefa_report_-_the_eleven_saudi.php

Kounang, Nadia. "Opioids Now Kill More People Than Breast Cancer." *CNN*, December 21, 2017.

Lamb, Christina. "Guantanamo Closure Delayed Amid Rehab Failures." *The Australian News* (2010). Published electronically January 11.

Lázaro, Fernando. "Extremo Control De La Yihad en Las Cárceles." *El Mundo*, February 18, 2018.

Martin, Robert R. *The National Park Service and Transnational Criminal Organizations: Is a Crisis Looming?* Charlestown, WV: American Military University, 2012.

McCaffrey, Robert H. and Barry R. Scales. "Texas Border Security: A Strategic Military Assessment." *Colgan LP*, 2011.

McNabb, J. J. "'Sovereign' Citizen Kane." The Intelligence Report, No. 139, Montgomery, AL: Southern Poverty Law Center, August 1, 2010.

Molloy, Molly. "The Mexican Undead: Toward a New History of the 'Drug War' Killing Fields." *Small Wars Journal*, August 21, 2013.

NAALPO (North American Animal Liberation Press Office). http://animalliberationpressoffice.org/NAALPO/

National Consortium for the Study of Terrorism and Responses to Terrorism. "Understanding Law Enforcement Intelligence Processes." www.start.umd.edu (July 2014).

Perlinger, Arie. "Challengers from the Sidelines: Understanding America's Violent Far-Right." *Combatting Terrorism Center, West Point*, 2012.

Pluchinsky, Dennis A. "Global Jihadist Recidivism: A Red Flag." *Studies in Conflict & Terrorism* 31, no. 3 (2008).

Rivinius, Jessica. "Proportion of Terrorist Attacks by Religious and Right-Wing Extremists on the Rise in United States." *START*, November 2, 2017.

Rodriguez, Olga R. "Mexico Cartel Stitches Rival's Face on Soccer Ball." *San Diego Union Tribune*, San Diego, California, 2010.

Simcox, Robin and Emily Dyer. *Al-Qaeda in the United States: A Complete Analysis of Terrorism Offenses*. London: Henry Jackson Society, 2013.

Sofer, Ken and Molly Bernstein. "17 Years after Oklahoma City Bombing, Right-Wing Extremism Is Significant Domestic Terror Threat." *Think Progress*, April 19, 2012.

"The Solution, Schaeffer Cox Speaks on the Future of the Liberty Movement." www.youtube.com/watch?v=tvRUcT0Z7uI (2012).

"Ten Years after 9/11: An Anarchist Evaluation." *Anarchist Developments* 1 (2011). www.anarchist-developments.org/

US Department of Justice. "35 Members and Associates of Barrio Azteca Gang Charged with Racketeering." *News Release*, Washington, DC, March 9, 2011a.

———. "National Gang Threat Assessment." Washington, DC, 2011b.

———. "Eleven Defendants Indicted on Domestic Terrorism Charges." Washington, DC, 2006.

———. "National Drug Threat Assessment." Washington, DC: National Drug Intelligence Center, 2017.

———. "Nine Members of a Militia Group Charged with Seditious Conspiracy and Related Charges." *News Release*, Washington, DC, March 29, 2010.

Winter, Jana. "FBI and DHS Warned of Growing Threat from White Supremacists Months Ago." *Foreign Policy*, August 14, 2017.

Žižek, Slavoj. *The Sublime Object of Ideology*. London: Verso, 1989.

CHAPTER 5

Soft Target Threat Assessment
Schools, Churches, and Hospitals

I would like to make it crystal clear, I do not regret what I did.

—Dylann Roof, pleading guilty to his racially motivated massacre at
the Emanuel African Methodist Episcopal Church (Zapotsky 2017)

INTRODUCTION

Every day, somewhere in the world, a terrorist, insurgent, or criminal group attacks a school, church, or hospital. Increasingly, these attacks are happening on our soil at our most vulnerable places—where we worship, study, and heal. The psychological vulnerabilities covered earlier in the book are only part of the challenge related to protecting people from these types of heinous soft target attacks. There are also physical vulnerabilities, making soft targets more attractive to would-be attackers—some we can mitigate, and others we cannot. Prior to discussing individual venues, we start with a strategic view of the United States to assess vulnerability of certain regions and cities, and then explore the targets themselves.

VULNERABILITY IN THE UNITED STATES

If I asked you to name the top four US cities most vulnerable to a terrorist attack, the natural response is those with large populations and symbolic targets such as Washington, DC, and New York City. Would it surprise you to know a government-funded study, conducted by mathematicians and statisticians, produced a wholly different list?

In 2007, a groundbreaking report rated 132 US cities on their vulnerability to terrorist attack using a newly developed statistical method. "Benchmark Analysis for Quantifying Urban Vulnerability to Terrorist Incidents" was written by Dr. Susan Cutter, a hazards and vulnerability expert and Dr. Walter W. Piegorsch, a leading statistician and environmental risk expert (Piegorsch, Cutter, and Hardisty 2007). The Department of Homeland Security-funded study yielded some unanticipated results.

The overarching goal in this study was to analyze the relationship between location vulnerability and terrorist outcome. Terrorism vulnerability involves three dimensions of risk—social aspects, natural hazards, and construction of the city and its infrastructure. Using this new approach, the study calculated the susceptibility of areas to terrorist attack, predicting the impact of an attack on the populace, and assessing the likely response of residents. The report considered natural geographic features and environmental hazards, as well as critical industries, ports, railroads, bridges, tunnels, water/sewage systems, and the age and fragility of the existing infrastructure. Finally, the team analyzed and factored in historical data from the terrorism knowledge base and the global terrorism database.

Although most Americans can only recount a handful of terrorist attacks if asked, the research considered more than 1,000 unique terrorist-related incidents in US cities, spanning a thirty-year period. A surprising result: contrary to typical threat assessment criteria, areas with nuclear power plants and military facilities did not come up as "high risk" in the analysis. Although the study is ten years old, it is still quite accurate; many of the factors used in computing vulnerability, such as aging infrastructure, are persistent or even may degrade over time, increasing vulnerability.

The final computation of factors resulted in a place vulnerability index, or PVI, rating. Overall results presented in Table 5.1 indicate the eastern and southern seaboards of the United States are at greatest risk and also show a large swath of vulnerability from Texas to Ohio. Cities scoring the highest place vulnerability index (PVI) are illustrated in Table 5.1.

Other major areas typically thought of as vulnerable were much lower in ranking, even falling below Columbia, South Carolina, which had a PVI of 1.117. For example, Los Angeles, California, had a PVI of 0.421; Dallas, Texas, a PVI of 0.447; and Denver, Colorado, a PVI of 0.171. Surprisingly, Seattle, Washington's PVI was very low, at—0.315. To view the map with color code results and more detailed computation information, please access the study (Piegorsch et al. 2007).

TABLE 5.1   Place Vulnerability Index
Cities Scoring the Highest Place Vulnerability Index (PVI)

City	PVI
New Orleans, LA	3.110
Baton Rouge, LA	3.061
Charleston SC	2.543
Norfolk VA	2.326
New York/Newark area	2.154
Washington DC area	1.978
Houston, TX	1.844
Philadelphia, PA	1.737
Boise, ID	1.696
Atlanta, GA	1.683
Chicago, IL	1.404

SMALL CITIES AND RURAL AREAS IN THE CROSSHAIRS

Cities previously hit or targeted by terrorists naturally spend more money to harden against attack, upwards of $100 million tax dollars in several cases. However, those few urban areas represent less than 5 percent of the US population; what about everyone else? Not only are the top four cities identified in the previous study as vulnerable surprising, but Boise, Idaho, with a population of 220,000, emerged as a new area of concern, the lone red "blip" in the northwest. Although funded by the government, the study's results were not widely disseminated to the public or covered by the news media. Boise city officials acknowledged surprise at the results, engaging with both Piegorsch and the state's Homeland Security officials for clarification. In 2008, I blogged about the study's results on the Internet and was contacted by several concerned citizens from Baton Rouge and chided by one for "painting a bull's-eye" on his city. Instead of responding emotionally to vulnerability studies, it is more helpful to appreciate how the emergent research illuminates a pathway to greater awareness, inspires businesses and community institutions to review security procedures and review terrorism insurance coverage, and can be used as a vehicle to lobby the government for target hardening funding.

Therein lies the conundrum: Do citizens truly want to know their vulnerability to terrorist attack? Isn't it far easier just to hope the storm clouds pass by? Bad actors hope we become passive bystanders or, worse, remain in blissful denial so they will not have to fight us on the way to the target.

The standard perception in our country is smaller cities and rural areas are not vulnerable to attack by international or domestic terrorists. For example, the Terrorism Risk Insurance Act (TRIA) was enacted in 2002 as a response to the 9/11 terrorist attacks as a public–private partnership requiring private insurance companies to provide terrorism risk coverage, with federal funding as a backstop if costs to insurance companies exceed $100 million. The law was renewed in 2005, 2007, and 2014, and is now set to expire on December 31, 2020. Critics argue not only does the law place an unnecessary burden on taxpayers, it puts an undue cost on those living in rural areas with "less of a terrorism threat" (Novak 2014). They are not looking at vulnerability studies or data from our law enforcement agencies showing how rural areas are now being preyed upon and exploited by violent gangs, drug cartels, and organized crime. Recent terror attacks in Orlando and San Bernardino further illustrate how no place is immune.

For instance, in 2009, the DEA discovered during Operation Xcelerator the Sinaloa's drug cartel hubs were not in major metropolitan areas as previously thought, but rather the cartel used unsuspecting rural areas to move product. One distribution center was located in Stow, Ohio, a quiet community of 35,000. The Sinaloas used the small airport to move drugs between Stow and distribution hubs in California (US Department of Justice 2009). In rural Rhode Island, the La Cosa Nostra (Mafia) allowed the Hells Angels outlaw motorcycle group to continue illegal trafficking activities on their turf without interfering, in return for the bikers paying a percentage to the mob (WPRI Newport 2008). Who would predict quiet Stow and rural Rhode Island would be host to such violent transnational actors? Recent cases of cartel activity shows the groups are stepping up activity in rural areas such as Ivanhoe, North Carolina, population of 300, where the La Familia Michoacana Mexican drug cartel was growing 2,000 marijuana plants. The presence of organized crime or cartel activities in a rural area is a red flag for an even more vexing threat: terrorists often prey on established routes, and groups with different goals are increasingly working together.

The place vulnerability study teaches us much about risk assessment, and its methodology can be applied in any country to similarly illuminate the gap between perceived and actual vulnerability. The study's surprising results indicate *probability*, is driving the government's security focus and funding streams, not *vulnerability*. Only focusing efforts to harden the location of the last attack makes the next one more vulnerable.

HOW BAD ACTORS CHOOSE TARGETS

Before discussing the soft targets themselves, it is essential to get inside the minds of criminals, especially killers. In 2014, I attended an international security conference in Dubai and was fortunate to meet Dr. Martin

Gill, a renowned British professor of criminology and author of several outstanding publications viewing crime through the eyes of the criminal (Gill 2014). His field work includes interviews with convicted killers about their crimes, to assess motives and the real versus perceived usefulness of closed circuit television (CCTV), store security guards, alarm systems, and other physical security apparatus. When posed the question regarding how criminals choose their targets, Dr. Gill's answer is simple: because they are easy. Gill found CCTV does not affect the way criminals commit their offenses, as they merely wear a disguise or pull a hat down low and look at the ground. They bet the cameras are not working or if they are caught and facing prosecution, the burden will be on the prosecutors to prove it is them in the video. In fact, some criminals share that if they believe during the course of the crime their image was captured on CCTV, the severity of the crime may escalate. One convicted murderer commented that if he was going to spend a long time in prison anyhow, he might as well kill, saying "They've taken away my incentive not to kill." Another stated, "If I'm going to jail for armed robbery and I need to kill someone in order to get away, I may take that next step." In fact, one man in prison for murder said in risky crimes, the decision to shoot and kill a lone security guard is actually easy. It eliminates the one piece of evidence that will always stand in court: visual recognition of the perpetrator. Criminals report being more concerned about being stopped by people than any type of technology. They also note favoring large, bulky security guards because they can be outrun. As shown in this example regarding the potential ineffectiveness of CCTV, seeing the potential crime scene through the eyes of a criminal is invaluable to the discussion of target hardening. Many criminals believe a camera is either not real, not filming, or no one is watching. They would be right in many instances. Dylann Roof, undeterred from his massacre mission, walked directly under a camera at the AME church in Charleston, South Carolina. Although cameras are usually not a deterrent to a determined actor, they do collect valuable evidence. Roof's photograph was immediately circulated to the community; police arrested him before he could carry out his next planned attack.

THE SOFT TARGETS

Although successfully hitting a hard target such as a government building, military base, or a symbolic target brings credibility to a terror group, a soft target attack would certainly damage the national psyche and discredit the government's ability to protect its people. Factor in the use of a chemical or biological agent, or radiation, and the impact could be immense on sectors such as tourism, shopping, and recreation.

All citizens have the right to learn, worship, and receive medical care in a safe environment. However, we all can easily slip into a false sense of security in these facilities and become complacent about safety. Security is also not the primary goal of these institutions, which are typically resource constrained and do not have money to spend on extra security measures or guards, adding to their vulnerability. Also, these are typically "gun-free" zones, so the only resistance a bad actor will meet is a security guard or two, typically not armed. This combination of factors makes schools, churches, and hospitals targets of choice for terrorists or homicidal killers.

SCHOOLS

On April 7, 2011, a 24-year-old man named Wellington Oliveira traveled to the Tasso da Silveira Municipal School in Rio de Janeiro where, as a former student, he had been subject to bullying. He methodically killed twelve students. A firefighter who responded to the scene told newspapers "There is blood on the walls, blood on the chairs. I've never seen anything like this. It's like something in the United States" (Johnson 2012). His statement illustrates the prevailing worldview toward the escalation of violence in our country, especially with the recent epidemic of school shootings and stabbings garnering wide press coverage.

Perhaps nothing more deeply affects the American public than an attack at a school. We never expect the targeting of innocent children, whether by a fellow student, a member of the community with a mental illness, a criminal, or a terrorist. Therefore, despite these events happening on a more regular basis in our country, we are shocked, and deeply saddened. The ripple effect of school attacks is also immense, traumatizing students, teachers, and first responders who view the scene, inducing posttraumatic stress and panic disorder in many. We have to assume the terrorists also see the immense vulnerability in our schools.

At any given time, there are at least 75 million Americans attending some type of school from kindergarten (K) through doctorate level courses, and there are five million teachers, administrative, and support staff on campuses (DHS 2012). Many schools also serve community needs and are used as places for meeting or polling, or shelters in times of emergency. Even if schools are not the terrorists' intended target and their act of violence is a city building or mass transit, we must protect children from physical and emotional side effects of being in proximity to such horrific violence. For example, there were four elementary schools and three high schools located within six blocks of the World Trade Center on 9/11, and thousands of children were exposed to the toxic dust clouds from the collapsing buildings. Children in at least three states had parents working in or around the World Trade Center that day; in the Washington, DC, area, schoolchildren faced similar stress during the Pentagon attack (CDC 2003).

Several of the deadliest mass shootings by a single person in US history occurred on school campuses. On April 16, 2007, 23-year-old Seung-Hui Cho killed two students in his dormitory and then went to a classroom building, barricaded himself inside, and shot fifty-three students and teachers, killing thirty in just nine minutes. On December 14, 2012, Adam Lanza killed his mother in their home and then went to the Sandy Hook Elementary School in Newtown, Connecticut. There, he bypassed the security door and shot through a plate glass window to gain entrance to the building. He killed twenty first-graders and six staff members in only six minutes. On February 14, 2018, in Parkland, Florida, former Marjory Stoneman Douglas High School student Nikolas Cruz pulled a fire alarm and then started his massacre. In just a few minutes, seventeen students and staff were dead, and another seventeen were severely wounded.

Since the 1999 Columbine attack by students Eric Harris and Dylan Klebold, which killed fifteen students and injured twenty-four, there have been forty other major school shootings in our country resulting in deaths, and more than 100 incidents with none killed but hundreds of injuries. Of course we can never measure the psychological damage. Beginning with Columbine in 1999, more than 187,000 students attending at least 193 primary or secondary schools have experienced a shooting on campus during school hours, according to a year-long analysis (Cox and Rich 2018).

Data now kept by the Educator's School Safety Network, a group that tracks school safety, confirms anecdotal thoughts regarding steep rises in school threats and incidents following a mass shooting. For example, in the six weeks following the February 14, 2018, mass shooting at the Marjory Stoneman Douglas High School in Parkland, Florida, there were nearly 1,400 "school-based incidents and threats" made, many through social media. Of eighty-three total incidents, a gun was found in forty cases and twelve were classified as "thwarted plots." The Network also tracked a huge uptick in school-based violent incidents following the massacre; typically they track around ten threats and incidents per day, but in the weeks after Parkland, they were tracking more than seventy each day (Educator's School Safety Network 2018).

As the scope of violence grows in our country, keeping schools safe is a constant challenge for administrators and law enforcement. The National Center for Education Statistics report entitled Indicators of School Crime and Safety (NCES 2017) is alarming and illustrates the vast number of students affected by violence in school. For instance, during the 2015–2016 school year, 69 percent of public schools recorded that one or more violent incidents had taken place on their property. Focusing in on secondary schools, consider there are 15 million students in grades 9 to 12 in the United States. The Youth Risk Behavior survey from the 2015–2016 school year showed 4 percent of high school students, or 600,000, reported carrying a weapon (gun, knife, or club) to school during the previous month. During the 2015–2016 school year, there were 1,600 reported firearm possession incidents at schools in the United States. Furthermore, 4 percent of students ages 12 to 18 reported that they had access to a loaded gun without adult permission. Also, in that same year, 6 percent of high schoolers stated they were threatened or injured with a weapon such as a gun, knife, or club on school property—this equates to more than 900,000 students. We cannot measure the impact of violence or fear on the quality of teaching and learning in schools, or how this later impacts the workplace (Indicators of School Crime and Safety 2017).

Although US-wide data is unavailable, large cities such as New York closely track the types of weapons confiscated in schools and might serve as a "barometer" for what is happening in the rest of the country. The number of deadly weapons found in New York City schools climbed for the third straight year. In the 2016–2017 school year, 2,120 weapons were seized from students, including 10 firearms, 1,176 knives, 607 box-cutters and razors, 53 BB guns, 34 stun guns, and 240 other dangerous objects. The total weapons seized for the 2016–2017 school year was 3.3 percent more than the 2,053 weapons seized in 2015–2016, and up from 1,673 in 2014 to 2015 (Edelman 2017).

School Violence: Not Just Students

We can't forget the danger staff with personal troubles may bring to schools. Eulalio Tordil of Adelphi, Maryland, killed his estranged wife, Gladys, outside of the Prince George's County school where she taught. Her daughters were students at the school, and one witnessed the murder. She saw Tordil confronting her mother; the girl dropped her backpack and ran to help her mother, who shouted. "Grace! Run! Run!" (Bui 2017). Those were her last words. Tordil shot and killed Gladys and left the scene. The next day, he shot two good Samaritans who attempted to help a woman in the parking lot of Westfield Montgomery Mall, as he tried to steal her vehicle. Malcolm Winffel died; the woman and other man were injured. Later that morning, Tordil shot and killed Claudina Molina as he tried to steal her SUV outside Giant Food on Connecticut Avenue in Aspen Hill. Tordil, a federal security officer employed by the Federal Protective Service, was on administrative duties after a protective order was issued against him to stay away from his estranged wife.

On April 10, 2017, Cedric Anderson, the 53-year-old husband of a special education teacher entered his estranged wife's classroom at an elementary school in San Bernardino, California, and fired ten shots, killing his wife and an 8-year-old student. He also injured a 9-year-old student before killing himself. Also in California, on November 14, after killing his wife the previous day, Kevin Neal, 43, shot his neighbors, then fired at random persons on his way to an elementary school, possibly in search of his neighbor's son. While the school was on lockdown, the gunman fired shots penetrating the outer walls injuring some. The attacker was ultimately killed by law enforcement. All told, he shot and wounded at least ten and killed five, including two of his neighbors and his wife (USSS 2018).

Stabbing Attacks on the Rise

Gun attacks are obviously the most feared assault, since mass casualties can be inflicted in a short period of time. However, more knives than guns are confiscated in schools across the country annually, and knifing incidents are increasing in the United States and are worthy of our attention.

Emergent Threat

Stabbing Attacks in Schools on the Rise

Gun attacks are obviously the most feared assault, inflicting mass casualties in a short period of time. However, as our focus naturally centers on keeping guns out of schools, we can't forget that knives are easier to conceal and transport and can also inflict significant bodily harm in a short period of time. We confiscate far more knives in schools across the country than guns. And the number of knives on school property appears to be on the rise; in New York City, there were 1,176 knives confiscated in 2016–2017 compared to 873 knives in 2015–2016. Since school behavior is reflective of societal trends, it is also important to note that knifing deaths in the US are prevalent and on the rise; the FBI Uniform Crime Report (UCR) for 2016 shows there were 1,604 people killed with "knives or cutting instruments" in the US, or 11 percent of all homicides for the year (FBI 2017).

One factor driving a perpetrator to use a knife instead of a firearm is knives are much easier to obtain. In many recent attacks, perpetrators simply used kitchen or hunting knives. Also, for those hoping to escape after the attack, knives are usually untraceable. The MS-13 gang has a penchant for using knives and machetes in their attacks versus firearms. Often, the stabbing or slicing weapons used by the group are purchased at hardware stores or mall kiosks and paid for with cash. Even if a knife used as a murder weapon is recovered, as in many MS-13 cases, they are virtually untraceable. Unless the weapon has a decorative handle, is an antique or unique in another way, it is very difficult to trace to the sale point and buyer. Also, MS-13 prefers knife attacks as they are more "up close and personal," appealing to a certain type of killer who wants to inflict prolonged suffering or a leave a lingering reminder of the attack. This type of information is helpful as we profile potential knifing attackers.

Recent Knife Attacks in Schools

Knife attacks are also fast, unexpected, and can be devastating in terms of injuries. Attacks on elementary schools are of great concern since small children as basically defenseless and unable to protect themselves. On December 14, 2012, just hours before the Sandy Hook shooting, a 36-year-old villager in the village of Chenpeng, Henan Province, stabbed twenty-three children and an elderly woman at the village's primary school during morning arrival. The attack took only a few minutes and the perpetrator was eventually restrained by teachers and arrested. All of the victims survived, however many lost fingers or ears, and some sustained serious internal damage to organs, requiring long-term care. In January 2018, two Russian students inspired by the Columbine and Charleston AME attacks stabbed fifteen fourth graders and their teacher. A few days later, a ninth-grade student attacked seventh-graders with an axe at a school in another part of the country.

Despite having an older population, high school attacks can also be devastating; on April 9, 2014, 16-year-old Alex Hribal used two kitchen knives to stab twenty-two victims in their stomachs and lower backs at Franklin Regional High School outside of Pittsburgh. The attack took less than five minutes and Hribal was eventually subdued by brave students and a gym teacher. In September 2017, during history class, Abel Cedeno, 18, whipped out a three-inch switchblade and stabbed Matthew McCree, 15, in the chest, killing him. He also allegedly knifed Ariane LaBoy, 16, who survived. The two wounded boys had been pelting Cedeno, who was bullied for being gay, with pencils. "I guess I just snapped," Cedeno said in an interview from his jail cell (Edelman 2017).

Stabbings at colleges are also on the rise; on April 9, 2013, fourteen people were injured in a stabbing attack at the Lone Star College in Texas. Dylan Quick, a 20-year-old student, used an X-ACTO knife and a scalpel, purposely stabbing victims in the head. The fast-paced attack ended when students subdued the suspect. In November 2015, ISIS sympathizer Faisal Merced used a hunting knife with a ten-inch blade to quickly and gleefully stab four students at the University of California. He was shot and killed by responding police when he refused to drop the weapon. Therefore, all types of schools have proven vulnerable to stabbing attacks, which can be very fast and lethal.

Another challenge is that the presence of a knife in school may not be alarming. A good example comes from a stabbing attack at a primary school in Sweden in October 2015. One witness, a student, told broadcaster SVT that the attack was initially believed to be a joke and attract students, pulling them in close: "He wore a mask and black clothing. There were students asking to take pictures with him and touch the sword." Obviously, a student wielding a gun would be treated quite differently. A recent stabbing attack illustrates the difficulty of profiling potential violent actors or vulnerable locations in the school. At 8:00 AM on November 2016, a straight-A student at Mountain View High School in Orem, Utah stabbed five students in the boy's locker room before turning the knife on himself. The boy had no previous discipline issues, and the stabbings were not racially or ethnically motivated. None of the victims had threatened the attacker in any way—the stabbing was completely random. That same month, a random knife attack at the entrance of their high school in Abbotsford, British Columbia, left one girl dead and another seriously injured. The perpetrator was not known to law enforcement officials and could not explain his motive.

Physical Response to a Stabbing Attack

The physical response to stabbings presents yet another challenge. In stabbing events, victims often do not realize what is happening until they start bleeding, delaying their "fight or flight" response and allowing the attacker more time to engage. During a knife attack involving puncture wounds, with the attacker plunging in and out of the body, victims often don't feel pain. There will be a cold, icy feeling at the stabbing site as the body goes into shock, and a person may only realize they are injured with the actual presence of blood. Panic, disbelief, and confusion will set in at the large volume of blood lost from the penetration site, rendering the victim even more unable to save themselves from an ongoing violent situation. Interestingly, there aren't many pain sensors inside our bodies; in fact, a large blade penetrating a critical organ results in death so quickly that most people pass out and die without much pain. Slashing attacks are quite different and painful, since the skin has many nerve endings. However, most premeditated stabbing attacks have the perpetrator plunging the knife or knives (one in each hand is a popular tactic) deeply into victims. The superficial slashing begins when the attacker is confronted and shifts to the defensive, vice offensive mode.

Mitigating a Knife Attack

In reviewing stabbing case studies, it appears people are more willing to engage and try to subdue an attacker with a knife, while choosing to run or hide from a gunman. However, physically confronting an enraged assailant wielding large knives is very difficult, and those who approach are likely to be severely injured or killed. Certainly, the use of committed, overpowering force by more than one person is necessary, or neutralizing the attacker with a disabling (or more) potent weapon like a firearm. This is where "bringing a gun to a knife fight" might actually be a good tactic.

In terms of mitigation, metal detectors at entrances are the best way to confiscate knives. However recent reports from school administrators suggest that some schools are decreasing use of metal detectors because they appear to increase students' fears and anxieties vice allay them. In the absence of metal detectors, random wanding in hallways is better than doing nothing. Unannounced locker inspections are a good way to stay on top of non-firearm weaponry such as knives, numchucks, brass knuckles, and batons. It is advised to regularly look in closets and restrooms for hidden knives, perhaps in ceiling tiles, taped in toilet tanks, and behind moveable objects. Also discuss the rising possibility of knife attacks when discussing active shooter scenarios or conducting desktop or live exercises in your schools. Think about response—how to engage and disable the attacker, as well as render first aid to stabbing victims when precious minutes can mean the difference between life and death. Finally, remember teachers, students, and staff are the new first responders, as most attacks are over and physical damage inflicted before the arrival of law enforcement and medical personnel. Annual first aid training, especially focused on lifesaving tourniquet application, should be mandatory.

Although weapons deterrence may increase physical safety, remember it does not address underlying reasons for students carrying weapons to school. Perhaps identifying root causes of those fears and motivations, then expending resources in related areas is a better long-term solution for addressing school violence.

The kindergarten through twelfth grade vulnerability differs from that on a college campus. First, a younger populace cannot defend themselves as readily and are more likely to slip into suspended disbelief as the situation unfolds instead of experience a flight or fight response. College campuses have their own vulnerabilities related to the culture of openness, physical location in the community, poor partnering with or distrust of external law enforcement, and nefarious elements to which they are already exposed such as drugs and even espionage. Examining the unique vulnerabilities associated with K–12 and colleges and universities helps to understand trends, the risk of attack, and mitigation challenges better.

K–12 in the Crosshairs

The first K–12 school attack in the United States was the Enoch Brown School massacre, which occurred July 26, 1764. On this date, four American Indian warriors entered a white settler's log cabin school in Greencastle, Pennsylvania, and used a tomahawk to kill and scalp the teacher and ten students. Throughout the years, primary and secondary schools have been the sites of revenge murders, racial attacks, gang violence, suicides, workplace violence, and lover's quarrels. They have

also been used by domestic terrorists as a way to express rage and garner attention to their cause. For example, on May 18, 1927, the Bath
Consolidated School was the scene of the deadliest act of mass murder
in a school in US history, a lone wolf, anti-government attack. Andrew
Kehoe, upset with policies and tax law he believed led to his farm foreclosure, murdered his wife at home and then detonated three dynamite
bombs at the Maine school, where he worked as the accountant. Kehoe
spent months planting explosive material throughout the building in a
premeditated act that stunned the country. When confronted at the scene
by law enforcement, he detonated a vehicle bomb, killing himself and
the school superintendent. In all, the attack killed thirty-eight schoolchildren and five adults. Andrew Kehoe left his five-word suicide note at his
house, wired to his fence (Figure 5.1).

Modern-day schools are used as political targets by international terrorist groups and embattled governments. Students are the victims of
bombings, shootings, and kidnappings and hostage situations. In the last
the forty years, there were massacres at the Ma'a lot school in Israel,
the Bahr el-Baqar school in Egypt, the Beslan school in Russia, and the
Nagerkovil school in Sri Lanka. Schools in the Gaza Strip, Iraq, and
Afghanistan are routinely targeted by insurgents, and, in Syria, schoolchildren are bombed by their own government, which is engaged in a
worsening civil war. Mass student kidnappings became a new fear when
terrorists from the al-Qaeda-linked group Boko Haram killed 2,200
teachers and is responsible for 1,440 schools closing in Nigeria since
starting their insurgency campaign in 2009. Some of their more heinous attacks involve the kidnapping of children. In 2014, Boko Haram
operatives posed as soldiers to gain trust and then kidnapped more than

FIGURE 5.1   Andrew Kehoe's Sign

276 girls from their boarding school in Chibuk. Boko Haram leaders threatened to sell them into marriage and the sex trade for $12 apiece, to raise money for the cause. They next attacked the village where the girls were from, killing 150 family members and search-and-rescue team personnel. Although some of the girls escaped or were released, many are still unaccounted for. Despite international outrage over this incident and pressure on the Nigerian government to protect schools and children from Boko Haram, the group was able to successfully strike again. In February 2018, they kidnapped 110 girls from the Government Girls Science and Technical College. The Nigerian army is still unable to repel Boko Haram attacks and protect citizens. The impact of a generation of children unable to attend school will likely be felt for decades and impact the country's prosperity.

The horrific 2004 Beslan school attack in Russia is difficult to read about, and the pictures are extraordinarily painful to view. However, to glean valuable information for hardening efforts, we must confront the harsh reality of these attacks. This case, in particular, provides insight into the mentality of terrorist groups and actors who will target defenseless children, as well as how poor response by the government to a mass hostage situation can lead to even more bloodshed.

Case Study: Siege at Beslan School Number 1—Innocence Lost (Fisk 2014)

Since the advent of modern terrorism in 1968, hostage taking is a tactic often used in terrorist operations, whether as a bargaining chip or to generate additional public fear. September 1, 2004, again proved another employment of the tactic, as more than thirty Chechen Islamic militants took control of Beslan school number 1, in Beslan, North Ossetin-Alania, Russia. Terrorists stormed the school and quickly took 1,200 hostages, including 705 children. Unfortunately, the siege had a horrific ending, but only by revisiting the case can we learn how to prevent a similar massacre in our own country.

Beslan is a picturesque town of 30,000 near the beautiful Caucus Mountains. Unfortunately, the North Caucasus region also serves as a base of operation for al-Qaeda operatives, among other jihadists. The "Day of Knowledge" is the first day of the new school year in Russia, when students attending for the first time are greeted in a festival-like atmosphere, and those entering their last year are given flowers by the younger children as a sign of congratulations and good luck. On this fateful day, parents were also in attendance, pushing the population inside the school to maximum capacity. School started in Beslan at 9:00 a.m. that morning, the celebration having been pushed up an hour because of the forecasted high temperatures. At 9:20 a.m., terrorists seized the school, gathering those who could not escape and herding them inside the gymnasium. The terrorists were wearing camouflage uniforms and appeared to be Russian security forces conducting a counterterrorism drill, so the adults were initially unsuspecting of their activity. Overwhelmed by the size of the terrorist group and their firepower, the adults could do nothing but obey the orders of the hostage takers and sit through three days of unimaginable terror with the children.

SHAMIL BASAYEV

To understand the Beslan school siege, one needs to understand the group's leader, Shamil Basayev, who approved, planned, and ordered the Beslan attack. Basayev was no stranger to Russian security forces, leading guerrilla operations against the Russian military in both the first and second Chechen wars, and as the leader of the radical wing of the Chechen insurgency. He is in a unique position to plan attacks, intuitively understanding how forces will respond and their tactics and vulnerabilities. His goal is recognition of the independence of Chechnya and UN and Russian withdrawal from Chechnya. No stranger to large civilian hostage operations, Basayev also planned the soft target attack against 916 civilians at the Dubrovka Theater on October 23, 2002, a case study covered in Chapter 6 of this book. In addition to attacks on government buildings, Basayev also ordered the suicide bombing of two Russian Civil Aviation aircraft on August 24, 2004. He directed an attack at the Rizhskaya metro station in northeast Moscow on August 31, the day before his Beslan operation. In all, more than 100 persons were killed in these three attacks.

TACTIC: BLITZ ATTACK

On the morning of the attack, children and adults dressed in their finest clothes and arrived at Beslan school number 1. Waiting in the distance were thirty-five Chechen militants in military vehicles, ready to conduct a surprise attack on the school and, with overwhelming force, seize as many hostages as possible. With violence of action and confusion as to whether they were members of the Russian military, their plan was successful and they corralled most of the students and adults into the school's gym. Fifty people escaped and alerted police, and several were able to hide in the boiler room. Upon responding, police, who were unaware of the scope of the incident, wildly exchanged gunfire with the terrorists; five police officers and one terrorist were killed. Realizing the situation exceeded their capabilities, a call was put in to the Russian army for assistance.

The terrorists moved a majority of the hostages into the gymnasium. Then, with tactical proficiency, they began to construct defensive fortifications. They established sniper positions and had male hostages move desks and chairs around the entrances of the building to block potential counterattacks. The terrorists also placed improvised explosive devices (IEDs) in a "daisy-chain" configuration in the gymnasium, placing some in basketball hoops and above the heads of

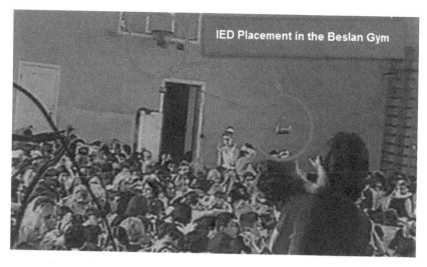

FIGURE 5.2   IED Placement in the Beslan School Gym

the hostages for the maximum casualty-producing effect (Figure 5.2). They tactically positioned terrorists in strategic locations throughout the school to repel an outside assault. Later in the morning, hostages, mostly children, were staged at the windows as human shields.

BLACK WIDOW INVOLVEMENT

As discussed in Chapter 3, the Chechen Black Widows are an asymmetric and formidable force in the terrorist group's arsenal. Another tactic used at the Moscow theater siege and during the Beslan operation was the use of female terrorists rigged as suicide bombers. By the conclusion of day one, it is believed three of the female suicide bombers were dead. One was killed by a fellow terrorist after protesting the treatment of the hostages, specifically the children, and another died during the malfunction of her bomb. A third may have been used to detonate a bomb to kill the strongest twenty male hostages, selected by the terrorists from the group in the gymnasium. Their bodies were dumped out of a second floor classroom into the schoolyard (Chivers 2007).

PSYCHOLOGICAL TERROR

At the beginning of the siege, two male hostages were killed in front of the others in the gymnasium, their bodies dragged through the crowd. Additional threats were made by the terrorists to the government response team assembled outside the school: if Russian security forces killed any terrorist, fifty hostages would be executed; if one was wounded, twenty hostages would be killed. Cell phones were confiscated to reduce the risk of hostages transmitting information to the outside, and the terrorists threatened to execute anyone caught with a cell phone, as well as anyone around the person. Furthermore, if disobedience or resistance was suspected, the hostage being disobedient would not be killed, but everyone around him or her would. The hostages could only speak Russian. To show their intent to follow through on these threats, the terrorists allowed a male to address the group. In an attempt to calm the hostages, he did not speak in Russian, and instead spoke in the local Ossetian language; he was shot and killed in front of the other hostages (Terror Operations: Case Studies in Terrorism 2007).

LOGISTICS

From the terrorists' perspective, food, water, and medical supplies were robust because they had total control of the school and its assets. They also had a large stock of ammunition and weapons; every terrorist was armed with a Kalashnikov rifle, and there was a cache of sniper rifles, RPG-7 grenade launchers, machine guns, hand grenades, pistols, dynamite, and at least 100 IEDs (TRADOC 2007). The sheer amount of weaponry and the terrorists' apparent familiarity with the building led some to speculate there was on-site reconnaissance and storing of supplies during the summer while the school was under renovation (McDaniel and Ellis 2009).

The hostages were deprived of food, water, and medical supplies by the terrorists during their captivity; children and adults even had to resort to drinking their own urine. By day three, a significant number of children and adults began showing signs of exhaustion, dehydration, and food deprivation. Many of the hostages began fainting as a result of not having any food or water and being forced to stand for lengthy periods of time. This deprivation and mental confusion was evident on day three when the attack and counterattack started, as some of the escaping hostages were seen running back into the school during the fighting. The terrorists were also growing weary of the standoff and became more brutal to the hostages.

DEMANDS

One of the survivors recalled her conversation with a terrorist; when she asked him why they had seized the school: "One of the terrorists said that a Russian plane flown from our airfield had killed his entire family. Now, he wanted to kill, and didn't care that it was women and children" (Leung 2005). Initial attempts to engage the terrorists in negotiations were futile; the terrorists only wanted contact with senior-level Russian officials. They also wanted three politicians and a pediatrician as part of the negotiation team. In addition to this demand, the terrorists had made three other demands: for Russian forces to end operations and withdraw from Chechnya, for the release of militants arrested in the raids on Ingushetia, and for the United Nations to recognize their independence. On the second day of the standoff the former president of Ingushetia, Ruslan Aushev (the only one of the four people requested by the terrorists to come to the scene who did so), arrived in Beslan. Aushev had also worked on the negotiations during the Moscow theater hostage crisis in October 2002 and was well respected in the Caucasus region.

During his meeting with the terrorist leader he secured the release of twenty-six hostages: eleven women (nursing mothers) and their infants. One nursing mother who had other children in the school was allowed to leave with her baby, but refused because her other children had to remain behind. She handed her baby to a terrorist, who in turn gave the baby to Aushev (Leung 2005). Aushev was also handed a written note from Shamil Basayev with his demand. This was the only face-to-face negotiation conducted during the siege.

CNN and other news networks carried the Beslan siege live, multiplying the fear felt not only by children and parents in Russia, but also around the world. This kind of publicity is a terrorist group's dream, as they and their cause are catapulted onto the world stage. Horrific images of the aftermath of the bloody final assault are widely available on the Internet, keeping the event alive.

THE BATTLE

During the late morning on September 3, the terrorists agreed to allow medical workers into the schoolyard to retrieve the bodies of the dead thrown out of the second floor window on day one. At approximately 12:50 p.m., four people moved toward the school yard to begin the process of retrieving the bodies; reports indicate the terrorists fired shots at the workers, an event with a cascading effect that would end the Beslan siege.

At 1:05 p.m., two explosions occurred in the gym, killing hundreds. It was never made clear if the explosions were caused by the terrorists or the Russian army. Fortunately, many children escaped through holes in the walls and broken windows. A full-out firefight ensued. Russian security forces detonated explosives as breaching charges to enter the gym and attempt to rescue hostages. The terrorists detonated their IEDs, setting the roof of the gym on fire; the roof collapsed, killing more of the hostages. Another breach would be conducted using a BTR-80 on the gym's western wall; this armored infantry tank fired its 14.5 millimeter machine gun as it rolled toward the school and breached the wall and the windows, likely killing more hostages.

THE CAFETERIA

While the situation in the gym unfolded, terrorists were moving the remaining children and adults, first to the hallways of the school and then to the cafeteria, which gave slight tactical advantage for the terrorists because security bars covered the windows. Terrorists made the women and children stand in front of the windows as human shields while Russian security forces and police fired at the building. Children and adults who were not standing in front of the windows hid in and under anything they could find; some children even hid in large pots and pans. Although they could clearly see these human shields, and women were waving white napkins and screaming not to shoot, Russian security forces, police, and local armed civilians continued to fire on the school (Chivers 2007).

The fight for the school continued, and Russian military tanks took up positions near the school and, on orders from security forces, fired 125 millimeter main gun rounds into the building locations still occupied by the terrorists. Thirteen of the terrorists, including two women, escaped the school and hid in an outbuilding on the school property. Using tanks and Shmel rocket infantry flame-throwers, the building was destroyed and all thirteen terrorists killed. Some of the terrorists escaped the fight and tried to blend into the local population. At least one was beaten to death and another lynched by outraged family members. Reports indicate some of the terrorists escaped, but Russian authorities say these are rumors. Only one terrorist was captured alive; he was convicted and sentenced to life in prison.

In the end, more than 330 people died at the Beslan School, including 108 children. At least 700 were wounded and required medical care. All survivors received deep psychological wounds that will stay with them a lifetime. Second only to the attacks on 9/11, the Beslan attack had the highest death toll of any terrorist attack in history.

EPILOGUE

Some of the casualties at Beslan came at the hands of the terrorists, but hundreds more occurred at the hands of responding forces. Aggravating factors included:

The apparent total disregard of hostage safety

The use of high-caliber weapons

Firing at human shields

Failure to establish a perimeter cordon and allowing parents and the local population to stand near the school and even arm themselves and fire at the building

Not having the appropriate first response assets such as medical and firefighting support

These actions and inactions played a major role in the final, disastrous outcome of this attack.

(Source: Fisk 2014. Mr. Ralph R. Fisk Jr., ATO, PCP-1, MEMS. Instructor/trainer, subject matter expert and thought leader in the areas of Emergency Management, Contemporary Risk, and Threat Assessment.)

Ten years later, 2,300 miles from Beslan, the town of Peshawar, Pakistan, was the scene of another school massacre at The Army Public School. In an eight-hour coordinated attack, Tehreek-e-Taliban, also known as the Pakistani Taliban (TTP) killed almost 150 children and staff, injuring another 100. TTP issued a statement indicating they specifically chose the school since the government of Pakistan was waging a war against the terrorist group. Many Army soldiers rushed to the school, only to find their children dead. Pakistanis were shocked at the carnage of the terrorist attack, the worst in the country's history, and often refer to the event as "Pakistan's 9/11."

Case Study: 2014 Peshawar School Massacre

The Army Public School and College in Peshawar, Pakistan, is an English language school managed by the Pakistani Army. The school holds around 1,100 students and staff members, and the students are primarily the children of members of the Pakistani Army. The school is located in a highly populated urban area, surrounded by several other schools and housing developments.

THE OPERATION

December 16, 2014, was a typical Tuesday at the Army School. Just before 11:00 a.m., a group of foreign militants affiliated with the Tehrik-i-Taliban (Taliban Movement of Pakistan, TTP) began a siege that would change Pakistan and shock the world.

The attackers first lit a van on fire in a graveyard at the rear of the school. This created a diversion that drew security staff away from their posts. At the same time, six to nine heavily armed Taliban militants, wearing suicide belts, began scaling the walls of the school. (Note: sources differ on the number of gunmen since several detonated suicide vests and others escaped in the melee). Upon entering the school, the militants opened fire on an auditorium full of eighth to tenth graders, who were being given instruction on first aid; this location is where most of the casualties occurred (Khan 2014).

The attack continued throughout the day, lasting more than seven hours. When the school was finally secured by Pakistani forces, the death toll stood at 144; 132 students (ages 8 to 18), nine school staff, including the school's principal, and three responding soldiers. It was later revealed by survivors that TTP militants used an execution style form of killing, resulting in most deaths coming from single gunshot wounds to the heads of the victims. Students were gathered and forced to watch these killings, including the execution of their principal (Khan 2014).

THE ATTACKERS

Created in 2007, the TTP, a Sunni-Deodandi organization, is the largest and most active Taliban umbrella organization in Pakistan, incorporating almost half of the total Taliban groups in Pakistan. From 2008 to 2009, the TTP united with al-Qaeda, under Osama bin Laden, to form the Shura Ittihad al-Mujahedee. This coalition was created in conjunction with the three commanders of the TTP, Baitullah Mehsud, Hafiz Gul Bahadur, and Maulvi Nazir, to combat US Coalition forces in Afghanistan. The partnership ended in 2009 due to internal conflict, and the TTP refocused on Pakistan. In February of 2017, the Pakistan Armed Forces launched "Operation Radd-ul-Fasaad" which targeted rogue terrorist organizations, like the TTP, by killing their leadership and destroying strongholds. The different factions and leadership of the TTP are notably diverse, but united under an ideology that strongly opposed female rights and strongly supported an extreme form of Sharia law (DNI 2018).

Survivors of the attack remarked that militants spoke to each other in foreign languages and did not look Pakistani. The militants were, in fact, of foreign origin; one was Chechen, three were Arab, two were Afghani (Rush 2014).

Muhammad Umar Khorasani, the TTP spokesperson who claimed the attack, stated that it was in retaliation to a Pakistan Army offensive in North Waziristan, Pakistan. Khorasani claimed that they chose the school, specifically, because the Pakistani Army was killing their own families and women.

THE RESPONSE

Army and police personnel responded to the school within ten to fifteen minutes of the attack. Due to the potential for a hostage situation inside the school, it was difficult for the counteroffensive to penetrate and regain control of the campus. The attackers went from classroom to classroom, executing students and teachers, often entering rooms by spraying bullets and throwing grenades. This method of attack slowed the terrorists down. Rescue operators were able to evacuate the bulk of the students early in the siege while militants went room-to-room. By 1:45 p.m., the counter-forces had cleared the main block of the school, isolating the militants to the administrative blocks, where it was believed they were holding hostages. At 3:10 p.m., police discovered some of the attackers already escaped by cutting barbed wire and fleeing the school. At 3:30 p.m., the conflict spilled into the streets, where police were trying to keep parents from entering the school (Boone and MacAskill 2014). By 3:50 p.m., the army isolated the militants to four areas of the school, with four of them confirmed dead. A short five minutes later, the militants were

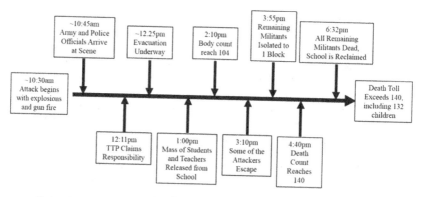

Timeline of Events from Live Updates on https://www.dawn.com/news/1151203

FIGURE 5.3   Timeline of the Peshawar School Attack

confined to a single block. The conflict lasted until 6:32 p.m., when the last remaining militants were killed (Khan 2014).

PLANNING

As shown in Figure 5.3, the planning cycle for this attack was very short, illustrating how devasting an unsophisticated attack can be against a soft target, especially children. Pakistani Taliban leaders started planning the attack just weeks prior to the operation. Planning occurred in Afghanistan, but the militants were trained in Pakistan, near Peshawar. The intent of TTP was to kill older children who could potentially join the Pakistani Armed Forces, although, once the carnage began, the militants were indiscriminately shooting children as young as 8 years old.

THREAT AND VULNERABILITY

In August of 2014, the government of Khyber Pakhtunkhwa, Pakistan, received intelligence and issued a warning of impending attack on a school. The National Counter-Terrorism Authority circulated the threat alert to the other providences. The government was also made aware of the militants who entered Peshawar just three days prior to the school massacre (Khan 2014). The school was walled in, had security and barbwire, and the administrators were even made aware of a potential attack, yet they were still overcome by militants.

AFTERMATH

The Army School attack had lasting implications for the people of Pakistan. Religious and political leaders, united in their condemnation

of the brutality, vowed to root out and destroy these Taliban organizations. For days after the attack, protestors took to the streets to
criticize and demand consequences for pro-Taliban preachers. Anger
turned to remorse, with candlelight vigils held in every major city.
Due to the demands of the people, the then-Prime Minister Nawaz
Sharif reinstated the death penalty, sentencing four Peshawar-linked
militants to death by hanging, and moving hundreds more TTP
prisoners to death row. Stronger security measures were added to
schools to prevent a similar attack. The military stepped up anti-
terror operations, arresting more than 2,000 suspected terrorists.
Pakistan started the Safe Schools Initiative, which funded more security, trained school officials, and engaged at the community and family levels to educate on the signs of a potential threat.

Years later, the Pakistani government is still criticized by citizens
for lack of action, even though there has been an overall decline in
the number of attacks.

(Source: Copello 2018. Mr. Evan Copello is a data scientist and
researcher at the University of North Florida, with a focus on the
psychology of terrorism.)

Could the Beslan siege or Peshawar massacre happen in the United
States? Although the likelihood of an incident on the scale of Beslan, with
attackers approaching a school in tanks with heavy firepower, is remote,
it is quite plausible that a large-scale attack such as Peshawar could happen. Considering the massacres at Columbine, Virginia Tech, Sandy
Hook, and Marjory Stoneman Douglas High were perpetrated by amateurs, it is irresponsible to think that a preplanned, coordinated attack
by a group of professional, trained terrorists would not result in more
destruction and casualties. All types of schools, in both urban and rural
areas are vulnerable. Local, county, and state law enforcement and first-
responder support organizations should exercise the possibility of a mass
hostage incident in a school, reviewing the Beslan case study and fine-
tuning their own response. The National Incident Management System
(NIMS) is a valuable tool for preparedness, and the incident command
system must be understood to prevent confusion at the scene. If a terrorist organization is involved in a school siege, federal law enforcement will
respond; therefore, prior coordination and relationship building would
be extremely helpful. A list of valuable FEMA courses regarding the
coordination of response is located in Appendix B.

Passive security measures, such as those discussed in Chapter 8,
would be helpful at schools, including a comprehensive identification
check system, and extensive background checks on all workers employed
by the institution, as well as those contracted and subcontracted to
support educational operations such as bus drivers and construction
workers. Entry control points and securing points of egress are critical

to repelling a school attack and catching the perpetrators. The arming of teachers might be a step toward hardening this soft target, as they could act as force multipliers during active shooter or kidnapping and hostage situations.

K–12 Vulnerability

Why are K–12 schools more vulnerable to attack? First and foremost, the student populace is younger and easier to overpower. Security measures are typically in place, but not consistent. For instance, as violence in our country began to rise in the 1980s, many schools began installing metal detectors at entryways. Although they work extremely well to catch weapons, school administrators found this type of screening to be time consuming, especially when trying to move hundreds of students to their classrooms every morning. Also, operating detectors or individual wands is extremely manpower intensive, so most schools abandoned the idea. The concept of school resource officers (SROs) took hold in the 1970s when protests and unrest related to the Vietnam War spilled over into school systems. SROs are sworn law enforcement officers who are detailed to the school system and work to enhance security at their institution. They may be armed and can make arrests.

However, SROs can also be of limited help when facing a determined gunman or gunmen with a practiced, solid plan and heavy firepower. For example, in the Columbine High School attack, Eric Harris and Dylan Klebold managed to kill fifteen people and injure twenty-four despite the presence of an armed guard. Jefferson County Sheriff's Deputy Neil Gardner, a fifteen-year veteran of the Sheriff's Office, usually ate his lunch with the students in the cafeteria, his car parked in front of the cafeteria doors between the junior and senior parking lots. On the day of the attacks, Deputy Gardner was eating elsewhere on campus, watching an area frequented by smokers. When shots were fired inside the school, he pulled up to the indoor/outdoor cafeteria area where Harris and Klebold had tried to set off two bombs and had already started killing students. Gardner engaged them in a gun battle; however, he was unable to hit the perpetrators. One injured teacher and a student were able to escape during the chaos and Gardner was responsible for later saving other students as he protected them when they were fleeing. He also exchanged gunfire with the shooters when they were killing students in the library, before they committed suicide. He likely saved lives in the end, but Gardner's daily presence on the school grounds obviously did not deter the shooters from their operation. In fact, they may have purposely chosen the area where Gardner typically had lunch to start the operation, intending to kill him first and remove their only obstacle to success.

The armed deputy at the Marjorie Stoneman Douglas massacre, a seasoned police officer who was armed, chose not to enter the active shooting scene and engage the shooter, despite hearing gunshots and people screaming. His attorney stated that former sheriff's deputy Scot Peterson had no legal duty to stop the slaughter at the school. He confirmed that Peterson took shelter rather than confront the killer, but asserted that since he did not act with malice or bad faith, he can't be held legally responsible for the death. The attorneys stated that allegations against Peterson suggest only that he "opted for self-preservation over heroics" (Kornfield 2018).

Therefore, the presence of an SRO should not alleviate the need for other security measure such as fencing, gates, metal detectors, and bag checks. Also, an SRO should be the last layer of defense, not the first; there are many other measures outlined later in the book that can protect a school from attack far beyond the hallway.

The Red Lake school massacre occurred on March 21, 2005. On that morning, 16-year-old Jeffrey Weise killed his grandfather, a tribal police officer, and his girlfriend at their home. Weise then took his grandfather's police weapons, vest, and vehicle, and drove to Red Lake Senior High School, where he had been a student some months before. Weise first shot and killed the unarmed security guard at the entrance of the school and then targeted a teacher and five students. After the police arrived, Weise was undaunted and exchanged gunfire with them; he was wounded and then committed suicide in a vacant classroom.

In May 2014, police in Waseca, Minnesota, arrested 17-year-old John David LaDue on charges related to an elaborate plan to carry out a massacre at a nearby school. According to his 180-page diary, which police found in his bedroom, LaDue plotted to kill his family members, start a diversionary fire to distract first responders, and then go to a nearby school. He was first going to kill the school resource officer and then set off bombs and shoot students and staff. A resident living next to a storage facility worker tipped off police to the suspicious teen; contents of his locker revealed a pressure cooker, pyrotechnic chemicals, steel ball bearings, and gunpowder. He had also stockpiled three completed bombs, an SKS assault rifle, a Beretta 9 millimeter handgun, hundreds of rounds of ammo, and a safe with several other guns at his home. LaDue tested his devices at a local elementary school playground and intended to attack the school on the anniversary of Columbine; however, it fell on Easter Sunday and school was not in session. Locals described LaDue as a polite boy who did well in school and had plenty of friends (Ford and Brumfeld 2014).

Many school shooters are insiders. They are known current or former students, staff, volunteers, janitors, cooks, or teachers. They know the school layout and class schedule, the school resource officer's habits, and when and where to strike for the least resistance and most effect. Deterring school violence under these circumstances is very difficult.

Cross applying insider threat mitigation, discussed in Chapter 8, may be helpful.

Religious elementary schools in the United States have also been the target of terrorists. In August 2011, federal law enforcement officers arrested Emerson Winfield Begolly in New Bethlehem, Pennsylvania. Begolly was a moderator and supporter for the internationally known Islamic extremist web forum Ansar al-Mujahideen English forum (AMEF). He produced and distributed a 101-page document with instructions for constructing chemically based explosives and a target list including Jewish schools (Investigative Project on Terrorism 2011). Secular schools must be especially vigilant since religious terrorism is the most dangerous, with actors believing their violent actions are sanctioned and just.

Colleges: Campus Culture and Vulnerability

Every type of bad actor now sees the university campus—facilities, programs, students, and staff—as a conduit to their illicit activities. Many cultural factors are at play resulting in this exploitation. For instance, a basic higher education tenet is academic freedom, which allows professors and students to explore topics in an environment free of repression or censorship, so they may fully participate in the learning process. Except for some instances of religious universities, this freedom also applies to research activities, where open inquiry means no query or methodology is out of bounds. Freedoms on campus are typically extended to student activities, school newspapers, and protest events, and universities are unable or unwilling to contain inciting or seditious speech. Also, formerly able to operate in a disconnected manner from society in their "ivory tower," the higher education system is more transparent than ever. Skyrocketing tuition rates and campus scandals have made parents, taxpayers, and political representatives angry and demanding disclosure. The combination of these internal and external dynamics contributes to a very open campus environment rich for learning, as well as for exploitation.

For example, due to the government's problems with cost overruns by major defense contractors, universities are increasingly relied upon for research and development (R&D) in sensitive areas such as cyber-warfare and weapons of mass destruction, including the testing and development of chemical, biological, and nuclear weapons and counter-weapons. In 2016, the government paid universities an estimated $30 billion for R&D work (AAAS 2017). Often, the projects involve future cutting-edge technology; therefore, schools compete for the work and associated funding and prestige. However, the mere presence of R&D activities makes the campus a target for anti-government anarchists or single-issue domestic terrorists such as animal or environmental rights activists. Annual government reports listing R&D funding to specific schools may paint a target for foreign actors who may also attempt to penetrate the campus. Nation-state and nonstate actors are stepping up collection activities against the US industrial base, which includes campuses conducting government research (ODNI 2011). According to the FBI, "The open environment of a university is an ideal place to find recruits, propose and nurture ideas, learn, and even steal research data" (FBI 2011).

Prevailing negative attitudes regarding security measures and agencies among our citizens may also contribute to the increase in nefarious activity in and around campuses. As time passes from the 9/11 tragedy and subsequent terrorist plots have failed or been interrupted, intelligence and law enforcement agencies fear a sense of complacency. Complicating the situation, it is important to note the American citizen's trust in the government is at a historic low point (18 percent), and one in three people believe the government is threatening their personal freedoms with post-9/11 security activity and laws (Pew Research Center 2017). Certainly these attitudes are conveyed on campus with the younger, more activist-minded generation and faculty trying to enforce principles of academic freedom. Therefore, any security measures put into effect on campus may be met with resistance, not the compliance we expect. The school may even back down to a lower security posture to pacify students and faculty, resulting in more vulnerability.

Also complicating matters is security fatigue in the population as a whole, with citizens tired of looking for threats and being vigilant. Wake-up calls such as the tragic Virginia Tech murders, an event which could be characterized as "higher education's 9/11," and subsequent campus shootings have shifted security focus to weapons and student lockdown/notification procedures. Although the lone-shooter threat is compelling, campus security must be careful not to lose sight of other vulnerabilities and threats. In other words, while we are specifically looking for guns at the entrance of a classroom building, a crude but effective bomb may be under construction in the basement.

Campuses Already Under Attack

Make no mistake: our schools are already under persistent passive attack. For instance, foreign intelligence services (FISs) and nonstate actors continuously prey on campuses to steal intellectual property and bypass expensive research and development. Also, FISs are actively recruiting students and professors for espionage and to use later as sources, with multiple cases on college campuses in the last five years and actors exhibiting increasingly bold tactics (FBI 2011). In March 2018, the FBI director testified to Congress about FIS infiltration in higher education, warning US universities about Chinese intelligence operatives active on their campuses, adding that many academics display "a level of naiveté" about the level of infiltration (Johnson 2018).

The case of University of Tennessee professor Dr. John Reece Roth illustrates lack of policy and procedure, and how the open academic environment is penetrable by "countries of interest." Despite statutory requirements, Roth was able to hire foreign national students from China and Iran to work on his classified, Department of Defense-funded plasma-related aerospace project on campus. The students recruited him, and he traveled at least eight times with sensitive material to China (FBI 2009). Roth is not the type of professor we might expect would be susceptible to this type of FIS activity; he was in his late sixties when approached by the students, an emeritus professor of electrical engineering who taught at Tennessee for nearly thirty years after his time at NASA. He also holds eleven patents and testified before Congress on nuclear fusion. The Chinese coerced Roth into thinking intellectual property should be open and available to all countries. Roth's academic colleagues feel his ego was stroked by attention from the students and host government and he believed he was making a significant intellectual contribution to the world (Golden 2012).

Intellectual property theft is not the only goal of foreign governments operating on our campuses. The 2009 case of Russian spy Lidiya Gurveva (using the name Cynthia Murphy) is particularly illustrative of how the campus environment can be exploited merely to collect information on professors and students. Gurveva was pursuing an MBA degree at Columbia Business School, Columbia University, in 2008 when her handlers gave her the following assignment:

> [S]trengthen . . . ties w. classmates on daily basis incl. professors who can help in job search and who will have (or already have) access to secret info . . . [r]eport to C[enter] on their detailed personal data and character traits w. preliminary conclusions about their potential (vulnerability) to be recruited by Service.

They also directed Gurveva to "dig up personal data of those students who apply (or are hired already) for a job at CIA" (US Department of Justice 2010). In yet another campus spying case, Andrey Bezrukov (also known as Donald Hatfield) was arrested in June 2010 for being an agent of Russia. He graduated from Harvard's Kennedy School of Government and, while a student, developed associations with professors at George Washington University and Oxford University. Bezrukov/Hatfield targeted a professor who was once former Vice President Albert Gore's national security advisor, as well as other policymakers at Kennedy School reunions and think tank events (Srivatsa and Zu 2010).

These cases clearly illustrate the vulnerability of professors and students to recruitment and the ease with which foreign nations can penetrate our universities.

Cyber-criminals are also present on campus; data theft is an emergent challenge as servers are breached to steal student information protected by law, putting the university at great risk and liability. For example, the University of Maryland regretfully announced in February 2014 that information had been stolen from its database since 1998 on 300,000 students and faculty who were issued identification cards (University of Maryland 2014). Although Maryland's breach may have been due to failure to protect on-site servers and recognize ongoing penetration activities, many universities are now moving their electronic student, faculty, and staff records to the virtual servers offered in the "cloud"—which presents new and significant vulnerabilities.

As if spying and cyber theft are not enough of a challenge for university security officials, campuses are increasingly seen as a "safe haven" for drug dealers. The activity is not what we might expect, such as students attempting to grow marijuana in their dorm rooms or selling dime bags at parties. Police are now discovering methamphetamine labs on college campuses, which not only pose health dangers to students, but also place explosive materials in high-occupancy buildings and bring an unwanted, dangerous element to campus property. In 2013, the cases were not just confined to urban settings, and it seems no university is now immune from this emergent threat. For example, meth labs were discovered in dormitory rooms at Georgetown University, in a music practice room at Southern Methodist University, on the roof of an on-campus student apartment building at the College of Charleston, and in a father-son operation in a house across the street from Winthrop University.

Finally, the J-1 Student Visa Program has been repeatedly misused and exploited, notably by nineteen convicted terrorists, since 1990, including Mohammed Atta, leader of the 9/11 cell (Kephart 2005). Over 100,000 foreign students enter the United States annually on student visas, but not all of them actually show up or stay at school. Despite new, rigorous post-9/11 laws to scrutinize requests and follow up after visa expiration, many still slip through the cracks. In 2006, eleven Egyptians with J-1 visas did not appear for class at the University of Montana. The school waited forty-eight hours after classes began to report the absence to the FBI, which then started a resource-intensive manhunt to find the eleven (workpermit.com 2006). Not all were captured.

The J-1 visa has also been used as a conduit to attain asylum. The case of Ibragim Todashev, friend of Boston Marathon bomber Tamerlan Tsarnaev and admitted murderer of three people in Massachusetts, is compelling. A Chechen, Todashev came to the United States on a J-1 visa and, instead of attending college, immediately applied for asylum and, later, citizenship. He was on a downward spiral with a lengthy criminal record, yet his newly obtained citizen status protected him from deportation. Law enforcement killed Todashev when he attacked investigators during an interview to collect evidence regarding the Boston bombings and the triple murder in Massachusetts. The University of Massachusetts-Dartmouth also became part of the bombing investigation because co-conspirator Dzhokhar Tsarnaev was living in his dorm room and storing evidence in his closet at the time of the event. Although Tsarnaev failed seven classes in the previous three semesters, was carrying $20,000 in student debt, and was a known marijuana smoker/distributor, the university allowed him to remain on campus, a decision they likely regret today (Goode and Kovaleski 2013). These cases show how university policy decisions can result in vulnerabilities.

In another case, in February 2011, law enforcement arrested Khalid Ali-M Aldawsari, a Saudi student studying chemical engineering at Texas Tech University, on a charge of attempted use of a weapon of mass destruction. Investigators found a notebook at Aldawsari's residence indicating he had been planning to commit a terrorist attack in the United States for years. One entry describes how he sought and obtained a particular scholarship because it allowed him to come directly to the United States and helped him financially, which he said "will help tremendously in providing me with the support I need for Jihad" (US Department of Justice 2011). The journal goes on to say: "And now, after mastering the English language, learning how to build explosives and continuous planning to target the infidel Americans, it is time for Jihad." Aldawsari had the blueprints of chemical IEDs and had already started purchasing the components for his weapons. Targets included former US military personnel, a nightclub, dams, and nuclear power plants.

Escalating Number of Attacks on College Campuses

Perhaps inspired by successful school attacks abroad, terrorists are now turning their sights toward our universities. El Mehdi Semlali Fahti, 27, came to the United States from Morocco in 2008 on a student visa. However, he flunked out of Virginia International University and the visa expired. Fahti traveled across the county and was arrested for a trespassing charge (dismissed), turned over to immigration officials in Virginia, and placed in custody. However, authorities allowed him to stay in the United States after manufacturing a story about imprisonment and beatings by Moroccan police. A judge was persuaded to approve his request for political asylum in 2011. Fahti traveled to the West Coast, and was arrested for theft in California; while serving his sentence, his case again went to the immigration agency, but a judge released him from custody in August 2013 (Investigative Project on Terrorism 2014d).

Fahti moved to Connecticut and by January plotted an attack on a university and a federal building using remote-controlled hobby planes packed with explosives, components of which he had started to gather. Fahti lived in an apartment in Bridgeport, Connecticut, with a man he met while incarcerated in Virginia. He told undercover FBI agents, who thankfully became aware of his plot during a sting operation, he studied the plan for months, learned how to pack the explosives while a student in his home country, and would be able to obtain the materials at the Mexican border. He also said the plot would be funded through "secret accounts" using laundered cash and drug-dealing profits. In a conversation with the FBI, Fahti says "the more he thinks about the case, he laughs because he cannot believe the judge believed him" and allowed him to stay in the United States for political reasons (Mayko 2014). He also stated three things cause fear in the American people: causing harm to schools, the economy, and their sense of security (Investigative Project on Terrorism 2014c). In other recent cases, the Russian sister-in-law of San Bernardino terrorist Syed Rizwan Farook, Mariya Chernykh, and her sister, Tatiana, both obtained legal resident status after overstaying J-1 visas and marrying citizens. Farook's wife, Tashfeen Malik, immigrated on a K-1 visa, the so-called fiancé visa, which gave her ninety days to marry an American citizen to ensure a green card. Both Farook and Malik were killed by law enforcement while fleeing the area. The sisters pled guilty to entering sham marriages and lying to the FBI.

The J-1 "summer study program" visa is now being exploited by human traffickers and so-called labor recruiters to bring young would-be students to the United States to participate in illegal or immoral activities. The problem came to light in 2010, when law enforcement officials found would-be students in Myrtle Beach, South Carolina, working in strip clubs, crammed into dirty apartments, eating at food kitchens, and even begging on the street. Summer study students are also recruited by the adult entertainment industry and have been used to smuggle cash and other goods back to their home country by criminal groups (Mohr, Weiss, and Baker 2010). The hopeful students' passports are seized upon entry to the United States and they are threatened into complying with the trafficking groups. Some students do attend programs on campuses, possibly introducing the criminal element. Despite State Department focus on the issue, the situation in Myrtle Beach (and other seaside towns) regarding exploitation of J-1 visas persists. In 2017, ten college students from the Dominican Republic came to the States to take part in the US State Department's J-1 Visa Summer Work Program. They each paid almost $2,000, but the "host" company put them in terrible living conditions, and paid them $1.50 an hour for their work (Hayes 2017). I recently spent time with law enforcement and a volunteer agency in Myrtle Beach, helping foreign students exploited by these "labor brokers" and sex traffickers. The young people get into a bad situation financially, and then are led down a path to prostitution and worse. Helping agencies are in touch, but the girls are afraid to come forward or give statements about the people exploiting them. A horrible cycle.

Terrorist attacks on college campuses are increasing worldwide. In the United States, 2005 University of North Carolina-Chapel Hill honors graduate Mohammed Reza Taheri-azar sought to "avenge the deaths of Muslims worldwide" and to "punish" the United States government. In March 2006, he drove a rented sports utility vehicle into a crowd of students with the intent to kill. Although no one was killed in the attack, nine people were injured (none seriously). Taheri-azar was born in Iran but moved to the United States at the age of two, growing up in North Carolina. He pled guilty to nine counts of attempted first-degree murder and was sentenced to thirty-three years in prison on two counts of attempted murder. In one letter, Taheri-azar wrote, "I was aiming to follow in the footsteps of one of my role models, Mohamed Atta, one of the 9/11 hijackers, who obtained a doctorate degree" (Schuster 2006). In another US case of terror on a college campus, the November 21, 2016, Ohio State University attack by ISIS-inspired student Abdul Razak Ali Artan is covered in Chapter 4.

Al-Qaeda splinter groups are actively targeting colleges in Africa in their campaign of fear. Boko Haram was responsible for a night massacre at a technical college in 2010 in Nigeria, and in 2013, gunmen entered the male dormitory in the College of Agriculture in Gujba, killing forty-four students and teachers in their sleep. Taking a page from Boko Haram's playbook, al Shabaab attacked the Garissa University College in 2015, executing the deadliest terrorist event in Kenya since the 1998 United States embassy bombings and the second deadliest in Kenya's history.

Case Study: Al-Shabaab Attack: Garissa University College

Al-Shabaab, formed in 2006, is an Islamist terrorist group centered in Somalia. According to the US National Counterterrorism Center, al-Shabaab forces are primarily focused on overthrowing the fragile Somali federal government and generally are not interested in a global jihad; although in February of 2012, the leadership of al-Shabaab pledged an alliance with al-Qaeda (DNI 2018). Since 2010, al-Shabaab has executed a number of high-profile attacks in Somalia, Kenya, and Uganda. These attacks included the 2010 bombing of a rugby club in Uganda, the 2013 Westgate shopping mall attack in Kenya, and the 2015 Garissa University College attack in Kenya. Kenya has fallen victim to a high volume of al-Shabaab attacks, as the county is home to a large number of Somali refugees and takes direct military action against al-Shabaab in Somalia.

THE ATTACK

Garissa University College is located in Garissa, Kenya, a sizable town of 67,861. The school is less than 100 miles from the Somali border. There were at least 887 students present at the time of the incident, both Muslim and Christian.

The attack began at approximately 5:30 a.m. local time on Thursday, April 7, 2015. Al-Shabaab militants killed two unarmed guards at the main gate to the university and entered the campus. Morning prayers were underway in the campus mosque, which was not attacked. Victim accounts described gunmen as moving through dormitories, opening doors and asking if occupants were Muslim or Christian. Those identifying as Christians were immediately shot (Odula and Muhumuza 2015). Many of those claiming to be Muslim were ordered at gunpoint to recite passages from the Koran to prove their faith.

As National Police and Kenyan Defense Forces converged on the campus, the attackers drew back to the female dormitories, taking more than 700 hostages. This started a siege that lasted more than twelve hours.

RESPONSE

Local personnel of the National Police and Kenyan Defense Forces comprised the initial response to the shooting at Garissa University College. Their response disrupted the attack, likely saving many lives, and forced the attackers to take refuge in one of the dormitories. Kenyan forces cleared and evacuated the other three dormitory buildings and contained the attackers to one building.

Soldiers from RECCE Company, the elite paramilitary arm of the Kenyan National Police, were deployed to the campus. The decision to deploy RECCE Company was delayed by Kenyan government officials, so the unit arrived nearly twelve hours after the incident started. The RECCE Company crisis response team is trained for high-risk operations such as counterterrorism and hostage situations. RECCE Company moved swiftly upon their arrival, with high impact tactics. Local media reported that RECCE Company ended the siege, killing or arresting all attackers within twelve minutes of their arrival on the scene (Kenya Today 2015).

RECCE Company shooters reportedly killed four attackers, while a fifth attacker detonated a suicide vest, killing himself and injuring seven RECCE soldiers. Another RECCE soldier was killed by an enemy grenade.

In all, al Shabaab took 147 lives in the attack, which included two guards, one police officer, three soldiers, and 142 students. The attack injured seventy-nine. A total of eight suspected gunmen were involved in the attack. Four gunmen were killed by RECCE Company forces, and one detonated a suicide vest. One gunman was captured fleeing the scene, and two were captured on the campus.

Students were taken to the nearby Garissa military camp where they were cared for by the Red Cross. By the end of the incident, all students had been accounted for. Kenyan officials established a dusk-to-dawn curfew in the region that lasted more than a week. Garissa University College was closed after the incident and reopened on May 5, 2015.

In the aftermath of the attacks, several men were apprehended and arrested for their suspected involvement, which included a security guard at Garissa University College who was suspected of facilitating the attacker's entry into the institution (Newsweek 2015).

ANALYSIS

According to the National Consortium for the Study of Terrorism and Responses to Terrorism (START), there were more than 3,800 terrorist attacks on educational institutions between 1970 and 2014 across 111 countries. These attacks comprised 2.7 percent of all terrorist attacks globally during this time period (Pate, Jensen, and Miller 2015). While attacks on educational targets have the capacity to be highly lethal, the number of fatalities from the Garissa University College attack were much higher than the average of 0.9 deaths per attack, and, in fact, makes this one of the deadliest terror attacks on an educational target on record since 1970.

On April 4, al-Shabaab issued a statement, indicating that the Garissa shooters want to "avenge the deaths of thousands of Muslims killed at the hands of the Kenyan security forces."

LESSONS LEARNED

Unfortunately, incidents occuring in many foreign nations are not well documented for the global public safety community beyond brief statements by government officials and scattered reports from news agencies. That, in itself, is an important lesson learned as the global public safety community continually seeks to learn from past incidents about terrorist groups, their targets and motivations, and the strategies and tactics used by attackers and responding forces.

There are, however, other lessons learned that we can extrapolate from what is known of this situation. For instance, there is no documented evidence of closed circuit cameras on the grounds of the campus or in buildings. Cameras can provide effective intelligence on the location, number, status, and armaments of attackers, as well as the location, number, and status of victims and hostages. Soft targets should consider placement of cameras so as to observe entrances to the grounds, entrances to buildings, hallways, and other key areas. Live video should be accessible locally as well as remotely.

The rapid response of National Police and Kenyan Defense Forces stationed in Garissa likely contributed to fewer deaths of students, faculty, and staff as the attackers were forced to abandon their methodical attack in favor of taking a defensive position. Swift and aggressive response to active shooter situations has become a standard of practice in many areas of the world.

The Garissa area, with its proximity to the Somali border, had suffered several attacks from al-Shabaab prior to the attack on the university. The university should have clearly been identified as a potential target, and as such should have had put better protections against any potential attacks into place. The number and capability of the university guards present at the onset of the attack was clearly inadequate for a confrontation of this magnitude. While documentation does not indicate the total number of guards present across the campus, it is clear that the guards were unarmed and overwhelmed immediately. Additionally, consideration should be given to physical barriers at the entrance to grounds, as well as controlled access to buildings, which would have prevented or delayed the attackers in entering buildings.

In the event of an active shooter or terrorist attack, tactical law enforcement resources must stand ready to deploy as soon as possible. In many situations, the attack is neutralized early by standard patrol resources, but this is an unpredictable outcome. The significant delay in the deployment of RECCE Company, which allowed the attackers to kill more hostages and to assume a better defensive position, was heavily criticized post-incident.

(Source: Riecker 2019. Mr. Riecker is a partner and principal consultant with Emergency Preparedness Solutions, LLC. He is a former head of training and exercises for the New York State Emergency Management Office and is a certified emergency and disaster professional.)

Bad Blood: Intelligence, Law Enforcement, and Higher Education

There is a possibility action (or nonaction) by security agencies may be contributing to campus vulnerability to domestic and foreign bad actors in the US. Unfortunately, the historically poor relationship between academia and intelligence and law enforcement agencies has led to difficulty with their partnering to address vulnerabilities and threats on campuses. This "bad blood" dates to 1956 with the FBI's Counterintelligence Program (COINTELPRO), a series of covert projects in which the Bureau conducted surveillance and disruption activities against domestic political organizations on campuses (Churchill and Vander Wall 2002). COINTELPRO infiltrated college campuses to monitor antiwar activity during the Vietnam War and, when this activity came to light in 1971, massive protests erupted on campuses, impacting the relationship between academia and the government.

Activities on campus by the Central Intelligence Agency (CIA) from 1967 to 1973 further strained the relationship. Operation CHAOS was the code name of a CIA domestic espionage program to unmask possible foreign influences on the student antiwar movement on campuses (Rafalko 2011). Project RESISTANCE was a parallel operation, in which the CIA worked with college administrators, campus security, and local police to identify antiwar activists and political dissidents without any infiltration taking place (Church Committee Reports 1975).

A review of official documents regarding COINTELPRO, CHAOS, and RESISTANCE, especially the Church Committee proceedings, yields great data regarding interaction between higher education and intelligence agencies during a period of extreme domestic unrest. Present-day concerns about government and law enforcement activities on campus re-emerged in 2011, when the New York Police Department admitted infiltrating colleges to monitor Muslim students and activities (Hawley and Apuzzo 2011). This case was a lightning rod for the media and led to state-by-state cases of intelligence community activity on college campuses documented by the American Civil Liberties Union (ACLU) in 2011 (ACLU 2014).

A new book by author Daniel Golden, entitled *Spy Schools: How the CIA, FBI, and Foreign Intelligence Secretly Exploit America's Universities* (Golden 2017), is raising new questions and suspicions about the relationship between the government and higher education. This includes a critical discussion about the National Security Higher Education Advisory Board (NSHEAB) discussed in the next section, and how college presidents were hesitant to belong to the group.

The literature regarding attitudes toward, perceptions of, motivation for, resistance to, and barriers to the relationship between higher education and the intelligence community highlights the cultural disconnects of two enterprises essentially sharing the same goal: protecting First Amendment rights and national security. In terms of the intelligence perspective, the FBI 2011 white paper entitled "Higher Education and National Security: The Targeting of Sensitive, Proprietary, and Classified Information on Campuses of Higher Education" gives great insight into the subject. The higher education view on the tenuous relationship comes into view through an essay in the *Chronicle of Higher Education* entitled "Academics and National-Security Experts Must Work Together" (Gansler and Gast 2008). In this article, the authors discuss legislative and environmental changes since the 9/11 terrorist attacks and the impact on higher education. They also address the cultural divide between higher education and intelligence agencies, asserting it is "so often at the root of poor policies and unnecessary roadblocks for both groups" (Gansler and Gast 2008). This balanced essay asserts how experts in the intelligence field don't fully understand how communication with other countries is crucial to scientific research, and universities and research institutions fail to appreciate the importance of securing technology and protecting sensitive information. Finally, an analysis of the impact of the Economic

Espionage Act of 1996 gives insight into how what was supposed to be a framework for success is not working to protect the academy (Brenner and Crescenzi 2006).

The institutions of higher education and the intelligence community have both witnessed great change and turmoil in light of the 9/11 terrorist attacks on our country. The events of 9/11 and subsequent investigations into the campus-related activities of the hijackers, new statutory reporting requirements, and continued, persistent collection on campuses by "countries of interest" have potentially aggravated an already strained relationship between the two enterprises. Both have undergone institutional reform, forced by uncontrollable environmental conditions, and both are inherently resistant to change. Due to the urgent nature of national security concerns following 9/11, there was no time to plan strategically for the change, to seek mutual agreement, or to communicate cross enterprises properly. The situation continues to evolve with current events and emergent challenges; therefore, an opportunity exists to bridge the gap and to partner strategically for future change events.

In response to increased concerns, the FBI created the National Security Higher Education Advisory Board (NSHEAB) in 2005. The NSHEAB consisted of nineteen university presidents and chancellors and strives to met on a regular basis to discuss national security matters intersecting with higher education. Previous panels included discussion on protection of weapons of mass destruction research and laws regarding domestic terrorism investigations on campuses. The NSHEAB became much less engaged over time and unfortunately was disbanded in 2018. The Department of Homeland Security instituted the Homeland Security Academic Advisory Council (HSAAC) in March 2012 to discuss matters related to homeland security and the academic community, mainly issues regarding security-related curriculum, recruitment of students to DHS, academic research, and cybersecurity on college campuses.

One of the subcommittees deals with campus resilience. The Resilience Pilot Program (CR Pilot) launched in 2013 for seven select US colleges and universities to help them take proactive steps to enhance preparedness and campus resilience. The CR Pilot is a joint initiative of DHS's Federal Emergency Management Agency (FEMA), the US Immigration and Customs Enforcement Student and Exchange Visitor Program, and the Office of Academic Engagement. The CRP will harvest best practices, lessons learned, and resources to help schools identify their vulnerabilities and be more resilient and prepared. Drexel University, Texas A&M, and others participated in the project (DHS 2013a). Out of this effort, DHS built an outstanding online resource for colleges: www.dhs.gov/academicresilience. The DHS Office of Academic Engagement (OAE), in coordination with the Federal Emergency Management Agency, also developed a new Exercise Starter Kit to assist colleges and universities build and refine response training and exercises to enhance their emergency plans and capabilities. In March 2018, DHS announced UMass Amherst Emergency Operations Center team would be the first to participate in an exercise using the kit. A group representing leaders from functional areas throughout campus responsible for carrying out response and recovery actions during an emergency will participate in a DHS-facilitated emergency exercise focused on an active shooter threat scenario.

In Chapter 9, we discuss hardening efforts for colleges including strengthening partnerships with law enforcement and harvesting best practices from around the country.

CHURCHES

Churches are another soft target where violent attacks are met with disbelief, especially when perpetrated by an actor with an extreme religious ideology. Or in Dylann Roof's case, extreme white supremacist beliefs. How can anyone's God condone the killing of another human being? We also now have a "black swan" phenomenon of Christians killing Christians and Muslims killing Muslims in the name of their extremist religious ideology. The worship space, formerly respected and shielded from violent crime, is exploited by bad actors, whether as a place to exact personal revenge against a parishioner, to steal money or artifacts to pay for drug buys, or to carry out an attack in which the institution and ideology are a target.

Despite these cultural changes, clergy may not see security of their building and faith community as a pressing issue. A survey conducted by LifeWay Christian Resources posed questions to more than 1,300 evangelical leaders from around the world to gather information about what they considered their most urgent concerns (Baptist Press 2005). The results of the survey, which included topics related to faith and life in modern society, did not return any concerns about safety, security, or terrorism. Carl Chinn, a church security expert, has been tracking US church-related crimes and statistics since 1999. Deadly force incidents (DFIs) include abductions, attacks, suspicious deaths, suicides, and deadly force intervention/protection. Between January 1, 1999, and December 31, 2017, Chinn reports 1,705 DFIs at faith-based organizations, with 811 people killed and 1,705 injured. Almost 30 percent of DFIs were related to robbery; 16 percent to domestic issues, and 13 percent to personal conflict or disagreement. Guns were the weapon of choice (996 incidents) followed by knives (267 incidents) and explosive devices/Molotov cocktails (91 incidents). There were seventy-six incidents related to what Chinn labels "religious bias" (Chinn 2018).

Chinn also points out there is no government organization responsible for tracking crimes specifically associated with churches. Following up on the LifeWay survey and data compiled by Chinn, Brian Gallagher, a former member of the US Secret Service and church security expert, interviewed a church planting organization about its perspective on safety and security related to its family of 100 churches in the United States. This particular organization, which asked to remain anonymous, revealed that less than 10 percent of their churches invested funds to provide proper security for their facility. The majority of the churches in the organization had never considered security or terrorism as a concern to their congregations (Gallagher 2014).

The advent of megachurches in the United States presents a unique vulnerability: there are fewer worship sessions, but they are attended by thousands of attendees. Lakewood Church in Houston, Texas, is the largest megachurch, with more than 16,800 worshippers attending popular author Joel Osteen's services at the former Compaq sports arena. Although the church has a high-tech security camera system and around-the-clock guards including off-duty law enforcement officers, it is still vulnerable. On March 9, 2014, possibly during services, a safecracker stole more than $600,000 in collection money. Lakewood generates $75 million in revenue annually, making it a lucrative target for theft. Nationally, thefts of money and securities constitute a significant problem for churches. Wisconsin-based Church Mutual Insurance Co., which insures about 95,000 churches, reported 178 such thefts in 2013. The total declined from 240 cases in 2011, but the value of money stolen rose to more than 9 percent of total theft claims paid (Turner and Hlavaty 2014). Church Mutual's website is replete with information for churches, camps and conference centers, K–12 schools, and senior living communities. Some emergent topics include preventing copper theft, senior bullying, embezzlement, and cyber hacks (www.churchmutual.com/5403/Trending-Topics).

Churches also have a unique vulnerability: in addition to supporting their congregation, they invite troubled members of society to worship, for counseling, or to attend support groups. This exposure is difficult to mitigate, although Chapters 8 and 9 discuss additional steps clergy and staff can take to secure the facility and populace. However, unlike school attacks, many church crime perpetrators have no association at all with the church; they have never attended a service and do not know the clergy members or parishioners. Therefore, the church attack may be more about opportunistic crime or could just serve as a symbolic target. The outward appearance of a hardened facility is therefore extremely important for churches so the terrorist or violent criminal shifts his or her intentions elsewhere.

The Proliferation of Church Attacks

Church attacks are common around the world, and most are perpetrated by enemies common to the United States. For instance, in Kenya, Christian churches are routinely targeted by radical Islamist terrorists from the Somalia-based al-Qaeda splinter group al-Shabaab. Tactics include use of bombs, semiautomatic weapons, or even machetes. Kenya is a natural target for terrorists; it has East Africa's biggest economy, is westernizing, and is a recipient of US counterterrorism funding. Also, the Nairobi government has sent troops into neighboring Somalia as part of an African Union force (AMISOM) to combat al-Shabaab, drawing their wrath. Christianity is the predominant religion in Kenya also making it a target for those with a radical Islamist ideology. In Nigeria, Boko Haram militants routinely target churches, often walking in doors closest to the altar and using semiautomatic weapons on stunned worshippers for maximum death in a short period of time. In 2013, the Vatican's ambassador to Tanzania was at the Roman Catholic church in Arusha, newly opened and holding its first mass, when hand grenades and a crude bomb were thrown into the crowd outside the church. He was unharmed, but three people died and thirty were injured in the first significant attack on Tanzania's Christian community. The operation was carried out by four Saudi Arabian nationals and two locals; no group claimed responsibility.

A 2013 terror case in England perfectly illustrates how a terrorist can enter a foreign country and quickly move to the execution stages of an attack against churches. Twenty-five-year-old white supremacist Pavlo Lapshyn, a Ukranian citizen, was a PhD student who won a competition for a work placement with Delcam, a specialist software firm in Birmingham, UK. However, Lapshyn never intended to work; the competition merely facilitated his plan to carry out hate crimes against Muslims in the United Kingdom. He practiced building and detonating hexamethylene triperoxide diamine (HMTD) devices packed with nails in the Ukraine and researched how to buy similar bomb components in Birmingham. He flew to England on April 24, 2013, on his work visa and had been in the country only five days when he started a campaign of terror. His first victim was 82-year-old Mohammed Saleem killed by Lapshyn as he walked home from evening prayers at a mosque in Birmingham. On June 21, Lapshyn planted explosive devices in a child's lunch box at the mosque gates, and seven days later, he placed a bomb on a roundabout near Wolverhampton Central Mosque. The most serious attack was on July 12 at the Tipton mosque, where Lapshyn packed hundreds of nails in a bomb on a railway embankment next to its car park and detonated it during what he thought was the prayer service. Thankfully, mass casualties were averted because, unbeknownst to Lapshyn, prayers were held an hour later than usual, so parishioners had not yet arrived. Using forensics from the scene and a shadowy picture of Lapshyn from CCTV, police were finally led to his workplace at Delcam, and his apartment and a trove of evidence. Lapshyn is serving a forty-year prison sentence for the killing and the bombings. Interestingly, he was on police radar in Ukraine, where a chemical explosion damaged his flat in 2010; he told authorities the blast was related to schoolwork in a lab project gone bad. Yet no travel restrictions were imposed and he was not being watched by authorities. The case illustrates how a perpetrator can go from planning stages to execution in a short period of time, even days after entering a foreign country. Police in the UK were on Lapshyn's trail during his attack spree, but the investigation was difficult and he continued his operation (Lumb and Casciani 2013).

Shared religion or nationality is not a deterrent when selecting targets. For example, in 1993, members of the Italian Mafia (presumably Catholic) bombed two of Rome's most venerable Catholic churches—San Giovanni and San Giorgio—to further their political goals. In our country, right-wing religious extremist Christians have killed other Christians without second thought to advance their goals. Islamist extremists have bombed mosques in Libya, Nigeria, and Mali. Even historic mosques and tombs, revered by Muslims, are targeted. For instance, the world was stunned in July 2012 when terrorists from the al-Qaeda splinter group Ansar Dine bombed the Yahya mosque in Timbuktu, a UNESCO World Heritage site. They even pried open a fifteenth-century door, which many Muslims believed would be closed until the end of the world and the return of the prophets. In 2006, Wahhabi militants who bombed the Askariyyah shrine in Samarra, Iraq, almost ignited a civil war. The shrine houses the graves of the tenth and eleventh holy imams, descendants of Muhammad. In 2014, members of al-Qaeda splinter ISIS destroyed the tomb of the prophet Jonah (depicted in the Old Testament as being swallowed by a whale) in Mosul, Iraq. These "crimes against history" are shocking, get widespread press coverage for a group, and can shift the core of a conflict. In another stunning case, more than 100 bomb threats were called into Jewish Community Centers in 2017. Assumptions about the likely culprits were proven wrong when a 19-year-old Israeli-American man was arrested in Israel and charged with calling in dozens of the threats. He was advertising his services on the dark web, and also made more than 2,000 other calls to airlines, embassies, malls, hospitals, and police stations. Therefore, we can't discount attacks or threats by those with similar religious beliefs.

US Churches as Targets

Unfortunately, terrorists took a page from the international playbook and are now targeting US churches. Levar Haley Washington, Gregory Vernon Patterson, Hammad Riaz Samana, and Kevin James were arrested in August 2005 and charged with conspiring to attack synagogues and other targets in the Los Angeles area. Kevin James allegedly founded Jamiyyat ul-Islam Is-Saheeh (JIS), a radical Islamic prison group, and converted Levar Washington and others to the group's mission. The JIS allegedly planned to finance its operations by robbing gas stations (Zuckerman 2014). The men were convicted and their sentences ranged from five to twenty-two years in federal prison.

In the 2009 "Bronx plot," James Cromitie and his three accomplices separately converted to Islam while in prison. After meeting at the Masjid al-Ikhlas mosque in Newburgh, New York, following their release, the men devised a complex plan to bomb the Riverdale Temple and Jewish Center in New York City and, using Stinger surface-to-air guided missiles, shoot down military planes flying out of a nearby air base. Each man is serving a twenty-five-year sentence (Investigative Project on Terrorism 2014c).

On May 31, 2009, Scott Philip Roeder, an antiabortion activist, shot and killed Dr. George Tiller in the foyer of the Reformation Lutheran Church in Wichita, Kansas, as he handed out church bulletins after services. Tiller was one of the few doctors in the country who performed late-term abortions. Roeder was sentenced to life in prison.

In October 2010, two packages shipped from Yemen to Chicago-area synagogues contained explosive materials of the same type used by airline attackers Richard Reid ("shoe bomber") and Umar Farouk Abdulmutallab ("underwear bomber"). The packages contained printer cartridges filled with explosive material and were intercepted while in transit on cargo planes in the United Kingdom and Dubai from intelligence tips from Saudi Arabian authorities. The Yemen-based al-Qaeda in the Arabian Peninsula (AQAP) claimed responsibility (Zuckerman 2014).

In May 2011, Ahmed Ferhani of Algeria and Moroccan-born Mohamed Mamdouh, a US citizen, were arrested by the New York Police Department after attempting to purchase a hand grenade, guns, and ammunition to attack churches and synagogues in Manhattan. The men planned on disguising themselves as Orthodox Jews in order to access the facilities. Ferhani, the mastermind of the plot, also sold Percocet, cocaine, and marijuana to finance weapons for the attack. Both pled guilty and are serving five- to ten-year terms (Investigative Project on Terrorism 2014a).

Amine El Khalifi, a Moroccan citizen illegally in the United States, was arrested in February 2012 on charges of plotting to attack the US Capitol. Before choosing the Capitol building as a target, Khalifi had proposed targets including DC office buildings, restaurants, and synagogues. He believed undercover FBI agents were al-Qaeda operatives and revealed his plots, even showing them his practice detonating test bombs with cell phones. Law enforcement arrested Khalifi as he left his parked car next to the Capitol building with a bomb that was, unbeknownst to him, inert (Investigative Project on Terrorism 2014b). Khalifi was sentenced to thirty years in prison.

On August 5, 2012, Wade Michael Page fatally shot six people and wounded four others at a Sikh temple in Oak Creek, Wisconsin. Page was an American white supremacist and US Army veteran with ties to white supremacist and neo-Nazi groups. He was part of the white power music scene and openly spoke and sang about the impending racial holy war. Page committed suicide after a responding police officer shot him. Sikh men are often confused with Muslims due to their beards and turbans, and they have been the targets of multiple hate crimes in the United States since the 9/11 terrorist attacks (BBC News 2012).

Unfortunately, attacks against churches in the US are not subsiding. White supremacist Dylann Roof shot and killed nine black parishioners at the Emanuel African Methodist Episcopal Church in Charleston, South Carolina, in a heinous attack on June 17, 2015. Roof's massacre stunned the country and reminded us of the vulnerability of churches and what happens at the intersection of hate and violence.

Case Study: Attack at the Emanuel African Methodist Episcopal (AME) Church, 2015

On the night of June 17, 2015, then 21-year-old Dylann Roof, who is white, entered the Emanuel AME Church. He was welcomed by the black parishoners, who invited him to their Bible study. After prayers began and heads bowed and eyes closed, Roof drew his .45 pistol and opened fire. The events of the next few minutes are best told through the words of the victims, given at Roof's trial (Shapiro 2017).

Felicia Sanders, a survivor of the shooting, testified that when Roof opened fire she clutched her granddaughter tight and told her to play dead. "I could feel the warm blood flowing on each side of me," she said. "I was just waiting on my turn," she added. "Even if I got shot, I just didn't want my granddaughter to get shot." Amid the chaos and the bloodshed, her youngest son, Tywanza Sanders, stood up and confronted the assailant: "Why are you doing this?" he asked, according to Felicia Sanders' testimony. And he told our son, "I have to do this because y'all raping our women and taking over the world," Felicia Sanders said. "And that's when [the gunman] put about five bullets in my son." We watched him take his last breath, she said of her son. "I watched my son come into this world, and I watched my son leave this world" (Shapiro 2017).

ATTACKER AND PLOT

Fortunately, the AME church had a security camera over the entrance and police were able to immediately circulate Roof's picture, his face and distinctive haircut clearly visible in the stills. Roof's father and uncle contacted police to positively identify him upon seeing security photos in the news.

Roof had two prior arrests, both made in the months preceding the attack. His admission to a narcotics offense should have prevented him from purchasing the weapon used in the shooting, Unfortunately, an administrative error in the National Instant Criminal Background Check System kept Roof's admission from appearing on his mandatory background check (Nakashima 2015).

Roof reportedly told friends and neighbors of his plans to kill people, including a plot to attack the College of Charleston, but his claims were not taken seriously. His website, www.thelastrhodesian.com, is permanently archived at https://web.archive.org/web/20150620134455/http://lastrhodesian.com/. Roof was an active participant in many white supremacist chat sites.

He planned the attack for around six months and targeted the Emanuel AME Church due to its prominent role in African American history. One of the friends who briefly hid Roof's gun from him said, "I don't think the church was his primary target because he told us he was going for the school. But I think he couldn't get into the school because of the security . . . so I think he just settled for the church" (Krol 2015).

Federal prosecutors said in August 2016 that although Roof was in contact with white supremacists, he had no personal associates who knew about or encouraged his plot, therefore he "self-radicalized" online. Roof's prominent display of the Confederate flag on his vehicle and in pictures led to a call for removal of the flag from the state capitol and other buildings. On July 10, 2015, just a few weeks after the massacre, the flag was lowered from the state capitol in Columbia. Many retailers stopped selling the flag and the controversy spilled over to monuments, park names, and memorials.

CAPTURE AND SENTENCING

Police pulled Roof over on a traffic stop in Shelby, North Carolina, approximately 245 miles from the scene of his attack. Police were tipped-off by an alert woman who recognized Roof's car and then identified him as the driver. She called her employer, who contacted local police, and then she tailed the suspect's car for thirty-five miles until certain authorities were moving in for an arrest. The murder weapon was in the vehicle.

Roof was sentenced to death on April 10, 2017. At his trial, Roof complained that "it's not fair" he had to hear so much from his victims. In a forty-two-page diary found in Roof's cell, he stated, "I do not regret what I did," and "I am not sorry. I have not shed a tear for the innocent people I killed."

LESSONS LEARNED

The security camera over the church door did not deter Roof, yet provided and immediate photo, which led to a quick arrest. Roof had a list of other targets and may have carried out another attack if not apprehended.

Roof's friends knew he was planning some type of attack but did not report him. Roof told friend Joey Meek he hated black people so much he was going to kill them at a South Carolina church. After seeing the news about the AME shooting, Meek did not call police and talked another friend out of calling. He also lied to the FBI about his conversation with Roof. Meek was sentenced to two years in jail. Unlike Roof, Meek was remorseful and cried in court about the shooting (AP 2017).

The AME Church was not Roof's first choice of target. He told friends he was planning an attack against the College of Charleston but ruled it against because of security on the campus. Although the hardened posture at the university prevented the attack there, soft targets abound and Roof instead focused his anger on a less secured facility, the AME church just a few blocks away (Krol 2015).

As with previous racially motivated attacks in the US, the definition of terrorism was disputed. Some politicians and law enforcement officials referred to the attack as domestic terrorism, yet others did not. Professor and terrorism expert Brian Phillips opined the attack was "clearly a terrorist act." He based this conclusion on a racist political motivation, and the "intimidation of a wider audience" criterion was met when Roof spared one person in the prayer group to "spread the message" (Phillips 2015). However, the FBI director at the time, James Comey, stated the AME attack was a hate crime, not a terrorist attack, citing the lack of evidence of political motivation for the suspect's action (WHAM 2015).

Unfortunately, a church was the scene of another mass shooting, this one in Sutherland Spring, Texas. Although the shooter, Devin Patrick Kelley, did not have political or religious motives, we can learn much from this case about what leads up to an attack and the aftermath.

Case Study: Mass Shooting at First Baptist Church of Sutherland Springs, Texas

On Sunday, November 5, 2017, just one month after fifty-eight people were killed and more than 800 wounded in the Las Vegas massacre, 26-year-old Devin Patrick Kelley walked up to the First Baptist Church of Sutherland Springs, Texas, shot and killed two people outside, then entered and opened fire on the congregation.

THE ATTACK

Armed with a Ruger AR-556 semiautomatic rifle, Kelley, dressed in black tactical gear, a ballistic vest, and a black face mask covered with a white skull, killed twenty-six parishioners, including an unborn child, and wounded another twenty. Inside, he yelled, "Everybody die, motherfuckers," as he proceeded up and down the aisle and shot at people in the pews (Cullen 2017). Police found fifteen empty magazines capable of holding thirty rounds each. A camera, set up at the back of the church to record services for uploading online, captured the shooting. The footage shows Kelley methodically and indiscriminately shooting the victims, pausing only to reload his rifle (Goldman, Pérez-Peña, and Fernández 2017). The final victim count was ten women, seven men, seven girls, one boy, and an unborn child. The oldest victim was 77 years old. One victim was the 14-year-old daughter of church pastor Frank Pomeroy, who was elsewhere the day of the attack. Visiting pastor Bryan Holcombe died, along with eight of his family members.

Kelley left the church and was engaged and shot in the leg and upper left torso under his tactical vest by a local resident, a former firearms instructor wielding an AR-15 (Pearce, Savage, and Adrawal 2017). The resident flagged down a truck driven by another Southerland Springs area resident, and both men pursued Kelley. Although wounded, Kelley led the men on a chase with speeds up to 90 mph before going off the road and taking his own life.

The Sutherland Springs attack was the deadliest mass shooting in Texas, followed by the 1991 Luby's massacre in Killeen in which twenty-three were killed and twenty-seven were wounded, and the fifth-deadliest mass shooting in the United States. It was also the deadliest shooting in an American place of worship in modern history, surpassing the Charleston AME church shooting of 2015.

THE ATTACKER

Kelley had a lengthy disciplinary record at New Braunfels High School, including seven suspensions for falsifying records, insubordination, profanity, and a drug-related offense (Cullen 2017). Despite his background, Kelley was able to enlist in the US Air Force and served for five years. While in the Air Force, Kelley was brought before a general court martial on four charges: assault on his wife; aggravated assault on his stepson, an injury that fractured his skull; two charges of pointing a loaded gun at his wife; and two counts of threatening his wife with an unloaded gun. Kelley also made death threats against the superior officers who charged him, and in an incident prior to his court martial, was caught sneaking firearms onto Holloman Air Force Base (Connor and Arkin 2017). Kelley pleaded guilty to the assault of his wife and stepson. In return, the weapons charges were dropped. He was sentenced to twelve months of confinement and reduction in rank to airman basic. His appeal was unsuccessful and, in 2014, he was dismissed from the Air Force with a bad conduct discharge. Around that same time, he made threats of self-harm to a coworker and was committed to a mental health facility, from which he escaped. His ex-wife said she feared for her life, as

Kelley threatened to kill her and her entire family. She stated: "For a whole year, he slapped me, choked me, kicked me, water-boarded me and held a gun to my head" (Rosenberg 2017). However, the Comal County, Texas, Sheriff's Office did not bring charges against Kelley, and "the case became inactive because the victim did not respond to four follow-up calls and messages from a sheriff's office detective" (Eaton 2018).

Post-Military Life

After his release from the Air Force, Kelley returned to New Braunfels, where he lived in a converted barn at his parents' home. Shortly thereafter, in 2013, he was investigated for sexual assault and rape, and for a physical assault of his then-girlfriend, whom he later married. The couple moved into a mobile home in Colorado Springs, Colorado, where he was charged in August 2014 for misdemeanor cruelty to animals after beating his malnourished husky.

At the time of the shooting, Kelley was again living at his parents' property in New Braunfels. He reportedly lied about his background to pass a background check and obtain a license from the Texas Department of Public Safety as a security guard and was a security worker at the Summit Vacation and RV Resort in New Braunfels. He had previously worked as an unarmed security guard at the Schlitterbahn Waterpark and Resort in New Braunfels but was fired after less than six weeks on the job (Bradshaw 2017).

On the night of October 31, less than a week before the shooting, Kelley attended a festival at the First Baptist Church wearing all black. According to two parishioners who were at the festival, he acted so strangely that people had to keep an eye on him. One also examined him to make sure he was not carrying a firearm.

Kelley's motive for the shooting was a dispute with his estranged mother-in-law. Kelley's estranged second wife sometimes attended First Baptist Church in Sutherland Springs with her family. Prior to the shooting, he sent threatening text messages to her mother. His wife and her mother were not at the church when the attack occurred, but he killed his wife's grandmother at the church.

LESSONS LEARNED

Kelley had a documented history of domestic violence, both in the military and as a civilian. He received a bad conduct discharge; this conviction meant he could never legally possess a firearm. The Air Force failed to record the conviction in the FBI National Crime Information Center database, which is used by the National Instant Check System to flag prohibited purchases. Therefore, this conviction was never available as a "flagging" action. As a result, Kelley was legally able to stockpile firearms over the course of several months, including the one he used to conduct his attack on the First Baptist Church.

In another instance of a missed opportunity to possibly stop Kelley, a former Air Force colleague who was temporarily reacquainted with him online, said Kelley claimed he would buy dogs and other animals and use them for "target practice." He also expressed his obsession with mass murders, particularly the Charleston church shooting, and joked about committing one himself. These comments prompted her to block him on Facebook (Silva 2017). The former colleague did not report his violent threats posted on Facebook. As with other mass shootings, the people in close proximity to the shooter usually have information that is of value to law enforcement, yet they fail to report it. Often they are afraid to get involved or risk safety to self and family.

(Source: Fisk 2019. Mr. Ralph R. Fisk Jr., ATO, PCP-1, MEMS. Instructor/trainer, subject matter expert, and thought leader in the areas of emergency management, contemporary risk and threat assessment.)

Church terror attacks continue. On January 29, 2017, an assault on the Islamic Cultural Center in Quebec City, Canada, killed six and wounded nineteen. Alexandre Bissonnette used an AK-47 rifle in his attack. He spent hours online reading about mass shooters and scouring Twitter accounts of alt-right figures and conspiracy theorists (Coletta 2018).

On September 24, 2017, Emanuel K. Samson, a black nationalist, opened fire with two pistols as Sunday services ended at the Burnette Chapel in Antioch, Tennessee, killing one person and wounding seven others. He injured himself and was arrested. Samson targeted white churchgoers in retribution for the Charleston AME church attack by Dylann Roof.

On October 28, 2018, Robert Bowers barged into a Pittsburgh, Pennsylvania synagogue and opened fire with an AR-15 rifle and 3 handguns, killing 11 people and critically injuring 6 others, including 4 police officers. He spewed anti-Semitic slurs during the assault, and previously posted hateful speech on social media.

Throughout history, churches were a place of sanctuary and refuge for those in need. However, we forget churches were caught up in wars for centuries. For example, during the Civil War, Ezra, Dunker, Salem, Baptist, and St. Mary's churches, landmarks in rural areas, were all ground zero for bloody battles. In World Wars I and II, hundreds of churches and cathedrals in Europe were destroyed, whether purposely or through collateral damage. During ongoing religious and political wars in countries like Syria, churches are targets and part of the war plan.

However, the mere idea of crime and terror affecting a US church seems new and surprising to our populace, despite recent massacres. After the Sutherland Springs shooting, there was an uptick in pastors seeking active shooter training and security assessments but, as with other attacks, interest in enhancing security fades with time. The unwillingness to believe a church may be a target for criminals or terrorists creates a large blind spot and gives the advantage to those who wish to do us harm.

Security must move closer to the top of concerns for US clergy and staff now, as crime and terror attacks are trending upward. Although the number of places of worship in the US versus the percentage of those attacked are small, churches cannot be lackadaisical on the security they provide for the safety of their congregations. They must protect the flock.

Safety and Security at Polling Places

Every year, millions of Americans exercise their right to vote by going to polling locations in their voting districts. In a long-held tradition, churches, schools, and community centers will open their doors to the public, many for thirteen hours or more. Groups like al-Qaeda and ISIS regularly attack polling places in Libya, Iraq, and other countries to scare voters from the polls and destabilize a government. On April 22, 2018, an ISIS suicide bomber struck a voter registration center in Kabul, Afghanistan, killing at least fifty-seven people. Since polling centers are legitimate targets to a group threatening our country, we should take action.

Election day is not only a celebration of our democracy but a growing security challenge. In general, there is an increase in violence in our country, and people are acting out on their anger like never before. Add a contentious election cycle, with supporters on all sides, parties are emotional about their candidates and important "hot button" issues like race, gender, and abortion. We also have terrorist groups targeting our country, possibly looking for an opportunity to impact an election or, at the very least, get wide press coverage. Crowded public places, which are basically unsecured, such as churches, schools, and community centers, are the perfect target. The report "Electoral Violence: A Study of the 2016 United States Presidential Election" (Araida et al. 2016) records, analyzes, and contextualizes electoral violence in the United States during the 2016 electoral cycle. Data shows a spike of violence around the primaries, much more so than on election day. Physical violence is the most prevalent type of violence during that period, followed by threats, intimidation, and vandalism. Finally, data shows rallies and protests are now flashpoints for violence, therefore host organizations must have an emergency plan and security personnel in place to protect their facilities and attendees.

Many venues stay open for business and polling, mixing facility users with the voting public. As the parent of a student attending a school that will be open on election day, or the user of a facility opening its doors to both you and the voting public, you have the right to ask questions of the venue about their safety and security plan for the day. Don't assume they have a plan or have even considered their location as a place where violence could occur. Very often, building owners have a severe blind spot about their vulnerabilities. They don't believe violence could happen on their property, especially those in rural areas or tucked away in quiet neighborhoods, and thus, do not adequately prepare.

Security in the form of a police officer, contracted security, or even just a parked security vehicle at the location may deter those who might do harm. Since most polling locations don't have the funds for increased security, I recommend they ask parents, parishioners, neighbors, or community members with experience in law enforcement or the military for voluntary assistance on election day. A simple solution!

Access control is a must at the polling location. For instance, there should be a specific parking area for voters, separate from facility users. Parking on voting day is always chaotic with vehicles in the grass, etc., so remember that fire lanes must be kept open in case of an emergency. Cones, ropes, or even chairs will work. Also, extra traffic generated by voters is a serious issue in areas with pedestrians (for example the elderly or children), so safe walkways at the location are a must. I recommend volunteers man the parking area and adjacent crosswalks to assist with pedestrian and vehicle flow.

Finally, voters shouldn't be able to roam all over the property of the polling place, or throughout the building. There should be one entry and exit for the voters, and enough manpower at the location to ensure crowd control.

No one wants to imagine the worst, but we must to properly prepare. No town, city, state, or region is immune from attack. If the public is educated on risk and response, they become force multipliers to resource-constrained law enforcement in our communities. The bottom line: you certainly have the right to ask the voting location or local officials about their security plan and measures before election day. Also, if you sense security or safety issues, unapologetically bring them to the attention of those in charge at the polling site and try to offer a solution.

HOSPITALS

Hospital violence is also on the rise. The tracked categories are violent crimes (murder, rape, robbery, aggravated assault) and disorderly conduct, simple assault, theft, and vandalism. Violent crime at US hospitals slightly rose from 2015 to 2016 yet is still lower than previous years.

However, incidents of assault, disorderly conduct, theft, vandalism, and burglary all rose from 2015 to 2016 (IAHSS 2017).

In addition to these criminal activities, there is discussion in the counterterrorism community about the possibility of terrorists stealing Cobalt-60 or Cesium-137 to make a "dirty bomb." A GAO report in 2012 found security of radioactive sources lacking at US medical facilities. The report detailed security lapses, such as unsecured research irradiators kept in unlocked basements, near the public or outside on a loading dock. At one hospital, an irradiator was in a locked room, but the combination was written on the door frame in a heavily trafficked hallway (GAO 2012). One of the major findings of the report regarded physical security of the medical facilities, stating "some are more vulnerable than others to potential sabotage and theft because of security weaknesses."

What about the hospital itself as a terrorist target? From 1981 to 2013, approximately 100 terrorist attacks were perpetrated at hospitals worldwide, in forty-three countries, killing at least 775 people and wounding 1,217 others. The record year for terrorist attacks against hospitals was 2005, when eight such attacks occurred in Iraq (six attacks), Thailand (one attack), and Israel (one attack). These attacks were perpetrated through bombings, suicide bombings, and car bombings (ICT 2013). Hospitals in the US are a critical infrastructure/key resource (CI/KR) under the national response framework, making them high-priority targets. CI/KRs are individual targets whose destruction could create local disaster or profoundly damage our nation's morale or confidence. In a multistage attack, taking hospitals and medical personnel out of play would surely lead to an increased casualty count. A terrorist attack against a hospital has not happened in the United States yet; however, these heinous assaults routinely happen in other parts of the world. Either the hospital itself is targeted or it is targeted after an event as a secondary or tertiary attack when the wounded are being rushed into the building.

As covered in Chapter 2, terrorists are often underestimated in terms of intelligence, and many have formal education. In this new type of warfare, those entrusted to save and protect lives have actually been the trigger pullers. Consider the perpetrators of the June 30, 2007, al-Qaeda-inspired attack at Scotland's Glasgow Airport and the failed bombings in London's nightclub district two days before. Four of the seven group members were physicians, two were in medical school, and one had a PhD in engineering. A hospital was also in their crosshairs; on the afternoon of July 1, police carried out a controlled explosion on two cars in the parking lot of the Royal Alexandra Hospital, where the suspects worked and had apparently intended to attack.

On November 29, 2008, members of the al-Qaeda affiliate, Lashkar-e-Taiba (LeT), began their four-day assault in Mumbai, India. The twelve coordinated shooting and bombing attacks shocked the world and lasted four days, killing 164 people and injuring hundreds. Targets included a train station, a Jewish community center, the Taj Mahal hotel, and the Oberoi Trident hotel. Overshadowed by the horrific events at these locations, not much has been written about one of the main targets in Mumbai: the Cama Hospital for Women and Children. The LeT terrorists specifically attempted to gain access to the maternity ward, after killing two security guards with an AK-47 and grenades at the entrance. The security doors of the ward kept them from entering, and scared patients barricaded and refused to open up, despite threats from the terrorists. The shooters wandered other hospital floors, killing other security guards and workers. When directly confronted, a frightened hospital orderly offered the shooters water; they took a drink before killing the man (IBN Live 2008).

As discussed in Chapter 3, the Tehrik-i-Taliban Pakistan (TTP), or the Pakistani Taliban, is a designated terrorist group specializing in hitting soft targets. TTP has already tried to attack soft targets inside the United States, most notably through the failed Times Square bombing. In an example of a secondary attack against a hospital, TTP militants in Pakistan's restive province of Baluchistan first bombed a bus carrying female college students, killing fourteen. The perpetrator was a female suicide bomber, who boarded the bus with the students and then carried out the attack. At the Bolan Medical Complex, a second suicide bomber sat in the reception area of the emergency room, waiting for the right moment to attack. As dead and injured bus victims arrived at the emergency room and parents and local officials gathered, he detonated his vest, killing eleven (The Telegraph 2013). Heavily armed militants then stormed the hospital, taking hostages and shooting from the windows, killing several police officers and local officials.

Other coordinated, violent attacks against hospitals by the TTP in the last few years include the 2008 DI Khan Hospital attack (thirty-two dead) and the 2010 attack against the Jinnah Postgraduate Medical Center in Karachi (thirteen dead). The resurgent Taliban in Afghanistan has also attacked the country's hospitals; in 2008, a lone suicide bomber struck in the cafeteria at the Kabul hospital, killing six people and injuring twenty-three during a surgery training session. The hospital is located in the "green zone," heavily guarded, and very close to the US embassy. Also in Kabul, three Americans were killed on April 24, 2014, when a security guard opened fire at a hospital funded by a US Christian charity, killing a father and son who were visiting from the United States and a doctor. The worst attack against a hospital in Afghanistan happened on March 8, 2017, when ISIS attacked a military hospital in Kabul, killing thirty and injuring fifty others. A suicide bomber struck the back gate to clear the way for four gunmen, disguised as medical staff, to enter the main building. They threw grenades and opened fire on patients and staff inside the seven-story building.

A brazen attack by al-Qaeda in the Arabian Peninsula (AQAP) against a hospital in Yemen on December 5, 2013, stunned the world (Figure 5.4). The primary target was a nearby defense building; however, stray militants entered a nearby hospital, killing two German and two Vietnamese doctors, and one Indian and two Filipino nurses during the assault. Most were executed in front of the staff. Closed circuit television footage of the attack was broadcast by state media, causing widespread outrage among Yemenis. AQAP portrayed itself as fighting for the average citizen against foreign drone strikes, so its brazen killing of hospital personnel was a shock to the populace. Whether outraged or sensing a rift between the citizens and AQAP, a member of the core al-Qaeda group issued the following apology: "We do not fight in this way, and this is not what we call on people to do, and this is not our approach. We warned fighters not to attack the hospital" (Al Jazeera 2013).

Here in the United States, there are indications that hospitals might be in the terrorist crosshairs. In November 2002, the FBI issued an alert to hospitals in San Francisco, Houston, Chicago, and Washington, DC, warning of a vague, uncorroborated terrorist threat. In August 2004, the FBI and DHS issued a nationwide terrorism bulletin indicating al-Qaeda might attempt to attack Veteran's Affairs hospitals throughout the United States, and in April 2005 the FBI and DHS investigated unusual incidents of imposters posing as hospital accreditation surveyors. The Joint Commission on Accreditation of Healthcare Organizations sent a security alert to hospitals. In January, 2017, in light of ISIS encouraging its followers in the US to perpetrate lone wolf attacks on cinemas, malls, and hospitals, the US Department of Health and Human Services sent

FIGURE 5.4   An al-Qaeda Gunman Lobs a Live Grenade at a Group of Civilians in a Yemeni Hospital (McCluskey 2013)

a letter to officials in the public health sector warning of potential terrorist attacks and included a list of resources designed to prepare public health facilities for the threat of an active shooter. The UK also recently stepped up security at its hospitals. The National Counter Terrorism Security Office released an updated "Crowded Places Guidance" document, which tells medical professionals: "The worst-case scenario is your staff, patients, and visitors could be killed or injured, and your premises destroyed or damaged in a 'no warning' multiple and co-ordinated terrorist attack" (NACTSO 2017).

Nefarious Use of Ambulances

Ambulances are used in conflicts as vehicle-borne (VB) IEDs (Pakistan in 2013), as shooting platforms (Gaza in 2001), to move terrorists (Pakistan in 2004), to hide suicide belts (Gaza in 2002), and as getaway vehicles (Gaza in 2004). We have much to learn from these case studies in terms of hardening our hospitals to protect ambulances from theft, enhancing our laws regarding re-selling first-response vehicles, and educating first responders on the threat.

Terrorists use ambulances as VBIEDs in creative ways. January 12, 2013, was a deadly day in Quetta, Pakistan, with 103 people killed and more than 200 wounded in four separate, coordinated, and planned soft target attacks by the TTP. First, there was an attack at a mosque killing twenty-two worshippers, followed by a mass shooting at a recreational area used by Pakistan's military commandos, with another twelve dead. Next, a suicide bomber detonated his vest at a billiards hall packed with families. As police officers, journalists, and rescue workers rushed into the building, a second blast emanated from a bomb hidden in a stolen ambulance folding itself into the pack of response vehicles. The total death toll at the billiards hall was sixty-nine (Associated Press 2013).

The Taliban in Afghanistan has also used ambulances extensively in its attacks. For example, on April 7, 2011, Taliban suicide attackers used an ambulance VBIED to attack a police training center in the southern province of Kandahar. If actual ambulances are not available, groups will simply create one for the attack. In January 2010, the threat of cloned first-response vehicles came to light when, during coordinated attacks in downtown Kabul, the Taliban detonated a VBIED in a van disguised as an ambulance. The worst ambulance bombing in Afghanistan was January 28, 2018, when the Taliban drove an ambulance packed with explosives into a crowded street in Kabul, killing 103 people, injuring 200. The attacker passed the first checkpoint by claiming he had a patient. A simple vehicle check may have save lives.

HAMAS also uses ambulances to further their goals. On May 11, 2004, an Israeli television station aired footage of armed Arab terrorists in southern Gaza using an ambulance owned and operated by the United Nations to support Palestine refugees. Palestinian gunmen commandeered the emergency vehicle as getaway transportation after murdering six Israeli soldiers in Gaza City. The footage shows two ambulances with flashing lights pulling onto a street. Shots and shouts rang out during the nighttime raid, and then a gang of militants piled into one of the ambulances, clearly marked "UN" with the agency's blue flag flying from the roof, and sped away from the scene (Malkin 2004).

Consider how often first responders leave ambulances idling at the scene or at the hospital entrance. In rural areas, I have witnessed idling emergency vehicles at convenience stores and fast food restaurants. There are reports of ambulances stolen in the United States, and some were never recovered. But if a bad actor does not want to steal an ambulance (or build a clone), it is now possible simply to buy one on the Internet. Cash-starved communities often sell their old emergency response vehicles to fund a new fleet. Websites such as Ambulance Trader and Fire Truck Trader could be exploited by terrorists and criminals flush with cash who want to make a quick buy (Figure 5.5). Ambulances are now for sale on eBay and payable in full through PayPal, a nonbank that can be funded anonymously (Hesterman 2013).

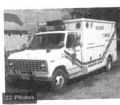

Ford : E-Series Van CHATEAU
1979 ford chateau e 350
ambulance

11h left
Friday, 12AM

$1,075.00
6 bids

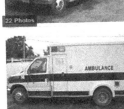

2002 Ford E350 Box Ambulance

$4,999.00
or Best Offer

⌃ 12 Watchers

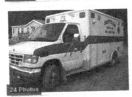

1994 E350 diesel ambulance
Runs Great !

14h left
Friday, 3AM

$2,025.00
17 bids
$3,500.00
Buy It Now

FIGURE 5.5   Ambulances for Sale at an Online Auction Site

Recognizing the growing threat, DHS issued an advisory in 2013, entitled "Terrorist Tradecraft: Impersonation Using Stolen, Cloned or Repurposed Vehicles" (DHS 2013b) with the following guidance:

Mitigating the Risk

Secure station or facility entrance and exit points, including apparatus bay doors.
Limit or lock unattended emergency vehicles.
Establish a policy for decommissioning vehicles.
Stay current on the "branding" of vehicles used by neighboring jurisdictions and mutual aid companies.
Consider using holograms on emergency vehicles for authentication.
Establish a stolen vehicle reporting process including "be on the lookout" warnings for high-interest vehicles.

Possible Indicators

Improperly marked emergency vehicles
Driver of emergency vehicle not knowledgeable about area of responsibility or service
Incorrect vehicle decal verbiage, colors, word font, and size
Visible identifiers such as phone numbers, license plates, or call numbers that are inconsistent with the vehicle's operating area or mission
Heavily loaded vehicle, possibly beyond capacity

In conclusion, schools, churches, and hospitals are places where citizens should feel safe and protected from danger. Unfortunately, there is an escalation in the number of attacks and scale of violence against these soft targets worldwide and here at home.

We are also no longer safe in the places we go for relaxation and entertainment; the next chapter explores the rising threat against shopping, sporting, and other recreational venues.

REFERENCES

ACLU (American Civil Liberties Union). "Spying on First Amendment Activity: State-by-State." New York City, New York, 2014.
American Association for the Advancement of Science. "Guide to R&D Funding Data: R&D at Colleges and Universities." Washington, DC: AAAS, 2017.
Al Jazeera. "Al-Qaeda Apologizes for Yemeni Hospital Attack." *Al Jazeera International Online*, December 22, 2013.

Araida, Saki, Evan Chiacchiaro, Georgia Garney, Elizabeth Lievens, Sundar Ramanujam, and Laura Sinclair. *Electoral Violence: A Study of the 2016 United States Presidential Election*. Washington, DC: Georgetown University, December, 2016.

Associated Press. "Bombings Kill 103 in Pakistan." *News Release*. www.nydailynews.com/news/world/bombing-pakistan-billiard-hall-kills-69-article-1.1237569 (2013).

———. "Friend of Dylann Roof Sentenced for Blocking Call to Police after Shooting." *The Guardian*, March 22, 2017.

Baptist Press. "LifeWay Christian Resources Survey: Prayer Is Most Urgent Concern for Churches." Nashville, TN, April 12, 2005.

BBC News. "Profile: Wisconsin Sikh Temple Shooter Wade Michael Page." www.bbc.co.uk/news/world-us-canada-19167324 (August 7, 2012).

Boone, Jon and Ewen MacAskill. "More Than 100 Children Killed in Taliban Attack on Pakistan School." *The Guardian*, December 16, 2014.

Bradshaw, Kelsey. "Sutherland Springs Church Shooter Went to New Braunfels High School, Worked at Schlitterbahn and HEB." *San Antonio Express-News*, November 6, 2017.

Brenner, Susan W. and Anthony C. Crescenzi. "State-Sponsored Crime: The Futility of the Economic Espionage Act." *Houston Journal of International Law* 28, no. 2 (Winter 2006).

Bui, Lynh. "Former Federal Officer Sentenced to Two Life Terms for Fatally Shooting Estranged Wife and Attempted Killing." *Washington Post*, September 6, 2017.

CDC (Centers for Disease Control and Prevention). *Schools and Terrorism: A Supplement to the National Advisory Committee on Children and Terrorism Recommendations to the Secretary*. Atlanta, GA: National Advisory Committee on Children and Terrorism, 2003.

Chinn, Carl. "Ministry Violence Statistics." www.carlchinn.com/deadly-force-statistics.html

Chivers, C. J. "The School." *New York Times*, March 14, 2007.

Church Committee, "Senate Select Committee to Study Governmental Operations with Respect to Intelligence Activities," Church Committee Reports, 1975.

Churchill, Ward and Jim Vander Wall. *The Cointelpro Papers: Documents from the FBI's Secret Wars against Dissent in the United States*. Cambridge, MA: South End Press, 2002.

Coletta, Amanda. "Quebec City Mosque Shooter Scoured Twitter for Trump, Right-Wing Figures Before Attack." *Washington Post*, April 8, 2018.

Connor, Tracy and Daniel Arkin. "Texas Gunman Devin Kelley Escaped from Mental Health Facility in 2012." *NBC News*, November 7, 2017.

Copello, Evan. "Case Study: 2014 Peshawar Massacre," 2018.
Cox, John Woodrow and Steven Rich. "Scarred by School Shootings." *The Washington Post*, March 25, 2018.
Cullen, Terence. "Survivors of Texas Massacre Recall Moment Gunman Entered Church." *New York Daily News*, November 7, 2017.
DHS (Department of Homeland Security). "The Federal Emergency Management Agency 428, Primer to Design Safe School Projects in Case of Terrorist Attacks." Washington, DC: FEMA, 2012.
———. "Homeland Security Academic Advisory Council Minutes." Washington, DC: Annual Meeting of the Homeland Security Academic Advisory Council, 2013a.
———. "Terrorist Tradecraft: Impersonation Using Stolen, Cloned or Repurposed Vehicles." https://publicintelligence.net/dhs-fbi-cloned-vehicles (April 3, 2013b).
DNI (Direction of National Intelligence). "Terrorist Groups, al-Shabaab." *National Counterterrorism Center*, 2018.
———. "Terrorist Groups, Tehrik-e Taliban Pakistan." *National Counterterrorism Center*, 2018.
Eaton, Emilie. "Comal County Authorities Didn't Charge Sutherland Springs Gunman with Rape, Even Though the Victim Described Brutal Attack." *San Antonio Express-News*, February 25, 2018.
Edelman, Susan. "New Stats Reveal Rise in Gun & Blade Seizures at City Schools." *New York Post*, September 30, 2017.
Educator's School Safety Network. "Fact Sheet: Thirty Days of Data after Parkland." http://eschoolsafety.org/parkland/ (October 27, 2018).
FBI (Federal Bureau of Investigation). FBI 2017 Uniform Crime Report (UCR) https://ucr.fbi.gov/crime-in-the-u.s/2017 (2017).
———. "Former University of Tennessee Professor John Reece Roth Sentenced to 48 Months in Prison for Illegally Exporting Military Research Technical Data." Knoxville, TN: US Attorney's Office, https://archives.fbi.gov/archives/knoxville/press-releases/2009/kx070109.html (2009).
———. "Higher Education and National Security: The Targeting of Sensitive, Proprietary, and Classified Information on Campuses of Higher Education." Washington, DC: US Department of Justice, www.fbi.gov/file-repository/higher-education-national-security.pdf/view (2011).
Fisk, Ralph R. "Siege at Beslan School Number One: Innocence Lost." Case Study, *Soft Target Hardening: Protecting People from Attack*, 1st ed., Boca Raton, FL: Taylor & Francis, 2014.
———. "Mass Shooting at First Baptist Church of Sutherland Springs, Texas." Case Study, *Soft Target Hardening: Protecting People from Attack*, 2nd ed., Boca Raton, FL: Taylor & Francis, 2019.

Ford, Dana and Ben Brumfeld. "Police: Minnesota Teen Planned School Massacre." www.cnn.com/2014/05/01/justice/minnesota-attack-thwarted/ (May 2, 2014).

Gallagher, Brian. "The Terrorist and WMD Threat in the Place of Worship." unpublished (2014).

Ganor, Boaz and Miri Halperin Wernli. *Terrorist Attacks against Hospitals Case Studies.* The Hague, Netherlands: International Institute for Counter-Terrorism, October 2013.

Gansler, Jamie and Alice Gast. "Academics and National-Security Experts Must Work Together." *Chronicle of Higher Education 54,* no. 44 (2008): A56.

Gill, Martin. *How Offenders Say They Get around Security Measures: Why They Say It Is Easy.* Dubai, UAE: ASIS Middle East 5, 2014.

Golden, Daniel. *Spy Schools: How the CIA, FBI, and Foreign Intelligence Secretly Exploit America's Universities.* New York: Henry Holt and Company, 2017.

———. "Why the Professor Went to Prison." *Business Week,* November 1, 2012.

Goldman, Adam, Richard Pérez-Peña, and Manny Fernández. "Texas Church Shooting Video Shows Gunman's Methodical Attack, Official Says." *The New York Times,* November 8, 2017.

Goode, Erica and Serge F. Kovaleski. "Details of Tsarnaev Brothers, Boston Suspects Emerge." *New York Times,* April 19, 2013.

Government Accounting Office. "Nuclear Nonproliferation: Additional Actions Needed to Improve Security of Radiological Sources at U.S. Medical Facilities" (GAO Publication No. 12-925). Washington, DC: U.S. Government Printing Office, September 2012.

Hawley, Chris and Matt Apuzzo. "NYPD Infiltration of Colleges Raises Privacy Fears." *Associated Press,* October 11, 2011.

Hayes, Theo. "J1 Students Describe Summertime Nightmare in Myrtle Beach." *WMBF News,* May 24, 2017.

Hesterman, Jennifer. *The Terrorist-Criminal Nexus: An Alliance of International Drug Cartels, Organized Crime, and Terror Groups.* Boca Raton, FL: CRC Press, 2013.

IBN Live. Terrorists Kill Man Who Gave Them Water." Mumbai, India: India Broadcast Network, November 27, 2008.

National Center for Education Statistics (NCES). "Indicators of School Crime and Safety." Washington, DC, https://nces.ed.gov/pubs2018/2018036.pdf (2017).

International Association for Healthcare Security and Safety (IAHSS). "Annual Healthcare Crime Survey." Chicago, IL, https://iahssf.org/crime-surveys/iahssf-crime-and-incident-survey-2017/ (2017).

Investigative Project on Terrorism (IPT). "USA v. Begolly, Emerson." Washington, DC: IPT, www.investigativeproject.org/case/554/us-v-begolly (2011).

———. "State of New York v. Ferhani et Ano." Washington, DC: IPT. www.investigativeproject.org/case/550/state-of-new-york-v-ferhani-et-ano (2014a).

———. "US v. El-Khalifi." Washington, DC: IPT. www.investigative-project.org/case/615/us-v-el-khalifi (2014b).

———. "USA v. Cromitie, James, et al." Washington, DC: IPT. www.investigativeproject.org/case/324/us-v-cromitie-et-al (2014c).

———. "USA v. Fahti, El Mehdi Semlali." Washington, DC: IPT. www.investigativeproject.org/case/662/us-v-fathi (2014d).

Johnson, Bryan. "Top 10 Chilling Quotes During School Shootings." http://listverse.com/2012/05/09/top-10-chilling-quotes-during-school-shootings/ (2012).

Johnson, Tim. "FBI Says Chinese Operatives Active at Scores of U.S. Universities." *McClatchey DC Bureau*, February 14, 2018.

Kenya Today. "Inside the Elite GSU Police Unit's RECCE Company That Took 12 Mins to Kill Garissa Terror Attackers." *Kenya Today*, April 4, 2015.

Kephart, Janice. "Immigration and Terrorism." *Center for Immigration Studies*, 2005.

Khan, Ismail. "Taliban Massacre 131 Schoolchildren: Principal among 141 Dead in Attack on Army Public School, Peshawar." *Dawn*, December 17, 2014.

Kornfield, Meryl. "Lawyers: Parkland Deputy Wasn't Legally Required to Stop Massacre." *South Florida Sun Sentinel*, June 15, 2018.

Krol, Charlotte. "Dylann Roof's Friend: Charleston Church 'Wasn't Primary Target.'" *The Telegraph*, June 20, 2015.

Leung, Rebecca. "New Video of the Beslan School Terror." Edited by *48 Hours Documentary CBS News*, 2005.

Lumb, David and Dominic Casciani. "Pavlo Lapshyn's 90 Days of Terror." *BBC News*, 2013.

Malkin, Michelle. "The Ambulances-for-Terrorists Scandal." *The Philadelphia Enquirer*, June 7, 2004.

Mayko, Michael P. "FBI: Drone-Like Toy Planes in Bomb Plot." *Connecticut Post*, April 7, 2014.

McCluskey, Brent. "Graphic CCTV Footage of Militant Attack in a Yemeni Hospital." *Podcast Audio*. www.guns.com/2013/12/14/graphic-cctv-footage-militant-attack-yemeni-hospital-video/ (2013).

McDaniel, Michael C. and Cali Mortenson Ellis. "The Beslan Hostage Crisis: A Case Study for First Responders." *Journal of Applied Security Research* 4 (2009): 21–35.

Mohr, Holbrook, Mitch Weiss, and Mike Baker. "U.S. Fails to Tackle Student Visa Abuses." *AP*, December 6, 2010.

Nakashima, Ellen. "FBI: Breakdown in Background Check System Allowed Dylann Roof to Buy Gun." *The Washington Post*, July 10, 2015.

National Counter Terrorism Security Office. "Crowded Places Guidance 2017." London, UK: National Counter Terrorism Security Office. www.gov.uk/government/uploads/system/uploads/attachment_data/file/701910/170614_crowded-places-guidance_v1a.pdf (June 2017).

Newsweek. "Kenya Arrests Five over Deadly Al-Shabaab Attack on University." *Newsweek Online*, www.newsweek.com/five-arrested-kenya-al-shabaab-attack-319666 (April 4, 2015).

Novak, Sophie. "Should Congress Speed Up Its Push for Terrorism Protection?" *National Journal* (April 14, 2014).

Odula, Tom and Rodney Muhumuza. "At Least 15 Dead as Gunmen Attack University in Kenya." *AP*, April 2, 2015.

Office of the Director of National Intelligence. *Annual Report to Congress on Foreign Economic Collection and Industrial Espionage.* Washington, DC: National Counterintelligence Center, Analysis Branch, 2011.

Pate, Amy, Michael Jensen and Erin Miller. "Background Report: Al-Shabaab Attack on Garissa University in Kenya." *START*, April 2015.

Pearce, Matt, John Savage, and Nina Adrawal. "In Texas, a Good Guy with a Gun Took on a Bad Guy with a Gun, Feeding Both Sides of the Gun Control Debate." *Los Angeles Times*, November 7, 2017.

Pew Research Center. "Trust in Government Nears Record Low." Washington, DC: Pew Research Center, 2017.

Phillips, Brian J. "Was What Happened in Charleston Terrorism?" *The Washington Post*, June 18, 2015.

Piegorsch, Walter W., Susan L. Cutter, and Frank Hardisty. "Benchmark Analysis for Quantifying Urban Vulnerability to Terrorist Incidents." *Risk Analysis* 27, no. 6 (2007): 1411–1425.

Rafalko, Frank J. *Mh/Chaos: The Cia's Campaign against the Radical New Left and the Black Panthers.* Annapolis, MD: Naval Institute Press, 2011.

Riecker, Tim. "Al-Shabaab Attack: Garissa University College." Case Study, *Soft Target Hardening: Protecting People from Attack*, 2nd ed., Boca Raton, FL: Taylor & Francis, 2019.

Rosenberg, Eli. "Texas Gunman's Ex-Wife Said He Once Put a Gun to Her Head and Asked, 'Do You Want to Die?'" *The Washington Post*, November 12, 2017.

Rush, James. "Peshawar Attack: Taliban Release Images of Gunmen Who Killed 132 Children as They Claim Massacre was Justified." *Independent UK*, December 17, 2014.

Schuster, Henry. "What Is Terrorism?" *CNN*, 2006.

Shapiro, Emily. "Key Moments in Charleston Church Shooting Case as Dylann Roof Pleads Guilty to State Charges." *ABC News Online*, 2017.

Silva, Christianna. "Texas Church Shooter Devin Kelley Said He Used Dogs As 'Target Practice.'" *Newsweek*, November 9, 2017.

Srivatsa, Naveen and Xi Zu. "Alleged Russian Spy Blends into Harvard." Boston, MA: The Harvard Crimson, 2010.

The Telegraph. "Gunmen in Pakistan Bomb Female Students' Bus Then Attack Hospital." June 15, 2013.

"Terror Operations: Case Studies in Terrorism." *TRADOC G2 Handbook* no. 1 (July 25, 2007): 6–19, Fort Leavenworth, KS: TRADOC Intelligence Support Activity (TRISA).

Turner, Allan and Craig Hlavaty. "Thieves Take $600,000 from Lakewood Church Safe." *The Houston Chronicle*, March 12, 2014.

United States Secret Service. "Mass Attacks in Public Places." Washington, DC: National Threat Assessment Center, 2018.

University of Maryland. "President's Task Force on Cybersecurity." www.umd.edu/datasecurity/ (2014).

US Department of Justice. "Affidavit, US v. Christopher R. Mestos et al." New York: Southern District of New York, United States Magistrate, 2010.

———. "Operation Xcellerator Press Conference." www.justice.gov/dea/speeches/xcellerator.pdf (2009).

———. "Texas Resident Arrested on Charge of Attempted Use of Weapon of Mass Destruction." Washington, DC: Office of Public Affairs, February 24, 2011.

———. workpermit.com. "Foreign Students to the U.S. Skip out on J-1 Visas, Become National Criminals." www.workpermit.com/news/2006_08_10/us/stud ent_visa_criminals.htm

WHAM Rochester, New York. "FBI Director: Charleston Shooting Not Terrorism." https://web.archive.org/web/20150628135934/http://13wham.com/news/features/nation-news/stories/fbi-director-charleston-shooting-not-terrorism-3408.shtml

WPRI Newport, Rhode Island. "Unusual Mob Partnership: Inside the Mafia Reveals Relationship with Gangs." www.youtube.com/watch?v=BYRreNJ-b9k (February 6, 2008).

Zapotsky, Mark. "Charleston Church Shooter: 'I Would Like to Make It Crystal Clear, I Do Not Regret What I Did.'" *Washington Post*, January 4, 2017.

Zuckerman, Jessica. *60 Terrorist Plots since 9/11: Continued Lessons in Domestic Counterterrorism*. Washington, DC: Heritage Foundation, 2014.

CHAPTER 6

Soft Target Threat Assessment

Malls, Sporting Events, and Recreational Venues

I think our name, Mall of America, is attractive to people that want to hurt America.

—**Maureen Bausch, executive vice president, Mall of America**
(Zwerdling et al. 2011)

INTRODUCTION

Not only are Americans targeted in the places in which they study, worship, and heal, but shopping and recreational venues are also now in the cross-hairs of violent criminals and terrorists. These profit-taking soft targets do not want to become fortresses and typically struggle with the challenge of balancing security with a pleasant customer experience. Unfortunately, the decision to lower the security construct in exchange for customer satisfaction and loyalty presents increasing risk to those who own and operate the venues. Although terrorism insurance protects loss of assets in the event of an attack, the loss of life on a property due to an attack is disastrous from an economic standpoint, as well as politically. The terrorist's main goals are achieved: instant notoriety for the group and the cause, a ripple of fear in the community, immediate impact to a business sector, and making the government appear to be unable to protect communities and civilians.

SHOPPING MALLS

The modern shopping mall is extremely large and glitzy, hosting more than just retailers; many also have crowd-drawing attractions. For example, most new malls in the Middle East have amusement parks with small roller coasters, Ferris wheels, laser tag, bumper cars, arcades, and bowling alleys. The Mall of America in Bloomington, Minnesota, is the largest in the country; it has a seven-acre indoor theme park, theaters, and nightclubs, as well as hosting the state's aquarium. The megamall has more than 500 stores, employing close to 12,000 workers and hosting more than 35 million visitors yearly, or 95,000 per day. On Black Friday, the mall's after-Thanksgiving visitor total is typically around 210,000, with thousands already standing in line before the 5 a.m. opening. This business owner's dream is also a security nightmare.

Malls have a unique vulnerability: there are many entrances versus limited or controlled checkpoints, making them extremely difficult to protect. As the opening quote in the chapter alludes, the mall's name alone may entice attack. For instance, the "Mall of America" and "Pentagon City" are not only soft target venues with thousands of unsuspecting, vulnerable shoppers, but also could be symbolic targets. The addition of attractions in or near a mall, such as a casino, could further anger radical Islamists, as was likely the case in the Westgate Mall attack in Nairobi. A collocated aquarium, zoo, or circus could draw the ire of single-interest terrorists such as ALF, putting the mall on their radar. If a mall store sells fur coats, that may also be a trigger. Indeed, intense protests against these venues happen worldwide on a regular basis by groups such as the Toronto Aquarium Resistance Alliance (TARA), Marineland Animal Defense (MAD), and Grassroots Ontario Animal Liberation (GOAL). Children's amusement park areas and daycare centers pose additional concerns as targets themselves or if the mall is attacked. These areas are typically located in a far recess of the building and are especially vulnerable. One of the worst daycare fires in history occurred at the new, luxurious Villagio Mall in Doha, Qatar, in May 2012, killing thirteen children and four employees, as well as two firefighters who tried to rescue them through the roof. Their single exit was at the top of a staircase, which collapsed, leaving them trapped in the room below.

Michael Rozin, an Israeli security expert, was formerly employed at the Mall of America as their special operations security captain and gave an informative interview about security at the facility. The mall calls its counterterrorism unit RAM, or risk assessment and mitigation. Rozin explains that, although detecting weapons is essential, assessing intent is equally if not more important. Therefore, his team was trained on behavioral recognition techniques to identify suspicious actors before they engage in a criminal or terrorist act. Rozin brought his experiences working security at the extraordinarily secure Ben-Gurion International Airport in Israel, where he learned behavioral detection and interviewing techniques (American Jewish World 2011). Human factors are extremely important in soft target situations where there are many access points such as malls and where technology, such as metal detectors and bag checks, is not available. Rozin's SIRA behavioral detection techniques are covered in Chapter 8 as an option for soft target venues without the ability to control entry points.

Mall violence has dramatically increased in the last few years, with violent fights, shootings, and even bombings. On December 26, 2011, the Mall of America was the scene of multiple violent fights with more than 200 youth involved. An Internet rumor about the presence of two popular rappers at the mall brought thousands of teenagers, who became enraged when they found no rappers or concert. This type of "mob violence" is on the rise in the United States and of concern in large venues. In 2011, in a racially motivated attack, a mob of fifty to one hundred African American teenagers attacked white patrons outside the fairgrounds at the Wisconsin State Fair. "Flash mob" attacks, fueled by the use of social media, have occurred in several US cities—Los Angeles, Chicago, Cleveland, Washington, DC, and Milwaukee. Philadelphia was the site of several flash mobs in 2017. On March 6, at least 500 teens who connected on social media turned up near city hall at 5:30 p.m. and wreaked havoc, resulting in assaults, shoplifting, store damage, and thirty arrests. On July 17, a rec center barbecue (which police deemed an unauthorized gathering) turned violent when 400 teens confronted police, throwing bottles and rocks, and jumping on vehicles. On November 22, more than 100 teenagers converged in a market area, terrorizing restaurant patrons and vandalizing stores.

This type of spontaneous violence, also dubbed "urban terrorism" is difficult to detect and prevent. However, the 2013 terrorist attack against the Westgate Mall in Nairobi, Kenya, showed sophisticated planning and methodical execution, raising the bar for mall security officials worldwide.

Case Study: The Nairobi Mall Attack

Saturday, September 21, 2013, was Kenya's annual International Day of Peace. However, the day was anything but peaceful; at noon, armed militants affiliated with the Somali terrorist group al-Shabaab stormed the Westgate Mall in Nairobi, Kenya. Over the next four days, at least sixty-seven people died, 175 were injured, and the mall was destroyed. Reports at the time were disjointed and confusing and after months of investigation by US, British, and Israeli experts, there is still little clarity about exactly what transpired, who was involved, or how the Kenyan security forces' response may have exacerbated the problem. However, the successful soft target attack provides insight to security experts and first responders regarding this new page in the terrorists' playbook.

THE ATTACK

The upscale Westgate Mall, owned by an Israeli businessman, sits across a park from the US and Canadian embassies and is frequented by Westerners and affluent Kenyans, making it a lucrative target. Even after a wave of bombings throughout Kenya in 2012 at the hands of al-Hijra, an al-Shabaab-affiliated group, security measures at the mall were described as cursory. Confidential documents accessed by the Sunday Telegraph newspaper showed the United Nations had been warned, in the previous month, that the threat of an "attempted large-scale attack" in Kenya was "elevated" (Pflanz and Alexander 2013). One week before the attack, Kenyan police claimed to have disrupted a major attack in its final stages of planning after arresting two people with suicide vests packed with ball bearings, grenades, and AK-47 assault rifles. A manhunt was also launched for eight more suspects (Pflanz and Alexander 2013). After the incident, Nairobi senator Mike Sonko claimed he warned the security services of a possible attack against the mall three months previously (Jambo News 2013).

The attack commenced when gunmen entered the mall and began shooting and throwing grenades. Initial reports of fifteen gunmen simultaneously entering the building from the main entrance, the rooftop parking lot, and a ramp into the basement (BBC 2013a) were disproven after reviewing CCTV footage. It appears there were likely only four to six gunmen, most of whom entered through the main entrance and then split into teams (Pflanz 2014). They carried hand grenades, AK-47 assault rifles, and ordinary munitions. Panic ensued as unsuspecting shoppers tried to flee or take cover. The initial attack was ruthless, including the killing of children who were attending a cooking competition in the parking lot. According to survivors, the attackers attempted to separate Muslims and non-Muslims and allowed most Muslims to leave unharmed. One woman declared to the attackers she was a Muslim; however, attackers shot her for not being dressed conservatively enough. Hostages were gathered and held in the cinema and casino on the second floor and in the basement. The situation was extremely complex, with responding law enforcement units likely unaware of the severity of the situation or the sophistication of the actors.

Despite the first calls for help, the police did not arrive on scene until 12:30 p.m. Thirty minutes later, they entered the mall to attempt rescue operations for the unknown number of people trapped inside. Kenyan Defense Forces (KDF) military personnel arrived at 3:00 p.m. and also entered the mall, engaging the shooters. The transition of command authority at the scene from police operations to military was poorly coordinated; the police later asserted that while helping people escape, they were mistaken for the attackers and fired upon by the military (BBC Africa 2013b). The police and military were using different radio frequencies, neither had mall blueprints, and the Kenyan military scrambled to fly their best-trained soldiers back from Somalia (Kulish, Gettleman, and Kron 2013). CCTV footage shows Kenyan security forces abandoning the search for the shooters and, instead, looting stores within hours of the siege. A jewelry store was emptied, and security forces looted watch and clothing shops, grabbed cash from tills and ATMs, and tried to shoot their way into a casino safe. At about 10:30 p.m., footage shows four attackers holed up in an office, one of them injured, while security forces stroll around the mall with bags full of merchandise and cash (Dixon 2013).

By Sunday, more than 1,000 people had been rescued from the mall, but government forces did not have control, and gunfire continued throughout the day. The death toll was up to fifty-nine and the attackers were still loose in the mall. Israeli commandos and specialized police officers arrived, along with American-supplied night vision goggles for the Kenyan forces. On Monday the government launched another offensive. There were loud explosions and sounds of gunfire, and smoke began to pour out of the building as the rear of the building collapsed; the death toll was up to sixty-two and it was believed there were more hostages inside. On Tuesday, the police declared the operation over, although there were still reports of sporadic gunfire as they cleared the mall. The final toll was at least sixty-seven people dead, including six security personnel and several terrorists who were in the rear of the shopping center when it collapsed. Some remains were burned beyond recognition and not capable of yielding DNA evidence; authorities believe the death count could have been as high as ninety-four (Butime 2014).

THE PLANNING

The attackers rented a small shop in the mall to gain access to otherwise prohibited areas such as storage rooms and service elevators. This also would have given them access before and after shopping hours, and they used this time to pre-position weapons and ammunition in a ventilation shaft (BBC 2013a; BBC Africa 2013b). Their presence in the mall provided opportunity to assess which areas would yield the highest casualties, and whether there were scheduled events to target, such as the children's cook-off outside the grocery store.

Western investigators from the United Kingdom, the United States, and Israel were called to help with the investigation. At one point the FBI had more than eighty investigators on scene, including members of the Evidence Response Team (ERT), who helped process the scene (FBI 2014). Despite initial reports of fifteen heavily armed attackers, investigators all concluded the attack was probably carried out by a group of four to six people with only a basic plan and light weapons, grenades to gain entry to the mall, and a few AK-47s. Kenyan officials disagree, insisting a larger force was involved in a detailed, intricate plan. A team of four to six gunmen thwarting

Kenyan government control for four days makes the government look ineffectual and ill prepared, especially given the known threats against Kenya. Therefore, it is easy to see why officials in Nairobi failed to embrace the investigative reports.

There is also confusion over the status of the attackers. Although it is possible some of the attackers may have put down weapons and left with the fleeing customers, there is no evidence to prove this theory. To add further confusion, after reviewing thousands of hours of CCTV footage, investigators from the New York Police Department said there is no evidence the militants were in the mall after the first day and they all most likely escaped in the confusion (New York City Police Department 2013). The FBI disagrees with this assessment, with their Nairobi LEGAT stating:

We believe, as do the Kenyan authorities, that the four gunmen inside the mall were killed. Our ERT made significant finds, and there is no evidence that any of the attackers escaped from the area where they made their last stand. Three sets of remains were found. Also, the Kenyans were on the scene that first day and set up a very secure crime scene perimeter, making an escape unlikely. Additionally, had the attackers escaped, it would have been publicly celebrated and exploited for propaganda purposes by al-Shabaab. That hasn't happened (FBI 2014).

Months after the attack, precious little information has been added to the initial investigations and few security forces have been held accountable for their ineffective and even deplorable behavior at the scene. There are four men on trial in Nairobi for aiding the attackers; all deny the charges (Pflanz 2014). Pseudonyms were released by Kenyan authorities less than a month after the attacks; however, a *New York Times* article in January 2014 listed what are believed to be the men's given names, including Hassan Abdi Dhuhulow, a Somali-born Norwegian national (BBC 2013a). Al-Shabaab claimed three Americans were involved in the Westgate Mall attack, naming Ahmed Mohamed Isse of St. Paul, Minnesota; Abdifatah Osman Keenadiid of Minneapolis, Minnesota; and Gen Mustafe Noorudiin of Kansas City, Missouri, via their Twitter account, @HSM_Press (http://jihadology.net/2013/09/21/new-statement-from-%E1%B8%A5arakat-al-shabab-al-mujahidin-claiming-responsibility-for-the-westgate-mall-attack-in-nairobi/). Al-Shabaab's claims have not been confirmed by American law enforcement. In addition, additional Twitter accounts claiming to be al-Shabaab-run have suggested that other Americans were also involved.

The threat in Kenya has not subsided, and US citizens are cautioned by the State Department regarding travel to the country and the threat of attacks against soft targets and kidnapping. For example, on March 17, 2014, a SUV packed with 350 pounds of explosives was found in the port of Mombasa and there may be two additional vehicles at large (Pflanz 2014). The FBI assessment is that attacks in Kenya will continue to be al-Shabaab's primary external focus.

(Source: Kinzer 2014. Ms. Kinzer is a Reserve Air Force intelligence officer and senior intelligence consultant at Patch Plus Consulting.)

Significant Overseas Mall Attacks

On July 22, 2016, a shooting started at the McDonald's outside the Olympia shopping mall, in Munich, Germany, and moved inside the mall. Ten people, including the perpetrator, were killed and thirty-six others were injured. The gunman, 18-year-old Iranian-German David (Ali) Sonboly, died from a self-inflicted gunshot wound. Although authorities established no direct link to terrorism, all of the victims were immigrants who frequented the McDonalds and it was Sonboly's main target. The final accounting determined the shooting was likely a hate crime against immigrants; Sonboly professed his adoration of Hitler and considered himself part of the Aryan nation. Hamas is also targeting shopping malls. Shin Bet, Israel's intelligence agency, foiled a bomb attack plotted by Hamas timed for the High Holy Days in September 2013. Two men employed as maintenance workers at the upscale Mamilla Mall were planning to smuggle the bomb into the shopping center and to hide it in a closet. Their handlers ordered them to plant the bomb in a restaurant, store, or trash can and to cover it with wrapping paper, in order to make it look like a gift in preparation for the upcoming Jewish holidays, and to detonate the device when the mall was packed with shoppers. One scenario included wrapping the device in a box of chocolates and placing it in a garbage can, according to the indictment (Lappin and Bob 2013). The Irish Republican Army (IRA) also targeted shopping areas; on the morning of June 15, 1996, a cargo van filled with 3,300 pounds of explosives exploded in the middle of a busy shopping center in Manchester, England, injuring more than 200 people. England was hosting the 1996 European Football Championship that year, and a match between German and Russian soccer teams was scheduled for the next day in Manchester's stadium.

Terrorist Threats Against US Malls

Al-Qaeda, splinter al-Shabaab (responsible for the Nairobi attack), and ISIS have all called for mall attacks in the United States; their videos

FIGURE 6.1   Screenshot From al-Shabaab Video Threatening the Mall of America, February 22, 2015

are still posted online. The United States has more than 1,000 shopping malls, although the industry is in decline, and experts predict about a quarter will likely close in the next five years, mostly due to changing shopping habits of Americans. The enclosed nature of malls, which used to cater to families, also lends itself to groups that "linger," such as gangs and large groups of teenagers, a factor also driving away shoppers. Some malls are tearing down the traditional three-story structures and rebuilding with an "open air" concept to address crime and add convenience for shoppers. Several mall terror plots were intercepted by law enforcement just after 9/11. Nuradin M. Abdi, a Somali immigrant living in Columbus, Ohio, was arrested in November 2003 and charged in a plot to bomb a local shopping mall and shoot the evacuating shoppers. Abdi traveled to Ethiopia purposely to receive training at an Islamist camp in construction of explosives for his operation (Investigative Project on Terrorism: US v. Nuradin Abdi 2014b). Abdi recently finished his ten-year term in federal prison and was deported to Ethopia.

Derrick Shareef was arrested in December 2006 on charges he planned to set off hand grenades in a shopping mall outside Chicago. Shareef acted alone and met with an undercover agent. FBI reports indicated the mall was one of several potential targets, including courthouses, city halls, and government facilities. Shareef, however, settled on attacking a mall in the days immediately preceding Christmas because he believed it would cause the greatest amount of chaos and damage (Investigative Project on Terrorism US v. Shareef 2004). Shareef was sentenced to thirty-five years in prison without the possibility of parole.

Tarek Mehanna, previously indicted for lying to the FBI about the location of terrorist suspect Daniel Maldonado, was arrested on October 21, 2009, on allegations of conspiracy to kill two US politicians, American troops in Iraq, and civilians in local shopping malls (Investigative Project on Terrorism: US v. Mehanna 2014a). He was sentenced to eighteen years in jail. His co-conspirator, Ahmad Abousamra, a former Boston resident who fled to his home country of Syria, is on the FBI's most wanted list for attempting to obtain military training in Pakistan and Yemen for the purpose of killing American soldiers overseas.

The first successful terrorist attack at a US shopping mall happened on September 17, 2016, at the Crossroads Center shopping mall in St. Cloud, Minnesota. At 8:15 p.m., 20-year-old Dahir Adan, a Somali-American inspired by ISIS, began his premeditated stabbing attack at a store just outside the mall then moved inside. Armed with two steak knives, one 10 inches and the other 9 inches, Adan made references to Allah during his attack, including shouting "Allahu Akbar" and asking people if they were Muslim. Adan stabbed nine people before Jason Falconer, a firearms instructor and part-time police officer, pursued and then fatally shot him in a Macy's store. Adan was previously employed part-time as a guard by Securitas and was wearing his uniform during the attack (*Star Tribune* 2016). Victims were stabbed or punched in the back, shoulder, head, neck, or face. They were aged from 15 to 53; all survived. ISIS took credit for the attack.

Just six days later, on September 23, 2016, five people were killed in a mass shooting at the Cascade Mall in Burlington, Washington, US. The gunman was identified as Arcan Cetin, a 20-year-old who emigrated from Turkey as a child with his family. Cetin bought a ticket to an evening showing of the movie Snowden and propped open the theater's exit door with his cell phone, an action reminiscent to the 2012 Aurora shooting. A moviegoer found the phone and turned it into a theater kiosk, where Cetin subsequently retrieved it. Shortly before 7:00 p.m., Cetin walked into a Macy's store with a stolen rifle and opened fire, killing four women and one man. Cetin told authorities he was interested in ISIS, but when asked if the terrorist group had inspired his actions he replied, "I can't answer that" (McNerthney 2017). On social media, Cetin posted photos of serial killer Ted Bundy and Islamic State leader Abu Bakr al-Baghdadi. ISIS also took credit for this attack. Cetin also had recent arrests, mental health issues, and a former girlfriend who worked at Macy's. On April 16, 2017, Cetin committed suicide by hanging himself in his jail cell.

On November 12, 2017, Mahad A. Abdiraham, a 20-year-old Minneapolis man, slashed two brothers inside Macy's at the Mall of America with an 8-inch blade, causing severe injuries. Abdiraham declared in court he was answering "the call for Jihad" on behalf of ISIS, who claimed credit for the attack.

Abdiraham had a history of psychiatric problems and read a statement in court professing his loyalty to ISIS (Walsh 2018).

In May 2018, 17-year-old American Matin Azizi-Yarand was accused of planning an ISIS-inspired mass shooting at a Dallas, Texas, mall, the Stonebriar Center in Frisco. He planned to release his manifesto "Message to America" pledging his allegiance to ISIS. Azizi-Yarand is spent $1,400 on weapons and tactical gear for his alleged attack. He accessed online radical Islamist propaganda and planned to construct pipe bombs using information regarding the Columbine shooting.

US malls have also been the scene of several attacks involving lone gunmen with no apparent motive, other than homicidal or suicidal intentions. On January 26, 2014, a suicidal 19-year-old man, Darion Marcus Aguilar, went to his favorite store, popular with skateboarders, and killed two employees and then himself at a mall in Columbia, Maryland. He also carried two makeshift bombs in his backpack, cobbled together with fireworks. In other random mall attacks, a 22-year-old man killed two people and then himself at a mall near Portland, Oregon, in December 2012; a 19-year-old man killed eight people and then himself at an Omaha, Nebraska, mall in December 2007; and an 18-year-old man killed five people before he was killed by police at a mall in Salt Lake City, Utah, in February 2007. Malls seem to be irresistible to violent actors who want to enter the scene without being challenged and kill a maximum amount of people in the shortest period of time.

Following the Nairobi mall attack and other incidents, the FBI and Department of Homeland Security stepped up exercises at major malls in the United States as part of the Complex Mall Attack Initiative preparedness initiative established in late 2013 to promote preparedness and strengthen public/private partnerships. Exercises were held at malls in at least twelve states in 2014, however the program has slowly lost momentum. See the section on malls in Chapter 9 for information regarding my work on a series of tabletop crisis response exercises.

Shopping Centers

Shopping centers are not lucrative soft targets due to their open, sprawling nature and dispersed populace, however a tenant of interest may draw terrorists to the location. For example, a new practice, particularly in the south, is to convert large retail spaces vacated by "block stores" into megachurches. Strip malls may house businesses which could trigger terror groups with certain ideologies, for instance adult entertainment, casinos, and alcohol stores. Businesses in the proximity of these potential targets should prepared to respond to "spill over" from an attack.

A more typical shopping center tenant is a military recruiting station, seeking visibility, easy access, and foot traffic for potential recruits. This desire to embed with the public makes these military operations vulnerable targets. Both al-Qaeda and ISIS routinely call for attacks on service members and their families, and anti-government groups lash out during times of heightened military operations abroad.

Routine malicious activities at strip mall recruiting offices consist of vandalism, graffitiing, and throwing pipe bombs. Major attacks against recruiting stations include the Times Square bombing in March 2008, when an unknown individual on a bike planted an incendiary device at 3:30 a.m.; there were no injuries. A June 2009 drive-by shooting attack at an army recruiting center in Little Rock, Arkansas, left one soldier dead, and another critically wounded. The attacker, American Abdulhakim Mujahid Muhammad, born Carlos Leon Bledsoe, radicalized while living in Yemen and was inspired by al-Qaeda in the Arabian Peninsula (AQAP). His attack plan started in Little Rock; first he drove to Nashville and threw a Molotov cocktail at an orthodox rabbi's house, but the device failed to detonate. His next target was an army recruiting center in Florence, Kentucky, selected due to its proximity to the highway and the Ohio border. Thankfully, the center was closed. He then returned to Little Rock, where he shot the soldiers at the recruiting station. The father of the deceased soldier, Private William Long, later remarked: "They weren't on the battlefield; but apparently, the battlefield's here" (Dao and Johnston 2009).

In October and November 2010, Yonathan Melaku, a former US soldier inspired by al-Qaeda, carried out a string of attacks in the northern Virginia area, including firing on the Marine Corps recruiting substation in Chantilly, and the Coast Guard recruiting center in Woodbridge, both located in shopping centers. The worst attack against a shopping center occurred in 2015 at the hands of al-Qaeda-inspired Mohammed Youssuf Abdulazeez.

Case Study: The Chattanooga Recruiting Office Shootings

On June 16th, 2015, the United States was rocked by an attack on two recruiting offices in Chattanooga, Tennessee, by a self-radicalized lone wolf actor. The attacks left four marines and one navy sailor dead, at two recruiting offices that were more than seven miles away from each other. The attacker, Muhammad Youssef Abdulazeez, started his rampage at the Armed Forces Recruiting Center (AFRC) and continued it by driving to the US Naval and Marine Reserve Center (NMRC).

The AFRC was located in a strip mall, situated between a wireless store and an Italian restaurant. The attack began around 10:50 a.m., with a volley of fire being directed at the AFRC, sending the army and marine personnel inside to take cover and barricade themselves in their offices. After the first burst of rounds, an eyewitness saw Abdulazeez back up his rental Ford Mustang, realign it, and started his second and final volley of rounds, never once leaving his vehicle. Only one marine was injured in this first attack. Abdulazeez then sped off to the NMRC, seven miles away.

At this time, police were responding to the first call at the AFRC, not knowing that the attacker had fled the scene. At 10:58 a.m., police received another "shots fired" call at the NMRC. The NMRC was a much more secured location than the AFRC and had an entry gate. Abdulazeez plowed through the entry gate of the Reserve Center and ditched his vehicle in front of the building. He carried a single assault rifle, a handgun, and a vest full of ammunition into the building, leaving one assault rifle in his vehicle. The twenty marines and two naval corpsman inside managed to get almost everyone out of the building. One serviceman managed to fire several shots at Abdulazeez, but it is unclear if he was hit during this exchange. At this point, he was able to storm the office and mortally wound Navy Petty Officer 2nd Class Randall Smith, who died two days later. Several marines went back into the center to attempt to provide cover for people who escaped through the rear gated motor pool. Abdulazeez fired into the group, wounding four marines. He then re-entered the building where Chattanooga police officers were waiting. There was an exchange of fire, wounding one police officer and killing Abdulazeez. By the time ambulances arrived at the scene, the four marines, Sgt. Carson Holmquist, Gunnery Sgt. Thomas Sullivan, Lance Cpl. Squire "Skip" Wells, and Staff Sgt. David A. Wyatt were already dead (Timeline from Bradbury 2015).

THE ATTACKER

Mohammod Youssuf Abdulazeez was a 24-year-old naturalized US citizen. He was born in Kuwait and had Jordanian citizenship. He attended high school and college in Chattanooga and was described as "polite" by those that knew him before the incident. Abdulazeez never pinged the FBI's radar, but his father, Youssuf Abdulazeez, was previously investigated for funding a potential terrorist organization (Fausset, Blinder, and Schmidt 2015). Abdulazeez's only signs of deviance were speeding citations and a driving while intoxicated arrest, for which he had an upcoming court appearance.

At some point, there was a change in Abdulazeez. He went from clean-cut to dawning a beard and blogging messages such as "life is short and bitter . . . do not let the opportunity to submit to Allah . . . pass you by" (SITE 2015). Federal investigators believe that Abdulazeez radicalized when he visited family in the Middle East in July of 2014. It also was revealed that he was a follower of the online teachings of the deceased al-Qaeda leader Anwar al-Awlaki (Khorram, Yasmin, and Zamost 2015). These revelations led investigators to officially call Abdulazeez an inspired terrorist.

PLANNING

Investigators determined the attack was planned but not far in advance. Abdulazeez made several trips to the Middle East between 2010 and 2014, but nothing indicated that he had planned the attack during those visits. One thing was clear to investigators, he wanted to commit Jihad in the United States. Al-Qaeda did not claim the attack, but they praised it and called for more lone wolf attacks.

LESSONS LEARNED

There were widespread policy implications from this attack. The governor of Tennessee at the time, Bill Haslam, mandated stricter sentencing for individuals who commit crimes against uniformed members of the military. Also, a nationwide debate about allowing members of the Armed Forces to protect themselves with personal firearms on bases ensued. Twenty-three states, including Tennessee, updated policies to allow selected trained guard members to carry personal or government issued firearms. The Pentagon also clarified a policy that gave authority to commanders to allow subordinates to carry firearms. The intent of these policies was to give highly trained individuals the right to protect themselves from future attackers.

(Source: Copello 2019b. Mr. Copello is a data scientist and researcher at the University of North Florida, with a focus on the psychology of terrorism.)

Vulnerable Open-Air Marketplaces

As the center of economy for poor villages and towns, open-air marketplaces are a soft target routinely singled out in war-torn countries. The open-air market is an attractive target because overwhelming firepower and planning are not necessary to cause mass casualties. For example, on February 5, 1994, during the Bosnian war, a 120-millimeter mortar shell fired by Serbian forces landed in the Markale marketplace in Sarajevo during the busy lunch hour. UN observers reported 168 people were killed and 144 more wounded. These types of attacks against innocent civilians as they go about their daily routine can even change the course of a war. Markale was struck eighteen months later, on August 28, 1995, again during lunch hour. This time, Bosnian forces fired five mortar shells, killing forty-three people and wounding seventy-five others. The event pulled an angry NATO into the conflict, and its punishing airstrikes against Bosnian Serb forces brought them to the table for the Dayton Peace Accords and a negotiated peace.

Hamas and the Popular Front for the Liberation of Palestine (PFLP) routinely target open-air markets in Israel. A PFLP-led suicide attack against the Netanya produce market on May 19, 2002, killed three people and injured fifty-six. The perpetrator dressed as an Israeli defense forces soldier and easily accessed the market. The entrance was selected for the attack because it historically had a bottleneck of customers and would yield the greatest number of casualties. Hamas struck the Mahane Yehuda Market on July 30, 1997, with two consecutive suicide bombings. The market is Jerusalem's main open-air fruit and vegetable market. Sixteen people were killed in the attack and 178 were injured.

We must consider the vulnerability of open-air markets in our country; for instance, farmers' markets and flea markets. Similar venues are popular on weekend days in large US cities, when blocked off city streets become marketplaces and entertainment venues, and they, too, are completely unprotected. Another vulnerability in cities are tall buildings, providing window and rooftop platforms for attackers. As with all mass gatherings of citizens, detecting bad actors and their weaponry is difficult; therefore, the best way to address this threat is through a hardened posture for deterrence, active crowd policing for mitigation, and emergency response assets positioned nearby.

SPORTS VENUES

Large sporting events are of perennial interest to terrorists, as this vulnerable soft target serves two of their needs. First, there is a large crowd of unsuspecting, vulnerable people and, second, the added benefit of live television coverage to amplify the terror effect to millions of viewers.

Stadiums and Arenas in the Crosshairs

More than 1,300 professional sport stadiums and arenas in the United States are used for a variety of events from school graduations to concerts, political events, and evacuation and sheltering locations in natural or national emergencies. As such, the Department of Homeland Security (DHS) identifies sport stadiums/arenas as critical infrastructure/key resource (CI/KR) key assets. However, as with all soft target locations, the government relies on the venue owners and operators to secure their properties and users properly. Perhaps college stadiums have the most vulnerability, since schools have fewer resources for security. Dr. Stacey Hall, an expert on spectator sports safety and security, has written several outstanding articles and books on the topic, worthy of review by all who own, operate, or secure these venues. According to Dr. Hall (2010), college stadium vulnerabilities include:

Lack of emergency and evacuation plans specific to sport venue.
Inadequate searching of venue prior to event.
Inadequate searches of fans and belongings.
Improperly secured concessions.
Dangerous chemicals stored inside the sport venue.
No accountability for vendors and their vehicles.
Inadequate staff training in security awareness and response to
   WMD (weapons of mass destruction) attacks.

Stadiums are high on al-Qaeda's list of targets. The Encyclopedia of
Afghan Jihad), found in the London residence of Islamic cleric Sheikh
Abu Hamza al-Masri, proposed football stadiums as possible terrorist
attack sites. In July 2002, the FBI issued an alert warning about suspects
with links to al-Qaeda affiliates who were downloading stadium images
from www.worldstadiums.com, including the Edward Jones Dome in
St. Louis and the RCA Dome in Indianapolis (Grace 2002). In response
to these and other threats, DHS developed an extensive national planning scenarios document to cover possible terrorist attacks specifically
aimed at stadiums. The 2005 document specifically addressed the potential of a biological attack on a sports arena, stating how the spreading of
pneumonic plague in the bathrooms would potentially kill 2,500 people.
DHS's 2006 planning scenarios included a light aircraft spraying a
chemical agent into a packed college football stadium, contaminating
the stadium and generating a downwind vapor hazard (DHS 2006). The
advent of drones strengthened the possibility of a WMD attack on a
stadium.
     The only good news is that, unlike malls, entrance points to most
sporting and recreating venues can be limited, bags checked, and behavior assessed. However, the cost to secure a stadium of 75,000 people
or an Olympic venue is exorbitant, especially if protecting against an
unknown threat. For example, in response to threats against its games,
the NFL instituted mandatory pat-downs at entrances, upsetting the venues and teams, which had to pay extra for security and to handle irate
fans. US taxpayers were outraged at the $300 million price tag for the
2002 Winter Olympics in Utah, yet the 2014 Sochi Olympics cost $50
billion, including extreme security measures to protect from terrorist
attacks.
     As an international event on the world stage, the Olympics have
always been a target for nefarious groups and actors. The first major
terrorist attack against a sporting event was at the 1972 Munich Games,
when the Palestinian terrorist group Black September took the Israeli
national team hostage, eventually killing eleven athletes and coaches
and one West German police officer. The world was transfixed on the
event, as the kidnappers and their hostages could be seen on television

through their hotel windows. German officials devised a sound rescue plan, Operation Sunshine; unfortunately, members of the International Olympic Committee went on television and gave the details. Unbeknownst to them, the terrorists were watching and learned of the plan. After more failed negotiations, a new rescue strategy was developed involving escape helicopters, with snipers targeting terrorists as they walked across the airfield with the hostages. However, the number of terrorists and their firepower were underestimated; the snipers were unable to gain control of the situation, and all of the athletes were killed in the rescue attempt.

The Olympic scene was quiet until Eric Robert Rudolph, a former US Army soldier and member of Christian Identity (a white nationalist group), attacked the 1996 Atlanta Games. At 1:20 a.m. on July 27, 1996, a bomb was detonated in Centennial Olympic Park, an entertainment and vendor area. The blast killed two people and injured more than 100. According to Rudolph, in a riveting *Sports Illustrated* oral history of the bombing, the attack was meant to shut the Games down, not kill people:

> The plan was to clear the park, and hopefully after clearing the park and the explosion, this would create a state of instability in Atlanta, potentially shut the Games down or at least eat into the profits that the Games were going to make. The idea was to use them as warning devices, not to target people. . . . In retrospect, it was a poor decision.
>
> (Zaccardi 2012)

After placing the bomb, which had a 55-minute timer, Rudolph called in two bomb threats to 911, anticipating the park would be cleared. As he watched from a distance, security officers inspected the bag and determined it was a bomb. Much to his surprise, people were still milling around the area when the device detonated: the bomb threat information was never transmitted to the scene. As Rudolph left the park, he detonated four unexploded devices in a trash can outside the park instead of planting them. Unfortunately, the security guard who originally noticed the suspicious bag containing the bomb, Richard Jewell, was named as the prime suspect while Rudolph slipped out of Atlanta. After seven years on the run and bombings at abortion clinics and a lesbian bar, Rudolph was caught by a rookie police officer in 2003 while scavenging food from a dumpster; he is currently serving four life terms at the supermax prison in Colorado. The only attack he ever apologized for was the one against the Olympics.

The Basque separatist group ETA targeted the 2002 European Champions Soccer League final in Madrid, Spain. On May 1, 2002, a car bomb exploded near Santiago Bernabeu stadium hours before the game, and a second car bomb exploded a half hour later about one mile away.

Seventeen people were injured in the attacks. However, in a show of defiance to the terrorist group, officials went ahead with the game with 75,000 fans in attendance. Also, the Boston Marathon was not the first running race targeted by terrorists. On April 6, 2008, a suicide bomber detonated a device at the start of a Sri Lankan marathon, killing fifteen people and injuring a hundred. The terrorist group Liberation Tigers of Tamil Eelam (LTTE) took responsibility for the attack (New York Times 2008).

There have been several sporting event threats or attacks in the United States. In June 2003, a bomb threat was made against Continental Airlines Arena during game five of the NBA finals, and responding police found ten cars on fire in the arena parking lot. In October 2005, an Oklahoma University student suicide bomber strapped a detonating device to his body outside the school's stadium during a football game, killing only himself. His apartment had jihadist and bomb-making material, as well as a cache of the explosive triacetone triperoxide (TATP), a favorite of al-Qaeda terrorists. In October 2006, the National Football League received an uncorroborated threat indicating the use of radiological "dirty bombs" against seven National Football League stadiums.

Finally, in the worst attack against a sporting venue in the United States, the Boston Marathon bombings on April 15, 2013, were carried out by brothers Tamerlan and Dzhokhar Tsarnaev, naturalized US citizens of Chechen descent. The attack killed three people, and wounded more than two hundred. Tamerlan was clearly the ringleader—a vicious killer who was posthumously implicated in a prior unsolved triple homicide of his best friend and two others in Boston. At some point, he was (at the very least) communicating with and inspired by radical Islamists. The brothers used an edition of al-Qaeda in the Arabian Peninsula's *Inspire* magazine to construct the pressure cooker bombs, which, interestingly, are used in many Chechen rebel attacks. However, in a show of psychological resiliency, the city hosted a marathon a few weeks later for those unable to complete in the main event. In April 2014, Boston held a full-up marathon event with thousands of security officers and the event itself went off without incident. However, a week before, a man dressed in black, screaming "Boston strong," walked down the middle of Boylston Street with two backpacks containing rice cookers; the bags were detonated by law enforcement. Although not a terrorism-related event, it rattled the nerves in the still-healing city.

The worst attack at a stadium occurred when the Kurdish Freedom Hawks (TAK), a breakaway group of the Kurdistan Worker's Party (PKK), conducted twin bombings in Istanbul on December 12, 2016. First, they remotely detonated a car bomb with 300–400 kilograms of explosives and shortly after, a suicide bomber targeted fleeing people at Macka Park, less than a mile away. Of the forty-four killed, thirty were police officers.

The al-Qaeda splinter group al-Shabaab, which recruits from the Somali population in Minneapolis, targets sporting venues in both Somalia and Uganda. The Mexican cartels are particularly cruel, targeting children's soccer matches and sports-themed birthday parties. As covered later in this chapter, ISIS attacked stadiums during their Paris operation and perpetrated the Ariana Grande concert attack in Manchester, UK. Therefore, the concept of stadiums and sporting events as targets is not new—their vulnerabilities are regularly exploited by criminal and terrorist organizations.

PERFORMING ARTS AND RECREATIONAL VENUES

Citizens attending the theater, concerts and amusement parks are particularly vulnerable since the venue is typically loud and animated. Attacks at these locations are not only unexpected, but people may mistake the sound of gunfire or screaming as part of the show. Seconds count in a mass shooting event and freezing in place instead of fleeing can be the difference between life and death. In addition to the cover of noise and confusion, terrorist attacks on these large, concentrated crowds have a higher potential for casualties.

We can learn much from past terrorist and criminal assaults against theater venues. The Dubrovka Theater attack in Moscow turned into a multiday hostage crisis that ended in tragedy, and critical study of the event and response yields many valuable lessons. I recently corresponded with Polina Bogacheva, who was a child performer in Nord-Ost show at the Dubrovka Theater in 2002. She is an aspiring theater producer, who recently worked on Broadway in New York City. She is a graduate of Columbia's Master of Fine Arts program, and her thesis, "Theatre Security and Security Theatre on Broadway" is mandatory reading for those securing these types of venues (https://academiccommons.columbia.edu/catalog/ac:203689).

Case Study: The Dubrovka Theater Attack

The Dubrovka Theater in Moscow is a similar venue to the Kennedy Center and was the scene of a horrific Chechen terrorist attack on October 23, 2002 (Figure 6.2). Around 9:00 that evening, during act II of a sold-out performance, forty-one heavily armed and masked men and women drove a bus directly into the theater's main hall, firing assault rifles. Within seconds, 916 people were taken hostage, including a Russian general, while ninety people managed to flee the building or hide. The terrorists had grenades, improvised explosive devices strapped to their bodies, and they wired large bombs throughout the theater. The terrorists stated they had

FIGURE 6.2   CCTV Still From Inside the Dubrovka Theater, Moscow

no anger toward foreigners and promised to release anyone who showed a foreign passport. About 200 hostages were released, including some children, pregnant women, and foreigners. The rest were kept in the theater at all times, using the orchestra pit as a lavatory. As the situation moved into its second day, both an outsider who entered the theater to find his son and a hostage who stormed a terrorist were killed.

The mass death toll resulting from the siege actually came at the hands of the Russians themselves during a poorly executed "rescue" on the third day of the standoff. After Special Forces troops stormed the theater, President Putin ordered security forces to inject a substance into the ventilation system, an aerosol anesthetic possibly weaponized fentanyl or Kolokol-1, an artificial, powerful, opium-like substance. Instead of merely going to sleep as the government hoped, people suffocated as their tongues relapsed in their mouths, blocking the airway passage. Medical personnel at the scene did not have the proper antidote, and in all, 130 hostages died. In a stunning admission, Moscow's health committee chairman announced that all but one of the hostages killed in the raid had died from the gas (BBC News 2002). Those who survived the attack faced a lifetime of health-related issues. The terrorists leveraged mass media to broadcast the event live to the world and allowed those in the theater to use their cell phones to call family and friends. Prior to the theater attack, the Chechens were merely fringe actors, an irritant to the Russian government. However, the siege brought Moscow to its knees as it negotiated with the terrorists, and the world critically judged the government's handling of the crisis. The Chechen Rebels were now a formidable terrorist organization.

Since the Dubrovka Theater attack, other theater and concert events were targeted by terrorist groups and had to increase security due to a general rise in the threat level. Substantiated terrorist threats were made against overseas venues hosting US singers such as Madonna (St. Petersburg and Moscow, 2012), Lady Gaga (Indonesia, 2013), and Aerosmith

(Indonesia, 2013). On July 3, 2013, New York City canceled a Jay-Z concert due to security concerns including the possibility of a terrorist attack. Also, intercepted al-Qaeda communications indicated the Lolla-palooza music event in Chicago was targeted in 2013. Suicide bomber Salman Abedi, 22, who attacked the May 2017 Ariana Grande concert had ties to both ISIS and al-Qaeda.

Large outdoor music festivals are also a concern. For instance, the Bonnaroo Music and Arts Festival in Tennessee is now ranked near the top of the list of potential terrorist soft targets in the state. With more than 80,000 music fans packed into a rural area and thousands of vehicles, the event is a security challenge. One solution has been to increase the number of undercover officers working the crowd. In light of the Las Vegas mas-sacre just six months earlier, officials increased the security budget and strategy at the April 2018 Coachella concert. The crowd of 100,000 was protected by surveillance drones and other sophisticated technology to detect threats. Also, officials ramped up emergency response with extra medics and an enhanced supply of tourniquets and other first aid items.

Unfortunately, the mass shooting at the Route 91 music festival in Las Vegas on October 1, 2017, illustrated the vulnerability of an outdoor music event, this one in the shadow of a high-rise hotel that served as the shooting platform for the killer. When I walked the festival grounds, I was struck by the very high fence and few exit gates; it appeared the construct, meant to keep non-ticketed people out of the venue, instead penned in those who may have been able to flee the gunman's bullets. This attack, like most, hit the "reset button" on hotel security and proac-tive hardening activities.

Case Study: Death From Above: Massacre in Las Vegas

On October 1, 2017, Stephen Paddock committed the largest mass public shooting in the United States when he opened fire on the Route 91 Harvest Festival in the Las Vegas Village in Las Vegas, Nevada, killing fifty-eight people and injuring more than 851, 422 of those by gunfire (Preliminary Report 2018).

BACKGROUND

According to the report, Paddock "lived a seemingly normal life" based on accounts from relatives and acquaintances. He began trav-eling internationally—usually alone—in 2012, going to Europe, Asia, and South America, and on cruises to the Bahamas, Mexico, and Alaska. He complained about pain and fatigue, but his primary care physician since 2009 said Paddock's only ailment was a previ-ously torn muscle. The doctor described Paddock as "odd" and said he showed "little emotion," and likely was bipolar; Paddock refused to discuss it or take antidepressants. He did accept anti-anxiety medication, but it is unknown whether he took it. His girlfriend, Marilou Danley, told investigators that Paddock's demeanor changed during the last year—he became "distant" and "their relationship was no longer intimate." He became "germaphobic" and had strong reactions to smells. During their stay at the Mandalay Bay in early September, Ms. Danley said Paddock behaved strangely, and constantly looked out the windows of the room and at the concert venue below from different angles.

WEAPONS AND PLANNING

From 1982 through the fall of 2016, Paddock bought twenty-nine firearms, including handguns, shotguns, and one rifle. His purchases accelerated starting in October 2016 and he bought more than fifty-five firearms in less than a year, mostly rifles. He also purchased more than 100 firearm-related items such as scopes, ammunition, and bump stocks in the year before the attack.

Paddock meticulously planned his atrocity beginning in May 2017 when he began searching topics online such as "summer concerts 2017," "biggest open air concert venues in USA," and "Las Vegas high rise condos rent." Two weeks later, he looked for "swat weapons," "ballistics chart 308," "SWAT Las Vegas," and "do police use explosives." Investigators also found child pornography on Paddock's computer.

He also searched for expected attendance of concerts held in Las Vegas and police tactics and procedures (Medina 2018). Paddock had other targets in mind (AP 2017). Paddock first considered attacking the August 3rd Lollapalooza open air concert in Chicago, booking two rooms in a hotel that overlooked the venue but never checking in. He next considered attacking the Life Is Beautiful music festival in Las Vegas, requesting rooms at the Ogden condominium complex that overlooked the downtown outdoor venue. He stayed in a room on September 17, and in video surveillance, Paddock was seen taking several suitcases from his vehicle to his rooms.

CONFIGURING THE ROOM

Paddock's plan for mass murder at the Route 91 festival started on September 25, when he checked into room 32–135 at the Mandalay Bay Resort and Casino. Four days later, he checked into the adjoining room under Ms. Danley's name. Paddock, with the unwitting help of a bellman, began transporting the first of twenty-three firearms concealed in suitcases and bags to his rooms using the service elevators, which he was afforded access because he was a "high roller" at the casino (Fox News 2017). Over the course of the days leading up to the October 1st attack, Paddock continued bringing more suitcases up to his rooms via the service elevators. On his first night at the hotel, Mr. Paddock had dinner at a hotel restaurant and returned to the front desk with five suitcases. The next day, he took seven more suitcases up to his room with the bellman.

On September 27, Paddock gambled all night, stopping at 7:00 a.m. On September 28, he went to Mesquite, Nevada, and purchased a .308 bolt-action rifle, deposited $14,000 into a Wells Fargo account and transferred $50,000 to an account in the Philippines for his girl-friend. He stopped at a gun range before going back to the hotel. He gambled through the night again. On September 30, he brought four more suitcases to his room just before 6 a.m. and two additional ones at 3:20 p.m.

Paddock ordered expensive meals delivered to his room, giving cleaning staff strange instructions on what they could and could not touch in the room. Meanwhile, he stocked the room with multiple rifles including bolt action rifles and semi-automatic rifles of which the AR-15s were fitted with bump stocks, scopes, binoculars, and plenty of ammunition for all the weapons. He arranged the room to enable ease of access to weapons and ammo-Paddock pushed chairs together to set rifles on top of and neatly piled extra loaded maga-zines near the window he fired from.

Before he started shooting, he set up a camera at the peephole in his door to monitor the hallway outside his rooms, and another on a room service cart, and observed the video from his laptop in the room. He also blocked the nearest stairwell door with an L-bracket to prevent anyone from easily breaching it.

THE ATTACK

On October 1, at about 10 p.m., hotel security guard Jesus Campos arrived on the 32nd floor to respond to an alarm set off by an open door in another room. Paddock shot him in the hallway and six minutes later, at 10:05 p.m., he began shooting into the crowd of the Route 91 Harvest Festival, attended by more than 22,000 people. As people began to flee they were soon impeded by only two exit points on either side of the fenced-in arena. The fences did not collapse out-ward, trapping more people inside the area of impact.

Three minutes later, Las Vegas Metropolitan Police Department (LVMPD) officers began responding to the call of shots fired from the Mandalay Bay. Due to confusion in the hotel, police did not imme-diately respond to the 32nd floor. However, Paddock stopped firing at 10:15 p.m., three minutes after the first Las Vegas Metropolitan Police Department (LVMPD) responded to the Mandalay Bay. An hour later, at 11:20 p.m., LVMPD SWAT Strike Teams entered Pad-dock's room using explosives to break down the door, and found him lying dead on the floor, with a self-inflicted gunshot to the head.

MOTIVE

In the hours and days following the events, the world speculated about what made Stephen Paddock, a man with no criminal history and very little law enforcement contact, commit the deadliest public shooting in the history of the United States. Paddock did not leave a suicide note or manifesto to explain himself. The Islamic State tried to claim Paddock as one of their jihadists, however US law enforcement quickly shut that possibility down. Investigations by both law enforcement and media deeply delved into Paddock's life, searching everything from his gun purchases to medical history, finances, and his relationship with his girlfriend, who he unexpectedly sent to the Philippines prior to the shooting. Paddock's motives remain unclear, adding a layer of mystery to the worst massacre in US history.

(Source: Flynn 2019. Second Lt. Flynn is an Air Force intelligence officer. She has a BA in criminal justice and MA in emergency management and homeland security.)

Just months before the Las Vegas massacre, ISIS attacked a concert in Manchester, United Kingdom. On May 22, 2017, a shrapnel-laden homemade bomb exploded as children and their parents were leaving Manchester Arena following a concert by the American singer Ariana Grande. Twenty-three people died, including the attacker. The attack was particularly heinous because it targeted an event for youth.

Case Study: Ariana Grande Concert Bombing

Ariana Grande is well known for her vocal talents, and she stands out as one of the most popular musicians today. In 2017, she traveled the world on her "Dangerous Woman Tour." The concert series made its way to the UK on May 22, stopping in Manchester, an urban English city of 2.5 million people. The venue, the Manchester Arena, has a capacity of 21,000 people, and caters to more than a million attendees every year. The arena is surrounded by office buildings and is located next to the highly active Victoria railway station, which averages 22,000 passengers a day. The stadium was packed with young people and parents. Just after 10:30 p.m. local time, the Manchester police received the first call about an explosion at the arena. A suicide bomber detonated a shrapnel-laden device outside the main entrance as the concert ended, claiming the lives of twenty-two and injuring more than 500 (BBC 2018b). It was the deadliest attack in the United Kingdom since the July 7, 2005, London bombings, which killed fifty-two. Due to the mass exodus of panicked concert goers, families struggled for days after the attack to reconnect with their loved ones who had attended the concert.

THE ATTACKER

The attacker was Salman Ramadan Abedi, a 22-year-old UK native, born in Manchester to Libyan parents. At one point he lived in London with his religious family, but moved back to Manchester, where his father sang the Call to Prayer at the Didsbury Mosque. He attended Salford University in Manchester, was active in the local football community, and, according to other students, consumed alcohol and smoked cannabis (Dearden 2017b). Friends and acquaintances claim that Abedi was short-tempered, gullible, and seemingly unintelligent. Abedi's classmates also thought he fit the profile of a suicide bomber; this was supported by Sheikh Mohammad Saeed, who claimed that after criticizing ISIS, he was given a "face of hate" from Abedi (BBC 2018b).

RESPONSE

Manchester police arrived as the 14,000 concert attendees fled the arena. Within minutes after the initial call, police and military were on the scene. However, fire department officials were instructed to stay three miles away from the arena, awaiting clearance from the on-scene leadership. Due to poor communications, fire officials did not arrive at the arena until two hours after the bombing (BBC 2018b), a major failure of emergency response protocol.

The day after the attack, police questioned Abedi's cousins and raided his home. The cousins claimed Abedi never admitted to extremist beliefs, but they believed he was radicalized overseas. The investigation showed that on holidays, Abedi and his father, Ramadan, would go to Libya to fight the Gadhafi regime; the same regime that caused Abedi's parents to flee Libya. Abedi's parents and brother, Hashem, were in Tripoli, Libya, during the Manchester attack. Hashem was brought in for questioning by RADA (Libyan Special Deterrence Forces) for suspected involvement in the bombing. Abedi's sister, Jomana, who was still in the UK, was also detained for questioning by the UK police. Her interviews revealed that Abedi had been talking about "dying for a cause" leading up to the attack, and claimed the attack was retaliation for American-led airdrops "against children in Syria" (BBC 2018b).

THE PLANNING

Between April 15 and May 18, 2017, Abedi was in Libya. Manchester police believe he used student loans to finance the plot, including his travel to learn bomb-making in Libya. Authorities in the UK, reviewing CCTV tape, saw Abedi purchasing bomb-making materials shortly after returning from his visit to Libya. Hashem, Abedi's brother, assisted Abedi in the procurement of bomb-making materials. RADA investigators claimed the brothers were radicalized by ISIS in 2015 via the Internet, which contradicted claims made by their cousins who stated they were radicalized in Libya. ISIS later claimed credit for the attack, indicating Abedi was indeed radicalized by the group at some point. It was posited that the attack was ISIS's way of maintaining public fear, as they were losing territories in ongoing battles in Syria and Iraq (Dearden 2017a).

Abedi was investigated twice for potential ties to terrorism, so he was a "known wolf." A citizen called a hotline five years before the bombing to warn police about Abedi's views, and the Libyans in the UK stated they had "warned authorities for years" about Abedi's radicalization. As many as five community leaders reported Abedi for his extremist views, and family members were banned from a mosque. Internal investigations into Mi5's actions indicated the attack may have been thwarted, had the agency put an alert out on Abedi. The alert would have triggered Mi5 when Abedi re-entered the country after his four days in Libya. However, Mi5 claims that there was nothing they could have done to thwart the attack (Mendick et al. 2017).

LESSONS LEARNED

As ISIS lost ground, they were also enforcing a dialogue through their newsletters, online magazines, and social media directing recruits to "fight from within" (James, Jensen, and Tinsley 2015) and Abedi heeded their call. Although the Manchester arena was not specifically targeted by ISIS, it was a target of opportunity for Abedi to carry out his attack. Soft targets like it must be better guarded and secured. Abedi was able to carry an improvised explosive device into a high traffic area of the arena, where he should have never been. Emergency response to mass casualty events must be practiced to avoid the communication issues between responders at the scene, as witnessed in this attack. The arena bombing came just months after two vehicle attacks on London's famous bridges; for the first time in ten years, the UK's terrorism threat level increased from "severe" to "critical."

(Source: Copello 2019a. Mr. Copello is a data scientist and researcher at the University of North Florida, with a focus on the psychology of terrorism.)

NIGHTCLUBS

Terror attacks on nightclubs are not a new tactic; they have limited exit points, and are packed with unsuspecting people, many under the influence of alcohol, which dulls their senses and response time.

On April 5, 1986, three people were killed and around 230 injured when Libyan-sponsored terrorists attacked the La Belle discothèque in the Friedenau district of West Berlin. The entertainment venue was commonly frequented by United States soldiers, and two of the dead and seventy-nine of the injured were American servicemen.

On October 12, 2002, in the tourist district of Kuta on the Indonesian island of Bali, Jemaah Islamiyah, a violent Islamist group perpetrated an attack killing 202 and injuring another 200.

The first example of a terrorist attack against a nightclub in the United States came on June 12, 2016, when Omar Mateen, a 29-year-old American security guard who professed his allegiance to ISIS, killed forty-nine people and wounded fifty-eight others inside Pulse, a gay nightclub in Orlando, Florida.

Case Study: Pulse Nightclub Attack, Orlando, Florida

At approximately 2:00 a.m. on June 12, 2016, 29-nine-year-old Omar Mateen approached the Pulse nightclub in Orlando, Florida, and started his shooting massacre. The attack began as an active shooter incident, and transformed into a hostage situation, not resolved until three hours after Mateen's attack. After shooting his way into the club, Mateen barricaded himself in the restroom with multiple hostages and victims. He also claimed (falsely) to have explosives during his communication with law enforcement. These factors slowed police response and may have delayed medical attention to injured individuals in the nightclub. The SWAT team finally breached the restroom wall at 5:02 a.m. and engaged the shooter (Straub et al. 2017). There were forty-nine deaths and fifty-three wounded at the Pulse nightclub, in what was the deadliest terrorist attack on US soil since the 9/11 attacks.

SURVEILLANCE AND TARGET SELECTION

The Pulse nightclub served the LGBT community, and, initially, the sexual orientation of the club's clientele was considered to be a primary factor in the target selection. Further evidence about target selection and motive has undermined this conclusion (Greenwald and Hussain 2018). During the incident, Omar Mateen communicated with emergency dispatchers and swore allegiance to ISIS (Florida Department of Law Enforcement).

Mateen conducted surveillance at Disney World in Orlando the night of the attack, and he and his wife visited locations in Disney several days prior. Mateen purchased a baby carriage shortly prior to the attack and it is suspected he planned to use it to conceal his rifle for an attack on Disney (Associated Press 2018). He also speculated with witnesses about which target would cause more outrage, an attack on Disney or a nightclub (Greenwald and Hussain 2018).

The initial FBI investigation indicated Mateen conducted pre-attack surveillance on the Pulse nightclub (Straub et al. 2017). However, the FBI now states there is no evidence to verify any surveillance or visits to the location prior to the night of the attack, when Mateen visited a series of targets, including Pulse. Before the attack, he visited Pulse and other targets, which he decided against because they had visible uniformed law enforcement presence (Greenwald and Hussain 2018).

ATTACK TIMELINE

Phase I: Pre-Attack Actions (Greenwald and Hussain 2018)

5:00 p.m. Mateen leaves his residence in Fort Pierce, Florida, more than 100 miles from Orlando.

8:00 p.m. Mateen purchased food in the south Orlando area.

10:00 p.m. Mateen is in the Disney Springs area, a location believed to be a target of his earlier surveillance and planning. Searched "Disney Springs" on his phone at 10:27 p.m. and "Disney World" at 11:05 p.m.

12:22 a.m. Cell phone data places Mateen in the vicinity of EPCOT, a Disney park in the Orlando area. Mateen searched "downtown Orlando nightclubs" at this time. Selected directions to EVE Orlando.

12:30–12:55 a.m. Mateen drove to the EVE Orlando club and remained in the area until 1:01 a.m.

1:01 a.m. Mateen re-ran the nightclub search on his phone, and accessed directions to Pulse nightclub. He arrived at Pulse between 1:12 and 1:16 a.m.

1:33–1:37 a.m. Mateen selected driving directions back to EVE nightclub and left the vicinity of Pulse, but at 1:35 am he returned to the vicinity of Pulse.

Phase II: Active Shooter Assault (Straub et al. 2017)

Prior to 2:00 a.m. Suspect parks rental car in neighboring business lot north of Pulse and later approaches Pulse nightclub around the east end of the facility, to the entrance on the south side.

2:02 a.m. Suspect armed with 5.56 millimeter semiautomatic rifle and 9 millimeter handgun enters the nightclub and shoots a patron inside the front parlor. Suspect continued to fire at patrons and staff.

2:02 a.m. A uniformed Orlando Police Department (OPD) detective on extra duty reports "shots fired" on the radio, then additional transmissions with the address and reported multiple casualties. Office takes cover behind a vehicle and fires several shots at the suspect, who was visible through the entrance doors.

2:02 a.m. Patrons begin escaping through several exits and the main entrance. Pulse security officer made a breach through a fence that limited escape from the east patio area, allowing more people to escape.

2:03–2:04 a.m. Two OPD officers arrive at Pulse approximately one minute apart.

2:05 a.m. The OPD detective radios that the suspect has an assault rifle. The detective fires three additional shots at the suspect and shooting inside ceases.

2:06 a.m. The detective forms a team of three arriving officers and moves to enter the east side patio entrance.

2:07–2:08 a.m. The watch commander, a lieutenant who also commanded the SWAT team, arrives. A sergeant replaces the detective as commander of the east side contact team. The lieutenant then assembles a second contact team with five officers on the south side. Contact teams begin directing survivors to evacuate the facility.

2:10 a.m. At least five additional shots are fired by the suspect. The SWAT commander's team breaks a large window and gains entry to the facility. They believe the suspect is barricaded in the restroom area and prepare to engage him. A patron inside a restroom calls 911 and reports at least ten other people are hiding in the restroom and the suspect was in the restroom, as well. This information and the cessation of gunfire from the suspect leads to a transition of tactics from an active shooter response to a hostage situation.

2:14–2:18 a.m. Police locate patrons and staff hiding within the facility and directed them to escape. More than thirty people were evacuated by this time.

2:17–2:18 a.m. SWAT commander verbally engages the suspect and then fires shots at the suspect. SWAT commander asked dispatchers for a "full SWAT callout."

Phase III: Barricaded Gunman With Hostages (Straub et al. 2017)

2:18–2:28 a.m. Police evacuate at least fourteen incapacitated persons from the facility.

2:35 a.m. The suspect called 911 and tells the operator that he "did the shooting in Orlando."

2:48 a.m. The crisis negotiation team calls the suspect and speaks with him for nine minutes. Suspect claims to be wearing a suicide vest and that he placed several Vehicle Borne Improvised Explosive Devices in the parking lot that could "take out a whole city block almost."

3:03 a.m. Suspect answers another phone call from negotiators but provides little information relevant to the incident during the sixteen-minute call.

3:20 a.m. A tactical robot is deployed to provide images of the restroom but it could not reach the suspect due to obstructions. The robot's PA system was used to broadcast messages to the hostages.

3:24 a.m. Suspect answers another three-minute long phone call from negotiators but only expresses his grievances and annoyance with their calls.

3:25 a.m. A false report of gunfire at the Orlando Regional Medical Center results in a one-hour lockdown at the facility during a critical time in the crisis.

4:03 a.m. The sheriff's office bomb squad arrives on the scene and a K-9 from another agency alerts on the suspect's vehicle. The bomb squad requests a 1,000 foot evacuation zone around the vehicle, but law enforcement personnel do not withdraw. The ICP, triage, and other responder activities are located well within the exclusion zone recommended by the bomb technicians. The command vehicle is relocated further from the facility on the opposite side of the suspects vehicle.

4:29 a.m. A hostage inside the club sends a text message claiming the suspect is going to attach bomb vests to four hostages. The breakdown in communication and the possible presence of explosive devices influences OPD command staff to switch from prolonged negotiation to actions to neutralize the suspect and rescue the hostages.

4:30 a.m. SWAT officers on the exterior remove an air conditioning unit from the wall and rescue eight individuals from a dressing room near the suspect's location. This action was coordinated with the SWAT team by cell phone with an employee inside the room.

Phase IV: SWAT Team Assault (Straub et al. 2017)

5:02 a.m. An explosive charge is detonated by law enforcement, creating a partial breach in the wall.

5:08–5:09 a.m. A SWAT team armored vehicle breaches the wall while loudspeakers broadcast a message to hostages to move away.

5:10–5:13 a.m. SWAT rescues thirteen hostages from the southwest restroom.

5:14–5:15 a.m. Suspect begins firing in north restroom. SWAT team engages using flashbang grenades and exchanges gunfire with the suspect. The suspect is neutralized while one officer was wounded by a round striking his ballistic helmet.

Phase V: Extraction of Remaining Wounded and Primary Search (Straub et al. 2017)

5:17–5:27 a.m. All remaining individuals and hostages are extracted from the nightclub. Five additional hostages are rescued from the north restroom after the suspect was killed. Due to the risk of explosive devices, law enforcement completely withdrew from the facility, having rescued at least ninety people.

5:27–11:15 a.m. Due to the risk of improvised explosive devices, technicians must methodically search each deceased victim. The responders clear the facility and declared it free of hazardous devices in about six hours.

THE ATTACKER

Omar Mateen was employed for the G4S Corporation as an armed security officer from 2007 until the attack. As part of his employment, he likely had awareness of active shooter response protocols. He also made several attempts to seek employment with other criminal justice agencies. His employment with the Florida Department of Corrections was terminated during his probationary period for threatening to bring a weapon after the Virginia Tech Shootings (Barry et al. 2016). Efforts to join the Florida State police and enroll in a police academy were also unsuccessful (Swisher 2016).

Mateen had a long history of disruptive behavior in school as a juvenile and displayed many alarming behaviors as an adult. His first wife alleged he was controlling and abusive. Allegations of other violent and stalking behavior during relationships and his second marriage were noted in the investigation (Barry et al. 2016).

The attacker took actions and made statements prior to the incident indicating he was possibly radicalized. While performing security functions at the St. Lucie County Courthouse, Mateen made inflammatory comments about being involved in terrorism and made threats toward employees. An FBI investigation in 2013 and another in 2014 did not result in criminal charges against Mateen. G4S transferred him to serve as an armed guard at another facility instead of terminating his employment (Barry et al. 2016).

THE ATTACK

The facility was a single-story nightclub with more than 300 people inside at the time of the attack. The facility was divided into three main sections, each with a DJ and separate music systems. The attacker used a semiautomatic rifle and 9 millimeter semiautomatic pistol in the incident. The crowded conditions, loud music, low lighting, and inebriated state of many of those in attendance made the location very susceptible to an active shooter style assault. The attacker killed or wounded approximately one-third of the people in the nightclub, including 102 victims with gunshot wounds and five non-gunshot injuries from debris or evacuation-related injuries (Straub et al. 2017).

The uniformed OPD detective was working contracted extra duty at the club. He and his vehicle were located along the street on the south side of the facility; Mateen's approach route shielded him from view by club bouncers at the door of the facility and the detective. His path ensured that when he became visible, he was between the detective and the facility, preventing the detective from preventing access to the facility.

Upon hearing gunfire, the detective radioed for assistance and approached the building to engage Mateen. He used a vehicle for cover because he had a 9 millimeter semiautomatic handgun and could hear that the suspect had a semiautomatic rifle. When the detective observed Mateen shooting two patrons at an exit door, he fired at him. He also fired through a window at Mateen, and he then moved deeper into the facility. Additional officers, including SWAT members, arrived within three minutes in response to radio dispatches (Straub et al. 2017).

Similar to the Bataclan Theater attack in France, due to the loud music and unfamiliarity with the sound of gunfire, many patrons initially failed to recognize they were caught up in a shooting. Some believed it was firecrackers, others thought it was a sound effect or a problem with the sound system. One of the DJs turned down the music and realized it was gunfire, telling people to evacuate. Patrons who did recognize gunfire believed it was a personal altercation between individuals that would end quickly. While many patrons and staff attempted to evacuate, play dead, or hide from the shooter, there are no indications anyone other than law enforcement made attempts to stop the shooter (Straub et al. 2017).

The shooter's change of tactics, to include taking hostages and threatening the presence of multiple improvised explosive devices, challenged law enforcement, increased the difficulty of decision making, and hindered the conclusion of the incident (Straub et al. 2017). Investigators utilizing information from the 911 calls, estimated that Mateen fired 200 rounds in five minutes during the initial assault. He then positioned himself in a restroom with approximately ten hostages and used his cell phone not only to make calls to 911 but to claim responsibility for the attacks on Facebook (Straub et al. 2017).

PRE-HOSPITAL CARE

Many ambulatory wounded self-evacuated to the Orlando Fire Department station located near the nightclub. Law enforcement officers established an improvised triage location, approximately 200 feet from the nightclub, behind another building. Approximately twenty-five individuals were transported to Orlando Regional Medical Center's Level 1 Trauma Center located nearby. These efforts removed the vast majority of the wounded from the facility who were not in the immediate vicinity of the attacker. Of the sixty-nine critically wounded evacuated by law enforcement, fifty-eight survived (Straub et al. 2017).

Family reunification efforts initially began at the Orlando Regional Medical Center. Due to the scale of the incident, the hospital was overwhelmed by the influx of visitors seeking news of potential victims. The reunification and next of kin notification was then moved to a hotel that could accommodate the operations. Intelligence analysts with the Florida Department of Law Enforcement identified victims and made notifications.

SECURITY AND RESPONSE CONSIDERATIONS

The report "Rescue, Response, and Resilience: A Critical Incident Review of the Orlando Public Safety Response to the Attack on the Pulse Nightclub" (Straub et al. 2017) provides insight into law enforcement and first response activities the night of the shooting with many lessons learned.

Facility design: the facility had three emergency exits, one on the south side of the building and two on the north side of the building. The exits led to a fenced-in patio area, surrounded by a fence and gate. The design meant people could not escape from the attacker.

Facility security personnel were present at the entrance and inside the facility. They did not screen patrons entering the facility, and were primarily focused on crowd control issues.

The initial response lacked a unified command and control structure, which limited cooperation between law enforcement, fire department, and emergency medical services. No one from OPD established an effective command post outside the facility to coordinate resources and response during the first hour of the incident. More than 300 officers, from several agencies, deployed to the scene within three hours. While the initial surge was critical to containing the incident, it complicated coordination and command issues.

Agencies, including the Orlando Fire Department established a separate Incident Command Post. Interagency communications and coordination were lacking, and many fire responders were locked down in their station or held back from the response area. While law enforcement officers provided great assistance with triage and transportation of the wounded, better integration with fire and EMS personnel would have improved this process.

LESSONS LEARNED

Private facilities, law enforcement, and medical responders must continue to prepare for mass casualty events. Although the Pulse shooting was a simple operation, it was made more effective due to the factors and failures explored in this essay. Future attacks may be even more complex and utilize unconventional tactics not anticipated by law enforcement personnel. Therefore, all hazards preparation and response is paramount.

(Source: Wade 2019. Mr. Wade is president of All Hazards Security. His primary focus is on violence prevention and preparedness.)

Further illustration of the vulnerability of nightclubs to attack and copycat attacks, just six months after the Pulse massacre, an ISIS terrorist opened fire at the Reina nightclub in Istanbul, Turkey, where 800 people were celebrating the new year. Uzbekistan-born Abdulkadir Masharipov opened fire with his AK-47 at 1:15 a.m. local time, killing the security guard at the door and an additional thirty-eight people inside, wounding seventy others. Masharipov was on the run for sixteen days and was arrested in Istanbul on January 17. The effectiveness of Turkish security was questioned since this event occurred just one month after an ISIS-inspired stadium massacre in the city. There were 25,000 policemen on duty in Istanbul on New Year's Eve; the gunman's taxi passed through three nearby security checkpoints to reach the club. Then he was able to escape and evade police in the city for more than two weeks (Dettmer 2017).

AMUSEMENT PARKS

Amusement parks present yet another security concern and challenge. Since 9/11, Disney properties have been assessed by terrorist groups as potential targets or have assumed an increased security posture due to an overall increase in threat levels in the United States. We should remember the Disney Springs entertainment complex was Pulse nightclub shooter Omar Mateen's first target, but he changed his mind due to police presence. Amusement parks know they are very vulnerable to attack, and many increased bag inspections and limitation of items allowed in the park in light of recent world events. Gate areas are often scenes of large crowds and must be protected by increasing flow through the dates or spreading people out. Since bringing weapons through the gate is unlikely, the threat of chemical or biological attack might be more probable inside the park, so food should be protected from contamination, and building ventilation systems secured. Insider threat at parks is also a concern; employees can carry out reconnaissance on possible targets and pre-position materials needed for an attack. Therefore, screening of potential workers and ongoing vigilance concerning their activities is paramount to preventing a deadly attack from within.

CITY CENTER

Since 2014, we've witnessed a sharp escalation in violent terrorist attacks in cities. The Lindt Chocolate Café siege in Sydney, Australia, in December 2014 was the first of its kind, a bold hostage-taking event on a main city street. The city was ill-prepared to deal with this scenario, and we can learn much from a review of the attack and aftermath.

Case Study: Sydney, Australia, Chocolate Café Attack

On Monday, December 15, 2014, at 9:45 a.m., a 16-hour long siege began in Sydney's central business district when a gunman took over the Lindt Chocolate Café. Customers inside the café first realized something was wrong when employee Tori Johnson had a gun pointed at him by a customer he was serving. Officials later identified the man holding the gun as Man Haron Monis, an Iranian born, self-styled Muslim cleric. Australian Prime Minister Tony Abbott told reporters that the "gunman was already well-known to authorities and had a long history of violent crime, infatuation with extremism and mental instability" (Pearson et al. 2014). Shortly after Monis took control of the café, a customer tried to enter the locked doors, but was sent away by Monis waving his gun. It was then that local police forces were alerted and a crowd started to gather around the unfolding hostage situation at the café.

THE ATTACK

There were eighteen people inside the Lindt café, five of which were able to escape through the side door/fire exit several hours after the siege began. Reports state that Monis was made angry by their escape and screamed at the hostages, telling them there were bombs in the building and they had to follow his orders. Images taken at the scene showed two hostages standing with arms and hands pressed against the window in the front shop. Shortly afterwards they held up a black flag with white Arabic writing. The flag was initially thought to be an ISIS flag, but was later identified as the Shahada: the Islamic creed "There is no god but God, Muhammad is the messenger of God." The same script appears on the flag of Saudi Arabia, the al-Qaeda linked group known as al Nusrah Front, and the radical group Hizb ut-Tahrir.

Throughout the day, Monis forced hostages to make phone calls to local radio stations or place posts on social media relaying his demands for an on-air live broadcast phone with Prime Minister Abbott, an ISIS flag, and a public declaration from the government that his act was an act of terror committed on behalf of ISIS (Doherty et al. 2014). All demands met would mean a certain number of hostages released.

At this point, police and Australian Special Forces were on alert outside the café for almost sixteen hours. A crowd of 400 people were allowed to gather outside the café and watch. Rumors ran wild all over the city about package bombs and other threats that were unfounded. The siege dragged on through the night. At approximately 1:45 a.m. on Tuesday morning, Monis was still refusing to negotiate with police and becoming more and more agitated. Around 0200, upon hearing a bang from inside the café, police stormed the building from two different directions. Some reports stated the bang was caused by a group of hostages breaking down a door to escape just minutes before police charged in, while others indicated the noise was from gunfire inside the cafe. Once the police entered the café, gunfire broke out. Police and emergency personnel reported three dead and multiple injured but in stable condition. Three hostages and a police officer were wounded by police gunfire during the raid. Two of the fatalities were Lindt employees Tori Johnson and Katrina Dawson. Katrina Dawson was pronounced dead at the hospital as a result of bullet fragments during the firefight, and Tori Dawson was directly shot in the head by Monis (Doherty et al. 2014).

THE ATTACKER

Monis' life was unraveling at the time of the attack. He was out on bail for forty-three counts of sexual assault and for being an accessory to murder of his former wife. He previously made a number of extremist videos and declared a fatwa against Barack Obama. Monis was convicted of sending offensive letters to the families of Australian servicemen who were killed overseas, and the National Security Hotline had received no less than eighteen calls about him in the week leading up to the siege (Snow and Begley 2017). A website associated with Monis included condemnation of the United States and Australia for their military actions against Islamic militants in Iraq and Afghanistan. News reports said the site also contained a posting saying Monis had recently converted from Shia to Sunni Islam, pledging his allegiance to the "Caliph of the Muslims." The posting appeared to refer to Abu Bakr al-Baghdadi and the Islamic State militant group, though it did not mention them by name (Innis 2014). Monis screamed at the hostages that he was "a representative of Islamic State" and "this is a terrorist attack." US law enforcement and intelligence sources said Monis was believed to be acting alone and didn't appear to be part of a broader plot. Monis was killed in the gunfight with law enforcement, so many questions remain about his motive and intentions.

COMMUNITY REACTION

Australian Prime Minister Tony Abbott stated: "These events do demonstrate that even a country as free as open as generous and as safe as ours is vulnerable to acts of politically motivated violence, but they also remind us that Australia, and Australians are resilient and we are ready to respond"(Pearson, Mullen, and Coren 2014). The grand mufti of Australia, Professor Ibrahim Abu Mohamed, and the Australian National Imams Council issued a joint statement about the hostage siege, saying they "condemn this criminal act unequivocally." In a show of solidarity, thousands of Australians offered to accompany people in traditional Muslim clothing and concerned about a backlash from the siege. The hashtag #IllRideWithYou was used more than 250,000 times on Twitter by late Monday evening. The country pulled together after the heinous attack, yet many questions remained.

LESSONS LEARNED

There were many lessons learned from the Lindt Café crisis. First of all, the crimes Monis was charged with were enough to keep him imprisioned and off the streets, however an administrative failure kept two systems from sharing the necessary information.

Next, why did police wait till shots were fired to enter the café? The "time is my friend" theory espoused by many tactical units may backfire when the hostage taker has nothing to negotiate for and a death wish. As one hostage later stated: "It was never going to be a happy ending, a peaceful resolution was never on the cards. . . . I wanted police to end it on their terms, at least then people would have had half a chance" (Snow and Begley 2017).

Law enforcement training (unsure how to engage) and equipment (vehicles, phones, and radios) were both flawed at the scene of the attack. Practicing for a scenario like this one would have identified these issues before people's lives were on the line. Text messages and phone calls from hostages with important information about the shooter's intentions and mental state were either not received due to communication failures or not considered in the overall tactical plan (Snow and Begley 2017).

The police chief in charge of counterterrorism left the scene to go home and deleted important evidentiary text messages about her decisions and direction giving during the event. Perhaps the event was best summed up using the "swiss cheese" analogy used by investigators in aviation accidents: that if all the holes in the slices line up, you get a crash.

Each slice of cheese had a hole: a policy slice, the communications slice, the equipment slice, a leadership slice, and an intelligence slice—all the holes in all those things lined up and so we had Lindt. If law enforcement was unable to deal with that lone individual, one has to ask, are they ready for a multiple location, multimodal attack? I think it's a huge vulnerability for and it still is (Snow and Begley 2017).

(Source: Johnson 2019. Ms. Johnson is a graduate from Clemson University with undergraduate degrees in Chinese and international health. She is an intelligence analyst in the United States Air Force.)

A few months after the Lindt Café attack, al-Qaeda struck the heart of Paris, with a massacre at the Charlie Hebdo magazine office. The attack was boldly carried out in the middle of the day, on a quiet street in a residential neighborhood. The attackers escaped, and their murder and hostage-taking spree spread to other locations in the city over the course of several days, until they were finally killed by police. The Charlie Hebdo attack was unique in many aspects, and worthy of further study.

Case Study: Je Suis Charlie: The Jihadist Revenge Attack on a Satirical Magazine

The offices of the French satirical magazine, *Charlie Hebdo*, were located in a quiet neighborhood of the 11th Arrondissement in Paris. Two French-born terrorists, Cherif Kouachi and his brother, Said Kouachi, attacked the office on January 7, 2015, in revenge for what they believed were derogatory cartoons blaspheming the Prophet Muhammad. The brothers began their assault around 11:30 a.m., at the time of the magazine's weekly editorial meeting. Using Kalashnikov rifles, the pair simply walked into the building where the offices were located, held a woman at gun point until she keyed in the passcode to open the secured newsroom door, and proceeded to kill eleven people in the office and one upon exiting the scene (BBC 2015). Among the dead were eight Charlie Hebdo employees, including the editor, a building maintenance worker, a guest of the magazine, and the personal bodyguard of the editor. It is reported that the brothers called out by name the editor, Stephane Charbonnier, and four cartoonists . . . killing each one as they were identified and then shooting the remaining people in the room. The brothers escaped the scene, but a two-day manhunt ensued across Paris, resulting in more innocent lives lost and the deaths of the Hebdo attackers. In the final accounting a total of seventeen people were killed in attacks on the satirical magazine *Charlie Hebdo*, a kosher grocery store, and the Paris suburb of Montrouge. The only items left behind in their eventually abandoned Citreon getaway car were Molotov cocktails and two ISIS flags. Clearly they were not armed for the type of police response they must have known would follow such a bold and bloody attack.

WHAT WAS CHARLIE HEBDO?

The raw satirical magazine first began publishing in 1970. It was ruthless in lambasting with targets including political persons and organizations, as well as the major world religions. The magazine drew attention to itself in 2006 when it republished 2005 Danish cartoons, drawn by Jyllands-Posten, critical of the Prophet Mohammed and Islam. In September 2011, Anwar al-Awlaki, the American-born Al-Qaeda on the Arabian Peninsula (AQAP) senior leader and cleric, called for the killing of cartoonists who insulted the Prophet. Not long after, on November 25, 2011, the Charlie Hebdo offices were fire bombed, a day after the Prophet Mohammed was named "editor in chief" for that week's issue. Even a bomb could not deter the Charlie Hebdo staff from inciting more hostility; in 2012, it published cartoons of Prophet Mohammed, some depicting him without clothing.

THE ATTACKERS

Cherif Kouachi was born in Paris to Algerian immigrants in 1980. By the age of 10, he was a ward of the state; the fate of his parents unknown. Cherif's education in jihad began in the early 2000s when he met Ferid Benyettou. Under Benyettou's guidance, a group of disenfranchised young men, referred to as the Buttes-Chaumont Park cell, met to discuss jihad and exercise to prepare themselves for the fight. And in 2004, after a year of watching news reports from Iraq, the group made a pact to travel to Iraq to fight the Americans.

Keeping his promise, Cherif boarded a flight to Syria in January 2005. Suspecting his ultimate destination was Iraq, authorities arrested Cherif before the flight departed. At the time of his arrest, Cherif described himself as a "ghetto Muslim." He was not overtly religious, really just someone looking for a family, an identity. What he was searching for would materialize while in prison where he met Amedy Coulibaly and Diamel Beghal. Their meeting in prison was accomplished easily as people of similar culture were housed together at that time in France (a practice since discontinued). Beghal was a leading al-Qaeda recruiter in Europe and in prison, and had a wealth of recruits at his fingertips. He cemented the jihadi education of both Coulibaly and Kouachi who continued contact with him after release from prison.

Said Kouachi was Cherif's older brother and not as visible on the radar of French police. Although questioned at the time of his brother's 2005 arrest, authorities considered Said to be in pursuit of honest work and of little threat. Eventually, however, his involvement with AQAP (particularly the cell in Yemen) was more troubling than the petty theft and radicalization of his younger brother. In July 2011, the brothers traveled together to Oman where they were smuggled into Yemen and received three days of firearms training before returning to Oman. After this event, their names were added to both the US and British no-fly lists (Chrisafis 2015). It is also possible that Said fought for AQAP in Yemen sometime in the 2011–2012 timeframe and reports further speculate that Said Kouachi met Anwar al-Awlaki before he was killed in a US drone attack on September 30, 2011 (Schmitt, Schmidt, and Higgins 2015).

Amedy Coulibaly, the child of Malian immigrants, was also born in France and grew up in one of the worst areas of Paris where he was ripe for radical recruitment. Unlike the Kouachi brothers, he swore allegiance to ISIS. His role in the Charlie Hebdo attack seems to be twofold; provide money to Cherif to buy weapons and supplies and conduct attacks on seemingly unconnected targets (as a distraction). Coulibaly was not present at the Charlie Hebdo event; his first attack was a few hours after the Hebdo attack in which he randomly shot a jogger in a Paris park. The following day, while an intense manhunt was on for the Kouachi brothers, he killed a Paris police officer and wounded a street sweeper while armed with a Slovakian machine gun and a Russian pistol. In the final day of the assault, Coulibaly took nineteen hostages at the Hypercacher Kosher market, killing four and demanding the Kouachi brothers be allowed to go free in exchange for the release of hostages. Just moments after his demand, police surrounded and killed the Kouachi brothers. Coulibaly was then killed as police stormed the grocery store, freeing the remaining hostages (BBC 2015a).

THE WEAPONS

The recruitment of the Kouachi brothers and Coulibaly is relatively easy to explain and fits the well-established pattern of disenfranchised young men with little opportunity who become romanced by the idea of defending Islam. But how did they get the weapons to carry out these attacks without alerting the police? In May 2008, the EU made assault rifles (AR) that can fire live ammunition illegal. The only ARs allowed were ones that had been converted to fire only blanks and would be decorative pieces for collectors.

However, the fine details needed to ensure the weapons could not be easily re-converted to shoot live ammunition were never put into place. Furthermore, the European black market became awash with millions of weapons from the Russian military and the former militaries of the Balkans. There is no vast terrorist network supplying jihadist with weapons. The jihadis purchase them as needed from the black market in small quantities and simply take the few steps to necessary to make them live-fire capable.

In the subsequent investigation of the Charlie Hebdo attack, police confirmed the Kalashnikovs used by the Kouachi brothers were of Balkan origin. The two Ceska Sa vz.58s used by Amedy Coulibaly were traced to KOL Arms in Slovakia, a source of thousands of "deactivated" weapons across Europe. In fact, these weapons can (still) be purchased online for as little as 300 euros (Candea et al. 2015).

SOFT TARGET LESSONS FROM CHARLIE HEBDO

The satirists who wrote and drew cartoons for Charlie Hebdo knew they were targets of Islamic extremists after the petrol bombing of their offices in 2011 and when AQ propaganda magazine *Inspire* named their editor as "Wanted dead or alive for crimes against Islam." Undeterred in their satire and knowing they were a target, the security measures the Charlie Hebdo staff had in place may have seemed reasonable. The editor was protected by a personal bodyguard and the building where they resided after the 2011 bombing had passcode-protected locked doors. However, both of these measures were easily overwhelmed by two men with assault rifles who knew they would be dead at the conclusion of their attack, martyrs for their religion.

(Source: Miller 2019a. Ms. Miller is a former Air Force Intelligence Officer.)

The Charlie Hebdo attack stunned Paris and the world. While officials focused their efforts on investigating the attack, analyzing their response, and helping the city return to normal, no one could predict the complex plan already underway by ISIS to attack the city just nine months later.

Case Study: The Coordinated Paris and Brussels Attacks

NOVEMBER 13, 2015, AND MARCH 22, 2016

The coordinated terrorist attacks on Paris by ISIL operatives on November 13, 2015, were Europe's worst in a decade. The death toll reached 130 in eight attacks spanning five locations commencing within thirty minutes of one another. The mastermind, a Belgian national recruited by ISIS and trained in Syria, Adbelhamid Abaaoud, was killed five days after the attack by French police in Saint Denis, a suburb of Paris. Even with the ringleader dead, European authorities knew other operatives were still at large. In the weeks and months following the attack, investigators worked to unravel the layers of players, financing, and logistics—but they weren't fast enough. On March 22, 2016, members of the same ISIL cell conducted near simultaneous attacks in Brussels at the airport and a busy metro station killing thirty-two and wounding 320. Understanding who the terrorist were, how they trained, and their planning methods are imperative to stop future attacks.

THE ATTACKERS: WHO AND HOW THEY MET

Of the ten men known to have been involved in the Paris attack, eight have been identified. All eight were European citizens; two Belgian and six French. Six had criminal records, and four had suspected ties to terrorism before the attacks. All eight of the known men had traveled to Syria for training. Authorities believe the two unidentified men were Iraqi nationals fighting in Syria, who entered Europe in October of 2015 via Greece posing as refugees using fake or stolen documents. The Brussels attack would solidify the picture. Six of the European men were of north African descent—three bombers, two would-be bombers, and a planner, all but one with criminal records, all traveled, or attempted travel to Syria, and all radicalized in Europe.

One of the cell leaders, Abdelhamid Abaaoud, was a 28-year-old Belgian national. He grew up in the Molenbeek neighborhood of Brussels to a relatively affluent, moderately religious immigrant family. He was kicked out of school and turned to petty crime, later imprisoned for dealing drugs. In 2014, he became extremely religious and traveled to Syria, where he quickly rose in the ranks of ISIS. Abaaoud was featured in several disturbing ISIS videos, and interviewed in jihadi publications (Graham 2015). He was known to

European intelligence officials as a threat, and reportedly returned to Belgium at least once before organizing and taking part in the Paris plot. Abaaoud is linked to at least three other unsuccessful terrorist plots in Europe, including the attack on the high-speed train foiled by American service members. The night of the Paris attacks, Abaaoud was involved in a café shooting, and was then observed outside the Bataclan theater on his phone, probably speaking with the terrorists inside regarding the police response. His fingerprints were found in a house rented by two of the Brussels bombers. Abaaoud was killed during the raid by French police in the Saint Denis neighborhood of Paris.

Brothers Salah (26 at the time of the attacks) and Ibrahim (31 at the time of the attacks) Abdeslam grew up near Abaaoud in Molenbeek, Belgium, but both obtained French citizenship. They drank and were not considered religious growing up. Ibrahim spent time in the same prison as Abaaoud, and they were friends. Salah was key in the logistics of the attacks, renting cars and apartments. The bar the brothers ran together was shut down for illegal activity, most likely drugs, in early November 2015 (BBC 2018a). Both brothers were supposed to detonate suicide vests during the Paris attacks. Ibrahim succeeded during the café attacks, but Salah lost his nerve at the football stadium and fled. Salah is the only surviving attacker, held by French authorities. In February 2018, he went on trial in Belgium on charges stemming from a shootout with police prior to his capture in Brussels in March 2016. A trial in France for his role in the Paris attacks won't take place until 2020 at the earliest. He has thus far refused cooperation with investigators (BBC 2018a).

A *New York Times* (2016b) exclusive on the attacks provides the foundation for understand the remaining seven actors, their connections to the cell, training, and role in the attacks.

Chakib Akrouh, 25 at the time of the attack, was a childhood friend of Abaaoud, also from Molenbeek. He and Abaaoud were recruited by ISIS and traveled together to Syria in 2013. Akrouh was sentenced to prison in absentia while in Syria. He was able to return to Europe, was involved in the Paris café attacks, and was killed with Abaaoud in Saint Denis.

Ismael Omar Mostefai, 29, was a French citizen. Like the others, he had a criminal record, traveled to Syria, and was known by authorities to have ISIS connections. French authorities confirm Mostefai was in contact with Abaaoud prior to the attacks. He was one of the three Batalan concert attackers.

It's not clear how stadium bomber Bilal Hadfi, a 20-year-old French citizen living in Belgium, became involved in the plot. While he had a criminal record, and reportedly traveled to Syria, there is no firm evidence linking him to Abaaoud prior to the attacks. However he was in contact with a phone associated with Abaaoud on the night of the Paris attacks.

Samy Amimour, 28, and Foued Mohamed-Aggad, 23, Bataclan attackers, were both French and traveled to Syria for training. Amimour was known to police for terrorist ties.

The two unidentified men, both stadium attackers, were referred to as "The Iraqis" on a laptop recovered in Belgium in March of 2016. They traveled from Syria and used fake documents.

At least seven other people were tangentially involved in the Paris attacks—proving safe haven or transportation to Salah Abdeslam, Abaaoud, and Akrouh, the only attackers to leave the scene alive. Most were friends and neighbors.

Hasna Altboulahcen, Abaaoud's cousin (and at one point, fiancé), provided support to Abaaoud and Akrouh after the attack, and was killed with them in the police raid in Saint Denis.

Mohamed Abrini, a childhood friend of the Abdeslam brothers ferried attackers into France. Abrini was in Syria with Abaaoud. While he was seen on video at the Brussels airport bombing, his suicide vest didn't detonate. He was arrested on April 8, 2016, in Brussels.

Najim Laachraoui, 24-year-old Belgian national of Moroccan decent, was an electrical engineer turned ISIS bomb maker. He was radicalized by a preacher in Molenbeek. He went to Syria in 2013, returning in September 2015 with Salah Abdeslam. He made the suicide vests used by the Paris and Brussels attackers, including his own, which he detonated at the Brussels Airport (Rubin 2016).

Ibrahim El Bakraoui, age 29, and his younger brother Khalid, age 27, both Belgian, of Moroccan descent, were convicted criminals—kidnapping, carjacking, and robbery—and were wanted for parole violations. The brothers traveled under false documents and had Interpol warrants out for their arrest for providing logistical support to the Paris attackers. Ibrahim was killed when he detonated his suicide vest at the Brussels airport. Khalid was killed when he detonated himself at the Maalbeek metro station.

Mohamed Belkaid, A 35-year-old Algerian living in Belgium, and perhaps the cell commander there, provided financing and logistical support to the Paris attackers, but was not present. He was planning further attacks in Europe when killed during a police raid in Brussels on March 15. He was a petty thief, radicalized while living in Sweden from 2010 to 2014 (Radio Sweden 2016). He, too, spent time in Syria before returning to Europe.

Osama Krayem, age 24, is a Swedish man seen outside the Malbeek metro station with Khalid. He purchased the luggage used by the airport bombers (BBC 2016). A second metro bomber lost his nerve and did not carry out the attack. Police found his DNA was found in an apartment used by the Paris attackers. He was arrested April 6, 2016.

PARIS ATTACK

Timeline of Events (*New York Times* Interactive Timeline 2016)

9:20 p.m. Stade de France: A suicide bomber detonates himself near Gate D. Two dead, including the bomber.

9:25 p.m. La Carillon and le Petit Cambodge restaurants: Gunmen open fire with assault rifles. Fifteen dead, ten wounded.

9:30 p.m. Stade de France: A second suicide bomber detonated himself near Gate H. Only the bomber was killed.

9:32 p.m. Café Bonne Biére: Gunmen open fire with assault rifles. Five dead, eight wounded.

9:36 p.m. Le Belle Equipe restaurant: Gunmen open fire with assault rifles. Nineteen dead, nine wounded.

9:40 p.m. Comptoir Voltaire restaurant: A suicide bomber detonates himself. One person is wounded.

9:40 p.m. Bataclan Concert Hall: Three men with suicide vests, assault rifles, and grenades enter the hall and begin their attack. They take hostages, and a two-hour standoff ensues. When the police storm the building, two terrorists detonated themselves. The third's vest detonates when hit by a police bullet. Ninety dead.

9:53 p.m. Stade de France: A suicide bomber detonates himself a quarter of a mile from the stadium. Only the bomber was killed.

Paris Attack Logistics (Lormel 2016; Cruickshank 2017)

With financing from ISIS, and prepaid credit cards to increase anonymity, the group set about purchasing materials for the attacks in early September. They rented at least two different safe houses in Belgium as early as September for attack planning and preparation. In early November, Abdeslam rented several cars, and he and Mohamed Abrini ferried the attackers from Belgium to Paris in the days leading up to the attacks. The group split up, the Bataclan attackers staying in a suburban hotel, while the stadium and café attackers stayed in a rented house.

The night of the attacks, the rental car driven by Salah Abdeslam headed to the stadium. A second car, driven by Abaaoud, headed to the cafe district. The third car carried three terrorists to the Bataclan. The terrorists were in contact with one another throughout the attacks using burner cell phones and encrypted messaging apps. After the attacks, only three attackers were still alive.

Salah Abdeslam left his rental car near the stadium, discarded his suicide vest in a trash can, and called a friend, Mohammed Amri, in Belgium, asking him to come to Paris and pick him up immediately. Amri and another friend, Hamza Attou, arrive in Paris a few hours later. On their return journey to Belgium they are stopped three times at police checkpoints, but the identities of the attackers were still unknown to authorities, and all the men had proper identification, so they were allowed to pass. The men arrive in Brussels where Abdeslam disappears until March.

Abaaoud and Akrouh retreated to a wooded area not far from the stadium where they stayed until November 17. Abaaoud's female cousin Hasna ait Boulahcen was apprised of their location via a contact in Belgium. The terrorists were planning further attacks in

Paris set for November 19, and Boulahcen assisted with logistics. It was Boulahcen—the untrained accomplice—who would lead the police to the men. She brought a friend along on one of her visits to the wood, and the friend reported what she saw to the police. The police began monitoring the wooded area and Boulahcen's phone. Police were aware when she moved the men into a rented room in the Saint Denis neighborhood of Paris at 10:30 p.m. on November 17, and they raided the residence hours later. The two men and Boulahcen all died in the standoff.

Racing against the clock, Belgian and French police conducted a series of raids over the next few months, rounding up those linked to the terrorists. A raid on March 15 was a success of sorts; police killed cell leader Mohamed Belkaid and barely missed capturing Abdeslam. They found his fingerprints in the apartment, and later learned he was there during the raid but escaped over rooftops (Rankin 2018). It was enough to spook the remaining cell members into a flurry of activity to carry out their operation. The arrest of Abdeslam on March 18 was the final straw.

BRUSSELS ATTACK

With Belgian police closing in on the remaining cell members, Laachraoui and Ibrahim Bakraoui decided to rush plans. On March 21, they informed their superiors in Iraq via an audio recording (recovered from a captured laptop) that they would be commencing their attack on Brussels the following day.

> The situation is such that we cannot delay in any respect you see. We have to work as quickly as possible and we have decided to work Insha'allah tomorrow, Tuesday March 22 . . . Insha'allah. During the morning . . . because we no longer have secure safe houses, and there's no one left. You see there are no longer any brothers left for logistics etc. And everybody is burnt you see . . . All the photos [of us] have come out etc.
> (Cruickshank 2017a)

Timeline of Events

7:58 a.m. Brussels Zaventem Airport Departure Lounge: A suicide bomber detonates explosives at check in kiosk 11. Nine seconds later there was another explosion at kiosk 2. A third bomber was thrown by the force of the explosions, and leaves the airport, unable to carry out his mission. Seventeen dead, eighty-one injured.

9:11 a.m. Maalbeek Metro Station: A suicide bomber detonates himself in a carriage as the train leaves the station. Fifteen dead, 219 injured.

Brussels Attack Logistics

On March 22, five men set out. Three of them, Ibrahim El Bakraoui, Najim Laachraoui, and Mohamed Abrini, hailed a taxi, and along with three oversized bags, went to Brussel's Zaventem airport. The taxi driver refused to take a fourth bag as it wouldn't fit in the car. At 7:48 a.m. two of the bombers detonated their bags near simultaneously at opposite ends of the departure hall. The third man was unable to detonate his device and escaped in the chaos.

Meanwhile, Khalid El Bakraoui and Osman Krayem traveled to the Pettillon metro station. Both men are seen outside the station on CCTV. Bakraoui entered the station and boarded a train to detonate his bomb four stops later at Maalbeek. The bomb exploded from the second carriage of a four-carriage train as it started to leave the Maelbeek station. The station is located under the Rue de la Loi/Wetstraat, a street best known for the many official buildings of the European Parliament, European Union, European Commission, and Belgian Government. Krayem left the scene—later confessing he also had a bomb but lost his nerve.

Within hours the airport taxi driver went to police with his description of the three airport bombers, and led them to their apartment. Police found Laachraoui's laptop in a trash can with a treasure trove of information, which help lead police to the suspects (Cruickshank 2017a). Authorities captured Abrini and Krayem in Brussels on April 8. Authorities continue to untangle the large web of ISIS sympathizers linked to the attacks. There are dozens of people still in custody on suspicion of involvement in both Paris and Brussels, to include nine Moroccan men arrested in Barcelona one year after the attack (Minder and Schreuer 2017).

EVADING AUTHORITIES

Intelligence agencies are at a disadvantage when it comes to tracking terrorist cells, and the men behind the Paris attacks were well trained in both evading detection and conducting operations. Both attacks were directed from Syria by a man named Oussama Atar (CNN 2017). A dual Belgian/Moroccan citizen, and cousin to Ibrahim and Khalid Bakraoui, Atar was involved with extremist terrorist groups since 2002. He spent time in prison in Iraq to include Abu Ghraib, before returning to Belgium in 2012. Belgian authorities, not concerned about ISIS during that time frame lost track of Atar, and at some point he traveled to Syria where he held a position of significance—both in ISIS and as the most senior Belgian extremist with credibility to recruit newly radicalized Europeans.

All of the Paris attackers were featured in an ISIS videotaped in Syria and released post attack (Cruickshank 2017b). The front lines in Syria provided the men both training as well as battle experience.

The fact most had European citizenship and could travel undetected across borders was most likely the reason they were sent back home to carry out an attack. According to interrogations of captured extremists, under Atar's guidance, Abaaoud was seeking recruits to conduct the Paris attacks as early as June 2015, at which point he already knew he wanted to attack soft targets where large numbers of people congregated.

ISIS set up an elaborate encrypted communication system to keep in touch with its European operatives undetected (Cruick-shank 2017b). They used a software tool called Truecrypt, which authorities found on a thumb drive. Operatives were taught to copy a message into the software, select an encryption option and then paste the message into a password-protected sharing site. It operated like a dead letter drop. Bataclan attackers used the "Telegram" encrypted messaging app with message "self-destruct" option. The group rented apartments and set up bomb-making facilities in run-down areas without much police oversight. Pre-paid credit cards and burner cell phones further helped the attackers avoid detection. Plans needn't be complicated to be effective.

It is easy to lay blame and wonder how authorities missed so many clues that might have prevented the attacks in both Paris and Brussels. The atmosphere in Belgium was ripe to harbor terrorists. There were, and still are, large pockets of unassimilated immigrants—sympathetic and segregated communities with distrust of the government. Belgium has more citizens in ISIS ranks than any other Western country and their intelligence services are stove piped and fragmented. Another complicating factor is the Belgian bureaucracy is among the worst in Europe; authorities don't share information well, and Brussels alone has nineteen separate municipalities, each with different chains of command and databases for tracking criminals. Authorities knew of several of the attackers, but connections weren't made, information not shared. Turkey provided information on El Barkraoui when they captured and deported him to Holland, but nothing was done (Calamur 2016).

Looking back and connecting dots is easy, ensuring the same mistakes aren't made again is difficult—but not impossible, as long as the will exists to invest the time, money, and effort into learning from the past, and extrapolating into the future. And not just in Belgium.

(Source: Kinzer 2019. Ms. Kinzer is a Reserve Air Force intelligence officer and senior intelligence consultant at Patch Plus Consulting.)

HOTELS

As discussed in Chapter 3, international terrorists have targeted hotels repeatedly in the last fifteen years, with attacks resulting in thousands of deaths and injuries. Indeed, hotels provide many security challenges; in Western countries, vehicles can drive right up to the entrance and are often left unattended during check-in. Baggage is unloaded and brought directly into the lobby, where, again, it may be left for periods of time. Most facilities include restaurants and conference and special-event facilities, greatly boosting the building's population during peak use.

Terror groups routinely target hotels. On August 5, 2003, al-Qaeda splinter group Jemaah Islamiyah detonated a car bomb outside the lobby of the Marriott Hotel in Jakarta, Indonesia, killing fourteen. On November 9, 2005, three hotels attacked in Amman, Jordan, were attacked by Iraqi al-Qaeda operatives. The Days Inn, Radisson SAS (now known as the Landmark), and the Grand Hyatt were simultaneously attacked by suicide bombers. In all, fifty-nine people died and 115 were injured. At the Radisson, a husband/wife team entered a Jordanian wedding reception of 900 people and detonated their belts. Fortunately, the female bomber's belt did not work, keeping the casualty count lower than it might have been but killing at least thirty-eight. At the Hyatt, the lone bomber went to the hotel coffee shop and ordered an orange juice. After drinking it, he left and went to another room, donned his suicide vest, came back, and then detonated the explosive device. At the Days Inn, the suicide bomber walked into the entrance toward the bar/dining area. An alert employee noticed the man and called for security; the man left the building and detonated his vest in the street, killing three members of a Chinese delegation.

On November 29, 2008, members of the al-Qaeda affiliate, Lashkar-e-Taiba, began their four-day assault in Mumbai, India. The twelve, coordinated shooting and bombing attacks shocked the world and lasted four days, killing 164 people and injuring hundreds. Targets included a train station, a Jewish community center, the Taj Mahal Hotel, and the Oberoi Trident Hotel.

On July 17, 2009, Jemaah Islamiyah struck again, with attacks again the JW Marriott and Ritz-Carlton hotels Jakarta, the bombings were five minutes apart. Nine people were killed.

Sharm el-Sheikh, on the southern tip of the increasingly volatile Sinai Peninsula, is a beautiful, seaside resort area with luxury Marriott, Sheraton, and Renaissance hotels. The Sheraton property has 835 rooms, a private beach, its own diving center, and eleven pools. Rooms often sell for an astonishing $35 a night, as the hotel industry tries to entice vacationers. Sadly, Sharm el-Sheikh is often the scene of horrific hotel terror attacks. In October 2004, al-Qaeda in Syria and Egypt carried out three bomb attacks targeting tourist hotels, leaving thirty-four people dead and 171 injured. One car bomber drove directly into the lobby of the Hilton hotel, killing thirty-five and injuring more than 100. Hilton was the subject of a lawsuit by and American family, who sued due to the lack of security measures to protect the hotel. In July of 2005, an attack by al-Qaeda in Lebanon, the Abdullah Azzam Brigades, claimed eighty-eight lives and inflicted 150 injuries. Although majority of those killed and wounded were Egyptian hospitality industry employees, many tourists from USA, Israel, Britain, Germany, and others were also injured. On April 24, 2006, were three bomb attacks by Islamist terrorists in Dahab, with explosions at restaurants attached to hotels and a supermarket.

The area was finally starting to see a resurgence in tourism, when ISIS claimed it put a bomb aboard a Russian Metrojet Flight 9268 passenger plane on October 31, 2015, which exploded mid-air and crashed on the Sinai Peninsula after taking off, killing 224. The UK instituted a flight ban, and their leading travel agencies canceled trips for the usually busy 2017–2018 winter holiday season.

In June 2015, Tunisia experienced a horrific terror attack at one of their beach side luxury hotels. The case study gives insight into the vulnerability of these soft targets.

Case Study: The Marhaba Hotel Beachfront Attack, Tunisia

At approximately 12:05 p.m. on June 26, 2015, 23-year-old engineering student Seifddine Rezgui opened fire on the tourist-filled Tunisian beach on the property of the Spanish-owned, five star Riu Imperial Marhaba Hotel, ten kilometers north of the city of Sousse. The chaos unleashed by Rezgui would last for twenty-five minutes before he was eventually gunned down while fleeing the scene (Figure 6.3). Carrying a single Kalashnikov rifle with four magazines and three grenades, one terrorist killed thirty-eight people, inflicted damage on Tunisian tourism industry and economy, and threatened the stability of the newly elected secular government.

ATTACK TIMELINE

11:30–12:00: Gunman arrives on the beach dressed in black shorts and a black t-shirt, carrying a beach umbrella hiding his rifle and grenades. Speaks casually to several people. Calls his accomplice on a cell phone to tell him he is starting the attack and throws phone into the ocean. Phone recovered later and plot evidence gathered by officials.

1205: Rezgui begins firing shots at tourists on the beach.

1210: Continues carnage at the hotel pool, before making his way inside the hotel where most people fled for protection; throws a grenade in the reception area, killing one woman.

1220: Returning to the beach, shoots some of the injured, then runs north past another beach property (Hotel Riu Bellevue Park) and then runs west on an access road trying to escape, is now being chased by locals.

1225: Gunman and police exchange fire.

1230: Gunman shot multiple times and killed.

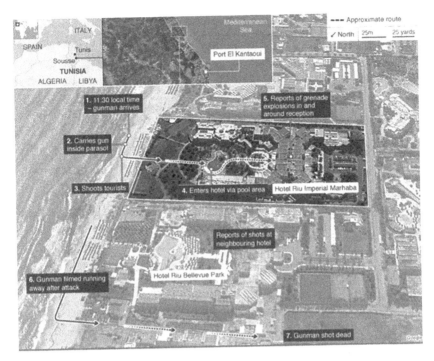

FIGURE 6.3   Marhaba Imperial Shooting Timeline and Map of Events
(BBC 2015b)

BACKGROUND

In the two years before the attack, the government failed to react appropriately to the growing threat to its fledgling democracy. Homegrown jihadists radicalized in Tunisian mosques were receiving militant training in Libya, and Tunisian fighters were rotating to and from the battle in Syria. The authorities knew radicalized youth were crossing the Tunisia/Libya border to receive training at a base affiliated with Ansar al-Sharia (Dearden 2015). Upon completion of their training, the men were assigned to sleeper cells, which authorities assumed were in the country. Although the group has not completely joined ISIS, Ansar al-Sharia's top official, Abu Abdullah al Libi, pledged allegiance to ISIS leader Baghdadi in early 2015 and several group members have defected (Joscelyn 2015). The gunman who conducted the Marhaba Beach attack was unknown to the government; however, ISIS, which said it was behind the attack, knew Rezgui and referred to him as "our brother in the Caliphate, Abu Yahya al-Qayrawani" and released a photo of him with weapons (Carty 2015). Officials later acknowledged Rezgui trained with the ISIS terrorists who attacked the Bardo museum (Dearden 2015).

Before this attack at the Marhaba Imperial, two other tourist venues in Tunisia were targeted by terrorists. On October 30, 2013, a suicide bomber was turned away from entering the Riadh Palm Hotel, located south of the Marhaba Imperial. Instead, he headed to the beach and started running towards hotel guests when his suicide vest exploded. On the day Khalil blew himself up, five others were arrested in Sousse on suspicion of planning similar attacks. His attempted attack on the hotel resulted in hundreds of police deploying to the resort area, but their presence dissipated as time went by and there were no further attacks. Just over a year later, on March 18, 2015, foreigners were again targeted by three jihadis at the Bardo Museum, with nineteen tourists killed. As a result of the Bardo tragedy, the President declared Tunisia was in a "war against terrorism." To demonstrate his resolve against terrorist who threatened the stability of his country and to reassure tourist they would be kept safe, he deployed troops to major cities. However, the beach resorts were largely left unprotected. Without significant security measures in place, the Marhaba Beach attack was easily executed.

Finally, in a bold warning that should have evoked a massive increase in tourist protection, the Ajnad al-Khilafa group, affiliated with Ansar al-Sharia in Tunisia, tweeted this in May of 2015 (Spencer 2015):

To the Christians planning their summer vacations in Tunisia, we cant accept u in our land while your jets keep killing our Muslim Brothers in Iraq & Sham (sic). But if u insist on coming then beware because we are planning for u something that will make you forget #Bardoattack. @Ajnad al-Khilafa.

The tourism industry in Tunisia took a massive hit in the days and weeks after the Marhaba beach attack. Over twenty hotels, including luxurious $500 a night spas closed their doors in the two weeks following the attacks as tourist fled home and others cancelled upcoming visits. The Marhaba Imperial closed the hotel due to the "difficult economic situation in Tunisia" and are attempting to reopen in Spring 2016. The parent company of the Marhaba Imperial, the Riu Spanish hotel chain owns ten hotels in Tunisia. Given there were one million fewer tourists in the first eight months of 2015 compared with 2014, and two million hotel nights expected to be lost in the year following the attack (Leach 2015), the future of the Marhaba Imperial and Tunisian tourism looks bleak.

Although guests at the resort who witnessed the shooting thought Rezgui seemed to know the layout of the grounds, there is no evidence he conducted prior surveillance. And given the lax twenty-five-minute response time to the scene by authorities, it is clear neither the hotel nor the local authorities were adequately prepared to respond. The Prime Minister's actions after the Marhaba massacre to close eighty mosques where radicalism and violence were preached (including Rezgui's Mosque) and the construction of a wall and sand trench for 100 miles along the border of Libya and Tunisia are steps in the right direction.

On July 10, 2015, in light of the Bardo Museum and Marhaba Hotel massacres, the Ministry of Tourism issued a press release outlining steps to protect tourists. An updated release was issued on October 7, 2015. The measures they directed put in place included the following (Ministry of Tunisia 2015):

1. Tourist police units have been armed and operational inside and outside any tourist area from July 1, 2015.
2. On top of the above, 1,000 security officers are deployed to enhance these measures.
3. Securing airports and border checkpoints.
4. Stationed and patrolled units have been deployed on the beaches and in the surroundings of all the resorts.
5. Security around cultural and archaeological sites has been reinforced.
6. Implementing a tracking security system of tours and excursions.
7. Strengthening of the supervisions of car parking areas for tourist vehicles in several tourist areas.
8. Running training courses for hotel security guards.
9. Allocating essential funds to provide hotels with necessary surveillance equipment.

Time will tell if a combination of these initiatives will keep ISIS and AQIM activity away from soft targets in Tunisia. As we protect hotels and other soft targets in the US against our common enemies, ISIS and al-Qaeda, it's important to consider cross-applying the updated anti-terrorism standards in countries already experiencing terrorist massacres.

(Source: Miller 2019b. Ms. Miller is a former Air Force Intelligence Officer.)

AQIM continues to attack hotels. Splinter al-Mourabitoun, bombed the Radisson Blu hotel in the Mali capital of Bamako in November 2015, killing twenty-one people. In January 2016, AQIM gunmen armed with heavy weapons attacked the Cappuccino restaurant, shooting into the crowd of 100 and then moved across the street to the Splendid Hotel in Ouagadougou, the capital of Burkina Faso. This attack killed twenty-nine people. Another AQIM assault came two months later when six gunmen attacked the Étoile du Sud hotel, in Grand-Bassam, Ivory Coast.

Eighteen people were killed in the shootout. A US delegation was staying at the hotel, also a favorite of tourists and expats.

Hotels remain a favorite target of al-Qaeda and affiliates around the world.

TOURIST SITES: A VULNERABLE TARGET

Attacks on tourist sites are also an operational tactic used by al-Qaeda and ISIS. On November 17, 1997, at 8:45 a.m., during peak tourist entrance into the park, six Islamist terrorists from Jihad Talaat al-Fatah, masquerading as Egyptian security forces, killed the two armed security guards and then stormed the Deir el-Bahri, an archeological site in Luxor, Egypt. Tourists were trapped inside the ancient buildings, and the terrorists went on a rape, mutilation, and killing spree, taking sixty-two lives. The terrorists escaped the scene in a tourist bus; at a checkpoint, they scattered into the hills. Some were later found dead, having committed suicide. This event deeply affected the tourist industry in Egypt, especially at Luxor, which has never fully recovered. The massacre did serve to turn Egyptian public opinion against al-Fatah and forced the government into action against the group, which later claimed it did not carry out the attack, and instead blamed Osama bin Laden.

A 2015 attack at a popular Tunisian museum by ISIS in Libya exposed their tactics for attacking a tourist site.

Case Study: Attack at the Bardo National Museum, Tunis, Tunisia

The Bardo National Museum is one of the top tourist destinations in Tunis, the capitol city of Tunisia, with an extensive collection of Roman mosaics. The museum is comprised of an eighteenth-century palace with a new modern wing and main entrance hall. The buildings are located in a large complex adjacent to the Tunisian Parliament buildings in central Tunis. The museum is a popular destination for Western cruise ship passengers on shore excursions.

On March 18, 2015, at least three gunmen wearing dark apparel and armed with Kalashnikovs and hand grenades passed unnoticed through an initial security check onto museum grounds where they waited for the arrival of tourist buses. Some accounts suggest the gunmen slipped past exterior security while the guards were conducting security checks on a tour bus. Other accounts suggest the security guards were on a coffee break and not at their posts at all. At around 1230 local time, as the buses from cruise ships began unloading, the gunmen brandished their weapons and began shooting into the crowd killing, several tourists instantly. The crowd scattered. It only took the police minutes to arrive, but the gunmen threw grenades at the police to impede their movement, fatally shot an officer

FIGURE 6.4   Still of Hostages From Raw Footage Inside the Bardo Museum (www.youtube.com/watch?v=RdCUnyHFq0M)

and his dog, and then followed a group of tourists through the glass doors leading into the museum's entrance hall. (Gall 2015) There were approximately 200 tourists present on the property at the time of the attack.

The attackers spent the next three hours inside the museum holding the tourists hostage (Figure 6.4). They spared the lives of Tunisian workers, targeting only foreign visitors. Accounts from an Italian tourist interviewed after the attack described how the tourists tried to find cover as the terrorists sprayed bullets around rooms. CCTV footage released by the Tunisian authorities shows two gunmen roaming the hall, hunting the tourists, and speaking to a third man. The standoff with police ended when Tunisian Special Forces secured the building. The death toll was twenty-three, including twenty tourists from Japan, Poland, Italy, and Colombia; one Tunisian police officer; and two of the three gunmen. There were fifty people seriously injured.

THE RESPONSE

Tunisian police immediately evacuated the area, to include the Tunisian Parliament, which was in session at the time. Television footage showed law enforcement escorting civilians to safety, and emergency medical response arriving to tend to causalities. Police and Special Forces snipers took positions surrounding the building, and a helicopter circled overhead. Counterterrorism police garrisoned nearby arrived on the scene quickly.

When the they entered the building, the team quickly killed two terrorists and secured the building. The Tunisian government identified the two dead gunmen at the scene as Yassine La Abidi, 20, and Hatem Khachnaoui, 26. Abidi was from Tunis, and well liked in his neighborhood. He recently became religious, and his name was known to Tunisian authorities, although friends and family could not believe he was involved in such a brutal attack. Khachnauoi was from Kasserine, near the Algerian border. In the days following the siege, the Tunisian authorities arrested four of Khachnaoui's relatives in connection to the attack. Both men had illegally left Tunisia to attend a jihadi training camp in Libya in December of 2014 (Stephen 2015b). A third gunman escaped, probably with fleeing tourists. Maher Ben Moudli Kaidi, who Tunisian officials believe coordinated the attack and may have been the third gunman is still at large. On March 29, Tunisian security forces killed the commander of the group responsible for the massacre, Khaled Chayeb, also known as Lokman Abu Sakhr, along with eight other Islamist militants.

THE PLANNING

The Bardo attack was a strategic move to hurt the newly formed secular government and disrupt tourism—the third largest sector of the Tunisian economy, at 7.4 percent of the GDP in 2014. From a tactical perspective, the planning was easy to plot and execute. The simplicity of the actions belies the impact.

The gunmen, and most likely several associates with planning experience conducted reconnaissance missions to determine the museum layout and security practices. They obviously concluded there was not sufficient security to simultaneously admit tour buses and ensure pedestrians were properly searched—or even noticed. If, as suggested in at least one media report, most of the guards were habitually away on a coffee break at a specific time each day, that would have been apparent to any surveillance team noting patterns of life. The same team could easily have noted peak arrival times for tourist buses full of cruise line passengers. Obtaining Kalashnikovs and hand grenades would have been easy across the porous borders with Libya or Algeria. One Tunisian official lamented the entire attack could not have cost more than 4,000 dinars—approximately $2,000 (Kirkpatrick 2015).

The results were dramatic for the Tunisian economy, and coupled with the Sousse resort attack in June of 2015, devastating. There is no dollar figure associated with lost revenue yet, but as of September 2015, tourism from Britain alone was down 80 to 90 percent (Stephen 2015a).

THE THREAT

Tunisia was the only country to benefit from the Arab Spring uprisings of 2011 and was enjoying relative peace and expanded democratic rights. In December 2014, national elections put a new, largely secular government in power. In contrast, Tunisia is also the largest supplier of foreign fighters to Syria, with an estimated 3,000 currently in the fray. In February 2015 alone more than thirty returning jihadis were arrested. Tunisia also shares long and porous borders with both Libya and Algeria, hotbeds of lawlessness and extremism.

It is easy for militant recruiters to cross into Tunisia to persuade disaffected youth to join their cause, and just as easy, would-be recruits can cross to attend jihadi training camps in Libya.

ISIS threatened Tunis in December with a video via the twitter handle "ghazwat Tunis" or "Raid of Tunis" and they were quick to praise—and on some social media sites take credit for—the Bardo Museum attack. However, Tunisian law enforcement ultimately determined the Okba Ibn Nafaa Brigade-a local splinter group of al-Qaeda in the Islamic Maghreb was to blame (Financial Times 2015).

LESSONS LEARNED

The Prime Minister of Tunisia dismissed six police commanders, including the Tunis police chief, for security failures brought to light after the attack (Gall 2015).

The fact the Islamic State and other jihadists groups to claim the attack in Tunis "demonstrates the interconnectedness of these loosely affiliated networks" (Kirkpatrick 2015). Lack of a clear recruitment or funding path for the gunmen is another problem for intelligence and law enforcement agencies trying to detect amateurs planning terrorist attacks. The interest of individuals and small groups to engage in attacks on soft targets is very visible on social media, where some aspiring jihadists have begun using the hashtag, in Arabic, "Lone Wolf." They are literally "hiding in plain sight" (Kirkpatrick 2015).

Small groups are much harder for law enforcement to infiltrate and stop, and as was demonstrated here, a few men with little planning and scant resources hitting a soft target had an outsized effect on the national economy and grabbed worldwide headlines for their cause.

Stopping lone wolf or small non-affiliated group attacks is extremely difficult for intelligence and law enforcement agencies, making bolstered security and increased vigilance at soft target destinations the first and only line of defense.

(Source: Kinzer 2016. Ms. Kinzer is a Reserve Air Force intelligence officer and senior intelligence consultant at Patch Plus Consulting.)

Several tourist sites in the United States could lend themselves to a similar attack, particularly soft target venues with a limited amount of hardening or security. For instance, in December 2017, the FBI arrested an ISIS-inspired former US Marine sharpshooter for plotting a Christmas terror attack target San Francisco's bustling Pier 39. Everitt Aaron Jameson, 26, attended basic training with the Marine Corps and graduated several months later, but was discharged for fraudulent enlistment because he failed to disclose his history of asthma. During his training, he earned a "sharpshooter" rifle qualification. Jameson selected the Pier 39 location because "he had been there before and knew it was a heavily crowded area" and was planning to carry out the attack using explosives between December 18 and December 25 because "Christmas was the perfect day to commit the attack" (Musumeci 2017).

These examples illustrate how recent history is replete with examples of attacks on or threats against shopping, sports, and recreational venues by groups threatening the United States. Now that we've covered the groups involved in soft target attacks and their traditional targets, we'll explore "what's next"—new tactics and emergent threats in soft target attacks.

REFERENCES

"Al-Shabaab Twitter Messages during the Westgate Mall Attack." http://jihadology.net/2013/09/21/new-statement-from-%E1%B8%A5arakat-al-shabab-al-mujahidin-claiming-responsibility-for-the-westgate-mall-attack-in-nairobi/ (2013).

American Jewish World. "Israeli Counters Terror at Mall of America." Minneapolis, MN: American Jewish World Press, February 2, 2011.

Associated Press. "Las Vegas Gunman May Have Targeted Lollapalooza & Life Is Beautiful Festivals." Los Angeles, CA: AP Online, October 5, 2017.

———. "Pulse Nightclub Shooter Intended to Attack Disney World." Orlando, FL: AP Online, March 28, 2018.

Barry, Dan, Serge Kovaleski, Alan Blinder, and Mujib Mashal. "Always Agitated: Always Mad: Omar Mateen, According to Those Who Knew Him." *The New York Times*, June 18, 2016.

BBC. "Charlie Hebdo Attack: Three Days of Terror." *BBC News Online*, January 14, 2015a.

———. "Tunisia Attack: What We Know about What Happened." www.bbc.com/news/world-africa-33304897 (June 30, 2015b).

———. "Brussels Explosions: What We Know about Airport and Metro Attacks." www.bbc.com/news/world-europe-35869985 (April 9, 2016).

———. "Salah Abdeslam Trial: Paris Attacks Suspect Lambast Anti-Muslim Bias." *BBC*, www.bbc.com/news/world-europe-42940636 (February 5, 2018a).

———. "Manchester Attack Fire Crews Sent Away from Arena Blast." www.bbc.com/news/uk-england-manchester-43548173 (March 28, 2018b).

BBC Africa. "Nairobi Siege: How the Attack Happened." www.bbc.com/news/world-africa-24189116 (2013a).

———. "Q&A: Westgate Attack Aftermath." www.bbc.com/news/world-africa-24274113 (October 21, 2013b).

BBC News. "Gas 'Killed Moscow Hostages.'" news.bbc.co.uk/2/hi/europe/2365383.stm (October 27, 2002).

Bradbury, Shelly. "Minute by Minute: A Timeline of the Chattanooga Attack Revealed." *Times Free Press*, July 23, 2015.

Butime, Herman Rujumba. "The Lay-Out of Westgate Mall and Its Significance in the Westgate Mall Attack in Kenya." *Small Wars Journal*, May 10, 2014.

Candea, Stefan, Jürgen Dahlkamp, Jörg Schmitt, Andreas Ulrich, and Wolf Wiedmann-Schmidt. "The Path to Death: How EU Failures Helped Paris Terrorists Obtain Weapons." *Speigel Online*, March 24, 2015.

Carty, Peter. "Tunisia Hotel Attack: ISIS Releases Picture and Names Killer of the 38 Tourists in Sousse." *International Business Times*, June 27, 2015.

Chrisafis, Angelique. "Charlie Hebdo Attackers: Born, Raised and Radicalied in Paris." *The Guardian*, January 12, 2015.

Calamur, Krishnadev. "Brussels Attacks: What the Belgians Missed." *The Atlantic*, March 25, 2016. www.theatlantic.com/international/archive/2016/03/belgium-terror-attack-intelligence/475464/

CNN. "2015 Paris Terror Attacks Fast Facts." www.cnn.com/2015/12/08/europe/2015-paris-terror-attacks-fast-facts/index.html (October 31, 2017).

Copello, Evan. "Ariana Grande Concert Bombing." Case Study, *Soft Target Hardening: Protecting People from Attack*, 2nd ed., Boca Raton, FL: Taylor & Francis, 2019a.

———. "The Chattanooga Recruiting Office Shootings." Case Study, *Soft Target Hardening: Protecting People from Attack*, 2nd ed., Boca Raton, FL: Taylor & Francis, 2019b.

Cruickshank, Paul. "Discarded Laptop Yields Revelations on Network Behind Brussels, Paris Attacks." *CNN*, January 25, 2017a. www.cnn.com/2017/01/24/europe/brussels-laptop-revelations/index.html

———. "The Inside Story of The Paris and Brussels Attacks." *CNN*, October 30, 2017b. www.cnn.com/2016/03/30/europe/inside-paris-brussels-terror-attacks/index.html

Dao, James and David Johnston. "Suspect in Soldier Attack Was Once Detained in Yemen." *New York Times*, June 3, 2009.

Dearden, Lizzie. "Tunisia Attack: Gunman 'Trained at Terror Camp in Libya with Bardo Museum Attackers." *The Independent*, June 10, 2015.

———. "Manchester Bombing: Isis Claims Responsibility for Concert Attack as Part of 'Shock and Awe' Tactics, Analysts Say." *The Independent*, May 23, 2017a.

———. "Salman Abedi: How Manchester Attacker Turned from Cannabis-Smoking Dropout to ISIS Suicide Bomber." *The Independent*, May 24, 2017b.

Dettmer, Jamie. "Nightclub Massacre Prompts Questions about Competence of Turkish Security." *Voice of America*, January 1, 2017.

DHS (Department of Homeland Security). "National Planning Scenarios." Washington, DC: Homeland Security Council, 2006.

Dixon, Robyn. "Video Shows Kenyan Soldiers Looting Besieged Mall." *Los Angeles Times Online*, October 3, 2013.

Doherty, Ben, Bridie Jabour, Brigid Delaney, Calla Wahlquist, Helen Davidson, Michael Safi, Oliver Milman, and Paul Farrell. "Sydney Siege: How a Day and Night of Terror Unfolded at the Lindt Café." *The Guardian*, December 19, 2014.

Fausset, Richard, Alan Blinder, and Michael S. Schmidt. "Gunman Kills 4 Marines at Military Site in Chattanooga." *New York Times*, July 16, 2015.

FBI. "On the Ground in Kenya, Part 2: Terror at the Westgate Mall." www.fbi.gov/news/stories/on-the-ground-in-kenya-part-2 (January 10, 2014).

Financial Times Reporters. "At Least 37 Killed in Attack on Tunisian Beach Resort." *Financial Times*, June 26, 2015.

Florida Department of Law Enforcement. "Florida Department of Law Enforcement After Action Report: Orlando Shooting: Pulse Nightclub." https://ric-zai-inc.com/Publications/cops-w0857-pub.pdf (2016).

Flynn, Jorja. "Death from Above: Massacre in Las Vegas." Case Study, *Soft Target Hardening: Protecting People from Attack*, 2nd ed., Boca Raton, FL: Taylor & Francis, 2019.

Fox News. "Las Vegas Shooter Reportedly Used Hotel Freight Elevator as High-Rolling Perk." October 11, 2017.

Gall, Carlotta. "Tunisian Museum Attack Leads to Firing of Chiefs." *New York Times*, March 23, 2015.

Grace, Francis. "FBI Alert on Stadiums." *CBS News*, July 3, 2002.

Graham, David. "The Mysterious Life and Death of Abdelhamid Abaaoud." *The Atlantic*, November 19, 2015.

Greenwald, Glen and Murtaza Hussain. "As the Trial of Omar Mateen's Wife Begins, New Evidence Undermines Beliefs about the Pulse Massacre, Including Motive." *The Intercept*, March 5, 2018.

Hall, Stacey. "Securing Sport Stadiums in the 21st Century: Think Security, Enhance Safety." *Journal of Homeland Security* (2010).

Innis, Michelle. "Sydney Hostage Siege Ends with Gunman and 2 Captives Dead as Police Storm Cafe." *New York Times*, December 15, 2014.

Investigative Project on Terrorism. "US v. Mehanna, Tarek." www.investigativeproject.org/case/282/us-v-mehanna (2014a).

———. "US v. Nuradin Abdi." www.investigativeproject.org/case/100/us-v-abdi (2014b).

———. "US v. Shareef, Derrick." www.investigativeproject.org/case/192/us-v-shareef (2004).

Jambo News. "Nairobi Senator Mike Sonko Reveals What He Knew about Westgate Mall Terrorists." Nairobi: Jambo News, October 10, 2013.

James, Patrick, Michael Jensen, and Herbert Tinsley. "Understanding the Threat: What Data Tells Us about U.S. Foreign Fighters." College Park, MD: START, 2015, 1–4.

Joscelyn, Thomas. "Ansar al Sharia Libya Fights on Under New Leader." The Long War Journal, June 30, 2015.

Johnson, Rebecca. "Sydney, Australia, Chocolate Café Attack." Case Study, Soft Target Hardening: Protecting People from Attack, 2nd ed., Boca Raton, FL: Taylor & Francis, 2019.

Khorram, Yasmin, Ben Brumfield, and Scott Zamost. "Chattanooga Shooter Changed after Mideast Visit, Friend Says." CNN, September 15, 2015.

Kinzer, Sarah. "Attack at the Bardo National Museum, Tunis, Tunisia." Case Study, Soft Targets and Crisis Management: What Emergency Planners and Security Professionals Need to Know, Boca Raton, FL: Taylor & Francis, 2016.

———. "The Coordinated Paris and Brussels Attacks." Case Study, Soft Target Hardening: Protecting People from Attack, 2nd ed., Boca Raton, FL: Taylor & Francis, 2019.

———. "The Nairobi Mall Attack." Case Study, Soft Target Hardening: Protecting People from Attack, 1st ed., Boca Raton, FL: Taylor & Francis, 2014.

Kirkpatrick, David. "Militants, ISIS Included, Claim Tunisia Museum Attack." New York Times, March 19, 2015.

Kulish, Nicholas, Jeffrey Gettleman, and Josh Kron. "During Siege at Kenyan Mall, Government Forces Seemed Slow to Respond." New York Times, October 1, 2013.

Lappin, Yaakov and Yohah Jeremy Bob. "Shin Bet Foils Hamas Bomb Attack Planned for Jerusalem Mall." Jerusalem Post, September 2, 2013.

Las Vegas Metropolitan Police Department. "Preliminary Report, 1 October Mass Casualty Shooting." January 18, 2018. www.lvmpd.com/en-us/Documents/1_October_FIT_Report_01-18-2018_Footnoted.pdf

Leach, Naomi. "Tunisia's Tourism Industry Plunges into Crisis amid European Travel Warnings with up to Two Million Hotel Nights Set to Be Lost over The Next Year." Associated Press, July 13, 2015.

Lormel, Dennis. "Lessons Learned from the Paris and Brussels Terrorist Attacks." ACAMS Today, March 29, 2016. www.acamstoday.org/lessons-learned-paris-brussels-attacks/

McNerthney, Casey. "Arcan Cetin Kills Five People at Cascade Mall in Burlington on September 23, 2016." *Historylink.org, File 20394,* June 26, 2017.

Medina, Jennifer. "A New Report on the Las Vegas Gunman Was Released: Here Are Some Takeaways." *The New York Times,* January 19, 2018.

Mendick, Robert, Gordon Rayner, Martin Evans, and Hayley Dixon. "Security Services Missed Five Opportunities to Stop the Manchester Bomber." *The Telegraph,* June 6, 2017.

Miller, Nicole. "Je Suis Charlie: The Jihadist Revenge Attack on a Satirical Magazine." Case Study, *Soft Target Hardening: Protecting People from Attack,* 2nd ed., Boca Raton, FL: Taylor & Francis, 2019a.

———. "The Marhaba Hotel Beachfront Attack, Tunisia." Case Study, *Soft Target Hardening: Protecting People from Attack,* 2nd ed., Boca Raton, FL: Taylor & Francis, 2019b.

Minder, Raphael and Milan Schreuer. "Spain Arrests 9 in Brussels Attacks Investigation." *New York Times,* April 15, 2017. www.nytimes.com/2017/04/25/world/europe/spain-brussels-attacks-arrests.html

Ministry of Tourism, Republic of Tunisia. "A Formal Statement from The Government of Tunisia About the Steps Taken to Prevent Further Attacks Which UK Tour Companies Can Use to Reassure Their Customers." www.tourisme.gov.tn/en/services/news/article/la-ministre du-tourisme-annonce-des-mesures-exceptionnelles-pour-secourir-le-tourisme.html (October 7, 2015).

Musumeci, Natalie. "FBI Thwarts ISIS-Inspired Christmas Terror Attack on San Francisco." *New York Post,* December 22, 2017.

New York City Police Department. "Analysis of Al-Shabaab's Attack at the Westgate Mall in Nairobi, Kenya." www.documentcloud.org/documents/894158-westgate-report-for-shield-website.html (2013).

New York Times. "Suicide Bomber Kills Official and 13 Others at Sri Lanka Race." April 7, 2008.

———. "Three Hours of Terror in Paris, Moment by Moment." November 9, 2016a.

———. "Unraveling the Connections among the Paris Attackers." March 18, 2016b.

Pearson, Michael, Jethro Mullen, and Anna Coren. "With Two Hostages and Gunman Dead, Grim Investigation Starts in Sydney." *CNN,* December 15, 2014.

Pflanz, Mike. "Nairobi's Westgate Mall Attack: Six Months Later, Troubling Questions Weigh Heavily." *The Christian Science Monitor,* March 21, 2014.

Pflanz, Mike and Harriet Alexander. "Nairobi Shopping Mall Attacks: Britons among Those Caught Up in Terrorist Assault." *The Telegraph,* September 21, 2013.

Radio Sweden. "Paris Attack Terrorist Radicalized in Sweden." November 30, 2016. http://sverigesradio.se/sida/artikel.aspx?programid=2 054&artikel=6576482

Rubin, Alissa. "Radicalization of a Promising Student Turned Bomb Maker in Brussels." *New York Times*, April 8, 2016. www.nytimes.com/2016/04/09/world/europe/najim-laachraoui-paris-brussels-attacks.html

Schmitt, Eric, Michael S. Schmidt, and Andrew Higgins. "Al Qaeda Trained Suspect in Paris Terror Attack, Official Says." *New York Times*, January 9, 2015.

SITE Intel Group. "Chattanooga Shooter Muhammad Youssef Abdulazeez Maintained Blog." *Jihadist News*, July 16, 2015.

Snow, Deborah and Patrick Begley. "What Really Happened on Night of Sydney Siege? Six Questions Inquest Must Answer." *Sydney Morning Herald*, May 20, 2017.

Spencer, Richard. "ISIL-Linked Terror Group Warned of Tunisia Attack One Month Before." *The Telegraph*, June 30, 2015.

Star Tribune. "Dahir Adan: What We Know." Minneapolis: *Star Tribune Online*. September 22, 2016.

Stephen, Chris. "Tourists Desert Tunisia after June Terror Attack." *The Guardian*, September 25, 2015a.

———. "Tunis Museum Attacks: Police Hunt Third Suspect in Shootings." *The Guardian*, March 22, 2015b.

Straub, Frank, Jack Cambria, Jane Castor, Ben Gorban, Brett Meade, David Waltemeyer, and Jennifer Zeunik. "Rescue, Response, and Resilience: A Critical Incident Review of the Orlando Public Safety Response to the Attack on the Pulse Nightclub." *US Department of Justice, The Community Oriented Police Services and The Police Foundation*, 2017.

Swisher, Skyler. "Omar Mateen Failed Multiple Times to Start Career in Law Enforcement, State Records Show." *Sun-Sentinel*, June 16, 2016.

Wade, Ted. "Pulse Nightclub Attack, Orlando, Florida." Case Study, *Soft Target Hardening: Protecting People from Attack*, 2nd ed., Boca Raton, FL: Taylor & Francis, 2019.

Walsh, Paul. "Man Who Stabbed 2 at Mall of America Tells Court ISIS Inspired Him." *Minnesota Star Tribune*, January 29, 2018.

Zaccardi, Nick. "An Oral History of the Bombing That Rocked the 1996 Atlanta Games." *Sports Illustrated*, July 24, 2012.

Zwerdling, Daniel, G. W. Schulz, Andrew Becker, and Margot Williams. "Under Suspicion at the Mall of America." *National Public Radio*, September 7, 2011.

CHAPTER 7

New Tactics and Emergent Threats

The art of war teaches us to rely not on the likelihood of the enemy not coming, but on our own readiness to receive him; not on the chance of his not attacking, but rather on the fact that we have made our position unassailable.

—Sun Tzu

INTRODUCTION

We routinely underestimate the sophistication of bad actors. Doing so gives us a severe blind spot and increases our vulnerability. As the case studies in this book illustrate, terrorists are constantly learning and their methods morphing, whether to avoid detection or to amplify the bloodshed and impact of their attack. We are always surprised after an attack by their ingenuity and creativity. Or frustrated that the same tactics are used but with an unexpected "twist," hitting the reset button, winning Black Swan game, and sending us scrambling to cover the ever-growing list of vulnerabilities.

After decades of playing defense, we must get on the offensive of this war on terror. Understanding evolving tactics allows for more effective hardening activities. Keeping an eye on the horizon for emergent threats means we will be ready to meet future danger with confidence, a plan and deterring and mitigating tools. Instead of quickly moving on after a terrorist attack, we need to spend more time studying the event, understanding how we failed, where we need to be, and what must change. Then we must create a plan to move towards the new construct.

Although this gap analysis is the backbone of every successful enterprise, it is rarely applied to target hardening after an attack. We do not feel comfortable "marinating" in the aftermath of our failures and therefore assume an attack was a "one off" and the terrorist or criminal was simply lucky. This short sightedness means yet another blind spot, ripe for exploitation by bad actors.

Delving into these cases, exploring new tactics, and visualizing emergent threats allows us to shift our thinking from "what is" to "what's next."

VEHICLES AS WEAPONS OF TERROR

Al-Qaeda in the Arabian Peninsula first encouraged its Western recruits to use trucks as weapons. The 2010 edition of the glossy online al-Qaeda magazine *Inspire* gave detailed instructions for carrying out vehicular attacks on crowds, urging would-be terrorists to "pick up as much speed as you can while still retaining good control ... to strike as many people as possible in your first run." Entitled "The Ultimate Mowing Machine," the article directs recruits to use a pickup truck as a "mowing machine, not to mow grass but mow down the enemies of Allah."

ISIS also endorsed the vehicle attack method. In 2014, spokesman Abu Mohammad al-Adnani called for lone wolf attacks with improvised weapons, "If you are not able to find an IED or a bullet, then single out the disbelieving American, Frenchman or any of their allies. Smash his head with a rock or slaughter him with a knife or run him over with your car or throw him down from a high place or choke him or poison him." In November 2016, ISIS issued the third issue of their online magazine *Rumiyah*, which included an article calling for followers to carry out vehicle attacks, specifying the ideal type, weight, and speed of a car needed for a terror attack, and encouraged targets such as "large outdoor conventions and celebrations, pedestrian-congested streets, outdoor markets, festivals, festivals, parades, political rallies." Palestinian terrorist groups also use vehicles to target Israeli citizens and soldiers in Gaza and have done so for at least two decades.

The Counter Extremism Project (CEP) documents vehicular terrorist attack (CEP 2018). Their data shows thirty-six attacks worldwide since 2006, resulting in the deaths of at least 196 people and the injury of at least 1,050 others. The US, Europe, and Canada showed a dramatic rise in the number of vehicle terror attacks and death at the hands of radical Islamists.

As discussed in Chapter 3, Mohammed Reza Taheri-azar drove a rented sports utility vehicle into a crowd of students at University of North Carolina, Chapel Hill, in March 2006 with the intent to kill. Following his attack, vehicle-ramming attacks continued for a decade, in locations ranging from Jerusalem (with a bulldozer) to Tel Aviv (outside a nightclub), Quebec (soldier), Austria (pedestrians), France (Christmas market), the West Bank (soldiers), and Ürümqi, China (attack against shoppers with explosives). In December 2010, DHS expressed concern over the rising use of vehicles as weapons and issued a warning, *Terrorist Use of Vehicle Ramming Tactics*, classified "For Official Use Only," but widely available on the Internet.

The attack in Nice, France, on July 14, 2016, set off a wave of ISIS and al-Qaeda-inspired vehicular attacks throughout the West. CEP documented these major vehicular incidents in just two years: Vienna (street), Ohio (university), Berlin (Christmas Market), London (mosque, bridges), Antwerp (thwarted), Stockholm (pedestrians), Paris (police), Barcelona (Las Ramblas shopping district), Edmonton (pedestrians), New York (bike path), and Toronto (public square). For more information about vehicular terror attacks, visit the Counter Extremism Project website at www.countexttremism.com.

Several of the attacks give helpful insight into target selection, attack preparation, and vulnerabilities, specifically Nice, Barcelona, New York City, and the two bridge attacks in London.

Case Study: Rise of New Terror Tactic: Vehicle Into a Crowd

A brutal, yet effective terrorist tactic is on the rise across Europe and the United States. Ramming vehicles into crowded streets is a method gaining popularity among terrorist and extremist organizations due to the simplicity of planning, low cost of the operation, and the overwhelming success in terms of deaths and catastrophic injuries.

Three specific attacks yield important information about how terrorists selected their target, evaded law enforcement,, and executed their attack.

Nice, France, Bastille Day, July 14, 2016
Barcelona, Spain, Las Ramblas Square, August 17, 2017
New York City, USA, bike path, October 31, 2017

NICE, FRANCE

On July 14, 2016, civilians across France were celebrating Bastille Day, a national holiday commemorating the turning point in the French Revolution. The closing parade was held at the waterfront Promenade des Anglais and drew a crowd of 30,000. The Promenade was closed to traffic and a long section converted into a pedestrian zone. The customary Bastille Day fireworks display took place between 10:00 and 10:20 p.m. As the fireworks ended, thousands of people who gathered on Promenade to watch were continuing their celebration when Moroccan terrorist Mohamed Lahouaiej-Bouhlel abruptly ended the celebration with his unexpected attack, driving a 19-ton truck into the crowd. Unlike other events with similar story lines, Bouhlel also wielded a gun and shot pedestrians as he drove down the road. The attack killed eighty-four and injured hundreds more. At least ten of the victims killed were children. The attack horrified the world; although Nice was not the first place to experience a terror attack by vehicle, the scale of loss of life and injury was shocking. It was the city's worst episode of violence since World War II.

ATTACKER

Bouhlel was born in Tunisia and moved to France in 2005. He married a French-Tunisian cousin with whom he had three children, and they lived in Nice. According to his wife's lawyer, he was repeatedly reported for domestic violence and the couple separated (Huffington Post-LeMond 2016). Bouhlel carried out the attack by himself, but after further investigation, it was discovered that he had five accomplices supporting his mission. Bouhlel and accomplices were previously unknown to French intelligence services, though Bouhlel was convicted of five prior criminal offences for threatening behavior, violence, and petty theft (Payton 2016). Per his family, Bouhlel also underwent psychiatric treatment before he moved to France.

THE ATTACK

Bouhlel was able to talk his way past security before the Promenade was closed to traffic at 3 p.m.; he told them he was delivering ice cream, and, despite the fact the truck was not refrigerated, security let him through to the Promenade (O'Brien 2016). Had they inspected the vehicle, they would have found no ice cream but guns, knives, and a grenade.

When Bouhlel was ready to attack, he drove the wrong way down a narrow access road, accelerated the truck and mounted the curb, pushed through a few lightweight crowd control barriers and lane separators. He sped down the promenade at 56 miles per hour in a zigzag fashion to maximize casualties, plowing through packs of people along a one-mile path. A motorcyclist drove alongside the truck, trying to reach into the cab; the bike went under the tires of the truck, which then slowed down (Willgress and Samuel 2016). The rider reached in the window and started punching Bouhlel, who pistol whipped him in the head. Police finally were able to engage Bouhlel in a gun fight, and he was pronounced dead at the scene.

INVESTIGATION

The investigation into the attack found Bouhlel performed surveillance several times on the Promenade in the days prior to the attack, using the rented truck and attempting to gain access (BBC 2016a). He also persuaded some friends to smuggle bundles of cash worth 100,000 euros to his family in Tunisia, a large sum for his modest lifestyle. An uncle stated that Bouhlel was radicalized a few weeks before the attack by an Algerian ISIL member living in Nice. According to investigators, Bouhlel had a "clear, recent interest in the radical jihadist movement," was friendly with a member of the al Nusra Front, expressed admiration for ISIS, and had pictures and videos of ISIS beheadings on his computer (Chazan, Morgan, and Turner 2016).

ISIS stated the attack was committed by one of its own soldiers after the fact, but no direct connections between Bouhlel and ISIS were detected. It is clear that he was self-radicalized, and the process was rapid.

Response: After the attack, emergency services, hospitals, and police forces realized they were underprepared for certain types of mass casualties. Across the state, initiatives for teaching first responders and hospital staff methods of treating large numbers of trauma patients, as well as equipping health professionals with knowledge of safe security measures are practical steps taken by the French in order to better prepare for future attacks.

BARCELONA, SPAIN

Barcelona is the most populous city in Spain and known for its vibrant culture. On August 17, 2017, a busy Thursday morning in Las Ramblas shopping district, locals and visitors alike were enjoying the afternoon when a large van pummeled through the street, killing thirteen people and injuring dozens more. This attack was brutal and unexpected, but the initial plan devised was much worse.

The evening before the Barcelona attack, one of the terror cell members misused triacetone triperoxide (TATP), causing an explosion at their safehouse in Alcanar. The explosion killed two of the ten Moroccan terror cell members, including their imam mastermind. A third man was injured and taken to a nearby hospital. Unbeknownst to police, the other seven terrorists fled the scene. The house was stocked with knives, trucks, and bomb-making chemicals, shedding light on the terror cell's deadly plans (Reinares and Garcia-Calvo 2017). Police found 120 gas canisters inside, which police believe the cell was attempting to make into one large bomb or three smaller bombs to be placed in three rental vans. The explosion forced the terrorists to change their plans and they decided to attack soon using the crude truck-into-crowd-method. Around 4:30 p.m. the next day, terrorist truck driver Younes Abouyaaqoub headed toward the city center of Barcelona, and about twenty minutes later his assault began in Las Ramblas square. After zigzagging his way into pedestrians, the airbags deployed and Abouyaaqoub abandoned his vehicle, fleeing the scene on foot. He carjacked a vehicle at knifepoint and was on the run for four days; a woman called in a tip that he was at a gas station; police responded and Abouyaaqoub, wearing an explosive belt, ran into a nearby vineyard where he was shot and killed (Parfitt 2017).

Nine hours after the Barcelona attack, five of the men from the terror cell drove into pedestrians in nearby Cambrils at 1:15 a.m., killing one and injuring six others. They jumped out of the vehicle and continuing their rampage with a stabbing spree. Police shot and killed all five attackers (Reinares and Garcia-Calvo 2017). Similar to the attack in Nice, France, ISIS took credit, further signaling its global presence to the world. In all, sixteen people of ten nationalities were killed: fourteen struck by the van in La Ramblas, including one who died from their injuries ten days after the attack; one fatally stabbed in Barcelona during the carjacking; and one in Cambrils. Over 100 people from more than thirty-four nations were injured in the attack, many severely (BBC 2017).

Response

After the attack, the Catalan set aside quarrels surrounding desired independence from Spain for a short time while the Spanish government dealt with recovery measures. The royal family issued statements of unification despite the harsh reality of a divided kingdom. The Barcelona attacks sparked global awareness and renewed solidarity in the war on terror and against jihadist extremism. Another practical response in the wake of this massacre comes in the form of large concrete bollards placed on Barcelona streets frequently visited by locals and tourists.

NEW YORK CITY, USA

Manhattan, New York, is busy year-round, bustling with Wall Streeters, wide-eyed wonderers, and everyone in between. Add in the spirit of Halloween and New York is transformed to an other-worldly scene. The celebrations came to a halt at 3:04 p.m. on October 31, 2017, when a rented Home Depot truck crashed through a crowded sidewalk on the Hudson River Greenway, a protected bike lane along the Hudson River, killing eight and injuring twelve others. The driver was 29-year-old Sayfullo Saipov, a former resident of Florida, Ohio, and New Jersey. Ties to ISIS were clear when investigators found a note in the truck saying ISIS would "endure forever." In addition to this note, two cell phones were confiscated, one full of ISIS propaganda videos and images, along with searches for "Halloween in New York." The driver also had a bag full of knives and a stun gun in the event of having to exit the vehicle and continue his massacre on foot. He crashed ten blocks into the massacre after crashing into a school bus carrying special needs children. NYPD Officer Ryan Nash shot and injured Saipov, ending the attack. The entire world mourned for those lost, especially Argentina, as five of the victims were Argentine citizens visiting the US to celebrate the 30th anniversary of their high school graduation.

Timeline and Actors

Born in Uzbekistan, Saipov moved to the United States in 2010 and lived a relatively normal life as a truck driver. Co-workers said he was aggressive and had a bad temper, which often cost his job. In 2015, federal agents interviewed Saipov about his contacts with two suspected terrorists, but a case was not opened against him. Since the bullet wound did not kill Saipov during his apprehension, officials were able to gain a plethora of information after he was treated for his injury. While he was not on the FBI Watch List, investigators learned of his desire to carry out an attack beginning about a year prior (Mueller et al. 2017). He rented the truck two months prior to the assault, to "get a feel" for how it drove. Saipov eventually decided on Halloween because he assumed there would be more people on the street, hoping to kill more in his wake. He told officers of his initial plan to prolong his rampage onto the Brooklyn Bridge, and was fairly open with officials throughout the rest of his interrogation, which was very helpful for analysts to break down ties to ISIS and possible future attacks (Chavez and Levenson 2017).

LESSONS LEARNED

Transportation Alternatives, a nonprofit organization in New York City which encourages city-friendly travel for bike riders and pedestrians, previously pushed for safety bollards ever since two vehicular incidents resulting in fatalities on the bike path in 2006, but the city ignored their safety concerns and made only aesthetic fixes to the path.

Since the attack occurred on Halloween, New York residents were hesitant to go out that evening for fear of a follow-up assault. This perfectly illustrates the amplifying effect of a terrorist attack. However, NYPD released statements encouraging people not to cancel their plans and continue to be "New Yorkers."

The commonality between all three events, Nice, Barcelona and New York City was the unsuspecting crowd, enjoying recreational activities. Holidays or other special events increase the likelihood of this type of attack, since a higher population is expected to gather in one area. This method of attack is widely successful and doesn't take much skill or effort; one simply needs to know how to operate and obtain a vehicle, and then choose a target. ISIS has presence across the globe, but to radicalize, a person doesn't have to have direct contact with ISIS members; their propaganda is easily accessed on the Internet as it was with Saipov. The truck-into-crowd terrorist tactic is expected to persist due to tremendous success in past attacks.

(Source: Sheller 2019. Mrs. Sheller is a graduate of Virginia Tech with a degree in political science, concentrating in national security studies. She works for the US government as an analyst.)

London experienced two terror attacks by vehicle within three-month period in 2017. Unfortunately, officials did not apply lessons learned from the first attack on the bridge near Westminster, to the second location, the London Bridge, a stated target of both al-Qaeda and ISIS for years. Therefore, just months after the first attack, a vehicle was able to mount the curb and carve a second path of destruction.

Case Study: Vehicle-Based Attacks on Bridges in London

Vehicle-based attacks are effective operations requiring few resources and easily accessed training via Internet propaganda posted by terrorist groups. In 2017, London experienced two vehicle attacks on its famous bridges, illustrating how a crude attack can still be deadly and achieve one of terrorism's main goals—fear.

254 Chapter 7 New Tactics and Emergent Threats

WESTMINSTER BRIDGE ATTACK

On March 22, 2017, Khalid Masood, a British-born 52-year-old, initiated a vehicle-based attack on London's Westminster Bridge at approximately 2:30 in the afternoon. Using almost the entire span of the bridge, he rammed his rental car into pedestrians, killing four people and injuring twenty-nine. One tourist was knocked into the Thames River and later died from her injuries. Upon exiting the bridge, Masood crashed his rental into the Carriage Gates, a guarded access point for members of Parliament. At that point, he abandoned the car and stabbed and killed the on-duty guard before police gunned him down. Khalid Masood acted alone in this vicious act of terrorism—at least in its execution (Payne and Engel 2017).

Immediately following the attack, pro-ISIS channels on the chat app, Telegram, exploded with coverage as events unfolded, a familiar pattern after attacks in Nice, Paris, and Orlando. ISIS eventually claimed Masood as one of their soldiers.

LONDON BRIDGE ATTACK

Just a little over two months later, the London Bridge was the scene of a copycat attack, also claimed by ISIS via their news agency, Amaq. This attack proved even more deadly than the original, and revealed new tactics employed by the terrorists. At approximately 10:00 p.m. on June 3, 2017, three ISIS soldiers started their attack. The driver and ringleader, Khuram Butt, conducting a trial run across the bridge in his rental van, began plowing the small rental van. Butt intended to hire a 7.5 ton truck but was refused due to his failure to provide payment details; had the transaction gone through, the victim count would have surely been higher. He then made a high-speed pass into pedestrians, eventually crashing the vehicle into a railing. After the crash, all three men escaped the van and began slashing and stabbing victims with kitchen knives as they made their way through Borough Market's restaurants and pubs. As the knife yielding assaults began, they shouted, "This is for Allah" (Joseph 2017).

Security guards stationed throughout the popular night spot were able to communicate about the ongoing attacks, but their only recourse and that of the crowd was to throw bottles and chairs at the attackers. The terrorists were not stopped until police officers arrived on the scene and shot the men. Once they neutralized the attackers, police discovered all three were wearing fake suicide vests. The vests were simple in construction and made of water bottles wrapped in duct tape. Clearly, the vests were intended to maximize the fear of their victims and possibly prevent police from firing on them in a hostage scenario. Investigators also found thirteen Molotov cocktail-type devices in the van along with two blow torches (Alexander 2017). These items suggest that the "plan" may not have gone as intended, and if executed more successfully, could have led to considerably more carnage. In the end, eight people died and forty-eight were injured.

Significantly more is known about the three men who attacked innocent victims in the London Bridge offensive than about the lone attacker of the Westminster Bridge. Butt, the driver of the van and the leader of this cell, was 27 years old, married with two children, and employed at a local gym. He was known to security services but not considered a threat or actively planning an attack. Butt was a known affiliate of Mohammed Shamsuddin, a London-based Islamic extremist calling for Sharia law in Great Britain. The second jihadist, Rachid Redouane, was 30 years old and claimed to be of Moroccan-Libyan ethnicity. He sought asylum in Britain in 2009, but his request was denied. Rachid was known to have lived in Ireland at some point and was married with a child. The last man in this trio—Youseff Zaghba—was 22 years old, significantly younger than the other men. Son of an Italian mother and Moroccan father, Zaghba had told his mother that he desired to live "as a pure Muslim." In 2016, he was stopped in Bologne, Italy, from boarding a flight to Turkey, with a final destination in Syria. At the time, US intelligence issued a general warning that Moroccans living in Italy were communicating in large numbers about joining the fight in Syria. When Zaghba was detained at the airport, he told police "I'm going to be a terrorist." Investigators confiscated his phone and passport and found propaganda videos and religious sermons on his mobile device. However, he was not jailed after the courts deemed there was not enough evidence to convict him of planning a terrorist attack (Booth et al. 2017).

It is not clear how long the three men knew each other or if they worked together to plan and practice the London Bridge attack. The only evidence giving some indication of their alliance is a video showing the three of them meeting outside the gym where Butt worked, recorded five days before the attack (Dearden and Bulman 2017).

RECRUITMENT AND TARGET SELECTION

At first glance, it is easy to assume that both of these attacks were simply ISIS-inspired and there was no direct command and control of either operation. However, an investigation by the BBC investigative show *Inside Out, London*, revealed that ISIS was recruiting British Muslims to carry out attacks on specific London targets since at least July 2016 (Adesina 2017). Two BBC reporters uncovered evidence of ISIS trolling the Internet looking for jihadis. With the knowledge of security services, they posed as fictional youth dedicated to the ISIS cause. Once they established a connection, the recruiter instructed them to further talks via a secured messaging site. He also inquired as to whether or not the recruit was familiar with Westminster; "a good target because it was busy and crowded." In December of 2016 one of the reporters was directed by a different ISIS agent to a terrorist manual on the dark web. "It outlined the strategy of using vehicles as lethal weapons and explained how to target vulnerable parts of the body with a knife." The reporter was also directed to web-based instructions on bomb making and to a video on assembling a fake suicide vest.

LESSONS LEARNED

These simple-to-execute attacks were highly effective; they instilled fear in the public, were low cost, and virtually undetectable. In both cases, the jihadis needed only to rent a car/van and carry easily purchased knives. A vast network is not required to support an operation of this kind. The only real requirement was an Internet connection.

ISIS suggested these two bridges as targets but did not mandate when the attack should occur or how the terrorists should execute the strikes. It must be assumed that ISIS has other such soft targets selected throughout the Western world. Simple and inexpensive prevention can take place in areas of high pedestrian traffic and tourists attractions to help protect the public from such indiscriminate attacks. Although barricades and bollards are good physical security protection for people and infrastructure, the way to stop these attacks is to infiltrate ISIS's communication platforms (broadcasts and publications) to monitor the leadership, the organization (to include recruiters in Western nations), and objectives. Western intelligence agencies must also work in conjunction with telecommunications corporation to continuously dismantle information and messages that are passed to would-be jihadis through dark web sites and private messaging platforms.

(Source: Miller 2019. Ms. Miller is a former Air Force Intelligence Officer.)

Vehicles for these types of attacks are procured in a variety of ways: insider threat—an authorized commercial vehicle driver carries out or facilitates the attack; hijacking—attacker gains control of a commercial vehicle by force; theft—attacker steals a commercial vehicle; rental—attacker rents a commercial vehicle; and purchase—attacker purchases a commercial vehicle. In one case, with no planning at all, an angry extremist used his own vehicle to mow down protestors on a main street. James Alex Fields, Jr., a 20-year-old from Ohio and member of a white supremacist organization, purposefully drove his vehicle at a high rate of speed into a group of protestors the Unite the Right Rally in Charlottesville, Virginia, in August 2017, and then backed up at a high rate of speed hitting more pedestrians, and left the scene. One person was killed, and nineteen others injured.

ISIS continues to ask followers to engage in vehicular terror; on May 17, 2017, the video "We Will Surely Guide Them to Our Ways," featuring the self-identified American fighter Abu Hamza al-Amriki, encourages lone wolf attacks with knives and motor vehicles. The video also features several short clips of US-based locations, including New York City's Times Square. Although the video was removed from the Internet, segments of the longer video keep reappearing on various social media sites. In May 2017, the Transportation Security Agency (TSA) issued For Official Use Only guidance in a report entitled "Vehicle Ramming Attacks: Threat Landscape, Indicators and Countermeasures." TSA shared the report with bus, trucking, and rental car companies. The report is available online.

Finally, in Toronto on April 23, 2018, Alek Minassian, a 25-year-old Richmond Hill man and college student, drove his rented white Ryder truck into a crowd, killing nine people and injuring sixteen.

See Chapter 9 for hardening tactics related to vehicle attacks. Figure 7.1 gives an idea of how sidewalks are hardened in France post-Nice attack.

FIGURE 7.1   New Sidewalk Hardening in Cannes, France

THE USE OF HUMAN SHIELDS

The cases of Beslan school and the Moscow theater sieges in Russia, and the Bataclan Theater attack in Paris were the largest terrorist kidnapping and hostage-taking crises at soft target venues to date. However, there were dozens of other smaller-scale events, like the Lindt Café in Australia, and the tactic is escalating among terrorist groups. Not only al-Qaeda and ISIS but all of the international terrorist groups, as well as Mexican cartels, routinely kidnap tourists as a way either to raise ransom or to secure the release of imprisoned colleagues. The recent trend: even if the ransom is paid, hostages are not released per the agreement or are killed anyway. Hostages of terrorists are doomed captives; there is nothing for the captors to negotiate for.

Managers and security personnel at soft target facilities and venues should also prepare for the possible use of children, women, and the elderly as human shields by terrorists (international or domestic) on our soil. Human shields tactics are the deliberate placement of civilians around targets or combatants to prevent the enemy from firing. The use of human shields is prohibited by the Fourth Geneva Convention, Protection of Civilian Persons in Time of War, which was passed in 1949 as a result of atrocities perpetrated by the Nazis during World War II. Specifically, the article states:

> The presence or movements of the civilian population or individual civilians shall not be used to render certain points or areas immune from military operations, in particular in attempts to shield military objectives from attacks or to shield, favour or impede military operations.

However, as discussed in Chapter 2, terrorists do not adhere to Geneva conventions or worry about worldwide condemnation of their activities, and therefore may use human shields when facing law enforcement or military response at the scene of their attack. Under international humanitarian law governing the legal use of force in an armed conflict, the use of human shields violates the principle of "distinction." Chapter 1, Rule 1 states: "The parties to the conflict must at all times distinguish between civilians and combatants. Attacks may only be directed against combatants" (ICRC 2018). Furthermore, the Geneva Convention states: "Children who have not attained the age of fifteen years shall neither be recruited in the armed forces or groups nor allowed to take part in hostilities."

HAMAS is one of the worst offenders; using innocent civilians for offensive and defensive operations is not just a tactic, it is part of their combat doctrine. Independent reports give detailed evidence that HAMAS used hospitals, schools, homes, and mosques to hide weapons and soldiers during the Gaza War, an Israeli military initiative from December 2008 through January 2009. At twenty-five miles long and six miles wide, with a population of 1.5 million, Gaza is the sixth most densely populated place on earth, providing a very complex battleground situation. The UN report on the war mentions the possible use of children, women, and the elderly as human shields by HAMAS; however, Malam, an Israeli intelligence think tank, produced a report using declassified material such as videotapes, maps, and operational plans recovered on the ground by Israel Defense Forces troops. The information indicates HAMAS hid improvised explosive devices in and around civilian homes and hospitals, and video taken from a helicopter appears to show the use of children and the elderly as human shields for soldiers engaged in operations.

The Liberation Tigers of Tamil Eelam (LTTE) was defeated by the Sri Lankan government in May 2009 in a final, violent offensive on a northern beach in the Vanni region. During the months leading up to the conflict, the United States used satellites to monitor the situation, releasing photos to the public to show how LTTE herded hundreds of thousands of citizens on the beach for use as human shields in their final standoff with government forces. Many died from starvation, execution, or government shelling, and some escaped only to be captured and put into government internment camps. The remaining civilians, approximately 130,000, were forced to stay in a one-square-mile area of beach and be part of the final battle. There is no final accounting of civilians killed in the final offensive; the United Nations (2011) estimated at least 40,000. A BBC documentary entitled *Sri Lanka's Killing Fields* documents the atrocities performed by the government and the rebels in "no fire" and "safety" zones, as well as hospitals, schools, villages, and convoys of refugees deliberately pulled into the conflict (Snow 2011). In 2012, a Sri Lankan general admitted to war crimes, including the extrajudicial killing of civilians. According to intelligence agencies, LTTE members who fled the country are regrouping in Canada, which is why the group remains on the US State Department's FTO list.

The use of human shields has become very commonplace with terrorist groups. The Chechen rebels used human shields in the Beslan school massacre. Al-Qaeda and the Taliban used human shields in Afghanistan in 2007; Syrian rebel groups herded Alawite men and women into at least 100 cages, paraded them through the streets, and placed them in various places to use as human shields against Assad's airstrikes; and ISIS used hundreds of thousands of human shields in both Mosul and Raqqa.

Although it seems inconceivable to us that a terrorist group, cartel, or lone actor would use human shields, we must remember the power of ideology, especially radical religious dogma, which empowers believers with a sense of justification for their illegal and immoral activities

FIGURE 7.2   HAMAS' Use of Human Shields (Israeli Defense Video 2007)

(Figure 7.2). The Beslan example reminds us the terrorists will use civilians to absorb the line of fire. Naturally, it is difficult to "go there" mentally, but we should prepare for even the most horrific of scenarios, including the terrorist exploitation of innocent civilians to further goals. How will we respond?

FIRST RESPONSE AND THE THREAT OF SECONDARY ATTACKS

It's what people like us do: without concern for our personal safety, we race to the scene of an attack to assist survivors. Law enforcement, medical professionals, those with a military background are hard-wired to respond this way, and our response is instinctive. Unfortunately, the instinct to run toward the fight, not away from it, could be deadly. My military colleagues often tell stories about the use of secondary and tertiary devices in Iraq and Afghanistan. The insurgents set off the first IED and wait until other soldiers rush in; then they set off a second device, sometimes a third. But this is not a new tactic; both international and domestic terrorists have employed it successfully for years. Facilities serving as shelters for people injured or fleeing an attack, such as schools, churches, malls, and sporting and recreational venues, can themselves become targets. As covered in Chapter 5, terrorists will even strike a hospital providing care to victims of the first attack.

International terrorist and criminal groups have successfully employed this "double-bomb" tactic to target first responders, and evacuating civilians are often caught in the fray. For instance, secondaries targeting responders in other notable attacks include the Jemmah Islamiyah hotel bombing in Bali in 2002, an anti-American attack by Hezbollah at the McDonald's in Lebanon in 2003, and the 2004 police station bombing in Athens by the Revolutionary Struggle group. In March 2010, in Dagestan, a Chechen suicide bomber dressed in a police uniform approached investigators and residents who had gathered at the scene of a car bomb explosion near a school and detonated his explosive vest. In April 2010, an al-Qaeda bombing in Algeria was followed by a secondary, detonated one hour later, killing a soldier. The same month, Chechen rebels bombed a train in Dagestan and remotely detonated a secondary device to target first responders. Cartels in Mexico have even kidnapped and used police as hostages to pull in others to the scene before they detonate a bomb, as they did with the VBEID in Juarez. According to a DHS memo, "First responders were lured into the kill zone with an emergency call stating a wounded police officer was at a specific location. Post event analysis revealed the attackers had dressed a wounded civilian in a municipal police officer uniform" (Esposito 2010).

Domestic terrorists also use this technique. Almost every attack perpetrated by Eric Rudolph included a secondary device specifically targeted toward emergency personnel. For example, prior to the Atlanta abortion clinic bombing in 1997, Rudolph called in a bomb threat and watched as office members evacuated and gathered in certain areas of the parking lot. He planned this into his operation months later; after he bombed the clinic, a second device went off an hour and a half after the first, injuring seven first responders. The Mexican cartels use secondary device tactics to ensnare and kill law enforcement. In fact, Louis R. Mizell, a terrorism expert and former US intelligence agent for the State Department, has compiled a database of 300 double-bomb attacks by more than fifty terrorist groups in the world over the last ten years. His advice is "the reality of today's double-bomb tactic dictates that first responders have three primary jobs at a site: attending to the wounded, dispersing the crowd, and finding a second bomb" (Gips 2003). The threat of secondary and tertiary bombing is real, and we must factor the tactic into soft target hardening and emergency response procedures.

Whether al-Qaeda's simultaneous bombings or ISIS operations to spread out attacks over a wide area and over a long period of time, terrorist attacks are designed to quickly exhaust first responder resources to add to the effectiveness of the attack and human suffering. Also, as responders in Mumbai and Paris found, a city attack with multiple scenes means the streets will be clogged with panicked citizens, the press, and helping agencies—you won't get to the scene in a timely manner.

Another concern is the deliberate targeting of first responders to "take them out of the fight." This tactic could be part of a larger plan to keep first responders from the scene of an attack, prolong the event, or increase the casualty count. Police and fire stations should keep their building secure and check for suspicious packages and people—also a good idea since violence in society is on the rise, and people are acting out on their anger like never before.

Consider all of these scenarios in your planning and exercising activities—forms of hardening.

WEAPONS OF MASS DESTRUCTION

According to the FBI (2018), weapons of mass destruction (WMDs) are defined in US law (18 U.S.C. § 2332a) as

> (A) any destructive device as defined in section 921 of this title (i.e., explosive device); (B) any weapon designed or intended to cause death or serious bodily injury through the release, dissemination, or impact of toxic or poisonous chemicals, or their precursors; (C) any weapon involving a biological agent, toxin, or vector . . . and (D) any weapon that is designed to release radiation or radioactivity at a level dangerous to human life. WMD is often referred to by the collection of modalities that make up the set of weapons: chemical, biological, radiological, nuclear, and explosive (CBRNE). These are weapons that have a relatively large-scale impact on people, property, and/or infrastructure.

Although we tend to worry about al-Qaeda, their splinters and ISIS groups using WMDs, chemical, biological, and radiological weapons are also on the table for use by domestic terror groups. A 2012 study conducted by Syracuse University's Maxwell School of Public Policy and the New America Foundation examined 114 cases of domestic terrorist acts and plots in the United States since 9/11, none involving al-Qaeda or groups/individuals motivated by Islamist radicalism. The ideologies that were studied span the spectrum from neo-Nazism and militant Christian fundamentalism to anarchism and violent environmentalism (New America Foundation 2012b). Among the vast number of weapons, destruction of property, and conspiracy charges, the research also found five plots of domestic terrorism involving chemical, biological, and radiological agents that could have killed thousands of Americans if executed (New America Foundation 2012a).

Naturally, al-Qaeda is at the very least interested in using WMDs against the United States. In the chemical and biological realm, a ten-volume *Encyclopedia of Afghanistan Resistance* found in Jalalabad contained formulas for manufacturing toxins, botulinum, and ricin and provided methods for dissemination. At Tarnak Farms, the former Afghan training camp near Kandahar, Afghanistan, al-Qaeda not only provided firearms training but also experimented with biological warfare in a special laboratory. Ahmed Ressum, the Algerian al-Qaeda member who was caught at the Canadian border before he could execute the 2000 "millennium attack" of the Los Angeles airport, testified that al-Qaeda taught him to poison people by putting toxins on doorknobs, and he engaged in experiments in which dogs were injected with a mixture containing cyanide and sulfuric acid. Also, al-Qaeda members were seeking to fly crop dusters that analysts believe might have been used to disseminate anthrax and chemical or biological agents (Boureston 2002). Regarding al-Qaeda and biological warfare, in 2009, Algerian newspaper *Anahar al-Jadeed* reported forty AQIM (al-Qaeda in the Islamic Maghreb) terrorists died at a training camp in Algeria from their infection with bubonic plague (Al Arabiya News 2009). Speculation abounded: Was it a dead rat causing the deaths or an experiment gone bad? We will never know; however, al-Qaeda's *Inspire* magazine has encouraged its readers to manufacture ricin, botulinum, and sarin in their homes, even encouraging them to get a Muslim microbiologist to assist, if needed.

Finally, al-Qaeda splinter ISIS considered weaponizing Y pestis, or the bubonic plague in 2014, as indicated on a laptop seized from a militant/ engineer in Syria. ISIS was keen to exchange American hostages for Pakistani neuroscientist Aafia Siddiqui, who is serving eighty-six years in US federal prison on terrorism charges. Also known as "lady al-Qaeda," Siddiqui, who received her PhD in the United States, was captured in Afghanistan with detailed plans to construct a variety of WMDs and employ them against US targets. Therefore, it is very concerning that ISIS sought Siddiqui to become part of their campaign to expand their self-labeled "caliphate."

Domestic terrorists may also use the al-Qaeda guides (widely available on the Internet) as a template for constructing their own weapons; in 2008, the FBI arrested Roger Bergendorff, who had ricin, a schematic for an injection pen, weapon silencers, and the jihadist Anarchist Cookbook in his Las Vegas hotel room. After recovering from ricin poisoning, he was sentenced to three and a half years in prison. Bergendorff never gave an exact motive behind his activities, but clearly it is dangerous to have private citizens tinkering with toxic biological and chemical compounds. We need to continue to work to get materials off the Internet and out of the hands of would-be attackers.

Perhaps the most accessible WMD is chlorine, an easily obtained chemical that could sicken or kill hundreds of people, under the right conditions. AQIM used chlorine in several vehicle-borne IED (VBIED) attacks against coalition forces in Iraq in 2006; although more casualties

arose from the bomb blasts, the terrorists kept trying different methodologies to perfect their technique and used it thirteen more times in the
war. Chlorine can be a silent killer; in 2005, two trains collided in Gran-
iteville, South Carolina, in the middle of the night, releasing sixty tons
of chlorine gas. Unsuspecting residents who heard the collision drove
through the cloud, stayed in their homes, or kept working their outdoor
night shift jobs. In all, nine people died and more than 250 were sickened
by the gas, which causes nausea, dizziness, and vomiting. Chlorine is
easy to obtain; therefore, we must educate suppliers on how and what
to report in terms of suspicious buys or patterns. Facilities with pools
should keep chlorine products stored in a locked facility.

Does al-Qaeda, ISIS, or other foreign and domestic terrorist groups
have WMDs? Those of us who live in the "open source world" do not
have the definitive answer to the question; however, we can turn to government reports and congressional testimony to provide an accurate
barometer. For instance, take the December 2008 report entitled "The
World at Risk," issued by the Graham/Talent Commission, a bipartisan
group that spent six months examining the WMD issue. When Senator Graham briefed Congress, he ominously stated, "Terrorists could
mount nuclear or biological attack within five years." Statements from
the report are also very telling:

> The commission believes that unless the world community acts deci-
> sively and with great urgency, it is more likely than not that a weapon
> of mass destruction will be used in a terrorist attack somewhere in the
> world by the end of 2013. The Commission further believes that ter-
> rorists are more likely to be able to obtain and use a biological weapon
> than a nuclear weapon.
>
> (Commission on the Prevention of WMD
> Proliferation and Terrorism 2008)

Synthetic manufacturing is causing increased concerns, as chemically
synthesized DNA can replicate DNA found in biological or chemical
agents occurring in nature and, more worrisome, enhance the effects.
According to Vahid Majidi, the assistant director of the FBI's Weapons of Mass Destruction Directorate, the agency is working to keep this
emergent technology from falling into the wrong hands (Committee on
Homeland Security and Governmental Affairs 2011).

What does this mean for soft targets? Bad actors have used WMDs
against civilians, notably the sarin gas attack by terrorist group Aum
Shinryko (now known as Aleph) in 1995, which killed thirteen people,
severely injured fifty, and causing temporary vision problems for nearly
1,000 others, including first responders who rushed to the scene without the proper equipment. In the United States, Bhagwan Shree Rajneesh
led a religious group in the Dalles, Oregon, area in the early 1980s. In

an attempt to keep voters away from the polls and sway a 1984 local election toward a candidate friendly to the group, he and his followers deliberately contaminated salad bars at ten local restaurants with salmonella. The incident was the first and single largest bioterrorist attack in US history. Vulnerabilities of soft targets include contamination of the food supply in cafeterias and the use of central ventilation systems to release a chemical gas or biological toxins. Anthrax transported through envelopes and the mail system is certainly a tactic we've seen, so mail rooms should take extra precautions with suspicious letters or packages. A WMD agent might also be attached to a bomb, making it the dispersal method for radiation or chemical or biological agents. As illustrated throughout this book, a WMD is in the playbook for a variety of bad actors wishing to do us harm; therefore, we must prepare.

DRONES

Terrorists are already using drones to advance their goals on the battlefield. Similar to other tactics and weapons borne of war, we should expect this tactic will spread into the West; we simply must prepare now.

Only imagination (and science) limits the ways bad actors may use drones. As often happens, weapons, and technology from modern and sophisticated militaries are adopted by militias and nonstate actors. For instance, ISIS has used drones in their battlefield operations since at least 2014, a very important, yet overlooked, development. They also produced how-to guides, widely available on the Internet. In 2017, ISIS used unmanned aerial vehicles (UAVs) in 129 attacks in just a four-month period. They continue to raise the sophistication and reach of their drone fleet— yes, fleet. ISIS drones are relatively cheap, made of homemade electronics or products readily available on the consumer market. ISIS currently uses drones for videos and surveillance, for indirect fire spotting, and weapons delivery. In fact, experts estimate there are thirty-two different models of drones operating in Syria and Iraq (Gettinger 2016). Of course, you can fly a more sophisticated unmanned aircraft remotely; the US military operates much of its drone fleet from an isolated location in Nevada.

To properly defend against this threat, we must understand basic definitions and the rules governing drone use. What is a drone? An unmanned aircraft system (UAS), sometimes called a drone, is an aircraft without a human pilot onboard; instead, the UAS is controlled from an operator on the ground. The FAA has stated that unmanned aircraft systems are aircraft, not toys, making operators subject to aviation laws and guidelines. The National Transportation Safety Board recently confirmed for the first time that all drones, regardless of size, are considered aircraft under federal law. As of December 2015, all commercial and noncommercial drones weighing 0.55 to 55 pounds must be registered via an FAA online system.

The rules get very complicated, so it is important you understand the specific FAA rules for drone use in the area you are trying to protect. Why? So you can more easily identify nefarious use of drones. For example, the FAA restricts flights over stadiums with a seating capacity of more than 30,000 people from one hour before until one hour after the game. Also, the FAA requires that airport operators and air traffic control towers receive prior notice of drone flights within five miles of the airport. The airport may also deny these flights. If your facility is within five miles of an airport and there is drone activity, make contact with the airport to see if it was approved.

FAA UAS Safety Guidelines include:

Fly at or below 400 feet and stay away from surrounding obstacles.
Keep your UAS within sight.
Never fly near other aircraft.
Never fly over groups of people.
Never fly near emergency response efforts such as fires.
Never fly under the influence of drugs or alcohol.
Understand airspace restrictions and requirements.
Only fly in daylight.

Terrorism and criminal activity aside, drones also carry with them the potential to invade privacy, injure people, and cause property damage, even if used properly and legally. As such, many college campuses are creating drone policies for safety and security, and they serve as a great model for businesses, churches, hospitals, and other institutions with a sprawling campus. Columbia University, Trinity College in San Antonio, Texas, and the University of Minnesota all have outstanding counter-drone planes posted on the Internet; just search for the college name plus drone policy. Also, many gated housing community associations are writing anti-drone policies, so there are many templates you can use for your organizations. Again, if you restrict drones from your institution and grounds, the sight and sound of one should cause alarm. Certainly drones have many good purposes, and are widely used in real estate, surveying, mapping, and other activities. The key is to know who and what is intruding in your airspace.

To further enforce the restriction of drones from your property, you may also point out these risks associated with haphazard drone use and their possible penalty:

Reckless endangerment (a felony).
Invasion of privacy (can easily be upgraded to a federal complaint).

Obstruction of police/emergency services duties (a felony).
Noise ordinance violation (local organization or community policy).
Misdemeanors related to endangering wildlife or felonies if disturb-
ing endangered species.

Many organizations I've consulted with believe they cannot restrict drone
use on their property, which is simply not true. They should err on the
side of the people and facilities they are protecting, not the hobby drone
user. If, when the technology becomes available, you plan to use your
own drones to provide security, understand more drones in your airspace
may increase your vulnerability. Drones can be counter-programmed and
used for nefarious purposes, as we've seen on the battlefield. Also, the
more drones in the air, the less likely you will identify the intruder.

CYBER AND PHYSICAL SECURITY

The Cloud: Just Someone Else's Computer

Most would agree globalization, fed by technological advances in the
information system and telecommunications realms, has overwhelmingly
been a "good thing." Our world is connected like never before, and those
formerly isolated are now part of the landscape, able to access critical
medical information, tap educational resources, and answer almost any
question in two clicks.
      Unfortunately, terrorists are similarly thrilled with globalization.
They, too, can answer any question in two clicks, including how to build
a crude bomb. They use Google Earth to identify targets and landmarks.
Somali terrorists used Facebook pages to liaise with recruits in Minneapolis, and insurgents on the battlefield have satellite phones and use
Telegram and Twitter to communicate. They are now able to directly
engage you through your home computer . . . or your child through his/
her web-enabled device . . . to spread radical ideology and fear. In addition
to waging societal warfare through crude attacks and fear mongering,
terrorists and criminals are also engaging in standard cyber-warfare by
deliberately targeting our systems to deny service or corrupt data. We
must remember that hackers don't necessarily have to create their own
tools, they have access to them on the Internet through the dark web and
other platforms.
      A few contributing factors led to the exploitation of cyberspace. If
you look at the domains we operate within, there is space, air, land, sea,
and cyber. The difference is that cyber is kinetic—it is invisible. Unlike
the other domains, we can't control what rides through and across our
system and our cyber work has to ride across other systems we can't

control. Not only do we have to adhere to our own national compliance, we have to comply and adhere to standards from other countries, as well.

The demand for cyber and wireless has propelled it into the $6 trillion range, meaning a race by companies to field applications and products (often without proper vetting). A final, significant challenge: the private sector has the lead, which means the government has little or no control. Recent discussion of the US government taking the lead in the development and fielding of the new 5G network was met with resistance by the telecommunications world. And the government was late to the discussion; AT&T announced they were nearly ready to launch, with Verizon, Sprint, and others to follow. Companies are racing for a piece of the 5G business and to meet a new global framework (3rd Generation Partnership Project, or 3GPP), which ensures all cell phone equipment can operate together throughout each of the world's markets.

A side discussion of what 5G will bring to the world includes: immersive virtual reality, real-time viewing, see-in-the-dark cameras, storage capacity for nearly an infinite amount of instant downloads from any location, virtual meet-ups with other people who appear in 3-D volumetric displays projected from your phone into the space just in front. By combining the increasing processing power of a smartphone with massive bandwidth, the ability to perform remote functions is greatly enhanced. Think of factories remotely operating machines and robots. Teachers projecting themselves into a virtual classroom. Doctors performing remote surgeries using their phone to operate hospital machines.

Now imagine this technology in the hands of terrorists and criminal syndicates. Recruiting, training, planning, funding. Trafficking, laundering, selling, buying. Gambling, drugs, pornography, hacking.

Partnerships like 3GPP are wonderful for the business world and customers (who doesn't want their smartphone to work in every country?) but still lacks a tie-in to security. Cyberspace is virtually "un-patrollable." We have a weak set of international laws and no overarching governing body for enforcement. Sovereign nations believing in freedom of speech and expression may monitor the web through their law enforcement agencies, but do not actively infiltrate and disable sites—this decision is left to companies that host the platform, and they typically decide based on what is best in light of the bottom line. In the rush to get cutting edge products to market, there is no pause to think about what I call "the 1 percent"—the terrorists and criminals that will exploit the technology. It is much easier and more comfortable to focus instead on the predictable 99 percent, customers without nefarious intentions, and what is intruding in your airspace.

Not only do terrorist groups use the same technology that we do on a daily basis, their financial assets are growing exponentially, allowing them to get the right people on the payroll, such as scientists, engineers, and technical experts. Social media apps allow people to connect virtually—as you and I might find fellow football fans or college alumni, jihadists can also find each other. For instance, in at least ninety-six countries, Facebook helped introduce thousands of ISIS extremists to each other using the "suggested friends" feature, per the Counter Extremism Project, a nonprofit group pushing tech companies to do more to remove known extremist and terrorist material online (Evans 2018).

Terrorist groups are even developing their own apps. In January 2018, a terrorist tech group on the "MuslimTec" Telegram channel distributed a link—posted in English and German—on the "MuslimCrypt," which was a purported self-developed steganography application for hiding and encrypting messages within images. The group's administrator encouraged users to test for viruses or trojans and attempt to break the application. Are you surprised?

Therefore, we've created an environment ripe for infiltration by terrorists who are sophisticated, have vast resources, and are patient. As such, the following assumptions must be made in the cyber realm:

Every new application will be exploited.
Every technological solution will be defeated.
Your operation will be targeted through system probes.
Your staff and facility users introduce vulnerability and will be exploited.

This book is not about cybersecurity, there are plenty of experts you can consult for assessment and advice. However, physical security and cybersecurity are now inextricably linked through the IP-enablement of everyday workplace functions. This phenomenon, called convergence, is creating an overlap of physical and cybersecurity issues and increased vulnerability. For example, hackers accessed Target corporation's network via an attack on a third-party maintaining their heating/ventilation/air conditioning (HVAC) system. Hackers were able to steal the financial information of more than 110 million customers.

Some physical security elements with an IT interface are closed circuit cameras; facial recognition; HVAC; lights; power, fire, and smoke sensors; sprinkler systems, electronic gates; badge systems; copiers; printers; some appliances; some soda; and snack machines. Some schools, churches, hospitals, and businesses are introducing virtual assistants, like Amazon's Echo (Alexa), Harmon Kardon Invoke (Cortana), Google Home, Lenovo Smart Assistant, or Apple HomePod—all of which connect to your Wi-Fi through a unique IP address. Also, be aware that third-party manufacturers are building connectivity to these virtual assistants into all kinds of devices, including phones, lamps, thermostats, TVs, and refrigerators. Don't forget Bluetooth-enabled devices such as wireless headphones, hearing aids, personal exercise monitoring devices, and phone headsets. Your employees and facility users are likely bringing these devices into your operating environment. Once connected, hackers can bombard your device with malware, steal data, or spy on you. Basically, if it has an IP address, it is vulnerable and a gateway to your system.

You can now think of scenarios where hackers could wreak havoc in your organization. Turning on the sprinkler system or turning off the air conditioning will damage sensitive electronic equipment. Turning off cameras, alarm systems, and badge readers means bad actors can enter the building and leave without detection. Hacking your printer could provide gateway to files or to send realistic-looking spear-fishing emails from the company system to employees.

This can be very disheartening—or very enlightening. Just understanding the enemy will go a long way toward protecting our infrastructure. For instance, often, two sets of people address these technology issues in an organization—yet in the face of this new convergent threat, the protection and response plans must be holistic and integrated. So be sure to get all those who "touch" your system on the same team. Know what devices are connecting to your system and make sure it is password enabled. Ensure your third-party providers are taking steps to protect their systems from hacking.

Don't forget to also protect against theft or loss of computer, laptops, electronic media, and files. Also, properly store and transmit Personal Identity Information (PII) and other sensitive information; protect and regularly change passwords; don't forget patches and updates for your system; pay for a good virus blocker; and properly wipe and dispose of computers and electronic media. Think about your vendors, what threat do they introduce to your organization? Have you asked them to assess their vulnerabilities and provide you, the customer, with a report so you can make good business decisions?

I recently met with a so-called white hat hacker—hired to penetrate an organization's system to expose vulnerabilities. No matter how sophisticated the system protections, he has never been stopped. He has been hindered, sidetracked, and slow rolled, but never stopped. He told me the two roadblocks for hackers are number one, people, and number two, process. People are the best dot connectors; they use their intuition, can quickly and holistically see what is happening and engage. There are two ways that he can defeat a system—poor patch management or social engineering, usually through phishing emails. We also spoke about ransomware, when the organization is "held hostage" by hackers. This form of extortion requires payment in the form of bitcoin or the hackers will continue to hold the system hostage, or worse, leak information to the public. The expert recommends that all companies should set up a bitcoin account now instead of waiting until the ransomware kicks in and they have to try to find out how to get and move digital currency. Just remember—having a strict policy and solid procedures is as good (or better!) than spending money on expensive firewalls and hardware. Also, technology should not replace training.

Even if there is a legal requirement, private companies are hesitant to report hacks to officials or admit they have a problem. They may be embarrassed by their inability to protect themselves from attack or think the event will be reputation damaging. Many will actually hide a cyberattack in its early stages instead of sharing that information with the public, so they can protect themselves from what will likely be a cascading event. This is similar to people around the country becoming ill from Salmonella. If hospitals don't share the data, and a contaminated product is still on the shelf, no dots are connected and more people get sick and/or die.

Also remember, hackers are patient. If they have a target, they will wait to make their move when it is least likely to expose their presence and intentions. They will wait until an employee is unstable, sloppy, or job shopping, then they will make a "lucrative offer." As with every security scenario, the threat of an insider going rogue is extremely dangerous—just consider the damage done to our national security by low level employees like Edward Snowden and Chelsea Manning.

Acknowledging the existence of an enemy, then keeping him in mind every step of the way, will prevent your system from being used in ways you have never considered, with devastating outcomes to your organization.

SHIFTING TACTICS

There is no such thing as a failed attack. Bad actors are constantly watching and learning, adapting and changing their methods and tactics to gain the most from their operations. We also underestimate their creativity, allowing them an asymmetric advantage. They attack, we respond with security measures to cover those specific vulnerabilities. They find another crack in the armor and create another way to engage.

For example, terrorist groups have a persistent fascination with the aviation industry, and they continue to find new ways to successfully attack. In the 1960s, 70s, and 80s, it was aircraft hijackings. On 9/11, terrorists turned airplanes into weapons, hitting the "reset" button on how we screen passengers, provide security to those onboard, and harden cockpit doors. Just a few months later, in December 2001, Richard Reid, also known as the Shoe Bomber, attempted to detonate an explosive device packed into his shoes on American Airlines Flight 63 from Paris to Miami. His actions led to the current procedure of extra shoe screening at airport security. In 2006, British authorities uncovered the transatlantic liquid bomb plot. They arrested twenty-four members of a cell attempting to simultaneously detonate explosives onboard seven airliners in route from the UK to the US and Canada using easily obtained substances. This led to scrutiny limitation of liquids taken aboard aircraft. On Christmas Day, 2009, Umar Farouk Abdulmutallab, concealed plastic explosives in his underwear, but failed to detonate them properly as his flight from Amsterdam came in for landing in Detroit. After this failed attack, the US expedited advanced imaging technology to screen passengers for metallic and non-metallic threats, including weapons, explosives, and other objects concealed under clothing that might normally go undetected. In March 2010, ten US airports received the first backscatter equipment.

On October 31, 2015, Russian Metrojet Flight 9268 disintegrated above the northern Sinai following its departure from Sharm El Sheikh International Airport, Egypt, en route to Saint Petersburg. All 224 passengers and crew on board were killed. ISIS Sinai Branch (formerly known as Ansar Bait al-Maqdis) claimed responsibility and posted a picture in their Dabiq magazine of a crude Schweppes soda can bomb that brought down the aircraft. A hole in the fuselage the size of a soda can seemed to confirm this claim and Russian and Egyptian investigators agreed a bomb brought down the jet. In this case, we had the targeting of commercial aviation and a successful downing of an airline by a fledging terrorist group.

The idea of laptops used as bombs once again hit the reset button for airport security. In 2015, I was flying out of Dubai, UAE, and passengers had to open their laptops and power up for security prior to boarding the plane, indicating early concern about this bombing technique. If your battery was dead and you had no power cord or charging source, the laptop did not accompany you on the aircraft. On February 2, 2016, an explosion occurred onboard a Daallo Airlines flight twenty minutes after it took off from Mogadishu. The aircraft returned to the airport, but there was one fatality (the bomber), who was sucked out of the plane by the explosion. Video showed two airport employees handing the laptop to a 55-year-old man boarding the flight (BBC 2016b). This case renewed the fear of insider threat at airports and the use of laptops as bombs. In early 2017, a new US–UK ban went into effect prohibiting certain electronic devices from the passenger cabins of flights from several north African and Middle Eastern countries. The ban was partly prompted by a yet-undisclosed plot involving explosives hidden in a fake iPad (McAskill 2017).

Air transport has responded to terrorism for more than forty years. With a staggering number of passengers traveling annually worldwide—3.7 billion in 2016 rising to 7.3 billion by 2034 (Menzel and Hesterman 2018)—security checkpoints prior to boarding aircraft are not perfect and likely unable to detect every banned item. Consider there are 450 major airports in the US and thousands of smaller airfields, and the security picture becomes even more complex. However, between technology and a robust uniformed security force, secure areas of airports are hardened to a point where they are likely deterring bad actors.

Naturally, the vulnerability then shifts to the softer target, public spaces at airports, first to the check-in areas. On July 4, 2002, Hesham Mohamed Hadayet, 41, an Egyptian who lived in the US for ten years, approached the El Al ticket counter at Los Angeles International Airport and, using two handguns, opened fire on dozens of people, killing two and wounding four others. On November 1, 2013, Anthony Ciancia entered Terminal 3 of Los Angeles International Airport with a semiautomatic .223-caliber rifle, five 30-round magazines, and hundreds of additional rounds of ammunition contained in boxes. He walked up to a TSA checkpoint and opened fire, shooting a TSA officer Gerardo I. Hernandez in the chest at point-blank range. He then went up an escalator but returned to the checkpoint and shot Hernandez again after seeing him move. He continued shooting TSA officers until he was finally shot by responding deputies. Ciancia described himself as a "patriot" and TSA as "pigs."

Next, the ISIS bombing at the Brussels airport (case study in Chapter 6) on March 22, 2016, illustrated the ease with which attackers can attack the departure area before security, usually packed with people and suitcases. Naturally, around the world, airports increased security in the departures area. Shifting tactics—on the evening of June 28, 2016, at the Atatürk International airport in Turkey, three ISIS gunmen armed with automatic weapons and explosive belts staged a simultaneous attack at the international terminal baggage claim and in the adjacent parking lot. Forty-five people were killed and more than 230 injured. Now there were new concerns about protecting the baggage claim area, typically unsecured and open to taxi drivers, vendors, and so on.

In the United States, a mass shooting on January 6, 2017, reinforced the vulnerability of the baggage claim area. Esteban Santiago, 26, flew from Alaska to the Fort Lauderdale airport with a gun in a checked bag. After he retrieved his bag, he went into the restroom, loaded his gun and opened fire in baggage claim, killing five people and wounding six others before he was taken into custody. Another thirty-two people were injured in mass panic and uncontrolled evacuation of thousands of passengers and airport employees, many ending up on the tarmac secure areas hiding among aircraft and vehicles. The airport lost 100 percent sterility in just three minutes. Despite rising threats, and the baggage claim terror attack in Turkey the year prior, the airport reduced the number of security guards in the year prior to the shooting and moved deputies out of the building to handle curbside traffic issues, leaving the arrivals area vulnerable (Sallah and Wellesley 2017). The sheriff's office report on the failures at the Ft. Lauderdale airport to protect against this threat and appropriately respond is mandatory reading for all soft target facilities (Broward County Sheriff's Office 2017).

After the Ft. Lauderdale shooting, there was a renewed effort to protect public spaces in airports. TSA issued the Public Area Security National Framework in May 2017. Again, this is a must-read document for facilities protecting visitors and employees in open, basically unsecured spaces (TSA 2017).

Terrorists and criminals will exploit our vulnerabilities. We must resist the knee jerk reaction to secure against the last attack, keeping an eye on emergent threats and "what's next" to stay ahead of those wishing to do us harm.

EXPLOITATION OF THE SECURITY GUARD INDUSTRY

As case studies in the book indicate, there is a recent trend toward violent actors having experience in the security guard industry. The New Jersey Office of Homeland Security Preparedness (NJOHSP) conducted a review of terrorism cases in 2016–2017, finding that extremists in the West sought employment with private security firms to "gain weapons experience and access to secure facilities" (NJOHSP 2018). The report reminds us that although not all security personnel receive weapons training, the position still affords credentials, uniforms, and access to otherwise restricted areas. A review of the cases from the last few years allows insight into the how and why bad actors might exploit the security guard industry to further their agenda and goals.

Omar Mateen, the ISIS-inspired Pulse nightclub shooter, was dismissed from the Florida Department of Corrections Academy. However, he was hired as a private security guard for G4S Secure Solutions and was licensed to carry a firearm; he worked for G4S for nine years. His jobs included guarding the St. Lucie County Courthouse, where he worked the metal detector, and at the PGA Village gated community, where he stood in the booth that checked in visitors. G4S was later fined $151,400 for falsely reporting the identity of a psychologist conducting screenings of 1,514 armed officers, including Mateen (Fleshler 2016).

In 2018, Nicholas Young, a former police officer with the D.C. Metro system was convicted of attempted material support to terror and will spend fifteen years in prison after he was caught in a terrorism sting operation. Young is the only US police officer to ever face terrorism charges. He was providing phone cards to an individual he thought was a member of ISIS but was actually a government informant. Also, he lied to federal agents about his travel and that of his "contact."

Ahmad Rahimi was responsible for a series of explosions at three locations in New York City and Seaside Park, New Jersey, on September 17 and 18, 2016, in which thirty-one people were injured. The first device exploded on September 17 in Seaside Park; the second explosion occurred on the same day in Manhattan, and a third set of devices were found September 18 near the Elizabeth train station. Rahimi was both al-Qaeda and ISIS-inspired, and both groups took credit. He was employed as a security guard through a private contractor in 2011 at a technology office in New Jersey, leaving the position after two months to travel to Afghanistan for training.

On September 17, 2016, in St. Cloud, Minnesota, Dahir Adan began stabbing individuals outside the Crossroads Center shopping mall and proceeded inside, continuing to attack shoppers. Thirty-one people were injured before Adan was shot and killed. This was an ISIS-inspired attack and ISIS claimed responsibility. Employed part-time at security firm Securitas, he was assigned for a few months to a factory near the mall. Adan resigned in June prior to the attack, but was wearing his guard uniform during the attack.

Khuram Butt and two other individuals drove a van through a crowd on London Bridge and crashed into nearby Borough Market, where they stabbed individuals at random on June 3, 2017. Eight people were killed and forty-eight injured before the terrorists were killed. ISIS claimed responsibility for the attack. Butt was employed as a security guard at the time of the attack, but had a scheduled interview for secondary employment at a security firm that handles large sporting events, such as the Wimbledon tennis tournament.

On August 12, 2017, in Charlottesville, Virginia, James Fields, Jr., rammed his car into a crowd of counterprotestors after the "Unite the Right" rally, killing one and injuring nineteen. Fields was a white supremacist extremist. He worked periodically as a security officer for a private firm in Ohio beginning in 2016.

Yousef Ramadan was arrested while attempting to fly to Jordan on August 25, 2017, in Detroit, Michigan. FBI agents found pepper spray, knives, a stun gun, and other items in his checked luggage. Ramadan was ISIS-inspired. He was employed as a security guard in Michigan and California and received a firearm permit in 2010, but it expired in 2014.

Other nations are facing the same issue. For example, in September 2017, seven Filipino security guards in Malaysia were arrested for being militants of the Abu Sayyaf Group and at least one was connected to ISIS-Philippines (Rodzi 2017). There are cases of embassy guards, bodyguards, and private security gone "rogue" in various countries of interest, involved with terrorists or organized crime, or looking the other way at the start of an operation as in the Garissa school kidnapping in Nigeria. Some seek the position to further their nefarious intentions, and others are recruited and "flipped." Either way, this trend requires our immediate attention; the access, insider knowledge, and ability to carry, employ, and pre-position weapons makes this type of insider threat extremely dangerous. Employment screening is important, but guard companies must find a way to actively monitor and manage employees to verify their ongoing suitability for these positions of trust.

Looking at "what's next" and preparing today will help us get on the offensive with terror threats. In the next chapter, we look at the human element of soft target hardening.

REFERENCES

Adesina, Zack. "IS Planned London Terror Attacks in 2016." *BBC Inside Out*, London, September 4, 2017.

Al Arabiya News. "Black Death Kills 40 Al-Qaeda Fighters in Algeria." www.alarabiya.net/articles/2009/01/20/64603.html (2009).

Alexander, Harriet. "London Bridge Attack-Everything We Know." *The Telegraph*, June 6, 2017.

BBC. "Nice Attack: Driver 'Researched Route' Earlier in Week." www.bbc.com/news/world-europe-36818719 (July 17, 2016a).

———. "Somali Plane Bomb: What Happened?" www.bbc.com/news/world africa-35521646 (February 13, 2016b).

———. "Spain Attack: What Do We Know about the Victims?" www.bbc.com/news/world-europe-40973119 (August 27, 2017).

Booth, Robert, Vikram Dodd, Lorenzo Tondo, and Stephanie Kirchgaessner. "London Bridge: Third Attacker Named as Yourself Zaghba." *The Guardian*, June 6, 2017.

Boureston, Jack. "Assessing Al Qaeda's WMD Capabilities." *Strategic Insights, Naval Postgraduate School* 1, no. 7 (September 2002).

Broward County Sheriff's Office. "Fort Lauderdale-Hollywood International Airport Active Shooter/Mass Evacuation Incident: Critical Incident Report." www.trbas.com/media/media/acrobat/2017-10/94837910-10093411.pdf (October 6, 2017).

Chavez, Nicole and Eric Levenson. "Terror Suspect Wanted to Attack People on Brooklyn Bridge, Documents Say." *CNN*, November 2, 2017.

Chazan, David, Tom Morgan, and Camilla Turner. "Bastille Day Terrorist Was Radicalised within Months and Sent £84,000 to His Tunisian Family Days before Attack." London: *The Telegraph*, July 17, 2016.

Commission on the Prevention of WMD Proliferation and Terrorism. "World at Risk: Report of the Commission on the Prevention of WMD Proliferation and Terrorism." New York: Vintage Books, 2008.

Committee on Homeland Security and Governmental Affairs. "Ten Years after 9/11 and the Anthrax Attacks: Protecting against Biological Threats." Testimony before the US Senate, www.centerforhealth-security.org/our-work/testimony/ten-years-after-911-and-the-anthrax-attacks-protecting-against-biological-threats (October 18, 2011).

Counter Extremism Project. www.countexttremism.com (accessed April 4, 2018).

Dearden, Lizzie and May Bulman. "London Attack: CCTV Video Shows Terrorists Laughing While Planning Atrocity at Llford Gym." *Independent*, June 8, 2017.

Esposito, Michael. "Mexican Drug Cartels' New Weapon in Border War—The Car Bomb." *ABC News Online*, August 12, 2010.

Evans, Martin. "Facebook Accused of Introducing Extremists to One Another through 'Suggested Friends' Feature." *The Telegraph*, May 5, 2018.

FAA. www.faa.gov/uas/

FBI (Federal Bureau of Investigation). "Weapons of Mass Destruction." www.fbi.gov/investigate/wmd (2018).

Fleshler, David. "Employer of Pulse Nightclub Killer Fined $151,400 for False Psychological Forms." *Sun Sentinel*, September 9, 2016. www.sun-sentinel.com/local/broward/fl-orlando-shooting-fine-20160909-story

Gettinger, Dan. "Drones Operating in Syria and Iraq." *Center for the Study of the Drone, Bard College*, December 13, 2016.

Gips, Michael A. "Secondary Devices a Primary Concern." *Security Management* 47, no. 7 (2003).

Huffington Post. "Le Monde Nice: Les Auditions Des Amants Et Maîtresses De Mohamed Lahouaiej-Bouhlel Emergent." July 18, 2016.

International Conventions of the Red Cross. "International Humanitarian Law." https://ihl-databases.icrc.org/customary-ihl/eng/docs/v1_cha_chapter1_rule1 (2018).

Israel's Foreign Affairs Ministry. "HAMAS Exploitation of Civilians as Human Shields." www.youtube.com/watch?v=70Oqo_wmuGo

Joseph, Yonette. "London Bridge Attack: The Implements of Terror." *New York Times*, June 11, 2017.

McAskill, Ewen. "Laptop Ban on Planes Came after Plot to Put Explosives in iPad." *The Guardian*, March 26, 2017.

Menzel, David and Jennifer Hesterman. "Airport Security Threats and Strategic Options for Mitigation." *Journal of Airport Management* 12, no. 2 (Spring 2018): 118–131(14).

Miller, Nicole. "Vehicle-Based Attacks on Bridges in London." Case Study, *Soft Target Hardening: Protecting People from Attack*, 2nd ed., Boca Raton, FL: Taylor & Francis, 2019.

Mueller, Benjamin, William K. Rashbaum, Al Baker, and Adam Goldman. "Prosecutors Describe Driver's Plan to Kill in Manhattan Terror Attack." *The New York Times*, November 1, 2017.

New America Foundation. "Non-Jihadist Cases, 2001–2011." http://homegrown.newamerica.net/nonjihadist (2012a).

———. "Right- and Left-Wing Terrorism since 9/11." http://homegrown.newamerica.net/overview_nonjihadists (2012b).

New Jersey Office of Homeland Security Preparedness. "Extremists Exploit Security Positions." www.njhomelandsecurity.gov/analysis/extremists-exploit-security-positions (February 5, 2018).

O'Brien, Zoie. "Nice Attack: Police Challenged Truck Terrorist Then Let Him Park on Prom for Nine Hours." *Daily Express*, July 15, 2016.

Parfitt, Tom. "How Barcelona Police Finally Tracked Down and Killed Terror Attacker Younes Abouyaaqoub." *Daily Express*, August 21, 2017.

Payne, Adam and Pamela Engel. "Police Officer Stabbed and Many Wounded in Apparent Terror Attack Near UK Parliament." *Business Insider*, March 22, 2017.

Payton, Matt. "Nice Terror Attack: Police Arrest Killer Mohamed Lahouaiej Bouhlel's Wife." *The Independent*, July 15, 2016.

Reinares, Fernando and Carola Garcia-Calvo. "'Spaniards, You Are Going to Suffer': The Inside Story of the August 2017 Attacks in Barcelona and Cambrils." *CTC Sentinel*, January 2018.

Rodzi, Nadirah H. "Seven Filipino Security Guards Arrested in KL Anti-Terror Raids." *The Straits Times*, September 22, 2017.

Sallah, Michael and Kristyn Wellesley. "Staffing Cuts Left Area of Fort Lauderdale Airport Shooting Unguarded." *USA Today*, January 21, 2017.

Sheller, Katelin. "Rise of New Terror Tactic: Vehicle into a Crowd." Case study, *Soft Target Hardening: Protecting People from Attack*, 2nd ed., Boca Raton, FL: Taylor & Francis, 2019.

Snow, Jon. "Sri Lanka's Killing Fields." *United Kingdom: BBC*, 2011.

TSA. "Public Area Security National Framework." www.tsa.gov/sites/default/files/pass_national_framework.pdf (May 2017).

Willgress, Lydia and Henry Samuel. "Hero Motorcyclist Attempted to Stop Nice Terror Attacker." *The Telegraph*, July 16, 2016.

CHAPTER 8

Soft Target Hardening and the Human Element

The human is the best weapon system.

—US Military Axiom

INTRODUCTION

Terrorism is a human issue. A terrorist attack is, by its very nature, a violation of human rights. There are humans on all sides of the security equation: the perpetrators, the victims and intelligence, law enforcement, and protection professionals trying to prevent tragedy. Security technology and equipment was meant to enhance and supplement—not replace—the human effort.

For instance, profiling is a human activity, as "the recording and analysis of a person's psychological and behavioral characteristics, to assess and predict their capabilities in a certain sphere or to assist in identifying a particular subgroup of people" (Oxford Dictionary 2018). In postmodern, asymmetric terrorism, physical profiling is a counterproductive tool, and we must dismiss the notion a terrorist "looks" a certain way. After 9/11, the law enforcement community focused on foreign-born male Arabs; yet we soon learned radical jihadists can be American non-Arabs and, in some cases like Jihad Jane, a woman. Although hard for us to conceive, the use of women, children, and the disabled is another proven asymmetric tactic shared among terrorist groups worldwide, preying on this blind spot. In 2008, two disabled women were unwillingly used by al-Qaeda in Iraq to attack an open market in Baghdad; the devices were strapped to their wheelchairs and remotely detonated. Also, in Iraq, a female suicide bomber attacked a group of women and children at a playgroup gathering, killing fifty-four people. In 2011, a man dressed as a cleric and a small boy were walking toward a government building in Karachi; alert police approached the pair and found they were both wearing bomb vests. In 2012, a 14-year-old suicide bomber walked into a group of his friends playing outside the NATO building in Kabul, Afghanistan, killing six. On August 20, 2016, an ISIS suicide bomber attacked a wedding in Turkey, killing fifty-one people. The attacker was a 14-year-old boy. If these are legitimate combat tactics for these groups to use on the battlefield, then we should expect them here. ISIS is using the children of their fighters, called the "Cubs of the Caliphate," to carry out attacks and threaten the coalition. One 10-year-old boy, Yusuf, stating his father is an American soldier, recently appeared in an ISIS propaganda video threatening our country. Dressed as an ISIS fighter, loading and shooting weapons while narrating how ISIS was "bringing the war to America," his accent and physical features are all too familiar and startling (Sulaivany 2017).

Profiling by age also does not work in the United States, as the al-Qaeda in America and ISIS in America studies covered in Chapter 4 illustrated—the age of radical Americans ranges from 15 to 63 years old and they are from all demographic groups and regions of the country. Profiling can also lead to tunnel vision: while focusing on one group or characteristic, the real threat is on the periphery, taking advantage of our myopia. We also must take care when profiling based on a person's activities, which may be quite harmless, such as taking photographs or sketching locations. Our efforts can lead us down a wrong path, distracting and expending resources while infringing on a person's rights in the name of security. Certainly, calling law enforcement is prudent if the situation exceeds what you can handle; however, be aware that if the Joint Terrorism Task Force becomes involved, suspicious activity reports (SARs) filed with the FBI may be kept on file for up to twenty years. Over-reporting is also a concern, as it burdens the system and causes "pollution," potentially obscuring the true bad actor or group. A popular saying in the security realm applies: If everyone is a terrorist, no one is a terrorist.

Further complicating hardening efforts, our asymmetric enemies keep reinventing tactics and improving, so we must not only tighten security based on past events, but, as the previous chapter illustrated, keep an eye on world events and emergent threats. This is a lot to ask of a church leader, school principal, hospital administrator, and business owner, when security isn't a primary mission and funding doesn't allow for a security "smorgasbord." There is one powerful resource all soft target venues have—people. Thus, this chapter focuses on the human element of soft target hardening.

STEADY STATE AND CRISIS LEADERSHIP

So now you may be thinking:

Profiling will not work. I do not want to make my facility into a fortress. The security environment is dynamic and unlike a government building, I cannot merely barricade my buildings and occupants into a cocoon of safety. The threat keeps changing as groups shift tactics and learn based on past successes and mistakes and I do not have the resources for high-end equipment and a legion of guards. How should I proceed?

Security begins and ends with the decisions and actions of the organization's leadership—not just the C-suite or front office, but everyone who has a key role on the leadership team. "Steady-state operations" is military vernacular describing periods of predictable activity, the day-in and day-out rhythm of an organization. During steady state, the leader directs the organization's operations and focuses on training, equipping, and resourcing. Steady state is the perfect time for growing and honing your crisis leadership skill set. A crisis is when a leader will either rise to the occasion or fail; there truly is no in-between state. People will look to you for direction, and even to save their lives. If danger crosses your doorstep, there will be a full investigation and history will judge your actions—and inactions. As leaders, we may get the glory for the wonderful things happening in the organization, but we are also held accountable for its failures, especially if they involve loss of life, property, revenue, or reputation.

Often, leaders fail during crises because they were not mentally or physically prepared for the acute stress of the situation. The skills are different than steady state. First, you will need to have self-control and not get swept away in the emotion of a situation which may involve violent death and/or destruction. Communication with your staff in this situation is not like your weekly staff meeting—there is mass confusion and you need to quickly gather facts and make impactful decisions like whether to evacuate or shelter in place. You need to be flexible, creative, and adaptable; if Plan A doesn't work, what's next? What if your strategy fails, are you open to input from the staff? What if you are incapacitated? What about the press, how will you engage? People will be on social media, shaping the narrative about what is happening in your facility, spreading false information. Should you engage? Although this can feel overwhelming, there is an entire body of research regarding crisis leadership worthy of your time. Simply reading (and re-reading) this book will add to the crisis toolbox. Connecting with other leaders to talk about these issues and share ideas is also important. Also, see Appendix B for a list of free online courses to build the leader crisis skill set.

A leader truly must fight the emotional trap of invulnerability: "It will never happen to me," and "It will never happen here." There are three kinds of crisis you should think about and plan for: the routine emergency, the crisis emergency, and the emergent crisis. One or all three of these situations will likely happen while occupying the front office. An emergent crisis the size and scope of the 9/11 attacks is rare, but we live in an unpredictable and unstable world. We all have our stories about that fateful day, but perhaps mine will help provide perspective in terms of fifteen years of steady state training, planning, equipping, and practicing—and how it paid off when it mattered most.

September 11, 2001, began as all other days, with a morning office meeting to discuss the daily schedule and downing a few cups of coffee to fuel the way ahead. I was an Air Force lieutenant colonel, the deputy base commander at Seymour-Johnson Air Force Base, North Carolina, an Air Combat Command base with several squadrons of F-15E fighter aircraft and thousands of military personnel and their families. We were gathered around the office television to watch live video of the "aircraft accident" in New York City and the increasingly thick smoke pouring out of the north tower of the World Trade Center. At 9:03 a.m., a collective gasp filled the room as we witnessed the second aircraft impacting the south tower. The mood immediately shifted from concern to horror with the realization that our country was under attack. And we instantly knew the only group with the resources and will to pull off such a massive attack was al-Qaeda.

Suddenly, I was in the unexpected position of trying to secure a major military installation and its panicked residents from an enemy with unknown intentions and capabilities. In the command center, my stunned colleagues and I watched the defense readiness condition change to DEFCON 3, the highest level since the Cuban Missile Crisis. The Pentagon, which I had just left three months earlier, was burning. I had to suppress thoughts about my E-ring office and colleagues in danger or possibly dying. With more hijacked aircraft airborne, our fighter jets were immediately loaded with weapons and crews put on alert. My husband, then a colonel, commanded the fleet of fighter aircraft and crew members; before allowing them to take off, he had to make sure his pilots were prepared to shoot down a civilian airliner on command—something they never trained for or considered a remote possibility prior to this fateful morning. We soon received the order to launch, and I could hear the aircraft thundering into the skies to fly Combat Air Patrol sorties over major East Coast cities to guard from further attacks.

My job at the helm of the Emergency Operations Center was chaotic for the next thirty-six hours. As the installation gates locked down, we had children (including our young daughter) outside the fence in community schools and worried parents who were trying to get to them. Scared citizens from the local community were asking for refuge on our secured base. Landlines and cellular phone networks crashed, and our most reliable way to communicate was through handheld radios, known as "bricks" for their cumbersome bulk. I ordered the communications squadron to break into deployment kits and access every other storage area on base to harvest bricks, batteries, and charging stations for commanders and first responders. Upon wise counsel from a staff member, I immediately executed a long-standing contingency contract to withdraw bottled water from the base commissary for safekeeping in case the installation became a self-sustaining island. Sure enough, within hours, base employees and family member inundated the grocery store and understandably stripped the shelves of basic essentials. My security forces defenders established Force Protection Condition Delta posture, the highest possible, emptying the base armory of battle gear, M-16s, and service revolvers. Snipers and counter-snipers took position around the base to protect us from attack. As I watched the surreal situation unfold, I remember thinking the hundreds of mundane exercises endured during our careers had paid off. We were a calm, precise, well-oiled machine during the most intense stress of our young lives.

As I executed seven binders of emergency checklists, my team was faced with several unanticipated threats, starting with the escape of an inmate from a minimum security federal prison on base. A convict with an "interesting" background took advantage of the 9/11 morning confusion to jump the base fence; a quick check of records revealed he routinely participated in work details all over the installation, in unclassified facilities, and along the flight line, mowing grass, picking up trash, and likely interacting with base personnel. The standard operating procedure was to put up search helicopters; however, the state police were denied flight clearance due to the national emergency. Instead, we implemented a coordinated ground search with local sheriffs, but without further intelligence about the 9/11 attackers and his possible connection, we were flying blind. The prisoner's intimate knowledge of our base and possible intentions were of extreme concern.

A few hours later, an FBI agent from a local office requested a secure phone call with our military federal agents, residing in the base Air Force Office of Special Investigations (AFOSI). We listened with surprise as his staff described ongoing surveillance operations and suspicious activities within the state and at nearby facilities, some frequented by military personnel. The base was suddenly not the secure "island" it had always seemed. I also quickly learned to operate within a new realm, that of ambiguity and the "inescapable unknowables." Thankfully, no threats to the installation materialized in the coming days, police recaptured the prisoner several states away, and our attention shifted from protecting the homeland to taking the fight 7,000 miles away to the enemy.

Some of the security measures we had to execute on the base were painful and inconveniencing. Naturally, on the day of the attacks and for a few weeks afterward, people did not complain about the long lines at the base gate or having to wear extra body armor and carry gas masks.

However, as time went by and there were no additional attacks, security fatigue set in. Even military members and their families became irritated and less cooperative. The problem from a threat standpoint is that with asymmetric attacks—when terrorist groups act at will on the day and time and at the place of their choosing—we do not know if the threat has subsided. Are they regrouping and planning? Will the next attack be a weapon of mass destruction (WMD)? Or was this their one big operation and the culmination of a decade of planning and fund-raising? No one knew the answers to these questions for a long time, not even our nation's director of national intelligence. We eventually lowered the security posture, taking baby steps back toward where we were on 9/10, trying to re-establish the balance of security and normalcy.

I've been there as a leader in crisis and was thankful for the years of "front work" the military invests in cultivating the necessary skills. Also, the military expertly leverages human capital to complement its vast array of technology.

INTUITION

One of our most underappreciated natural gifts is our intuition or the ability to know something from instinctive rather than conscious reasoning or proof of evidence. Almost every case study in the book contains statements from either the families of the perpetrators, their friends, colleagues, or people at the scene saying "Something just didn't feel right," or, worse, "I knew something like this could happen" or "When I heard about the shooting, I knew it was him." Trust your gut feeling, honed by years of experience and wisdom. If something looks or feels wrong, it likely is. Humans are the best sensors and have the edge over current technology as they feel emotions like fear, can build (or lose) trust, and be critical and creative thinkers. We are constantly observing and scanning the environment, compiling knowledge and experience, in what experts call "accumulated judgment" over time. Intuition taps into all these subconscious bits and pieces.

The US military is very interested in understanding and using intuition. US Marine Corps doctrine includes honing and trusting the sixth sense as the "art" in the art and science of war fighting. Based on stories from combat veterans returning from Afghanistan and Iraq about situations where intuition saved countless numbers of lives on the battlefield, the Office of Naval Research (ONR) launched a four-year, $3.85 million program to explore the phenomenon. The project, called "Enhancing Intuitive Decision Making through Implicit Learning," is a joint project with Massachusetts Institute of Technology, Northwestern University, and government agencies. ONR states: a "Research in human pattern recognition and decision-making suggest[s] there is a 'sixth sense' through which humans can detect and act on unique patterns without consciously and intentionally analyzing them" (Office of Naval Research 2014). The US Army also studied intuition, finding two kinds of American troops in combat areas were better able to detect hidden improvised explosive devices (IEDs). Troops raised in rural areas in a natural environment and involved in hunting and similar activities were the first group. They had better instincts and were more alert to nearby dangers. The other category was the troop who grew up in tough urban settings where he or she had to be aware of danger from crime and assault (Hammons 2015). I strongly recommend the book *The Gift of Fear: Survival Signals That Protect Us from Violence*, written by Gavin de Becker (1998), a leading expert on personal protection. His book helps people recognize various warning signs and precursors to violence, so they may avoid harm. Another theme is how individuals can learn to trust the inherent "gift" of their gut instinct.

Detecting Surveillance

Humans are also the best at detecting surveillance activity. As discussed in previous chapters, terrorists and criminals will often accomplish surveillance of the target prior to acting, sometimes returning to the scene more than once. Surveillance is an art and science; our federal agents and counterintelligence personnel spend a great deal of time learning this tradecraft. Most terrorists and criminals are amateurs at surveillance and can be quite careless, so if you and your staff is trained on what to look for, you can detect a plot in the making.

The human mind quickly recognizes patterns. This happens subconsciously every day as we go about our normal activities. In terms of security, you may think—didn't I see that car yesterday? Or why is that person hanging around at school pickup and leaving without a child? It is within your right as the facility operator or manager to *unapologetically* ask a stranger if you can help, using direct eye contact and a firm approach. This gives you a chance to assess verbal and nonverbal behavior—is the person avoiding eye contact, startled, stuttering, or even sweating? The mere fact you engaged may deter further actions. Bad actors want to act at the time and place of their choosing, with little resistance. Putting them on the radar frustrates their plans.

Amateurs conducting surveillance often suffer from "burn syndrome," the belief that the people they are watching have spotted them. Feeling "burned" will cause them to do unnatural things. Perhaps they will instinctively hide their faces or suddenly ducking into a doorway. If they may eye contact with security, they will abruptly turn and go the other way instead of casually walking by. These are physiological and physical responses that only training can override and are easy to spot, once you understand what to look for.

Naturally, if an individual looks threatening, it is best to call security or the local police department instead of confronting. After any suspicious event, take notes on the person's physical appearance and what he or she was wearing and carrying. Write down details about their physical appearance, an anything that seemed out of the ordinary with clothing, facial hair, certain hair style, etc. If the person drives away, note the make and model of the car, and even the license plate number. If you can, carefully snap pictures so police can zoom in for details. You will likely never need the information, but it will be of great help to investigators if your gut feeling was correct. Also, share this information with the staff. As with all hardening activities, you may never know the impact of your actions. The entire staff can be force multipliers when "watching for the watchers."

Emergent Thinking

All Hands Security

Security directors often view security enhancements through a technological prism. If you wish to harden a soft target, they may argue (with some justification) that it makes sense to look at hardware and associated software. Bollards, barriers, access control systems, cameras, and facial recognition programs all have their place. They also have their cost. The hard truth is that no soft target has an unlimited security budget, and many smaller facilities may have no budget line items specifically for security.

However, each of these locations has an invaluable resource: people. Whether they are employees, volunteers, or a combination of the two, each person working at your site has a vested interest in security. It only makes sense to provide them with security-focused training, making them de facto members of your security team. At some soft targets, like houses of worship, training can also include those people coming in to make use of a facility.

In the United States Army, the saying "every soldier is a sensor" means that everyone on the battlefield, from the lowest ranking private on up, has an intelligence collection responsibility. Translate this to a 400-room hotel where every employee has security training and related responsibilities, and you now have approximately 100 extra pairs of eyes looking for trouble, protecting people and property. The net effect, borrowing again from military terminology, is called a *force multiplier.* Your limited security staff cannot be everywhere, but your newly trained security "sensors" will have eyes and ears in so many more places.

Persuading Leaders to Engage

Increasing the number of security-educated staff requires training and persuasion. Persuading senior management may be the greatest challenge. No one organizational leader will say security is unimportant, yet this statement alone is not enough to mitigate twenty-first-century threats. It is up to the security professional in the room to be the agent of change.

Following are some potential talking points to use when discussing training force multipliers in your organization with the C-Suite. Some points may be better suited for organizations with existing security departments, others for those without, and some might be valid for both.

- Minimal capital expenditure is required when training is conducted in-house. Both the trainer and the trainees are already on the payroll.
- Training everyone to prevent or react to terrorism and active shooter events has the tangible benefit of reducing overall security incidents including assaults and theft, resulting in fewer lawsuits and other legal issues. As a result, insurance carriers may offer discounts.
- Empowering employees with security training makes them feel safer at work, builds loyalty, and reduces turnover costs.
- Employers have a legal Duty of Care obligation to provide a safe working environment for employees. Negligence in doing so can result in lawsuits, fines, and severe damage to brand reputation and public good will. In some countries, management could even face criminal sanction.
- Advertising increased security is a competitive advantage and enhances brand reputation in a media climate that fixates on mass casualty events.

Unique Challenge for Non-Profit Organizations

Some of the points just listed might also carry over to similar conversations held at nonprofit organizations. These entities, however, face unique challenges, not the least of which is a chronic shortage of funds. Although smaller nonprofits like local churches, food banks, and charities struggle to pay for security, large international nongovernmental organizations also have challenges. While many NGOs operating in the world's conflict zones have security departments and provide training to field personnel, offices in donor nations may be operating with a false sense of security, a huge vulnerability.

In nonprofits of all types, most operational conversations center around monetary requirements. Talking security will be no different, but it should not be difficult to turn this to a pro-security advantage.

- Donors like security and safety. A major security incident at an NGO, especially if casualties among staff are involved, could result in a precipitous drop in donations. A small nonprofit may never recover.

- Volunteers and paid staff alike want to work in, and deserve, a secure environment. Many of the same Duty of Care obligations placed on for-profits are in play here, as are the consequences for negligence.
- Private security consultants will often provide security assessments for nonprofit facilities, and training for staff and volunteers on a pro bono basis.
- Public awareness of enhanced security could result in positive press coverage that includes enhanced visibility of your work. This may lead to increased donations and more volunteers.
- Outsiders seeking to harm a soft target are likely to look elsewhere if it is well known you are prepared.

Another way to ensure management buy-in is through accountability. At many facilities, the general manager (GM) is the crisis team leader. Once charged with that responsibility, the GM should be your natural ally. Especially so in higher threat areas, the highest level of onsite management is held to account if the minimum approved security level is not maintained. Organizational assessments, external audits, and even red team testing all serve to promote compliance.

Employee Buy-in

Employees must also buy-in. While it might be tempting to simply issue an edict commanding staff compliance, resist the thought as it will get your training off to a bad start. While participation should not be voluntary, spending just a little time communicating the project's importance will pay off from day one with a more receptive audience. Lead with the fact that everyone will learn how to enhance their own security on the job. Answering the "what's-in-it-for-me" questions can be a powerful motivator.

Tailored Training

Hand-in-hand with getting the top brass and your audience onboard is readiness to launch a training plan once given the green light. An all-hands security training plan should not be overly complex, and it requires enough flexibility to train workers who have different job functions across an organization. Tailor training to your organization's size, employee mix, and specific needs.

Houses of worship, or other small nonprofits with only one location and a handful of volunteers can train effectively as a single group. At the other end of the complexity spectrum, security directors for large hotels and office buildings will benefit from training their staff in smaller groups based on primary job functions or where they work within the facility. Actual training group size also plays an important role in training effectiveness. While lecturing hundreds is possible through technology, consider the ideal number of students to whom you can deliver quality, hands-on training in a single session. Also, consider how many experienced trainers can you bring to the table. Answering these questions helps effectively focus your efforts and resources.

Larger multinational operations will face language challenges if training products and personnel use only the home office's primary language. Take the time to translate classes into the languages used by your future trainees. Whenever possible, use trainers who are fluent in these languages or who know how to work with interpreters. Working effectively with an interpreter is a skill more difficult to master than one might expect. Rehearsal is essential.

If you have multiple locations but few trainers, you will want to focus your energies on a single site before moving on to the next. If you have a large security talent pool, consider training-the-trainers together and dispatching them in teams to provide training at several locations at once. Critical to training large, geographically diverse organizations is developing a clear, methodical campaign plan. Your plan will require budgeting, a phased timeline, measurable and reportable milestones, and a clear understanding that there is no finish line. Think of security training as being in perpetual motion. Once an organization is trained to an acceptable baseline, the calendar soon tells you sustainment or refresher training is due.

Maximize Training

Effective training should maximize hands-on experiences, while keeping the lectures and slide shows short. Think innovative practical exercises rather than classroom time. Don't just tell housekeepers what is expected if they encounter dangerous items or suspicious circumstances when cleaning a hotel or hospital room, show them. Cement the training through concrete examples. Set up different scenarios in a few vacant rooms. Have your trainees deal with the situation from beginning to end. Do you need to restrict access to your kitchen, loading dock and other service areas? Show employees what to do, then conduct practical exercises where role players attempting to enter restricted areas are challenged. If you plan to train front-of-house staff in detecting terrorist pre-attack surveillance, illustrate what it looks like when someone is sizing up your lobby or taking surveillance video from across the street.

Challenge your trainees and assess their response. If they are to approach a person behaving oddly in the building's lobby and ask, "may I help you," then they should practice in training. If the policy requires housekeepers to back out of the room and call their supervisor, who then calls security, those calls are placed and security responds as if it was a real life situation. By realistically training, you are building the "muscle memory" that moves security policies and procedures from the abstract to the real world.

Too many trainers first show their trainees how not to navigate a security problem or send them into a scenario blind, then provide the solution afterwards. Do not fall into this trap. Train properly from the beginning. Ingrain positive responses through your actions and theirs. Show your employees what "right" looks like.

Is It Working?

How will you know that your all-hands approach to security is effective? With everyone now a part of the security team, you should see reductions in overall security incidents. Hotels often see a sharp decline in in-room theft and missing items in public areas. Facilities with service entrances, loading docks, and staff entrances can expect fewer successful intrusions and losses in those areas. Incident reporting will likely increase, but so should the early and successful resolution of those incidents.

Security personnel, if you have them on staff, must not be overlooked and should receive additional training, as well. Security officers are your front line, and are the people called to respond when other employees report an incident. In higher threat areas, the overt presence of uniformed security is welcomed and will convey your hardened security posture to the public and likely influence their decision to enter the facility as a user, shopper, etc. If also trained on customer service methods, guards will enhance the overall feeling of security as they greet and interact with your customers, clients, and other employees while making their rounds. All the while, your officers are making people feel safe, their own enhanced training ensures that feeling is not misplaced.

One issue many soft target operators struggle with is determining whether a newly upgraded security posture should be communicated to the public. While this decision is not one you make wholly based on advice in a book, it is worthwhile to consider views on both sides of the issue. Some who favor keeping security matters close-hold argue that public disclosure can provide valuable information to those bad actors who would put your facility in their crosshairs. A negative public reaction is also a worry for some. The concern here is that people may believe security was upgraded for some specific, yet undisclosed reason. They may ask—what threat is the management hiding?

Again, with the understanding that soft target operators must decide what is best under their unique circumstances, there are some compelling reasons to let the world know you aren't so "soft" and vulnerable anymore.

Potential active shooters may decide to look for a softer target. Deterrence is the watchword here. You don't want your defenses to have to physically hold off an attack. Rather, you want the knowledge of your preparations to prevent an attack early in the planning stage. In the event an attack occurs, and all-hands security plays a role in getting people to safety and reducing harm, this should become a key point in your post incident media interactions.

Actions that minimize loss of life and property during a soft target are lauded in the media for a day or two, then that incident quickly disappears from the headlines. From a public relations perspective, that is exactly what you want. Recall the 2018 school shooting in Parkland, Florida. Due to the high death toll, post-incident student activism, and the political debate that followed, this shooting was in the news for months. Not long after Parkland, another school shooting was decisively terminated by a School Resources Officer, who fired shots at a gunman, who then took his own life. For a few days, media hailed the officer as a hero, then it was back to the normal news cycle. Does anyone outside the local area remember the name of that school today?

The reality is that in the twenty-first century, people do not shy away from more security, they embrace it. In fact, they *demand* it at soft target locations—and it is our job to provide it.

(Source: O'Rourke 2019. Mike O'Rourke is the CEO of Advanced Operational Concepts, and a retired US Army Special Forces soldier.)

INSIDER THREAT: A FIFTH COLUMN

As if the soft target hardening situation was not already complex enough with myriad actors and tactics, we need to factor in the growing insider threat to organizations. When you ask a security professional the question, "What keeps you up at night," the insider threat is likely the answer. In military terminology, the insider threat is a "fifth column"—one or a group of insiders who secretly sympathize with or support an enemy and engage in acts of espionage or data gathering for the larger group's planning efforts, or subversion, thus destabilizing the organization from within and further "softening" the soft target. Consider the sabotage perpetrated by insiders Edward Snowden and Bradley Manning; they never pulled a trigger, but certainly put many others in the crosshairs with their sharing of extremely classified government information with the world, which included state enemies and terrorist groups. The insider could also be a lone actor—perhaps the most dangerous situation of all as the planning activity will often go undetected. The insider is a force multiplier to an attack, with intimate knowledge of your facilities, operations, and vulnerabilities. This individual can also pre-position supplies for himself or herself or others, as well as assess the perfect time to strike and obtain the maximum results, whether casualty counts or damage to the physical plant or the organization's reputation. Another type of insider is one whose is not connected to terrorism or organized crime, but their life is unraveling, and they need money—so will sell information or access.

Everyone has a public life, a private life and a secret life. The secret life is what we know little or nothing about yet need to access in order to root out a malicious insider. There is a persistent lack of research and data analysis regarding the insider threat, making it the least understood and least appreciated danger to an organization or venue. Compounding the problem, there are organizational and cognitive biases leading managers to downplay this danger. Also, indicators we use to detect outside threats fall short and thus our countermeasures fall short. There is a myth these employees are disgruntled or have outward signs of hostility at work; although some workplace attacks and breaches occur by recently fired employees, many others come as a complete surprise. The human resources life cycle is a good model to use when developing your insider threat detection and mitigation plan.

Good Hiring Practices—First Line of Defense

Countering the insider threat takes a multifaceted approach and this chapter offers a variety of viewpoints. The body of academic work regarding the insider threat is fairly small, but I strongly recommend the book, *Managing the Insider Threat: No Dark Corners*, by Nick Catrantzos (2012). He applies the Delphi methodology to this security challenge and arrives at the conclusion that infiltrators are more likely to be a threat than disgruntled insiders. In other words, the terrorist or group is more likely to try to plant one of their own than to leverage an insider (although the threat of the latter must not be overlooked). First, the infiltrator needs to get through your screening process and then on the payroll and into your facility. Certainly, a thorough employee background check is necessary, and I recommend using an approach similar to the government's security clearance process. In terms of past employment, absolutely call past employers, but do not ask only about the former employee's work ethic, etc. Take the opportunity to probe a little. In the name of security and the workplace violence issues in our society, ask about the emotional state of the employee and whether there were any signs of anger or disloyalty. At the end of the discussion, ask an open-ended question: "Is there anything else you think I should know about this person?"

When interviewing the potential employee, stay within the law but ask everything you can about background, family, and even financial status. Always interview a potential applicant in person. Note their behavior when you ask tough questions. Consider applying psychometrics to your hiring process to tap into attitudes and personality traits and make sure the prospective hire is a good fit for your organization and unearth any latent negative traits. There is plenty of information on the Internet about these practices, but if you aren't comfortable delving into this realm, hire an external company to do all of your pre-employment screening.

Understand the screening process itself has many flaws; deception experts believe 40 to 50 percent of applicants lie on their resumes and job applications and 80 percent lie during the full screening interviews (Whetstone 2014). The potential employee is trying to impress the hiring official by inflating past work experience or abilities or, possibly, he or she does have something to hide that might preclude hiring. For those who try to read body language during an interview, untrained screeners are usually about 50 percent accurate, but body language deception experts are 80 to 90 percent accurate. Therefore, a pre-employment screening by experts is a good frontline of defense for your operation.

Background Checks

A growing movement in our country to enact "fair chance laws" helps citizens with criminal records access the job market. The National Employment Law Project (NELP 2015) estimates 70 million US adults, or one in three, has an arrest or conviction record, though not all of these are felonies. There are laws to allow businesses and organizations to conduct background checks on potential employees who will come in contact with children in schools, churches, and hospitals. These checks are often performed by both state and federal law enforcement, often through simple fingerprinting and processing at the local police station, which will determine whether the person was ever convicted of a crime. Be advised, this system does not have information on arrests, pending legal processes or instances where the charges were dropped. So you may or may not be able to run background checks. However, the employment application (private and confidential) should include questions regarding the applicant's criminal history like arrests. However, a new movement is complicating this process: thirty-one states passed "ban the box" laws barring employers from asking potential employees about past convictions, believing the information creates an unfair barrier to employment. Also, eleven states—California, Connecticut, Hawaii, Illinois, Massachusetts, Minnesota, New Jersey, Oregon, Rhode Island, Vermont, and Washington—have mandated the removal of conviction history questions from job applications for private employers. State-level checks are not as thorough as you may want; keep in mind you will not receive any information from a crime committed outside your state. Therefore, you may need to complement your screening process with professional help and through Internet searches and other legal avenues. The time and money involved with verifying the background of a potential employee are worth it.

After gaining employment, the mole, as we refer to a nefarious insider, must gather information and determine how best to exploit your vulnerabilities. Detecting a radical jihadist or other religious or political extremist is very difficult. The government uses professional mole hunters to find spies in an organization. Perhaps one of the best books I have ever read on this topic is *True Believer: Inside the Investigation and Capture of Ana Montes, Cuba's Master Spy*. The author, Scott Carpenter (2007), was a mole hunter at the Defense Intelligence Agency; his sole job was to identify insiders who were colluding with or spying for other governments (the "fifth column"). In the book, he is honest about how he failed to act upon his early gut feelings regarding Montes, who, interestingly, was recruited while a night school student in a master's degree program at Johns Hopkins. Montes was able to spy for Cuba several more years, and the intelligence she gave them resulted in the deaths of several Americans at a classified outpost. Carpenter retrospectively looks at the case and the indicators Montes was not a "friendly," despite her ability to pass two polygraph tests. If a highly trained professional struggles with insider threat detection, we are in trouble.

The "no dark corners" approach offered by Catrantzos (2012) helps illuminates the shadows in the work space. First of all, a cultural shift is needed: all of your employees should be seen as force multipliers in terms of security. One person in an organization does not "do" security; rather, everyone is responsible for securing the workplace. Therefore, hire your employees on a probationary basis and treat the situation like a pilot/copilot scenario; stay close or have one of your long-term, trusted employees act in the mentoring role. The "no dark corners" concept means new employees are never left alone during this on-boarding period, thus communicating to the insider that "someone" is watching at all times.

The workplace should be very transparent in terms of physical work spaces and accessibility. Cubicle partitions should be low to create an open feeling. Employees have a constitutional right to privacy, but an employer has a legitimate and legal right to protect the workplace. Some laws, such as those preventing workplace harassment, require such monitoring.

Other than the manager, employees should not be the sole source of information or access; for instance, only one person has a combination to a safe, or employees have an email account or files to which only he or she has the password (not accessible by IT). What about the use of company phones and computers—should any communication conducted on those instruments be private? The desk is another hotly contested area regarding privacy. The key is to have sound policies and procedures in the workplace. Also, in the spirit of transparency, have regular audits, then if you suspect an employee is a threat, it is easier to approach and gather evidence prior to calling for outside help. The chart in Figure 8.1 shows the innovation of the "no dark corners" theory for securing against the insider threat.

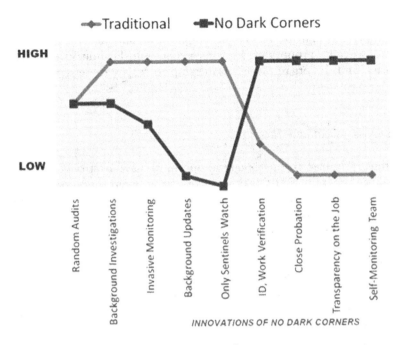

FIGURE 8.1   No Dark Corners Approach

The "no dark corners" applies to physical security, as well. Managers and security personnel should regularly walk the perimeter of their property, looking for cut fences or other indications of stockpiling or operational planning. If the perimeter is too large to walk, enlist the help of someone who owns an ATV. Several cases discussed in this book involved insiders pre-positioning explosives and weapons, sometimes over the course of months. Inspect storage areas and compartments in building. Look up at ceiling tiles (a favorite place to hide a weapon, cash, and drugs) and down at floorboards (another favorite), and every place in between. Shine that light in the dark corners in your organization. Staying vigilant will not only deter the insider but also detect any suspicious activity early in the planning cycle.

Reporting System

If you have an insider threat program without a reporting system, then you do not have an insider threat program. If people don't report, you don't know what's happening. The organization's culture must be such where people feel safe coming forward and their information protected. Also, a repository of reports is a necessity to connect the dots. Sleepers are patient and employees and managers come and go; files are your continuity through the years. The organization should have an Insider Threat working group with legal representation, IT, human resources, security, and the organization's leadership to review these reports on a regular basis.

Employee Assistance Program

To thwart insider threat, organizations must have a strong employee assistance program (EAP). EAP is a work-based intervention program to identify and assist employees in resolving personal problems. Common challenges addressed by the EAP are marital, financial, and/or emotional problems, family issues, or substance and alcohol abuse. The EAP is meant to help the employee address issues that may be adversely impacting his or her performance. When people are starting to "meltdown," the EAP is a safe place to go for help before they become vulnerable to outside recruitment, or feel the need to sell or give away proprietary information.

Much work is done to mitigate the insider threat from one critical, secretive, isolated workplace: nuclear power plants. Insider threats are the most serious challenge confronting nuclear facilities, and in every case of theft of nuclear materials the perpetrators were either insiders or had help from insiders. Sabotage is also a threat; in 1982, an employee detonated explosives directly on a nuclear reactor at South Africa's Koeberg nuclear power plant and in 2012 an insider sabotaged a diesel generator at the San Onofre nuclear facility in California. Matthew Bunn and Scott Sagan (2014) authored a very informative piece about worst practices and failures in the industry regarding the insider threat, with takeaways that may be cross applied to soft targets. The authors encourage facility owners and security managers to fight their assumptions, stating:

Don't assume that serious insider threats are NIMO (not in my organization).
Don't assume that background checks will solve the insider problem.
Don't assume that red flags will be read properly.
Don't assume that insider conspiracies are impossible.
Don't assume that organizational culture and employee disgruntlement don't matter.
Don't forget that insiders may know about security measures and how to work around them.
Don't assume that security rules are followed.
Don't assume that only consciously malicious insider actions matter.
Don't focus only on prevention and miss opportunities for mitigation.

Fighting these assumptions, use of psychometrics in the screening process, taking the "no dark corners" approach and a strong EAP will go a long way toward thwarting the insider threat.

Apply the same rigor to checking the background of your volunteers and seasonal staff. Many soft target venues use volunteers, whether in school libraries, running church groups, staffing the reception desk at a hospital, or during sporting and recreational events. Due to budgetary woes, organizations may even replace paid staff and use volunteers in key front office positions, a security "tip of the spear." Someone with illicit plans may think volunteering is one way to get inside an organization and its facilities by skipping employment background checks. Risk assessments usually do not include insider threat, but they should to fully protect the organization or venue and its occupants. Move it to the top of your list of risks.

THE SIRA METHOD

As already stated, physical profiling efforts will likely come up short when identifying suspicious actors. However, behavioral profiling is a powerful tool as humans are unable to suppress certain physical changes resulting from stress and adrenaline surges. Michael Rozin, the aforementioned Israeli security specialist who was also the security manager and captain of Special Operations at the Mall of America from 2005 to 2011, developed a methodology based on his experiences called the "Suspicion Indicators Recognition and Assessment" (SIRA)™. SIRA is an innovative behavior deterrence, detection, and security program, a proactive system to prevent acts of violence. Mr. Rozin believes (and I agree) there are some basic problems with the way organizations conduct their security programs. The allocation of resources and effort is based on perceived threat level (e.g., "We've never had a shooting or a bombing here before, so the security posture is low"), there is a lack of comprehensive security assessment and design, and ineffective security objectives are in place. SIRA is based on human factors, in a complementary manner to physical security and security technology. Effective security objectives are to deter, detect, prevent, and respond; however, tangible activities to deter, detect, and prevent are often given less weight than the response element. Mr. Rozin asserts the right approach is to believe the threat is constant; and an incident can happen at any time ("Today might be the day"). The relationship between suspicion and threat should be suspicion is a threat until refuted. The optimal approach: "If there is a doubt, there is no doubt." A doubt is a *threshold* for action, and but depending on the circumstances, sometimes a doubt is *reason* for action. Intuition certainly plays a role in planting the seed of doubt. "Suspicious" does not mean "guilty"; a violent act is the definitive evidence of guilt.

There is a gray area involved with doubts and suspicions, but a pre-incident indicator is enough to take investigative action. Major pre-incident indicators include inexplicable presence. Most people are walking with purpose, have keys in their hands, are carrying packages to and from somewhere. Someone who is adrift should be of interest; engage and ask what they are up to. Inappropriate clothing for the conditions such as heavy jackets in warm weather, the person may be hiding something. A stranger asking inappropriate questions of security guards or employees is another indicator. Partnering with this activity is another indicator, something known as grooming. People with bad intentions may try to look casual and avoid spooking others. Casual grooming actions include scratching or wiping the face, smoothing hair with fingers, for women, pulling hair behind the ear, or any similar usually unconscious gesture. Like a fake smile, these grooming behaviors look very contrived and unnatural when done consciously. If you see someone trying too hard to look natural, that is unnatural and an indicator. Again, trust your gut feeling, let your intuition connect those dots for you.

I strongly recommend the SIRA program for those responsible for securing soft targets as it provides tools for engaging when something does not seem right with an individual, whether a stranger or an insider. It draws on a leader's intuition and gives permission and a methodology for engagement (Rozin 2018).

SUICIDE TERRORISM

Suicide bombings typically result in higher casualty counts because the actor can access areas packed with people or a critical place in the facility and detonate the weapon at the time of his or her choosing. It is very hard to wrap our minds around a human turning themselves into a walking bomb and mingling with a group of other humans to commit suicide and homicide.

Suicide bombings are a relatively new phenomenon; Islamic Jihad Organization's attacks in 1983 during the Lebanese civil war are the first examples of modern suicide terrorism. They have been used extensively as a war-fighting and propaganda tool by every radical Islamist terrorist group in the last thirty years. Between 1983 and 2016, there were 6,594 suicide bombing attacks worldwide (START 2018). Although suicide attacks amounted to around 3 percent of all terrorist incidents in that period, they were responsible for 48 percent of all fatalities, not counting deaths resulting from the suicide attacks via airliner on 9/11. In addition to strategically placed IEDs, suicide bombings are the primary tactic used in conflicts in the Middle East and Southwest Asia and typically used against soft targets. In the ten years after September 11, 2001, there were 336 suicide attacks in Afghanistan and 303 in Pakistan, and there were a staggering 1,003 documented suicide attacks in Iraq between March 20, 2003, and December 31, 2010. Notable al-Qaeda suicide attacks since 9/11 include the July 7 attacks in London in 2005, which killed fifty-two people, and hotel bombings against US properties in Bali, Casablanca, Jakarta, Istanbul, Jordan, and Islamabad. Failed attempts at suicide bombing on airliners include the shoe bomber and the underwear bomber. ISIS suicide bombings include the Brussels airport and train station attacks, the Ariana Grande concert, the Stade de France in the Paris attacks. The Chicago Project on Security and Terrorism (CPOST) maintains a searchable database on all suicide attacks from 1974 through June 2016. The database includes information about the location of attacks, the target type, the weapon used, and systematic information on the demographic and general biographical characteristics of suicide attackers. The average deaths per suicide bomber attack is twelve, with another twenty-six wounded (CPOST 2018). Suicide bombings are very effective, low-cost attacks for a terror group. They can also shift the center of gravity of a battle and break the will of fearful citizens. The effect is amplified when the suicide attack is against a soft target like an open market, a church, or a school. When the planning begins, the suicide bomber would have already decided to give up his or her life for the cause. If backed into a corner, this type of attacker will jump straight to the execution stage of the operation, even if the timing is off. In many suicide bombings where the individual is challenged before reaching the actual target, he or she detonate the explosives. Therefore, never attempt to investigate, to engage, or to unravel any type of plot or attack on your own. Call local law enforcement at the first sign of any of the preceding activity.

According to Dr. Daniel Kennedy (2006), a forensic criminologist, the following are seven signs of suicide terrorist activity (along with my elaboration); we can use this methodology to detecting any type of terrorist or criminal preoperational planning activities.

1. Surveillance: The actor may observe the target area to determine security strengths and weaknesses, and the number of security personnel that might respond to an incident. Taking pictures, videotaping, drawing maps of the area, and stepping off distances are signs of terrorist surveillance activities. The 9/11 hijackers performed such surveillance on Disney properties and other soft targets. The Mumbai terrorists had a front man, American David Headley, who accomplished extensive surveillance on the targets. However, surveillance is not always necessary, as in the case of insiders or angry opportunists.

2. Elicitation: The actor attempts to gain information about certain operations: for example, asking questions about building infrastructure, class or worship schedules and attendance, and the posting of security personnel. The terrorists in the Nairobi mall shooting asked for and obtained blueprints of the building when securing shop space in the months prior to the attack.
3. Test of security: The individual may try to access unauthorized areas of your facility to test physical impediments or response time. Exit areas will be tested and possibly altered to prevent escape, such as in the Virginia Tech shooting when the shooter chained the classroom building escape doors closed; he was seen testing the chains the day before. David Headley walked the ground in Mumbai and knew every emergency exit at the hotels, later instructing the terrorists how to enter the building and block exits for high casualty numbers.
4. Acquiring supplies: The purchase or theft of explosives, weapons, ammunition, or security badges or uniforms in the local area is a red flag of possible impending attack. Insiders will also start stockpiling items in the facility such as in the case of the Westgate Mall attack.
5. Suspicious people: The actor may come to the future attack scene more than once. Looking out of place or wearing odd clothing, several of the perpetrators of mall shootings walked the same path they took the day of the shootings.
6. Trial run: Before the final attack, the terrorist may conduct a "dry run" to identify obstacles. A dry run might involve calling in a bomb threat to observe emergency response, evacuation plans, and rally points for those leaving the building, such as the tactic used by Eric Rudolph prior to the abortion clinic bombing. Terrorists also may try to assemble weapons or bombs in the facility.
7. Deploying assets: In this last stage, the attacker and any operational supplies are moving or being moved into position. This is the last chance to prevent the attack.

Humans are the best detectors of these activities. Law enforcement is currently testing technology to detect would-be terrorists with explosive suicide vests at train stations in major cities. Authorities expedited testing of the system after a suicide bombing attempt during rush hour at Penn Station in New York in December 2017. Obviously, this type of system is highly desirable, but it should complement behavioral detection activities, not replace it.

FACE OF RAGE

Your security personnel, people working near building entrances, or at check-in areas are your first line of defense. They can learn to visually scan crowds or individuals for the following (Whetstone 2014):

"Faces of threat" such as rage, anger, or guilt of a premeditated criminal act

Threatening mannerisms

Unusual nervousness

Body language that could indicate having a concealed weapon

If your facility has a main reception area or front office, you may consider tailored training for those staff members. Anger is the most dangerous emotion; in this stage, a person is most likely to hurt another. Extreme anger, or unbridled rage, is extremely dangerous, as the capacity for rational thought and reasoning is lessened and the person will likely act out in a violent manner against the source of the rage until the target is destroyed.

Recognizing the "face of rage" is important to react properly to an imminent act of violence. Rage is an extraordinarily strong emotion, a feeling of intense, violent, or growing anger. There is a high adrenaline rush associated with a "fight or flight" response that can give extra strength and endurance; senses are sharpened, and physical pain sensations are dulled. The enraged person may experience tunnel vision as he or she approaches the object of the anger. Due to elevated blood pressure, the person's sense of hearing is diminished and he or she may actually "see red" due to bursting blood vessels in the eyes. Time may seem to slow, due to the impact on temporal perspective.

We can distinguish rage from other emotions by certain distorted facial expressions which cannot be reproduced and are the same regardless of race, ethnicity, or gender. The skin above the bridge of the nose folds in a certain way (think of the shape of the letter A), the lips become thin, and upper and lower teeth are visible. Also, the face remains fixed in a state of rage for approximately four hours before relaxing back to its normal state. Based on expression, which one of the people depicted in Figure 8.2 (interpreted from top to bottom and left to right) is the biggest threat to your organization?

Picture 1: His face shows possible elements of rage, but because his hands are in the air, he better demonstrates "posturing," meaning he is mad and he wants you to know he is mad.

Picture 2: This is a good example of "stage 1 of rage," where anger is turning into rage. The man's eyebrows are scrunched together and he is showing the whites of his eyes, but the nose bridge of his face is not unnaturally wrinkled and his lips are pressed, indicating anger.

Picture 3: This woman is showing "stage 2 of rage." The nose bridge is wrinkled, nostrils are flared, the white areas of the eyes are more profound, and the lips are beginning to separate.

FIGURE 8.2   Faces of Rage

Picture 4: The woman is posturing, as evidenced by the display of her hand and arm. Her nose is crinkled and her upper lip is raised, which indicates disgust, not anger or rage.

Picture 5: She is posturing and there is no scrunching of the nose bridge or the eyebrows being drawn together, which would indicate rage. The fact her eyebrows are not lowered suggests she is not even truly angry.

Picture 6: This face reflects anger, but not rage. Anger is best defined by lowered eyebrows and lips pressed together.

Picture 7: His arm suggests posturing and there is no scrunching of the eyebrows or nose bridge, which would indicate rage. He is protesting and he wants you to know he is mad, but he is not in a state of rage and will probably not react violently.

Picture 8: While this man is displaying a scrunched nose bridge, his raised upper lip is more indicative of disgust, not rage.

Picture 9: The expression is not natural; the picture is staged. The man is posturing, and the lowered eyebrows might suggest anger, except the lips are not pressed together.

Picture 10: This is a good example of "stage 4 of rage" due to the scrunched nose bridge (with the letter A visible), showing the whites of the eyes, possible flared nostrils, and display of teeth with the lips forming a square. This is the look of animals (including humans) who are in unbridled rage and about to attack or are in the process of attacking.

For more information on reading facial expressions such as rage, I recommend *Unmasking the Face*, by Dr. Paul Eckman (2003), who is likely the best facial expression and lie detection expert in the world. Dr. Eckman consults to the popular television show *Lie to Me*, which uses his theories to explore criminal cases and deception.

As opposed to terrorist rage, which is aimed against those who represent an opposing political or religious system, criminal rage is more likely tied to low self-esteem where a person is bullied or perceives ill treatment at the hands of others. A good example is 22-year-old Elliott Rodger, who went on a shooting rampage on May 20, 2014, at the UC Santa Barbara campus and community after several years of methodical planning. Although he did not have the "face of rage" in the video he posted the day prior to the shooting (www.youtube.com/watch?v=zExDivIW4FM), he clearly states his rationale for the murders he is about to commit. The day of the shootings, he was likely in a state of rage; for example, even though he had high-powered rifles, his first act was to stab his three roommates to death, a very "up close and personal" killing. He then went on a shooting spree throughout the campus, killing six more people.

Not all terrorists, even suicide terrorists, are enraged. Some will methodically plan and rehearse the attack, and on the day of the event, stay very calm and cool as they approach the target. Others may even laugh or show joy once the event begins. Religious terrorists may believe their reward in heaven is just seconds away, sometimes causing a state of euphoria. However, in the case of an enraged opportunist, such as the white supremacist shootings at the Holocaust museum in Washington, DC, and the Jewish center in Kansas City, Kansas, the individual is pushed over the brink by some environmental factor and moves quickly to the execution stage. Or maybe there is no exact plan, but a church, school, college campus, hotel, or concert event provides the venue for the rage attack. In any case, recognizing the face of rage is important for response. Engaging enraged persons is extremely dangerous and you are unlikely to be successful either talking them down or changing their intention. Call for help immediately and take actions to save your life.

Ending the chapter as we started, the human is the best weapon system. After reflective thought on steady state and crisis leadership, honing intuition, training, and comprehending the general types of threats and possible avenues of response, you are ready to build your organization's plan to detect, deter, mitigate, and respond to the threat.

REFERENCES

Bunn, Matthew and Scott D. Sagan. *A Worst Practices Guide to Insider Threats: Lessons from Past Mistakes.* Cambridge, MA: American Academy of Arts and Sciences, 2014.

Carpenter, Scott. *True Believer: Inside the Investigation and Capture of Ana Montes, Cuba's Master Spy.* Annapolis, MD: Naval Institute Press, 2007.

Catrantzos, Nick. *Managing the Insider Threat: No Dark Corners.* Boca Raton, FL: CRC Press, 2012.

The Chicago Project on Security and Terrorism (CPOST). http://cpost-data.uchicago.edu/search_new.php (2018).

De Becker, Gavin. *The Gift of Fear: Survival Signals That Protect Us from Violence.* New York: Dell Publishing Group, 1998.

Eckman, Paul. *Unmasking the Face.* Los Altos, CA: Malor Books, 2003.

Hammons, Steve. "Navy Research Project on Intuition." *Culture Ready Blog,* April 6, 2015.

Kennedy, Daniel B. "A Précis of Suicide Terrorism." *Journal of Homeland Security and Emergency Management* 3, no. 4 (2006).

National Consortium for the Study of Terrorism and Responses to Terrorism (START). "Global Terrorism Database [Data file]." www.start.umd.edu/gtd (2018).

NELP (National Employment Law Project). "Faulty FBI Background Checks for Employment: Correcting FBI Records Is Key to Criminal Justice Reform." www.nelp.org/publication/faulty-fbi-background-checks-for-employment/ (December 8, 2015).

Office of Naval Research. "Basic Research Challenge: Enhancing Intuitive Decision Making through Implicit Learning." www.cultureready.org/blog/navy-research-project-intuition (2014).

O'Rourke, Mike. "All Hands Security." Case Study, *Soft Target Hardening: Protecting People from Attack,* 2nd ed., Boca Raton, FL: Taylor & Francis, 2019.

Oxford English Dictionary. *OED Online.* Oxford: Oxford University Press, March 2018.

Rodger, Elliott. "Retribution." *Video Posted on YouTube Day Prior to Massacre: Podcast Audio.* www.youtube.com/watch?v=zExDivIW4FM

Rozin, Michael. "Suspicion Indicators Recognition & Assessment (Sira) Training." www.rozinsecurity.com/sira/ (2018).

Sulaivany, Karzan. "Watch: American Boy in IS Video Warns Trump 'Fight Has Just Begun.'" Kurdistan 24 Online News, www.kurdistan24.net/en/news/4d131acb-ba8a-428c-ae03-9d41b139d1b8 (August 24, 2017).

Whetstone, Douglas. "'Catch the Lie': Importance of Body Language Deception Detection for Security Officials." Presentation given in Doha, Qatar by the Whetstone Security Group, Inc., 2014.

CHAPTER 9

Deterring and Mitigating Attack

The supreme art of war is to subdue the enemy without fighting.

—Sun Tzu

INTRODUCTION

The goal of soft target hardening is simple: look hard so when bad actors size you up, they move on to another target. Don't worry about where they may go, just protect the facility and people you are responsible for. Consider Omar Mateen's surveillance of targets the night of his massacre. Four hours before his assault at the Pulse nightclub, he drove to the Disney Springs shopping complex, his target of choice, which he previously surveilled with his wife. Mateen's plan was to smuggle the weapon into the complex in a baby stroller, which he purchased, along with a lifelike doll. However, he was deterred by the presence of armed police officers at the location and decided to change targets. Surveillance video captured Mateen walking near the House of Blues club, looking behind him at police officers standing nearby. About two hours later, his phone pinged a cell tower near Epcot. At 12:22 a.m., Mateen searched Google for "downtown Orlando nightclubs" and a club called EVE Orlando and the Pulse nightclub showed in the results. He got directions from Google Maps to EVE, a high-end nightclub in downtown Orlando. Mateen drove near EVE at 12:55 a.m.; he likely saw the substantial security at the entrance and that everyone was being searched before entering the club. At 12:52 a.m., he did another Google search for clubs in downtown Orlando and got directions to Pulse. He drove around the area for a while, finally walking up to Pulse, buying a ticket, and entering the club. He came out ten minutes later, went to his vehicle and retrieved his weapon. At 2:00 a.m., Mateen started his assault (CBS 2018).

If a bad actor breaches your access points or strikes from inside, you must swiftly engage with the ability to mitigate the attack and save the lives of your staff and occupants. As discussed in Chapter 2, hardening begins with you: with the acceptance that the threat exists, and that your operation and facilities are vulnerable. You likely have taken on some amount of risk by not having the resources to fully protect your operation, whether due to insufficient funding, lack of support from your leadership, or for business-related reasons. However, there is a spectrum of hardening actions you can take: from nothing to everything, from free to exorbitantly expensive. The key is to understand the desired effect and make a plan to use your resources effectively to lower your risk. I was fortunate to live the United Kingdom twice, once during the mid/late 1990s when the IRA was still a threat, and again in 2007–2008, during al-Qaeda attacks. I also lived in the Middle East for two years, from 2013 to 2015. Many of my experiences in these world hot spots shape my perspective on hardening tactics for soft target venues, and I have included personal stories and photographs in this chapter.

The first step is to educate yourself on tools available to help in your hardening efforts. In 2018, DHS published the Soft Targets and Crowded Places—Resource Guide. The opening paragraph is very telling about the threat and the urgency of response:

> Segments of our society are inherently open to the general public, and by nature of their purpose do not incorporate strict security measures. Given the increased emphasis by terrorists and other extremist actors to leverage less sophisticated methods to inflict harm in public areas, it is vital that the public and private sectors collaborate to enhance security of locations such as transportation centers, parks, restaurants, shopping centers, special event venues, and similar facilities. Securing these locations and venues is essential to preserving our way of life and sustaining the engine of our economy. The Office of Infrastructure Protection (IP), part of the U.S. Department of Homeland Security (DHS) National Protection and Programs Directorate (NPPD), is committed to improving the security and resilience of soft targets by providing relevant tools, training, and programs to both the public and private sectors, and the general public. This guide is a catalog of IP soft target resources, many of which were created in collaboration with our partners to ensure they are useful and reflective of the dynamic environment we live in.
>
> (DHS 2018)

As a companion to the resource guide, DHS also issued the Soft Targets and Crowded Places Security Plan (2018) to provide those engaged in public and private sector hardening activities, including representatives from industry; academia; associations; state, local, tribal, and territorial governments; law enforcement; faith based communities; nongovernmental organizations; and international partners an overview of how DHS is working to enhance the security and resilience of Soft Targets and Crowded Places (ST-CP) across the United States.

After accessing the DHS resources, the next step is to assess your vulnerabilities. Prior to creating or improving upon your security plan, complete the FBI's vulnerability assessment in Appendix C. Note this document must be safeguarded because it spells out all of your vulnerabilities. If the total score for the organization exceeds 256, and if local law enforcement was not involved in the assessment, notify them at once. Hand carry the document, do not email or send it through a postal service. Next, complete the all-hazards assessment in Appendix H. After you identify and think through your vulnerabilities, you can create a plan to reduce risk in your operation. Your security plan should be an all-hazards approach, meaning it applies to every emergency situation. This approach shifts the focus to preparedness, rather than the specific kinds of weapons or tactics the bad actor may use at your facility. For instance, a bollard or barricade doesn't care if the careening vehicle has a terrorist at the wheel or someone who just had a heart attack. It protects no matter the threat. Also, secure your facility for the most sophisticated attacker and plot. This approach accomplishes two goals; first, the level of effort corresponds to the hardened posture you present to would-be bad actors. Second, protecting from a terrorist attack also addresses crime challenges. For instance, one mall started routinely checking storage space to make sure no weapons were stockpiled. They found a stash of stolen merchandise a store employee was hiding, for later transfer out to her car. Doing random bag checks in retail areas may deter shoplifters. Just having signage stating there is an increased level of security (to create a better shopping, worshiping, studying, etc., experience) is hardening and deters. Soft target hardening is an orchestrated, all hazards approach. And trust me when I say, as the officer who was responsible for the security of Air Force One and the President of the United States while he transited our base at Andrew Air Force Base, you cannot have too much security when faced with an unknown threat and an actor who will violently engage on the day and in the manner of choosing.

EFFECTS-BASED HARDENING (EBH)

We simply cannot apply all resources toward all threats; we need a methodology to effectively cover your unique vulnerabilities against the threat and lower risk. Prior to Operation Desert Storm, the Air Force's aerial campaign strategy was that of attrition—to bomb targets repeatedly and shoot down as many aircraft as possible until the enemy lost either the will or the firepower to fight. However, to successfully prosecute the war against Iraq, with restraint to spare civilians and not destroy the infrastructure of Baghdad, Air Force strategic thinkers devised a new approach: effects-based operations (EBO). An EBO approach is one where "operations against enemy systems are planned, executed, and assessed in order to achieve specific effects that contribute directly to desired military and political outcomes" (Carpenter 2004). EBO provides a strategy for the application of resources, phased in a particular way to achieve the desired cumulative effect. For instance, on the first night of the war, F-117A stealth aircraft (my unit) went into Baghdad and selectively destroyed communication towers and antiaircraft batteries. Later in the war, after the battlefield was "softened," targets shifted to military headquarters and enemy airfields.

EBO provides a good theoretical foundation for our efforts to harden soft targets, and for these purposes we call it EBH—effects-based hardening. This proposes a new (or improved) way of thinking and a specific process on both physical and psychological planes. Accept several axioms prior to implementing this approach:

Actions cause results.
Inaction also causes results.
Deciding not to take action IS an action, with consequences.
Not seen does not mean not there.
The goal is to remove the enemy from the fight before it starts.
Actions are not universally applicable and must be tailored to your
    situation.
The plan is fluid; you must constantly assess and adjust based on
    changes in the environment.
The "fog of war" means you do not know everything about the
    threat; there are inescapable unknowables.
You have no experience with the situation that might occur in your
    organization; nothing that happened in the past can prepare you.

EBH provides a system for visualizing violent scenarios that might happen to your organization in an unemotional, data-driven way. In order to identify the Achilles heel discussed in Chapter 8 and other vulnerabilities increasing your risk and susceptibility to attack, you must "go there" and visualize and map out the worst possible scenario in your facility. At the least, consider an enraged outsider, a plotting insider, an active shooter, and a kidnapping and hostage situation.

The good news? You are fighting this "battle" on your own territory. No one knows the vulnerabilities and strengths of your operation better than you; you are in the position of power over bad actors when it comes to deterring or mitigating their attacks. No matter how much preplanning or surveillance takes place, or even if you face an insider threat, you have the upper hand. Accordingly, keep certain details about your plan close, think of your employees' "need to know," and draw a diagram of concentric circles with the critical operations and people at the center and continue outward to the periphery, where you may have building custodial staff and volunteers. They need security and response training, but do not need to understand the security apparatus in place or your plan for protecting the facility and its occupants. This approach is similar to the military method of compartmentalizing classified information keeping certain sensitive methods and operations on a "need to know" basis.

There is an art and science to security. The science part is physical: barricades at certain locations, walk-through metal detectors to keep out weapons, and security personnel stationed at entrance points for presence. The art is using your resources efficiently and effectively to achieve strategic security objectives. EBH is a way to harmonize, synchronize, and prioritize hardening activities and can complement (or replace) your current efforts. Any new security processes should be incrementally phased in to shape the behavior of your people (and the enemy), perhaps in a time-phased manner or from most to least critical. However, security is not just a program; it must permeate everyday operations and decision making. By baking security into the organization and not just leaving it to the security guard at the front door, you tap the full spectrum of your most valuable assets, people, equipment, and physical attributes of the building and location. The latter is the theory behind Crime Prevention Through Environmental Design (CPTED), a multidisciplinary approach to deterring criminal behavior by leveraging the organization's environment. You may never know what types of terrorists or violent criminal acts you have thwarted using EBH, but at the very least you will have a data-driven plan effectively using your resources to cover vulnerabilities.

Move forward unapologetically with your security plan. Leaders at soft target locations have confided to me their sense of regret about how efforts to tighten security inconvenience their staff and visitors. Those operating a for-profit operation are often concerned with customer satisfaction and whether measures will drive patrons away. I tell them to imagine, for a second, a horrendous attack at their facility. It could be an angry ex-spouse exacting revenge, a fired employee, a disturbed teenager, or a terrorist or group seeking to make the news and further their religious or political cause. As the leader or head of security, you must face the devastated family members and explain how you failed to protect their loved ones. Being a leader means taking responsibility, not only for the good things happening at your place of work, but also for the bad, and the very, very bad.

EBH, by its very nature, encourages the harmonizing and synchronizing of actions. For example, during an active-shooter event, the front office has a plan: one predesignated person calls 911, one makes an announcement on the loudspeaker, and one locks and barricades the door. These types of actions take training and practice. Like pilots who are thrown impossible situations to handle in the flight simulator, if you practice for the worst possible scenario, small security issues will be handled effortlessly by the staff, working together as a team. They will also be confident of their ability to handle a large-scale emergency, and this confidence makes them force multipliers to you and your security team.

Matrixing your vulnerabilities, desired effects, the means to lessen your vulnerability, and the capabilities you have and need helps with the decision-making process. Table 9.1 is an example of an EBH decision matrix for a church or school.

How do you know if your EBH efforts are working? You can test your system by having an outside security company do a red teaming

TABLE 9.1   Effects-Based Hardening Matrix

Prioritized Scenario	Desired Effect	Means	Capabilities and Cost	Implement/ Partially Implement/ Table
1. Highly visible location on busy highway draws opportunists	Lower "heat"	Remove external signage facing road	In house, volunteers; free	Implement
2. Too many people with keys to the main door	Restrict building access	Install electronic key lock on main door and obtain keying equipment and cards	Contracted; $3,000	Partially implement; rekey current lock, reissue keys; budget electronic key system for summer 2015
3. Holding meetings after hours for outside groups, attendees wandering in building	Restrict access to the rest of the building	Install locking door between basement and upstairs offices	Contracted; $1,500 with labor	Implement

exercise on your property, a tactic addressed later in the chapter. If you don't feel comfortable with outsiders, ask colleagues to help. Also, you should ask the people who work in and use your facilities if they feel safe and if not, how you could do better. Not only will you glean valuable information, but the mere process of asking for and then acting on their ideas will strengthen your relationship and open the lines of communication about vulnerabilities. A strong organization united against threats is a hardened, resilient organization.

The rest of the chapter contains best practices and ideas harvested from industry experts—information to guide your EBH efforts.

CAPABILITY ASSESSMENT

You already have many capabilities in your organization to harvest and apply toward hardening efforts. Identifying, growing, managing, and leveraging these innate resources will help you effectively to gain an advantage over bad actors and build capacity to deal with emergency situations. In the military we call this a "capability assessment." For instance, your location, building, property, vehicles, communications set up, whether you have a kitchen, basement, a generator, water source, etc., are physical assets. Your staff and facilities users have skills and competencies they bring to the table. Other capabilities include strong leadership, organizational resiliency, ability to innovate and improvise— these are intangible capabilities. Create a list of these organizational assets and consider how you can leverage them to deter, mitigate, manage, and recover from emergency situations. Capability based preparedness will build confidence that your organization is ready for the unexpected.

Emergent Thinking

Capabilities-Based Preparedness

In the days following a large-scale incident, we typically see discussion center around defensive security systems and methods. These systems and methodologies are often pitted against one another in a competitive, if not entrepreneurial, manner.

Active shooter incidents alone have created numerous response models aimed at preparing an employee base against the active shooter threat— *Run, Hide Fight*, ALICE, and others. While the methodologies have merit, they are frequently presented at the micro-level: a specific methodology aimed toward a specific type of threat. The acronyms may not provide the best course of action for someone under duress; for instance, maybe running is not a good idea, but hiding is under certain circumstances. Whether a public safety professional with the responsibility for jurisdictional preparedness or a private sector security director tasked with protecting an employee base, a broad focus on building capabilities can be more impactful than a series of narrow systems or approaches.

Example

An example of capabilities-based preparedness in action is the emergency management profession. Presidential Policy Directive Eight (PPD-8) is the enabling doctrine that defines the approach to capabilities-based preparedness planning. A jurisdiction, based upon a sound threat and risk assessment, will build capabilities to build preparedness. And by building capabilities against the threats of greatest concern, the jurisdiction inherently builds preparedness for other threats with similar response needs. A jurisdiction on the Gulf Coast building the capability to evacuate for an impending hurricane has also built the capability to evacuate for a Hazmat incident. For the operator of a soft target location, the principle is the same. Think of how this translates to the soft target environment, and the affected employee base.

Leveraging Advantages

In hardening a facility, operators should leverage every advantage against the challenges of operating in a soft target environment. Leveraging the response commonalities to various threats and hazards and building the capabilities to respond accordingly is one approach. In many instances, school systems struggle with building preparedness for an active shooter event. However, these capabilities already exist within the school system to a certain extent. On a basic level, we have taught children to escape a threat for decades by training for and executing fire drills. The underlying principle of evacuating from an active shooter event is the same. And while, for the purpose of this discussion, this is an oversimplification, the reality remains that we have built this capability to evacuate for decades.

Nuances certainly exist in how we execute capabilities in the face of a threat. The salient point is we are fine-tuning a *base* capability as opposed to creating a new system for each threat. These basic capabilities prepare a population based to respond as desired, regardless of threat. Broadening the school example to the operation of any soft target, by building the capability to evacuate we can prepare the population base of the facility to apply this capability to a fire, hazardous material event, active shooter, or for any other threat that would require an evacuation. In terms on impact, this approach becomes far more effective than creating specific systems to each specific threat a soft target facility faces.

The Importance of People

As you examine the threat and hazard picture for the facility, the occupants become a large part of the preparedness discussion. Not only do people want fears and concerns alleviated about the threat, but they often become the first face of response. By demystifying the turmoil surrounding a high-impact event, you allow the employee base to focus on consequences and mitigation. Once the sensationalism is removed, you can direct the focus toward the capability required to respond to the threat. Stripping away part of the apprehension about the threat will help direct the focus toward competence in response. However, the response capability itself should not contribute to incident-time stress.

The human response to stress of fight, flight, or freeze is well-documented. Realizing the impact of stress on the people we aim to protect in our facilities, we must ensure our methodology is not an additional source of stress. For one, with a diminished capacity in the face of a stressful event, our personnel will not be able to decipher a complicated acronym or specific system geared toward a specific threat. Two, the time spent deciphering an acronym or the application of a specific system is time away from addressing the threat at hand. Finally, if any component of the response is task-intensive or fine motor skill-specific, we are setting people up to fail. They simply will not be able to perform in a complex way during a stressful time.

The Big Picture

By no means should a facility owner discount the specialized training available to various threats and hazard of concern. Instead, focus on the tangible capabilities you are trying to build. Tailor the training to the people, not the people to the system. Focus on direct, actionable tasks a person can perform under stress to ensure their safety. Leverage those actions applicable to as wide of a base of threats and hazards your facility may face. Evaluate what value the training may bring to the organization, while keeping the base capabilities in the forefront.

School children of the 1980s were not encumbered by the sensationalism and politics of nuclear war. However, these children became proficient at seeking cover under desks, and knew the safe route to the fallout shelter. This action is simple in nature and could equally apply to taking shelter in a tornado. Within these children, we built a base capability to respond to several different threats. Regardless of soft target facility, the same methodology applies.

Finally, evaluate how building these capabilities can apply across the business spectrum. The capability to shelter is as much a physical design capability as it is a human response capability. An infrastructure meeting the needs of its users can help alleviate stress during a major incident. A facility that has invested in infrastructure, whether a mitigation project or future capital expenditure, will allow occupants to execute the basic capabilities needed to survive any event—this will surely will pay dividends down the road.

(Source: Gerkin 2019. Mr. Gerkin is a Lieutenant in the Baltimore Police Department, a security consultant, and an adjunct instructor at the National Emergency Training Center. He is a Certified Emergency Manager (CEM) through IAEM.)

USE OF DECEPTION

All warfare is based on deception. Hence, when able to attack, we must seem unable. When using our force, we must seem inactive; when we are near, we must make the enemy believe that we are away; when far away, we must make him believe we are near.

—Sun Tzu, *The Art of War*

Since the dawn of history, warring factions used deception to asymmetrically engage their enemy. Whether through feigned retreat, making an army look larger than actual size, using smoke to hide forces, using fires to make a camp appear where it wasn't, history is replete with examples of how this tactic gave the underdog an advantage. Over time, military deception developed from a tactic to full-fledged doctrine. The government employed misinformation and visual deception during World War I and the tactics came into even greater prominence during World War II. In the buildup to the 1944 invasion of Normandy, the Allies executed one of the largest deceptions in military history, Operation Bodyguard, which gave them full tactical surprise. Before storming the beaches of Normandy, the allies staged one of history's greatest military deceptions using rubber tanks, decoy landing crafts, inflatable tanks, body doubles, fake radio chatter, and double agents to divert Adolf Hitler's attention away from where the troops would actually land. After the attack on Pearl Harbor, the state of California hid defense department factories and air bases under a sophisticated system of camouflage netting. They even created entire mock towns with fake vehicles, storefronts, and streets. In Seattle, the gigantic 26-acre Boeing Aircraft complex was blanketed under netting; the area was disguised as a suburb complete with municipal buildings, parks, schools, and homes. A quick online search yields fascinating photos of these elaborate and expensive deception operations.

Moving forward to the modern day, tactical deception is a disruptive tool regularly used by the military to gain the advantage. Army Field Manual 90–2, Battlefield Deception (1988) defines military deception as measures taken to deliberately mislead adversary decision makers about friendly capabilities, intentions, or operations in ways that may be exploited by friendly forces. They include denial and deception, concealment, camouflage, and perception management.

As a young captain, I was a trained tactical deception officer for a classified, black world flying operation, and used the tactics to disguise our operations and deceive intelligence collectors. Deception is an art and a science, where you take the enemy's hand and lead them down the wrong path, protecting your assets and operations. Naturally, we had to assume sophisticated "countries of interest" were doing the same to us with their operations. The Russians, in particular, are famed for *maskirovka*, their camouflage, denial, and deception activities.

Unlike the rest of the book, I will not offer prescriptive advice about using deception tactics when hardening soft targets or explain how I used this tactic to protect sensitive military operations. The objective is merely to introduce a new concept and plant the seed for further thought. For instance, cell phone towers disguised as trees have been around since 1992. Besides trees, antennas are also concealed in fake grain silos, art, flagpoles, signs, cacti, and church steeples. Electric substations are often hidden in buildings that look like homes or office buildings. Many urban water treatment facilities are disguised as parks, such as Sherbourne Park in Toronto. Some parts of the rail and subway in London are concealed by false townhome facades. Although done primarily for aesthetics, the camouflaging of our critical infrastructure could certainly pay off in the event of a conflict where adversaries seek to take out communications, power, and water sources.

Conditioning is a form of deception. One facility I have consulted with is located on a large property. They concealed cameras in "birdhouses," mixed in with regular birdhouses. However, there are many more birdhouses without cameras than with. On a few of the houses closest to main roads, they've "slipped up" and exposed a part of the camera. For the passerby, this conditions them to believe all birdfeeders on the property likely have cameras. Another example: often, prior to a high visibility event, there is "practice" for the arrival of a dignitary. You can condition anyone watching to believe it will happen at a certain location, when it fact it will be elsewhere. Deception is not only about hiding things but also revealing something at the time, place, and manner of your choosing, when the bad guys are watching.

The act of drawing attention away from a target is called "diversion." Consider the security detail moving Princess Diana around London. In 1996, I saw the royal entourage pull up to the front of Harrods department store, where there was a large, excited crowd. Meanwhile, the princess slipped in through the back door, dropped off in a nondescript SUV. Motorcades for government officials often use this type of concealment to confuse would-be bad actors as to which vehicle contains the primary. Same for helicopters shuttling dignitaries around war zones.

Disinformation through language is another tactic. Ever since the advent of the radio, the military has used false radio calls to mislead the enemy and other forms of psy ops to confuse bad actors, plant messages, and shift their thinking. For example, some high security, closed events are advertised to occur on the wrong day, usually days after the actual gathering. Celebrities often do this with their weddings to prevent a frenzy of press, helicopters, drones, and fans, ruining their special day. Rumors are an exploitable form of communication which could be used to the benefit of an organization trying to secure an event or a location. Leveraging social media amplifies the effect. This change forces bad actors to change tactics, frustrating their efforts.

Signage is an easy and powerful deception tool to make your facility appear hardened when resources are too low to cover all bases. For example, a small church with a low security budget near my home posts menacing signs saying there is a guard dog on the property, even though there is no dog other than the pastor's poodle. Later in the chapter, we discuss how burglars are deterred by dogs, as "early warning devices." Some cash-strapped facilities post signs about extensive CCTV use and have a combination of a few real security cameras and an array of realistic looking dummies. Most home improvement stores sell all sorts of signage to warn trespassers they are on private property, property under camera surveillance, etc. Signage deters. Think of it this way—a burglar casing homes on a street will pass by the ones with signs indicating there is a security system on the property. Bad actors want an easy target with nothing standing in the way of their success.

Don't forget criminals and terrorists also use Google; Pulse Nightclub shooter Omar Mateen searched the Internet for information regarding several nightclubs the night of his attack. Therefore, language on your website about the security of the property, bag checks, armed guards, etc., may have a deterrent effect. Don't be afraid this will repel visitors or customers; in this day in age, it will pull them in. Another example: a megachurch in the northeast has an elaborate looking well-marked "safe" in which they put a small amount of cash after the weekend collection. The bulk of the collection money is actually kept in a vault disguised as an air conditioning vent. A compound in the Middle East had a guard tower that was always manned. However, on closer inspection, the "guards" were cardboard cutouts, which they moved around, adorned with sunglasses, binoculars, etc. Deception is used to get people's attention; often, police will park a cruiser in the median, sometimes with a dummy at the wheel to slow traffic—a tactic that inevitably works. Finally, as mentioned earlier in the book, bad actors may target people fleeing a building. Keep them guessing. Have several evacuation plans, say A, B, and C. Practice for all, and rotate locations. Expect someone is watching.

Deception is regularly used in cybersecurity. Perhaps you've heard of the "honeypot," a computer program or system designed to act as a decoy to lure cyberattackers, where they are detected and studied. Another tactic is to load a single server or file with tempting information like fake credit card numbers, with the hopes that hackers will take the bait, leaving real assets alone. There are so-called breadcrumbs, or pieces of data, purposely left unprotected, meant for the attackers to gather. Or, trip wire data, that, when accessed, alerts the system administrators of malicious activity. Systems can also be designed to detect data leakage and insider threat. These are all tactics you may adapt in some way for your organization. Use your imagination; the enemy certainly does.

When planning a deception event, defining the end state is the first step—ask, what is it that we are trying to achieve? Joint Publication 3–13–4, Military Deception (2012) describes three considerations in the planning process: (1) see: What does the target see from our operations? (2) think: What conclusions does the target draw from those observations? (3) do: What action may the target take as a result of the conclusions based upon those observations? Once you decide on the purpose of the operation and objective, there must be a clear plan, one person in control and a small group of people "read in" to the operation.

A good deception plan leads would-be attackers down a controlled path, diverts them from organizational assets, and hides vulnerabilities. It could be another asymmetric tool in your soft target hardening toolbox.

LAYERED SECURITY (DEFENSE IN DEPTH)

To protect its most valuable assets, the military and those responsible for protecting critical infrastructure, like nuclear power plants, use a construct called defense in depth. This layered security concept can easily be cross applied to soft targets. The purpose of defense in depth is to put layers or walls of security, or trip wires, between the protected asset and the adversary. It is also a delaying tactic, intended to slow down the advance of an enemy. As it advances toward the objective, security increases, and the adversary meets more resistance, losing momentum. These challenges cause frustration, a change in plans or tactics, and alter the timetable of the attack. Also, the enemy risks detection, therefore loses the element of surprise. The good guys start to gain the power and advantage; so as you can see, defense in depth isn't really a defense, it's more of an offense.

To visualize layered security, let's use concentric rings and the example of a high school. The building occupants, students, teachers, and staff are the critical node, or the asset, at the center of the circle. Each classroom, lab, office space is protected by a door with no glass that opens outward into the hallway so it cannot be kicked in and a secure locking mechanism on the inside. The asset the very last line of defense—the focus must be the outer circles to prevent danger from getting close to the asset, since the probability of success increases with each advance on the target. Many people don't realize that on a military installation, no one is armed except for military police. Despite being targets, and well trained in firearms, they rely on rings of security to protect them and their families from attack.

Surrounding the asset are people with direct contact, such as volunteers, janitors, food service, and maintenance staff. They, and everything they bring onto the property, requires special screening and scrutiny. They have access to the critical node and may introduce threats. The building itself should have access control, for instance, locked doors, metal detectors, cameras, and badging.

Moving out beyond, the second ring consists of the school grounds and parking lot. The layer of defense should be perimeter fencing, if possible, with access control via gates, manned if possible. Also, barricades and bollards to protect student gathering areas like outdoor activities, dining and bus stops from curb jumping vehicles. In this ring are bus drivers and groundskeepers; again, they enter the area surrounding the asset, thus introduce vulnerability and require special screening.

Further out, the third ring is the area around the school complex—neighborhoods, businesses, adjacent streets, parks, convenience stores, bus stops, train depots. This area provides a critical overwatch role, designed to identify danger before it arrives at the school. For instance, most recent terrorist attacks at soft targets include pre-operational surveillance. As previously discussed, many amateur bad actors lack the requisite skill set, thus are sloppy and easily detectable—if someone is aware and watching. Military installations have relationships with fast food, gas stations and other facilities outside the base perimeter fence for this very reason—they will see people taking photographs of the gates, doing dry runs, or even trying to cut holes in the fence or stack objects to help them get over (these are real-life examples from my own military experiences as a base commander). Soft targets must extend security out to this layer, build relationships, and provide contact information so the trip wire works and provides notification.

When discussing students who wish to do harm to their own school, the fourth ring is their home. There are many cases of parents who did not know what was happening in their child's room, when they were building bombs or stockpiling weapons, writing journals filled with violent thoughts and plans. Or parents look the other way at odd behavior during periods of stress, like bullying or relationship drama. Take the case of John David LaDue, arrested in April 2014, charged with attempted murder and property damage. In months of planning the attack on his school, he rented a storage locker and stockpiled three completed bombs, bomb-making materials, and weapons. In his room, there was a 180-page journal detailing plans to kill his family, then go to school, kill a resource officer, and carry out a mass shooting and bombing. When confronted with this evidence, discovered by police, his parents said they did not believe their son would have gone through with his plan. You can now see how layered security works. If this ring fails, the others closer to the asset are designed to frustrate and hopefully stop the attack.

In the outer ring is social media as "virtual community." There are plenty of cases where school shooters communicated on social media while in emotional decline, even stating their future actions. Columbine's Eric Harris posted violent essays on the Internet; UC Santa Barbara shooter Elliot Rodger posted a YouTube video; Marysville Pilchuck High School's Jaylen Fryberg melted down on Twitter; the Umpqua community college shooter posted his intentions on 4chan; and Independence High, Arizona, shooter Dorothy Dutiel posted "goodbye" on Twitter the night before she shot her best friend and killed herself at school. Sometimes parents and friends see these posts and do nothing. As difficult as it may be, when you confront someone who is making a violent plan, you frustrate their goal—the element of surprise. Knowing they are on the parent and school radar may serve to frustrate their plan.

Conducting a vulnerability assessment on each ring may uncover a fracture leading all the way from the outer ring to the asset. This gap may be lack of communication vehicle, a culture preventing open reporting between the "gatekeeper" of each ring, or inconsistent or incongruent policies that prevent timely reporting of important data points that, when connected, will prevent an attack. As a leader or manager, you will not be able to identify these disconnects unless you map out the rings.

The defensible space theory is also of value to soft target venues. In his 1998 book *Design Guidelines for Defensible Space*, architect and city planner Oscar Newman discusses ideas about crime prevention and neighborhood safety. He presents a study showing how a higher crime rate existed in high-rise apartment buildings in New York City than in the city's housing projects. Newman felt it was because residents felt no control or personal responsibility for an area occupied by so many people. His main point is you will gain a higher level of security by breaking down the macroenvironment into smaller, more manageable areas. There are five factors that make a defensible space:

Territoriality: the idea that one's home is sacred
Natural surveillance: the link between an area's physical characteristics and the residents' ability to see what is happening
Image: the capacity of the physical design to impart a sense of security
Milieu: other features that may affect security, such as proximity to a police substation or busy commercial area
Safe Adjoining Areas: for better security, residents obtain higher ability of surveillance of adjoining area through designing the adjoining area

For instance, to encourage people to have a more active role in owning and securing their space, break down large buildings or sprawling campuses into smaller areas with their own identity, perhaps their own access. In terms of natural surveillance, a parking lot adjoining a building should not be obscured by trees. Any would-be criminal is visible from the building, so would be deterred from vandalism, theft, or physical assault. Newman's book is available for free download at www.huduser. gov/publications/pdf/def.pdf.

You can use rings of security, layered defense, defense in depth, defensible space—whatever vernacular works best at your location. Just remember the principles and put up walls and layers to protect your most precious assets.

PHYSICAL SECURITY

(Thank you to Brian Gallagher, former physical security specialist at the US Secret Service and member of the Board of Directors for the Faith Based Security Network (www.fbsbamerica.com), a not for profit 501c(3) for assistance with the following section.)

The best way to find out what deters a bad actor is to simply ask them. Convicted thieves are an accessible populace and give valuable insight. Figure 9.1 shows responses from 360 burglars about physical security measures serving as the biggest deterrents to their activities (Kuhns 2013).

The presence of people is the number one deterrent, followed by an officer nearby, noise, and seeing neighbors. This type of data is useful when making security decisions. If you are considering a costly camera system, perhaps the money is better spent hiring an off-duty police officer to stay at your property overnight. Alarms are effective deterrents, but a bad actor may still probe to see if the system is engaged. The limited escape route is something to consider as well; criminals want to get in and out without anything in their way. This is where fencing and secure gates come into play. Although it might be easy to breach a fence to enter a property, getting out may be difficult, especially if running away from security or carrying stolen goods, weapons, etc.

The exterior of your building, the grounds, and the parking lot are all critical to the security of your occupants. Physical hardening of your property could be as simple as installing a security fence or raising the height of current fencing to keep out intruders. Fencing that conceals your building and its occupants (such as children in a schoolyard) is optimal and certainly projects a hardened posture more so than chain link. Always check the perimeter fence for breaches or the stacking of wood or objects that could allow someone to climb over the fence or establish a sniper position. Industry experts recommend the following fence standard: seven feet high, with three strands of barbed wire, six inches apart.

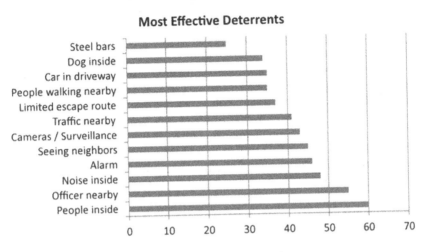

FIGURE 9.1   Most Effective Deterrents to Burglary

Also consider the psychological effect of walls, borders, and fencing; perhaps they are not constructed only for repelling intruders but for a sense of security for property users. Thoughts of possible attack plus related fear and stress are damaging and distracting.

Shrubbery should be no higher than three feet, and set back one yard from buildings, and tree branches trimmed eight feet above the ground. Outdoor lighting should not only illuminate buildings, but also the surrounding property, very important to deter trespassers. Motion lights will keep your electricity bill lower and startle any would-be intruder. There are many other industry standards for external security lighting; see IESNA, ASNI, and OSHA guidelines online.

Parking Lots

Consider your parking lot or parking garage an extension of your building. As illustrated in previous case studies, several international and domestic terrorists used these areas to stage an attack, plant the primary bomb in a vehicle, or place secondary or tertiary devices aimed at injuring response personnel and evacuees. At the very least, a bad actor is likely going to pass through your parking lot or garage to get to the building, so install a layer of security. The preferable situation is to have the parking lot inside the fence line, with a greeting area/entry point to control visitors. Think about when your parking areas are most at risk. For example, churches are especially vulnerable to burglary, with service times posted outside on signage and a lot full of unattended vehicles for an hour or more. A roving parking lot security team provides an extra layer of protection.

Operations with large parking lots or garages such as megachurches, large schools, malls, and sports and recreational venues might consider training for parking attendants called "First Observer" (www.parking. org/2017/03/01/online-course-first-observer-plus/). The free, online course is jointly operated by the Department of Homeland Security (DHS) and the Transportation Security Administration (TSA) to train parking attendants to identify a potential threat. The program also educates the parking attendants with background information on terrorist groups, their tactics, and trends as well as an understanding of weapons. Training of this type turns a parking attendant into a force multiplier for your organization.

Prepositioned Vehicle

Police departments use decoy security cars around the country to deter crime. Perhaps you could ask your local police department for a marked police cruiser not in service be placed at the entrance of your building. At some shopping centers, an officer will his or her personal vehicle in the lot while on patrol, and park the cruiser there when off duty. The marked vehicle serves as a visual deterrent for those who might be performing surveillance on the facility. If the marked cruiser is not possible, possibly a member of your church, school, hospital, or organization will give up an old SUV or truck, which you can mark to look like a security vehicle from afar using fluorescent tape and other tools. In the Middle East, I lived in a housing compound. The security posture was enhanced by a fleet of "security vehicles" parked at locations which a bad actor could see through a break in the fence or the gated front entrance. The vehicles were in fact just older trucks and jeeps with reflective striping and decals (Figure 9.2). If you use this tactic, remember to rotate the vehicles to keep the watchers on their toes and keep the tactic quiet so word does not get out.

There is no scientific data to prove the pre-positioning of law enforcement vehicles deters attack; however, anecdotal stories support the theory. Ventura County, California, and Dallas, Texas, both report lower crime in areas where they park a decoy vehicle. On the night he attacked Pulse, Omar Mateen decided not to attack the Disney Village

FIGURE 9.2   SUV Repurposed as a Mock Security Vehicle at a Compound in the Middle East

and another nightclub due to heavy security presence. There is reason to suggest Sandy Hook Elementary School shooter Adam Lanza's initial target was actually Newtown High School. According to a source familiar with the investigation, Lanza's car was identified on the school surveillance footage circling the school parking lot. The official believed Lanza saw two police cars parked in the lot and decided to move on (Lysiak 2013). Lawyers used the absence of such procedures as a contributing factor in several "negligent security" lawsuits; for instance, in 2007, a man was killed by a shooter with an AK-47 in a case of mistaken identity in a Waffle House parking lot in Pensacola, Florida, at 3:30 a.m. In the successful lawsuit filed by the family: "The plaintiff alleged the restaurant was located in a high crime area. The plaintiff's security experts opined the defendant was negligent in failing to have an armed, uniformed sheriff's officer on the premises with a marked police car which would have deterred the crime" (Rose, Vangura, and Levin 2009).

Traffic Duty

Soft target facilities have predictable schedules: schools have drop off/ pickup, church services start and end at the same time every week, sporting and recreational events have traffic issues at the beginning and end of events, and malls are typically their busiest on Friday and Saturday nights. Choke points outside your facility present a security hazard and you need to keep traffic moving. Mir Aimal Kansi, a Pakistani citizen residing in the United States with phony immigration papers and a forged green card, became enraged while watching CNN news coverage of US operations in Iraq and CIA involvement in Muslim countries. A courier, he often drove by the entrance to CIA headquarters, noting the two lanes of traffic waiting at the light to turn left onto the agency's ground. At 8:00 a.m. on January 25, 1993, Kansi drove his courier vehicle to that very spot, emerged from his vehicle with an AK-47 semiautomatic rifle, and walked up and down the lines of vehicles, firing a total of ten rounds, killing two CIA employees, and injuring three others. Kansi escaped the country and was arrested by FBI agents in Pakistan in 1997; he was convicted and sentenced to death by lethal injection, which was accomplished in 2002. The military actively tries to avoid choke points, such as long traffic lines at gates, where people are vulnerable to attack and are blocking emergency response vehicles, if required.

Many states and counties require some sort of intersection control for larger churches, schools, and sports and recreational events. Although tempting simply to use volunteers with reflective vests, it is important to have a uniformed police officer directing traffic along with a marked vehicle with flashing lights, not only to slow vehicles but also to show presence to any opportunist who may decide to strike during the congested, chaotic time. A possible solution is to use a member of your church congregation or the spouse of one of your school, hospital, or sports/recreational venue employees who happens to be a law enforcement officer. However, if you need to hire an officer, go directly through the county or local police departments instead of using a contractor, which is costlier and will likely outsource to the same organization.

SECURITY

We accomplish four goals through robust physical security features: portray to would-be bad actors that the facility is hardened and deter their actions; protect our property and its occupants in the event of penetration or attack; make staff feel safe, improving productivity and provide a better experience for users whether learning, worshiping, or healing. In for-profit organizations, a strong security infrastructure and program will positively affect your bottom line, especially for customers who make decisions about what venues they will entrust with their lives and those of family members.

Locks

Some facilities have only a few doors and others have many; no matter your situation, know that locks are critical to securing your property. Locks can be very easy to defeat if they are not constructed or installed properly. For instance, someone with basic knowledge gleaned from the Internet can defeat locks installed on home doors in a matter of minutes. A simple padlock can be cut with a bolt cutter. A file cabinet can be breached by a crowbar. So how do you keep out those with bad intentions?

Exterior doors must have, at the least, a dead bolt, and must never contain glass or be surrounded by glass window panes. In the Newtown, Connecticut, shooting at Sandy Hook Elementary School, the school's security procedures had just changed, requiring visitors to be admitted individually through a set of security doors after visual and identification review by video monitor. On December 12, 2012, doors to the school were locked at 9:30 a.m. after morning arrivals. Adam Lanza arrived at the school at 9:35 a.m. According to the official report: "The doors to the school were locked, as they customarily were at this time, the school day having already begun. The shooter proceeded to shoot his way into the school building through the plate glass window to the right of the front lobby doors" (Office of the State's Attorney Judicial District of Danbury 2013). See Figure 9.3 for a view of the front entrance of Sandy Hook Elementary after Lanza's attack.

Once inside, Lanza had a distinct advantage because he had attended Sandy Hook and had intimate knowledge of the inside of the building. However, there were infrastructure weaknesses detailed in the Newtown report, disadvantages allowing Lanza to kill twenty innocent children and six teachers and staff members in just five minutes before turning the gun on himself when the police arrived. For instance, the report discusses the office and classroom doors: "The doors in the hallway all locked

FIGURE 9.3   Front Entrance of Sandy Hook Elementary School

from the outside with a key. The interior door handles had no locking mechanism. All doors opened outwardly toward the hallway. All doors were solid wood with a circular window in the upper half of the door." Although investigators did not discuss how these doors failed to protect the building occupants, the report is replete with examples of how Lanza was walking up and down the hallway trying doors and looking through windows. If the doors also locked from the inside, with a double key lock, the extra security would have saved lives. Also, having windows on the doors provides visual advantage to the shooter and another way to get through the door if it is locked from the inside. Photographs taken at the scene show the classroom windows were the type opening inward just a few inches, with not enough space for a child to escape. The classrooms were on the first floor and students could have fled the scene through the windows if they slid on a track. The Sandy Hook tragedy gives much to consider when assessing external and internal building security.

Sadly, four years later, the Marjory Stoneman Douglas High School in Parkland, Florida, had the exact same doors that doomed Sandy Hook. Teachers couldn't lock classroom doors from the inside, but had to grab a key, open the door and turn the lock from the outside. The doors also had small windows that allowed Nikolas Cruz to fire into locked classrooms, leading to several deaths (Spencer 2018). Fourteen students and three staff members died in the February 14 shooting and seventeen others were wounded. It is imperative that schools learn from these horrific attacks and spend the money necessary to protect their students, and parents and staff must demand action. Who has access to your building? How many people have keys to your building? Do they all need a key to the front door? Typically, too many people have keys to a building. Keys should be numbered, issued by signature, and stamped "do not duplicate." The types of locks are also important; for instance, a standard lock has a cylinder inside with a series of pins moving up and down. When you insert a key into the cylinder, it moves the pins up and down vertically; when the pins line up correctly, the cylinder rotates, and the lock opens. Locks with more pins are harder to defeat; for instance, a filing cabinet lock may have three pins whereas the lock on your front door may have six or more. The depth of the pins also helps make the lock more secure, to prevent opening by mere jiggling of the cylinder using a pin. Professional locks have pins that are not merely vertical, making them extremely difficult to defeat.

Locks can also have "smart cards" or electronic chips in the key, allowing for remote access and the ability to activate or deactivate a key and to control and track access to a room. For example, using keys and locks with electronic chips allows the facility manager to give access only on certain days (church services or school days). Naturally, we should not assume people with keys to our facility have bad intentions; however, keys are routinely stolen or lost. In government facilities, lost keys often mean locks must be changed and new keys issued. Electronic keying allows for instantaneous changes that immediately prevent access in the case of nefarious intent by a thief or a person finding a lost key. The basic principle is to limit access.

Interior doors should have locks, including supply closets, which are notorious hiding places for a bad actor and/or the stockpiling of supplies for an operation. Business offices must be further hardened to protect not only from the theft of confidential information, but also the occupants who might be the target of a criminal act or an attack. Strictly ensure keys to these doors are only given to those who need daily access. Although some large hospitals now have sophisticated systems which automatically lock all doors and stop elevators in the case of a lockdown, consult with law enforcement and fire officials prior to installing such a system, as it could trap people trying to flee.

Alarms

So, what is the backup plan if your key system is defeated? Some soft target facilities have sophisticated alarm systems and others have none.

If you do not have an alarm system, why not? Security companies can install alarm systems at your facility for minimal cost and charge modest monthly monitoring fees. If you do have an alarm system, is it the right one and are all of your bases covered? It may be time for a security assessment and upgrade.

An alarm system protects your building and its occupants, but also acts as a powerful deterrent to many would-be intruders. When 422 convicted burglars were surveyed, approximately 83 percent of the offenders said they would attempt to determine if an alarm were present before the burglary and about 73 percent said they would seek an alternative target if so. Among those who discovered the presence of an alarm while attempting a burglary, half reported they would discontinue the attempt, and another 37 percent said they would leave the property. About one-third of the respondents planned their crime; the rest were opportunists, mostly looking for money or drugs (Kuhns 2013).

If you have a central alarm system, it can be wired or wireless. Monitored is available by a central location or you can have a "bells only" system, in which you hope the loud alarm deters the penetrator, who then departs the property. Remember, the alarm code is just as valuable as the master key and you should try to limit distribution of this code to staff who come to work early to open the building and stay late to close, or those who need to enter at odd hours. However, all staff should have the silent duress code number they can punch into a panel, alerting the alarm company to call law enforcement, a feature only possible with monitored systems.

If you choose a monitored alarm system, technicians will place sensors on doors and windows. You may also add motion sensors to catch movement inside the building and glass breakage detectors on sliding doors. When triggered, the alarm signal travels via a telephone or Internet line to a central monitoring location where an employee receives information such as your address and a schematic of your building with the exact location of the breach. The alarm company will have several contacts on file and will first call you before calling law enforcement, to prevent false alarms. Typically, you will have a prearranged, easy to remember telephone password confirming your identity. You must think redundancy when deciding on an alarm system for your facility; if the person is hiding inside the building when you lock up for the day, you need a motion sensor to detect activity. If the intruder can breach the external door lock and alarm (pressure pads are easy to defeat, magnetic pads, not so easy), again, the motion sensor will work. Glass breakage detectors are important on sliding doors, as the actor may try to avoid the sensor on the track by entering through the broken glass.

As previously mentioned, if your system is monitored, an employee can simply enter a duress code into the panel to alert authorities, and law enforcement will immediately respond to the location. Also, panels typically have hot buttons to push for medical help, fire, and police; these are time-savers during an emergency when seconds count. An alarm system is a great investment, and most insurance companies offer discounts for their use.

You should also have a panic alarm built into the reception area; this is a simple button located under the desk that staff can discreetly push in the event of an emergency to signal silently for help. The signal can be set up in different ways; for instance, it can be wired so the duress call will go straight to the local alarm company, which will immediately send the police. Or, the panic signal button does not have to be programmed to notify the local alarm company or police department; it is possible to have it signal a colleague to come to the area and provide backup. The button should be pushed only in a situation where there is the danger of physical violence; train the staff not to enact the duress signal if someone is merely acting demanding or overly emotional. Banks are served very well by these silent alarms, with police typically arriving while the robbery is being committed or shortly thereafter. Naturally, bank robbers know that banks have these alarms and yet are undeterred. Similarly, we need to realize security features will not keep all determined bad actors from engaging.

Visitor Access and Badges

Having a solid visitor management program to control access to your facility is incredibly important. If there are several access points to the building, have clearly marked signage funneling visitors through one set of doors. Have the visitor sign a log with name, time, and cell phone number, and produce photo identification for entry, preferably a government-issued card such as a driver's license. You may hold this identification in exchange for a visitor's badge. Many secure government buildings, such as the Pentagon, require two forms of government-issued photo identification. The best practice is to have the visitor wait in a designated area while you contact the individual he or she came to see; do not let the visitor wander aimlessly around the building. Having positive control of the visitor is important. Secure schools do not let parents walk items to classrooms (forgotten lunches, books, musical instruments); they may leave the items in a designated area in the front hallway and the child comes later to collect. Sign-in logs must be kept for a designated period of time, as they will provide evidence if the visitor commits a crime on the property, is in a parental custody battle, and so forth. The rosters also allow other due diligence activities, such as running the name through the sex offender database. Although these activities may feel uncomfortable or intrusive, remember you are responsible for the protection of hundreds, if not thousands, of innocent people. Inconveniencing a visitor is a small price to pay.

Closed Circuit Television (CCTV)

We have already discussed cameras in terms of terrorists and violent criminals, who barely see them as a deterrent, hoping they aren't taping or their image is obscured enough to cause doubt of their identity. On the other hand, more than 40 percent of convicted burglars, taking part in less violent activity, indicated the presence of surveillance cameras would deter them from a target. Still, 60 percent would be undeterred. We have discussed how some terrorists often conduct surveillance of their targets while planning, while others simply hit a target of opportunity. A key tenet of this book is that facility owners should not base hardening activities on guesses as to who might attack or how. Therefore, my opinion is all soft target locations should have CCTV, preferably monitored real-time, but, at the least, taping for later reference or evidentiary purposes. Many systems refresh on a cycle; forty-eight hours is probably a good point to start taping over old data. CCTV acts as a set of eyes when people are not available, and it helps gain convictions and even win court cases for you and your insurance company in the event of a lawsuit or claim.

Admittedly, CCTV does not deter a suicide terrorist or an enraged violent criminal who is not thinking rationally. However, if the actor believes the cameras are being monitored, they know there will be an immediate law enforcement response, compressing the timetable for the criminal act. Use camera systems to watch not only the front door, but also other exterior doors, hallways, classrooms, and other multipurpose rooms, and the parking lot. There are state laws against filming in certain areas such as bathrooms, locker rooms, changing areas, or nursing mothers' rooms. New camera systems transmit images over the Internet, so you can watch the feed from your computer or even through applications on wireless devices such an iPhone. One church security professional for a megachurch with a very large weekly collection can monitor safe activity through alarm and video feed. The mere fact that employees know he is watching is a deterrent from a malicious insider, and if an outsider did get in, security can call law enforcement right away and also take screenshots. Another notable feature of CCTV systems is pan, tilt, and zoom (PTZ) cameras with remote control capability if you need to get a closer look at an individual. For outside cameras, you could also employ infrared (IR) technology to see better in the dark; in fact, many companies are now installing IR cameras indoors to capture criminal activity occurring in dark corners or with flashlights. You can purchase systems over the counter and install them yourself; however, security system companies would be happy to bring their experts to your property to discuss CCTV coverage, and this is the preferred method for proper placement and operation.

Public Address System

I strongly recommend facilities have a public address system for broadcasting emergency information to the entire building. During the Sandy Hook Elementary shooting event, one of the injured staff members unknowingly tripped the loudspeaker system when dialing 911 for help. Her phone conversations were heard throughout the building, as were the gunshots in the front office area. This alerted the teachers and staff to the crisis and they had precious seconds to lock doors and hide students. The librarian called the front office and the staff to see what was happening and the staff member told her there was a shooter; again, this was broadcast to the entire school.

The Winnenden School, located in southwestern Germany, was the scene of a mass shooting when former student Tim Kretschmer entered with semiautomatic weapons on the morning of March 11, 2009. Immediately following the start of the attack, the school's principal broadcast a coded announcement saying "Mrs. Koma is coming," which is the word "amok" spelled backward. The message was a safety measure installed to alert the teachers of a school shooting and give them a chance to help students escape or shelter in place; it was established in Germany after a previous school massacre at Erfurt.

Intercom systems are also excellent ways to transmit specific threat and emergency information immediately. Hospitals have elaborate code systems that would be easy to adapt to other situations; for instance:

1. Code blue/code 99: CPR team
2. Code red/red alert/Dr. Firestone: fire alarm, activate department fire protocol (close fire doors, move people past fire zones, evacuate if ordered)
3. Code orange/code purple/code silver: internal incident (psychiatric patient missing, active shooter in building, active bomb threat, etc.; activate case-specific disaster plans)
4. Code black/code yellow/code 10: external incident (natural or man-made disaster, mass casualties; activate department disaster plan)
5. Code pink/code Adam/Amber alert: missing infant/child (lock down all exits, be on lookout for suspicious persons)
6. Code green/code 00/all clear: all clear, resume normal duties

In one school district, a "code 303 meeting" was known universally, even among the students, as the code for a bomb threat. "Mr. Falkes" and his parents being in the office meant a bomb threat, "Professor Norris" needing to meet his wife in the teacher's lobby meant weapon/stranger on site, and an "ROTC Club meeting" being canceled meant something very bad was happening and required immediate staff-wide attention (via email or intercom). At an exhibition center in London, loudspeaker calls include, "Will Mr. Goodfellow report to the security suite"—the code for a fire. A report "Mr. Goodfellow has left the building" is all-clear code for the fire situation. "Staff call 100" is the code for a bomb threat, and "Staff call 100 has been canceled" is the code for the bomb threat passing. At one college, instructors use a phone code to alert security if a student they are meeting in private may turn violent. If they want a security guard to come to the office as a precaution, they call the outer office and say "I'll be a little late for our meeting with 'Dr. Barry'"; if they want a guard to come in immediately, they say the appointment needs to be postponed.

The combination of the intercom and a code system can save lives.

Gunfire Detection System

Every second counts in an active shooter situation. Many government installation and major cities have gunfire detection systems, designed to recognize the sound of gunfire and immediately pinpoint the location and send emergency response. Knowing the location is also valuable for those under attack for more informed decisions about evacuation, shelter in place, and security response. In light of growing violence towards soft targets, companies, K–12 schools, universities, and other civilian-centric venues are installing gunfire detection solutions. I trust and recommend two companies. ShotSpotter is deployed throughout the country and offers the ShotSpotter Mobile ™ app to law enforcement. Each year ShotSpotter compiles gunfire data from their active coverage areas, then they aggregate, analyze, and publish for communities, federal, state, and local law enforcement agencies. The true volume of illegal gunfire activity is startling. They also found eight in ten incidents of actual gunfire are not reported, making a detection system all the more valuable for saving lives and getting criminals and guns off of the streets. Their National Gunfire Index is worthy of review, www. shotspotter.com/2017ngi. Shooter Detection Systems is another outstanding company, with more than 15,000 systems deployed in the field.

Ventilation System

We discussed the threat of weapons of mass destruction (WMDs) in Chapter 7 and, for closed buildings and venues, it is extremely important to understand your central air conditioning and ventilation systems. For example, find out if your building has fresh air intakes or recycled air intakes; newer systems are likely a combination of both. Are the units located on the roof, where they may be harder to reach (ideal) or are they on the ground and easily accessible? If an attacker is using a chemical or biological weapon against the property, he or she may introduce it through the intake system for maximum dispersal in the building. Even over-the-counter pepper spray will affect building occupants if introduced this way. If the unit is on the roof, make sure hatches are padlocked. If the unit is on the ground, consider building a fence around the unit with a lock on the gate. If possible, try to monitor these locations with security cameras and, if your organization cannot afford security cameras, then include these locations in a walk through for your security team or administrative staff.

Kitchens and Dining Halls

For facilities with kitchens, consider whether you have a "clean" environment; for instance, when they are not in use, do you secure items that an attacker could use as a weapon, such as large knives? Are food items secured in tamperproof containers or locked refrigerators, so a bacterial agent cannot be introduced? In churches, kitchens may only be used once a week, so they may be a good place for an insider or potential attacker to store supplies. Dining halls are particularly vulnerable to a mass shooting or kidnapping/hostage situation because there can be many people in a confined space; several attacks already profiled in this book have occurred in cafeterias, especially related to school shootings. Crisis planning and exercises should include this scenario, having students and staff practice sheltering and escape.

EMERGENCY PREPARATIONS

Hardening your facility includes being prepared for any contingency, whether there is an emergency in your town or city and you are receiving scared or hurt people, or whether you have a security incident on your property and need to provide medical care and possibly shelter in place until help can get to you. The first action is to take the applicable free FEMA courses listed in Appendix B, such as IS-360, "Preparing for Mass Casualty Incidents: A Guide for Schools, Higher Education, and Houses of Worship," or IS-362.a, "Multi-Hazard Emergency Planning for Schools."

Specifically, you should have a four-pronged approach to cover all bases: a "hold room" to secure your leadership, a command center for you and your key staff, a strong medical program, and the ability to shelter in place.

Hold Room

A hold room is a place where you and other key staff or important visitors can retreat in the event of an emergency and hold for an undetermined amount of time. The room should be located in an evacuation area or point of the building where law enforcement can most easily get to you and you can get out as needed. The hold room can be as simple as a room with a door and lock or as elaborate as an underground facility. It may be worth the money to purchase a security door for the hold room—whether an "intruder" door resistant to breach or a ballistic door protecting from forced entry, but also repels .30-06 caliber rounds. At the very least, you want to make sure the door can lock from the inside and it has no windows. Although it seems counterintuitive, it is best to select a room with no exterior windows for additional security. The hold room must have a landline phone in case cellular service is not working, and you may also want to have a charged cell phone in the room in the event the phone lines are not working. Also pre-position a case of water and energy bars in case you need to sustain those in the hold room for more than a few hours. Flashlights are a must in case the electricity goes out, as well as a battery-powered radio so you can get news updates on the unfolding situation. The goal in an emergency is to get out of the facility; however, if you cannot escape, the hold room will buy you time until law enforcement arrives. Be sure to add checking the hold room phones, supplies, and door lock mechanism to your facility walk-through checklist.

Emergency Response Team and the Command Center

In the event of a major incident in the surrounding community or at your facility, you may want to stand up an emergency response team and have an area serve as your command center. The command center might be the same as the hold room. You will need a landline, flashlights, a radio with extra batteries, water, and a supply of nonperishable food such as energy bars. Handheld radios that are charged and ready are a plus if someone needs to leave and communicate with the command center. Pads of paper, pens, and even a whiteboard with dry erase markers would be helpful. This room is the central repository for information and checklists.

Next, assess your potential emergency team. You may want to poll your employees to evaluate the additional skills and resources they bring to your operation. For instance, do they have a conceal carry permit and do they regularly carry a weapon? Do they have medical training, private security or a military background, or experience as a volunteer firefighter or paramedic? When formulating the emergency team, think about the skill set and also the mindset: Can he or she handle an extremely upsetting, emotional event and be an asset to the team, instead of a liability? Once your emergency team is identified, create an "alert roster" with their names and cell, home, and email contact information. Make sure to check the information regularly to ensure currency.

Who should be around your table? If your staff has directors or heads of specialized sections, they should each be there—security, facilities, communication, human resources, legal, etc. Also, if you have any counselors on staff, one should be designated to sit on the emergency response team. Additionally, have someone on your team in charge of handling the press and social media. If your building is under attack or there is a mass hostage situation, others will blog, tweet, and Facebook; take control of the "message" and transmit what you want people to know about what is happening inside. Also, information you transmit could save the lives of others; for instance, during the strong earthquake on the Eastern seaboard on August 23, 2011, citizens in New York City saw the Twitter alerts about an earthquake originating in Virginia fifteen to twenty seconds before seismic waves struck the city. According to Facebook, the word "earthquake" appeared in the status updates of three million users within four minutes of the quake. Twitter said users were sending as many as 5,500 messages ("tweets") per second.

You may want to have Twitter and Facebook shell accounts established for the purpose of keeping control of the message and transmitting data that could warn others of danger. Naturally, do not transmit any information about law enforcement activity in the building, for example, which responders are on site, numbers, and their plan. In many cases, such as the Westgate Mall siege, the terrorists are also using the media to transmit and television and radio to assess the activities of law enforcement outside. Also, never transmit the number of injured or fatalities, or any pictures that could be used as propaganda by the bad actors or disturb family members.

I recommend you have a binder with checklists for each situation that could arise. Yes—good old-fashioned paper. When running exercise events, I will often remove access to electricity early in the scenario, and organizations solely relying on their computers fail. I previously mentioned my job on 9/11 running the support operations center for a base of thousands. My checklists were up to date and I was able to go through and annotate what actions we had taken, problem areas, and so forth. After the fact, this paper trail was invaluable to prepare for future events. One thing you must have on hand are maps of the building and/or blueprints, as these are critical for first responders and law enforcement, especially if there is a hostage or active shooter situation. These floor plans must have cardinal directions and specific distance by feet (and even steps); walk your buildings and grounds and then map it out. Law enforcement will want to know everything about the ventilation system ducts, whether doors open in or out, and the location of light switches. This is why you must know every single inch of your property; you will be the expert they turn to for answers.

Your binder should include checklists for different contingencies your facility might face. The best way to ensure your team is prepared and ready to handle an emergency is to practice through exercises. Take the FEMA courses listed in Appendix B, specifically IS-120.a, "An Introduction to Exercises"; IS-130, "Exercise Evaluation and Improvement Planning"; and IS-139, "Exercise Design." In addition to full-scale practices, crisis "table top" exercises where you and the team report to the command center and simply talk through the event are also a must, perhaps quarterly. There are experts who can create scenarios tailored to your organization, or you can simply draft the scenario yourself based on past events such as the Beslan school and Moscow theater sieges, the Boston Marathon attack, Columbine, and so on. Run through it with the team and keep throwing in unexpected problems such as the phones dying, a family member breaching the cordon and entering the building looking for a loved one, or the electricity going out. Remember the "pilots-in-the-simulator" approach; make it very difficult or even impossible for your team to handle and they will rise to any future challenge and succeed. During contingency operations drills in the military, a card may be handed to the leader within the first few minutes of the exercise indicating he or she is out of the fight—either killed in the attack or otherwise incapacitated. This forces the team to consider who would step up and lead and gives the person the opportunity to sit in the "hot seat." Of course, you are not on your property 24/7, and there is a possibility a crisis will strike while you are away. Do not be the single point of failure for your team.

Something to ponder are the trigger points for action. Let us say there is an emergency in the community and it is infringing on your property, threatening your facility and the people within. When should you abandon the facility and how? I was fortunate to attend a conference session in Dubai regarding hotels in the Middle East and their contingency plans. During the 2012 uprisings in Libya, several US hotels were caught in the middle of the crisis in which a US ambassador and his team were killed in Benghazi and the embassy burned to the ground. One hotel unexpectedly was the recipient of an influx of people after the embassy made an announcement (without coordinating) that all Americans should go to this particular hotel. The hotel manager looked out the window and saw a line of cars and Americans outside his property's gate, which he had locked down. Naturally, he took all of the Americans in and bedded them down with the rest of the hotel customers and staff. But at some point, he had to make the difficult decision to leave the property, possibly forever because it would likely be overrun and destroyed by militants. They needed more buses than originally planned, and people could only take one small bag, leaving the rest behind. Travel arrangements had to be made with airlines, and the now-large convoy of Americans to the airport required security. A bad situation quickly degraded to the worst scenario. Fortunately, they all made it out of the country; however, the property still sits vacant.

The manager of the hotel in Libya told us he wished he had three plans on the shelf that day, instead of just one. He called them the "alpha, bravo, and zulu plans," Zulu was the worst-case scenario of no rescue possibility and ditching the facility. The account of the hotel manager and others profiled in this book teaches an invaluable lesson: expect the unexpected and plan accordingly.

Bomb Threat

Organizations all over the country receive bomb threats every year by phone, mail, email, or note at the facility. Most of these threats are geared toward one main purpose: to disrupt everyday activities, whether final exams, a church service, or a major event. Although most threats turn out to be benign, attention-getting mechanisms, you should not guess—call law enforcement immediately and they will conduct a thorough sweep of the building, possibly bringing dogs to detect explosives and other high-tech equipment to ensure the building is clear. The bomb threat sheet provided in Appendix D should be close to all telephones so the call recipient can immediately write down the details from the call. Train those who answer your phones to stay calm and keep the caller on the phone as long as possible to gather information about gender, background noises, etc. The conversation might even allow your staff member to ask when the bomb will go off, to include the time and date, and to query about whether the bomb has already been placed in the building and, if so, where. Practice is key to ensuring your employees respond properly when receiving a phoned-in bomb threat. Appendix E has the evacuation distance chart to use as a plan to immediately move people and vehicles the proper distance away from the location. Have an evacuation plan, post it, and practice often.

In 2017, I presented at the ASIS International conference in Dallas with Brad Spicer, founder of SafePlans, a firm specializing in all-hazards emergency preparedness technology and active shooter defense training. Our topic was unique—perhaps, based on data and emergent threats, evacuating as a result of a bomb threat may not actually be in the best interest of an organization. As discussed at length in this book, terrorists often target fleeing people or evacuation assembly points; they may call in a bomb threat to flush people into the actual attack zone. Your building may offer greater protection to occupants than the parking lot, where they are exposed to a potentially catastrophic vehicle bomb. Also, most "bombs" are crudely made explosive devices like a pipe bomb, placed in a trash can, locker ,or other receptacle that may absorb part of the blast. The blast radius around a small device is much smaller than that of a vehicle bomb.

Let's discuss the connection between bomb threat and actual bombings. The three largest bombings in US in the last fifty years are covered in this book—Bath, Michigan, school attack (1927); the first World Trade Center attack (1993); and the Oklahoma City bombing (1995). None of these attacks were preceded by a threat. The 2017 Explosives Incident Report (EIR), an informational product prepared by the United States Bomb Data Center (USBDC), further illustrates the relationship between bomb threat and bombing. The Bomb Arson Tracking System (BATS) receives data about explosions and bombings from 2,600 interagency partners and 12,845 registered users. First of all, the overall number of explosion incidences dramatically dropped from 1,242 in 2012 to 687 in 2017, of which 335 were bombings (down 24 percent from 2016).

Understanding the explosive threat landscape is paramount to having a sound evacuation protocol. In 2017, 26 percent, or 180, of the explosions were accidental. Another 23 percent, or 157 explosions, were undetermined, meaning unknown perpetrator or methodology. Of the 335 actual bombs, 168 were fireworks, military-related or homemade. Another 113 explosions were caused by Incendiary Explosive Devices (IEDs), thirty-three were over-pressure devices and twenty-one unknown.

The EIR also tracks bomb threats. Per the 2017 EIR, total bomb threats made in 2017 stood at 1,228, down from 1,536 in 2016, including the 100+ threats called into Jewish community centers and synagogues. Of the 1,228 bomb threats in 2017, the top three realms receiving threats were schools (237); residences, hotels, and dorms (154); and businesses, including banks and retail stores (148).

Of note—of the 5,317 explosions in the US in the last five years, none were preceded with a threat. Threats are more like promises than guarantees. Some who make threats do pose a threat. Many who make threats do not pose a threat. The important takeaway—most bad actors who are a bombing threat will never make one.

Consider the bomber who wants to kill people and/or destroy a building. If the goal is to destroy a structure, the bomb may will likely be placed at a time when no one will find it or interfere with the bomber. Therefore, he or she will strike when the building is unoccupied and will not call in a threat. If the goal is to kill people, calling in a threat would likely result in evacuation, which means fewer deaths in the building. Therefore, a threat is counterproductive to either of these goals.

However, the actor may try to attack the fleeing group outside the facility, with pre-positioned bombs at evacuation points or in parking lots. This is why you must strongly consider how your organization should respond to a bomb threat instead of immediately heading outdoors. There are four possibilities when it comes to bomb threats: criminal hoax (most likely), ambush (rare, but a tactic used by both international and domestic terrorists), explosive device outside, or explosive device inside.

In 2015, a bomb threat was sent to both the New York City and Los Angeles school districts, which handled the situation in dramatically different ways. A review of this case helps illustrate the questions you may ask prior to taking action when faced with this scenario.

Case Study: Anonymous Bomb Threat and a Tale of Two Cities

On December 15, 2015, anonymous threats were emailed to officials with the Los Angeles Unified School District (LAUSD) and the New York City Department of Education (NYCDOE). The threats, for all practical purposes, were identical. The responses were not.

THE THREAT

The emailed threats spoke of teams of jihadists armed with nerve gas, bombs, and automatic weapons. They were sent to board members of each district via anonymous email service and routed through Germany. Full text of the email sent to officials at LAUSD:

> I am emailing you to inform you of the happenings on Tuesday, 12/15/15. Something big is going down. Something very big. It will make national headlines. Perhaps, even international ones. You see, my last 4 years here at one of the district high schools has been absolute hell. Pure, unmitigated, agony. The bullying, the loneliness, the rejection . . . it is never-ending. And for what? Just because I'm "different"?
>
> No. No more. I am a devout Muslim, and was once against violence, but I have teamed up with a local jihadist cell as it is the only way I'll be able to accomplish my massacre the correct way. I would not be able to do it alone. Me, and my 32 comrades, will die tomorrow in the name of Allah. Every school in the L.A. Unified district is being targeted. We have bombs hidden in lockers already at several schools. They are strategically placed and are meant to crumble the foundations of the very buildings that monger so much hate and discrimination. They are pressure cooker bombs, hidden in backpacks around the schools. They are loaded with 20 lbs. of

gunpowder, for maximum damage. They will be detonated via Cell Phone. Not only are there bombs, but there are nerve gas agents set to go off at a specific time: during lunch hour. To top it off, my brothers in Allah and I have Kalashnikov rifles, Glock 18 Machine pistols, and multiple handheld grenades. The students at every school in the L.A. Unified district will be massacred, mercilessly. And there is nothing you can do to stop it.

If you do end up trying to, by perhaps, beefing up security, or canceling classes for the day, it won't matter. Your security will not be able to stop us. We are an army of Allah. If you cancel classes, the bombings will take place regardless, and we will bring our guns to the streets and offices of Los Angeles, San Bernardino, Bakersfield, and San Diego.

I wish you the best luck. It is time to pray to allah, as this may be your last day.

New York Police Commissioner Bill Bratton told CNN that an email received by a NYDOE superintendent was "almost exactly the same as received in Los Angeles."

THE RESPONSE

Los Angeles

Los Angeles School Chancellor Ramon C. Cortines, who once ran NYDOE, collaborated with law enforcement and decided to close schools. At a 7 a.m. (Dec. 15, 2015) news conference, Cortines stated "I as superintendent am not going to take a chance with the life of a student." LAUSD serves more than 640,000 students enrolled in nearly 1,500 schools and support buildings across more than 720 square miles. LAUSD estimated the cost of closing at roughly $29 million. However, the California Superintendent of Public Instruction Tom Torlakson estimated the number might actually be closer to $50 million.

New York

Officials from New York discounted the threat as a hoax and schools remained in session; but they operated schools under heightened security. NYDOE serves more than 1.1 million students enrolled in more than 1,700 schools. The district services all five boroughs.

Analysis

Neither city was aware the other had received a similar threat during their analysis. It is likely the December 2 San Bernardino terrorist mass shooting attack, which killed fourteen and wounded twenty-two, factored into the LAUSD decision to close schools. The husband and wife terrorist were killed in the attack and the possibility they considered targeting schools was still under investigation when the threat was received. L.A. police chief Charlie Beck stated "All of us make tough choices. All of us have the same goal in mind: We want to keep our kids safe. Southern California has been through a lot in recent weeks."

In New York, Bratton reviewed the threat received by NYDOE and decided it was a hoax. New York Mayor Bill de Blasio stated "We've come to the conclusion that we must continue to keep our school system open. . . . In fact, it's important—very important not to overreact in situations like this." Bratton, who once served as the police chief in Los Angeles, publicly stated he felt the LAUSD response was an "over-reaction."

Factors that supported the "hoax" determination:

Overly grandiose claims (i.e. "The students at every school will be massacred, mercilessly.")

A cell of 32 "comrades" is extraordinarily large; even larger than the team that carried out the attacks 9/11/01.

A Glock 18 is a highly unusual weapon.

A devout Muslim would not spell "Allah" with a lower-case "a."

Terrorist take credit after attacks, they typically do not warn in advance.

LESSONS LEARNED

While no threat should ever be ignored, anonymous threats are far more like promises than contracts. They are made to obtain a desired response; which is typically anxiety and confusion.

Centralized reporting and case management systems can aid in situational awareness and improve threat assessment.

Finally, had LAUSD been aware that NYDOE received a nearly identical threat, it is likely LAUSD would have concluded the threat was a hoax. While it may be impractical for New York and Los Angeles to immediately share threat information, threats received within a community or state should be managed within a common platform; providing better situational awareness and better analysis.

Just remember—a grandiose threat is not more credible. Anonymous threats must be assessed on their credibility, and not severity.

(Source: Spicer 2019. Mr. Spicer is the founder of SafePlans, a firm specializing in all-hazards emergency preparedness technology and active shooter defense training. He is an army veteran with twenty years of state and local law enforcement. He can be reached at brad@safeplans.com.)

Medical Program

A good medical program is a very important part of your security plan. During a medical emergency, unless at a hospital, your staff, building occupants, and visitors may not be able to think clearly and respond while being part of an intensely stressful situation, such as violent shooting. Therefore, it is important to have medical protocols in place that everyone is familiar with and to train to the worst possible scenario. I will say upfront that with the increase of violent crime, particularly mass shootings with high caliber weapons, you must train your staff and understand yourself how to stop bleeding. Having tourniquets on hand in the facility is a must, and understanding how to improvise in a lockdown situation using ties, belts etc. is a good idea. There are plenty of training videos from civilian and military medical authorities online for viewing as a group or individually.

There are many cases where people froze, unable to dial 911. It was not because they did not know the number "911" but rather because an additional digit was needed to get an outside line, like dialing 9 first. To prevent these kinds of situations, simply place a sign or sticker on every phone reminding the caller to dial 9 for an outside line and then 911 in case of an emergency. Recall that part of your hardening efforts will be to ask the staff if they have special skills, including first aid, CPR, or advanced emergency medical care. During an emergency, have a plan to find these people and get them to the scene. Your organization may want to sponsor training days with on-site classes delivered by the American Red Cross, American Heart Association, or the National Safety Council. Check with your staff, church membership, and parents of your students; you may have certified trainers who can teach one of these classes. CPR training for all is a must, and your organization should also consider purchasing automated external defibrillators, known as AEDs, now located in public areas such as airports and shopping malls. These devices are used to shock a person's heart back into a healthy rhythm and are designed for the lay person who has no training, as the unit gives verbal commands to the user on how to use the apparatus. Based on the size of your facility, you may want more than one AED. Make sure you perform routine checks to ensure the battery is charged; add this to your security checklist.

There are many helpful smartphone applications on the market with CPR and tourniquet instructions you and your staff could preload into your phone or tablet computer. I have compiled a list of emergency-related apps in Appendix F for your consideration.

Training is a hardening activity that will save lives. Consider this: after US Airways Flight 1549 landed in the water, out of 155 passengers only ten took their floatation devices, per the National Transportation Safety Board. And several of those passengers were wearing the device incorrectly. Zoom in on the pictures of people standing and sitting on the wings and floating slides—you can count a few yellow vests. Note how visible they are on dark water and next to people in dark clothing.

In the April 17, 2018, incident regarding the Southwest Airlines flight with catastrophic engine failure, video taken of passengers in the aircraft showed most were wearing the oxygen mask incorrectly, as it was only placed over their mouth and not their mouth and nose. These examples show that in times of great stress, unless training kicks in and we respond instinctively, we will fall short on lifesaving procedures. Also, humans learn by doing; had people been asked to demonstrate putting the mask on correctly, instead of half-heartedly watching someone else do it, perhaps all of the passengers would don them correctly. Practice with your staff. Break out equipment, loosely tie tourniquets, let them put their hands on every piece of lifesaving equipment possible.

OSHA's medical service and first aid regulation, 29 C.F.R. 1910.151(b) states: "In the absence of an infirmary, clinic or hospital in near proximity to the workplace which is used for the treatment of all injured employees, a person or persons shall be adequately trained to render first aid. Adequate first aid supplies shall be readily available." The American National Standards Institute (ANSI), an organization dedicated to the health and safety of consumers and the environment, works with OSHA to develop safety standards. ANSI Z308.1–2008 "Minimum Requirements for Workplace First Aid Kits and Supplies" provides requirements that are compliant with OSHA intent (https://safety.grainger.com/facilities/class-a-class-b-first-aid-kits.)

A first aid station or a central repository for supplies is a good idea. Based on the size of the facility, you may want one on each floor. These range in all types of sizes, shapes, and prices. However, it is important to have at least a rudimentary first aid supply available in the event of an emergency, with many gauze pads and dressings, roller bandages, adhesive bandages including butterflies for deep cuts, tape, scissors, antibiotic and antiseptic salve, "space" blankets, and latex gloves. You may also want to have breathing barriers with one-way valves in case you need to administer CPR to multiple victims. Some kits have the equipment needed to run a peripherally inserted central catheter (PICC) line IV with fluids, as necessary. I recommend keeping these supplies packed in backpacks, as "go kits" for easy transport to the scene of the emergency. Finally, your organization should consider joining the Red Cross Ready Rating Program, which is outstanding and free. The program offers an online 123-point readiness evaluation for businesses, churches, schools, and other organizations to assess preparedness for an emergency and help to address vulnerabilities (American Red Cross 2014).

Finally, consider purchasing hoods for your employees. A product I used extensively in the Air Force is now available for purchase by individuals and companies. The victim rescue unit (VRU) escape hood is a head and respiratory protective hood that can be donned quickly and is compact, lightweight, and totally enclosed with its own oxygen supply. The

VRU will protect the user from smoke, chemicals, biological agents, and radiation. It is available for order online (http://myescapehood.com/). You may want to place hoods in your vehicles, and pre-position enough for your ERT in the command center.

Shelter in Place

During emergencies happening either outside your property or on it, you may choose to direct the staff and building occupants to "shelter in place." This term is widely used by the military and government agencies; the concept originates from procedures taken during a nuclear, chemical, or biological attack. You should prepare for this worst scenario where you need to create a barrier between yourself and potentially contaminated air outside, a process known as "sealing the room" as a matter of survival. This type of sheltering requires prior preparation, planning, and practice.

First, designate a room or rooms with the least numbers of windows, a landline phone, and stocked with water and nonperishable food supplies such as energy bars. Have a pre-positioned emergency kit with flashlights and a battery-powered radio, and do not forget extra packs of batteries. Gather all building occupants into the room(s), bringing in your first aid backpack "go kits," and then lock the doors and close the windows and all air vents. Turn off fans, air conditioners, and forced-air heating systems. Seal all windows, doors, and air vents with thick plastic sheeting and duct tape. Consider measuring and cutting the sheeting in advance to save time; it must be wider than the opening you are trying to cover. Secure the four corners first with duct tape, pulling the sheeting tightly across the opening. Then tape down all edges to form a seal.

"Shelter in place" is now a term commonly used during active shooter or other violent situations, as a way to keep people inside locked rooms. If sheltering during a violent attack, first lock the door from the inside and cover any windows on the door. Turn off the lights. Move as much heavy furniture as you can in front of the door to prevent it from being kicked in. Move to the back of the room. Tip over long tables and hide behind them in the far corner of the room, lying flat on the ground to lower your profile. Silence all cell phones and pagers and be absolutely quiet. If you are hit by debris or a stray bullet, do not cry out; remain as quiet as possible and play dead. US Secret Service studies show mass shootings are over in 480 seconds, or 8 minutes, on average, and 60 percent ended before law enforcement arrived on scene. Always keep in mind that each event is unique, but you can use this type of open source data in your planning. For more on how to prepare your staff and building occupants for an active shooter situation, I also recommend viewing the DHS (2017) video entitled "Options for Consideration Active Shooter Preparedness" at www.

dhs.gov/options-consideration-active-shooter-preparedness-video. Again, watch with your work group, classroom, families, etc., to stimulate discussion and discuss fears related to this type of emergency. Education and team building are hardening activities.

A new idea builds group cohesion and collaboration around emergency response topics and serves as an engaging and effective hardening tool for organizations. A new preparedness program initiative, Marco Program©, is perfect for schools, churches, hospitals, small companies—any organization that may not be able to afford expensive in-person security assessments. The organization receives a box with a facilitator's guide, assessment tools, and information on a topic of their choice, scaled for a group of twenty. The subject of most interest to soft target locations is disasters and emergencies. Some of the questions the group will explore include: What lessons can your organization learn from existing threats, risks, and vulnerabilities? What processes and protection systems will protect all personnel regardless of physical, mental, and emotional capabilities to react? Specific topics include weather; chemical, biological, radiological, and nuclear outbreaks (CBRN); terrorism and civil unrest; technology; and psychology and health. A virtual facilitator is provided, but not required, for the completion of the Marco Program. After completing the workbooks, the organization sends them back in a prepaid envelope to security experts for analysis, and the final product has strengths, vulnerabilities, and recommendations for you and your participants. See their website at https://criticalops.com/.

K–12 SCHOOLS

While accomplishing research for this book, I watched video from scenes of church bombings, school stabbings and shootings, the mall massacre in Nairobi, the Moscow theater siege, and the attack at Beslan. Although each event is disturbing and was horrific in its own way, the three-day Beslan attack was the most heinous. Schoolchildren are particularly vulnerable due to their size and inability to protect themselves. Children have more difficulty than adults discerning between real life and fiction; in the middle of a hostage situation or an active shooter event, they are likely to freeze in a state of suspended reality while trying to decide if it is a staged event or real life. A teenager or adult in today's society is more likely to realize the gravity of the situation and take some type of action to run, hide, or fight.

Therefore, I asked a colleague, Ralph Fisk, who works in the emergency management field and has experience with school preparedness, for advice regarding the challenges and tactics for hardening elementary schools. Please see the checklist in Appendix G.

In terms of school attacks, often the disgruntled actor has ranted on social media about his plight, like UC Santa Barbara shooter Elliot Rodger, who posted a long YouTube video prior to the shootings and had a 145-page manifesto detailing his disgust with his fellow college students. Social media is not only a place to rant but also an outstanding recruiting tool. A disgruntled employee who is vocal about his or her dissatisfaction with your organization makes them a target for bad actors looking for an insider to help plan an attack. Stay vigilant and monitor social media and the Internet through keyword searches to see if anyone is discussing your facility and operation.

Marisa Randazzo is a former chief research psychologist for the US Secret Service who applied a "threat assessment" model to examine the behavior of forty-one school attackers over the previous twenty-six years. She found there was no good "profile" of the type of person who becomes a school shooter. However, there were similar patterns of behavior. School shooters did not just "snap" and begin shooting impulsively; they planned. The attacker was vocal about his or her angst or intentions, trying to procure weapons, writing about the situation in journals and schoolwork. Randazzo states that "paying attention to changes in kids' behaviors and regularly conferring with one another about smaller threats is key to heading off bigger ones." Of the shooters she profiled in the study, Randazzo found: "These are not kids who were invisible—they actually were on multiple radar screens" (Toppo 2014). In 2014, there were several cases of concerned parents and friends reporting odd and worrisome behavior to school officials and law enforcement, a practice we must encourage, even though the informant likely does not want to get involved.

As a result of the spate of school attacks in the recent year, law enforcement officials have stepped-up efforts to hold active shooter drills at schools—sometimes, in a controversial move, using students as role players. On May 19, 2014, at Jefferson Middle School in Tennessee, emergency responders converged on the school after a "report" of shots fired and injuries. The school system fully participated and practiced the evacuation of hundreds of students by bus to a nearby church. Officers and paramedics had to find and subdue the shooters, as well as tend to twenty-two casualties, and school officials had to "lock down" the school and evacuate the students (Marion 2014). This type of realistic exercising is the best possible preparation for the school staff, teachers, students, and local law enforcement in the event of an active shooter situation. Parents may also consider listening to taped sounds of gunfire with their older children; several videos online now have sound files for a variety of weapons. When seconds count, thinking maybe it's firecrackers (as we often hear after an attack) will eat up precious time that could be spent locking doors, barricading, turning off lights, escaping out windows, etc.

Schools are targets and hardened in the Middle East. For example, international schools typically have high walls and a low profile. The name of the school is not advertised, and no host country flags are seen from the outside. Students are transported in small buses with both a driver and another adult; the curtains are always drawn. Buses are cleared by security and then are driven into a special secure area obscured from public view, where children walk directly into the school. Students who walk to school, teachers, and visitors access the grounds through entry control points with standoff protection, manned with at least two guards. All students and visitors pass through a metal detector. Bags are checked. The process only took an extra five or ten minutes in the morning—worth the wait! Despite its austere look from the outside, once on the property, schools are very open and lush, with gardens, fountains, and lovely buildings. Students can study without fear, knowing every person who comes on the campus goes through the same screening process. There are models for success and best practices in international school hardening for US schools to adapt—no need to reinvent the wheel.

Colleges have the same level of security. For example, at the Education City in Doha, Qatar, universities from the United States, including Georgetown, Cornell, MIT, and Texas A&M share a secure campus with stunning architecture and landscaping (Figure 9.4).

There are seven colleges located in on a secure campus compound. All visitors drive through gates, then park and simply walk to the college they are visiting. This compound method eliminates the duplication of security each school would require. The schools also share facilities like the gym, library, and dining hall.

FIGURE 9.4   United States Universities in the Secured Education City Complex, Doha, Qatar

HARDENING THE COLLEGE CAMPUS

Although the physical security procedures previously covered are suitable for college campuses, target hardening is not just about barricades and cameras but also relationships, psychological preparation, and resiliency. Soft target hardening must also harness and apply the soft sciences.

Building Relationships

Several opportunities already exist for schools to partner with law enforcement to address vulnerabilities on campus and harden against threats; however, few engage. This is also a good model for other countries wishing to increase partnering activities between academia and government security organizations. The local FBI office can assist schools with points of contacts for these programs:

1. The National Security Higher Education Advisory Board (NSEAB). In response to increased concerns about security on college and university campuses and to open the lines of communication between academe and law enforcement, the FBI created the NSHEAB in 2005. The NSHEAB consisted of nineteen university presidents and chancellors who met on a regular basis to discuss national security matters that intersect with higher education. Previous panels included discussion on protection of weapons of mass destruction research and laws regarding domestic terrorism investigations on campuses. A cyber subcommittee addressed computer vulnerabilities on campuses.
2. The College and University Security Effort (CAUSE). FBI special agents in charge meet with the heads of local colleges and universities to discuss national security issues and share information and ideas. CAUSE is a conduit for schools to understand how to harden against the counterintelligence threat.
3. National Counterintelligence Working Group (NCIWG). NCIWG was designed to establish strategic interagency partnerships at the senior executive level among the US intelligence community, academia, industry, and defense contractors.
4. Regional Counterintelligence Working Group (RCIWG). The RCIWG is a subset of the NCIWG and focuses on special vulnerabilities of local institutions and the threat.

Productive dialogue between education and law enforcement leadership will enhance security efforts. Colleges and universities would be better informed on the threat and mitigation opportunities and can in turn educate government security officials on the rights and protections afforded by the First Amendment in academia and the unique challenges facing our schools. In terms of procedure and policy, college administrators responsible for creating and executing human resources, training, and other programs designed to reduce vulnerability to infiltration and recruitment on campus will benefit. The dialogue will also educate legal personnel in higher education and technology transfer offices at higher education institutions responsible for the execution of sensitive government contracts. The following are suggested questions for colleges and their off-campus law enforcement counterparts:

1. What is the health of this relationship, perceived and real?
2. What is working between the two "tribes"?
3. What are the perspectives regarding which entity is ultimately responsible for protecting the higher education enterprise?
4. How do internal and external factors contribute to the relationship?
5. What policies, procedures, and training would enable a healthy partnership?
6. How can we ensure that faculty and students are part of the solution through increased awareness and decreased vulnerability?
7. How can we open the lines of communication between higher education and the intelligence community?

Students and Staff as Force Multipliers

Often, we fail to share vulnerability information with those who can help us the most: the population we serve. As previously stated in the book, civilians are now the target and therefore have the right to engage in protective activities. Rationale for withholding threat information ranges from not wanting to scare people to not making the organization's weaknesses or vulnerabilities public for business or accreditation reasons. The culture must shift to one in which having a vulnerability and threat dialogue with customers and staff is seen as a sign of strength, not weakness.

As a result of our unwillingness to convey the threat, the "see something/say something" campaigns are largely ineffective and can flood the system with useless data. If citizens do not know the specifics, we will not fully leverage this incredible tool. A better approach would be: if you see (fill in the "what"), you say (fill in what data we want them to collect) to (agency they should contact).

For instance, with respect to meth labs on campus, we may want town pharmacies to be cognizant of repeat pseudoephedrine buyers and give the information to a local drug task force. Agriculture schools have a special resource coveted by bomb makers: fertilizer. Therefore, they must know how to protect the material and report any theft or suspicious activities. Small local airports should be trained to recognize suspicious drug or human trafficking activities. Schools hosting sensitive government research and development (R&D) contracts should ask law enforcement experts to train professors to understand their value to countries of interest and to recognize elicitation attempts by students and report them to the local FBI office. Students participating in sensitive R&D activities, in military ROTC units, and degree programs such as criminal justice and national and homeland security might also receive specialized training to make them force multipliers on campus. The administrative staff that handles the J-1 visa process should know who to contact if a student is a no-show for classes or leaves the university. Clearly, just starting the conversation is a hardening method.

Exercising Due Diligence

If you ask a college president who is responsible for protection from foreign theft, terrorist threats, or a criminal element on campus, he or she may point toward the local police department and FBI office. If you ask law enforcement, they may point to the campus leadership. In the past, schools have very much acted like victims when a national security or major criminal incident occurs, instead of accepting any type of responsibility. When a school reports a violation of government rules regarding R&D programs, it is typically only "slapped on the hand" and funding is not pulled. In April 2011, the FBI Counterintelligence Unit issued a white paper indicating the escalation of targeting and collection activities, asking universities to please engage to protect their programs (FBI 2011). Who is responsible for the existence of a major spy ring on a research campus, a meth lab in a dorm, or a student whose J-1 visa has expired, yet is still on campus? There is an urgent need for an honest dialogue about responsibility and establishment of punitive action against those who fail to engage properly. This could be the withdrawal of government R&D funds from a campus or a higher-level government investigation into failure of local law enforcement to protect the school. As it stands, the lines of ownership are blurred—another vulnerability.

Colleges and universities are soft targets and extremely vulnerable to nefarious activities ranging from misdemeanor crimes to drug trafficking to infiltration by agents of foreign governments. As routine targets become less accessible, domestic and international terrorist groups might also prey on the open campus environment to recruit, spread propaganda, or even stage an attack. In addition to physical hardening, soft targets can be further protected by activities to educate the populace on the threat and build relationships to open lines of communication and ensure unity of effort during a crisis. The successful partnering of academia and law enforcement is essential for both to meet their critical missions. The overarching goal is a balanced and rational approach that preserves our tenets of academic freedom and accessibility yet protects colleges and universities from exploitation.

CHURCHES

Church clergy and parishioners are understandably nervous after the Charleston AME, Sutherland and Pittsburgh synagogue massacres. For instance, if doors open during the service, you may notice the pastor looking up and churchgoers turning around. A simple solution—lock the doors. A locked door prevented white supremacist Gregory Bush from shooting black worshipers at a church in Louisville, Kentucky on October 24, 2018. Sadly, he killed two black people shopping at a grocery store across the street. I had a college professor who was tired of students coming into class late, causing a distraction. He locked the doors when the class started. At first, several students were outside, jiggling the door handle, trying to get in. As time passed, fewer were late, and eventually, no one was late. You can shape your security environment. By simply locking the church when services start, imagine the improved worship experience for all inside. People adapt. We take our shoes off at airport security, measure our liquids, open our laptops. This is the price of admission to an airliner. Take control of your security construct—be on the offensive.

Those of the Jewish faith have a history of persecution. Naturally, in the face of so many enemies, the Jewish people have unique concerns about securing their facilities. Many synagogues employ armed plainclothes security officers, who not only work the perimeter and entrances, but are also seated among the service attendees. Security was tightened with the shooting at a Jewish community center in Los Angeles in 1999, the al-Qaeda attacks of 9/11, and the shootings on July 28, 2006, by Naveed Haq, a self-proclaimed "Muslim American, angry at Israel," at the Jewish Federation office in Seattle. The attack at the Holocaust Museum in Washington, DC, on June 10, 2009, and at the Jewish Community Center in Kansas City, Missouri, on April 15, 2014, further reinforced the need to protect those of the Jewish faith not only from radical Islamists but also American white supremacists. Sadly, the Tree of Life synagogue in Pittsburgh had no security plan on the day of the attack.

The SAFE Washington program (www.safewashington.com/) provides an outstanding model of cooperation between religious facilities and federal, state, and local law enforcement. For its eighty Jewish entities, SAFE also "develops best practices for disaster response, community security, community preparedness, and provides low cost or no cost training for community partners through annual training." The website has a password-protected area with secure files only for SAFE members.

I would hope there is some intelligence sharing and analysis between law enforcement and SAFE. An outstanding tutorial entitled "Synagogue Security: The Basics" (Moses 2014) gives five pages of security pointed at those leading or securing synagogues. Guidelines for handling visitors, suspicious packages, and security incidents are thorough and tailored to the religious environs. Following the attack on the Sikh temple in Wisconsin in August 2010, the Sikh community also took actions to better secure their facilities. Using security "sevadars" or volunteers, the temples are protected by trained individuals and the guidelines are to "act without fear, act without anger, act to defend the weak, act to protect the innocent" (Sant Sipahi Advisory Team 2018). As with the Jewish community, much can be gleaned from the activities of those previously targeted to secure their facilities and congregations. Some countries in the Middle East are allowing megachurches to be built for their Catholic, Anglican, and Coptic Christian expatriate populations (Figure 9.5). One uses the model where Christian churches are grouped together on property outside the city and secured in a compound-like setting with security and limited entry points. Everyone parks in a lot (despite searing heat—no parking garages for security reason) and enters through security checkpoints. Once on the campus, you simply go to your church of preference. No crosses are visible from the outside; this posture and lack of signage also "lowers the heat" on the religious area, instead of taunting would-be attackers.

FIGURE 9.5   Courtyard of Church City, Doha, Qatar, Hosting Catholic, Anglican, and Coptic Christian Churches

A new initiative in the United States will help churches network, understand best practices, and receive threat intelligence. Carl Chinn, mentioned in Chapter 5, is a leading authority on church security in the United States and the force behind the only compendium of act of violence in churches, Ministry Violence Statistics. On October 18, 2017, he stood up the Faith Based Security Network, Inc. (FBSN) as a 501(C)(3) public charity (www.fbsnamerica.com/). His efforts will take ministry readiness to new levels, and it's time to act. There must be a balance between security and the open, welcoming environment that is part of religious doctrine; however, ignoring risks and vulnerabilities is not prudent in today's world.

HOSPITALS

Most hospital crisis planning efforts center on response to a natural disaster or mass casualty incident in the local community. Also, there is in-depth planning and training for staff on how to react to common hospital crimes such as violent outbursts in the emergency room, attempts to steal drugs, and domestic situations with spouses and parents. OSHA 3148 requires hospitals and healthcare organizations to do annual workplace violence assessments, and more than thirty-three states also require enhanced protection of hospital and healthcare staff, typically from enraged patients.

However, depending on their operations, hospitals themselves are targets for domestic terrorists such as antiabortion and animal rights activists. Examples presented in Chapter 7 show al-Qaeda and splinter groups are actively targeting first responders at the scene of the incident and then later at the hospital when victims and family members arrive for care. After a few near-misses at its own facilities, the United Kingdom seems to be leading research on the threat of terrorist attacks against hospitals. Recommended studies include "The Vulnerability of Public Spaces: Challenges for UK Hospitals under the 'New' Terrorist Threat" (Fischbacher-Smith and Fischbacher-Smith 2013), which started the conversation in England regarding the vulnerability of healthcare facilities.

Similar to churches, hospital culture dictates that doors are always open to the masses, and restricting entry usually is not possible or desirable. Hospitals not only carry great liability for patient care but also many state patients' bill of rights/state licensing regulations direct patients "receive care in a safe environment." This naturally extends to protection from criminal and terrorist elements and attack. DHS recognizes that nonprofit soft targets such as hospitals need financial assistance to bolster their security and include money in their budget for security enhancements; however, this money is usually apportioned to the states for further dissemination. FEMA has a direct funding program through the Nonprofit Security Grant Program (NSGP). In FY 2017, NSGP was funded to $25 million and plays an important role in the implementation of the national preparedness system by supporting the development and sustainment of core capabilities.

Core capabilities are essential for the execution of each of the five mission areas outlined in the national preparedness goal. The FY 2017 NSGP's allowable costs support efforts to build and sustain core capabilities across the goal's prevention, protection, mitigation, response, and recovery mission areas (FEMA 2017). Several hospitals received NSGP grants, including John T. Mather Memorial Hospital in New York, which used $75,000 to upgrade its security system, including a new camera system and cards and a card reader for one section of the hospital. Researching how hospitals are using the NSGP grants is a good idea before applying, in order to better tailor the request and posture the hospital for success.

Emergency room entrances are not the only concern; hospital loading docks also present vulnerability. International Association for Healthcare Security and Safety President Lisa Pryse describes loading docks as "volatile" and "often overlooked" and notes there were two instances where active shooters entered hospitals through unsecured loading dock doors (Canfield 2013). Security cameras should be installed on loading docks as an absolute minimum and a vehicular access control system is also desirable. Doors to loading docks must be locked during periods of inactivity.

Hospitals in the Middle East are massive structures with plenty of standoff protection attractively disguised as grassy knolls, decorated stairs, fountains, and sculptures (Figure 9.6). The emergency room,

FIGURE 9.6   Hospital in Doha, Qatar

ground zero for many terrorist attacks, is hidden and secured. Citizens cannot approach the emergency room; procedures are in place for injured to be transported securely by hospital personnel from the perimeter to the building and into the ER. Security guards are constantly patrolling the grounds and cameras capture every angle. Window are blast resistant. The result is a beautiful, yet secure facility.

MALLS

Naturally, as businesses that are trying to attract customers and make a profit, malls prefer to avoid heavy-handed security measures like metal detectors, armed guards, and bag screenings. They typically gravitate toward more passive measures, such as mass crowd surveillance and using human behavior theory to identify would-be troublemakers.

However, the Westgate Mall massacre, discussed in Chapter 6, served as a wake-up call to malls worldwide, which are now upgrading cameras and adding layers of security to protect their businesses and shoppers. Several lessons learned from the strategic response must be addressed in communities hosting malls. First, Kenyan officials did not act to protect their lucrative soft targets despite intelligence reporting on increased capability and threat of active, known, and capable al-Qaeda groups and chatter about their targeting of malls and other civilian venues. Therefore, the mall staff and security officers had no idea the threat was high and likely did not raise the security posture. Second, the police and military had no ability to coordinate and had never practiced communicating or working through thorny first-response issues such as who is the incident commander at a mass shooting event. This lack of coordination resulted in police being fired upon by the military while trying to rescue shoppers. Furthermore, military forces had only exercised a rescue scenario one time and this was their first real-life experience with a mass hostage situation; they were late to the fight and wholly unprepared, lacking even basic equipment such as night vision goggles. As noted in the case study, the behavior of security forces at the Westgate Mall lacked professionalism and discipline. Their rampant looting that trumped finding the terrorists prolonged the siege and exposed a degree of corruption that shocked the public and tarnished confidence in the forces' ability (and desire) to keep the population safe. There are many lessons learned from the Nairobi disaster to incorporate into our training and exercises.

In light of the Nairobi attack, several malls in the United States have held large counterterrorism and mass casualty exercises in 2014. Typically led by the FBI, these exercises happen after mall hours. My work pushes malls to have these exercises in the daytime, when the parking lot is full and people are around to get in the way of response activities. I was fortunate to take my soft target hardening methodology to a major US city and participate in a federal government-led plan to harden six shopping malls against crime and terror attacks. Some malls relied heavily on security on foot, others more so on cameras. Malls were located in urban or suburban areas and were different sizes with different types of stores and customers. Through red teaming (using a group of trained off duty law enforcement) we identified the one "Achilles heel" for each mall and then designed a tabletop exercise for their facility. At the exercise we had the mall leadership and their security managers, as well as representatives from the local fire department and police agencies. We also brought in the 911 dispatchers who would take the calls from the mall during an emergency. Using the rings of security construct, we invited stores and other properties on the mall periphery to participate—restaurants, apartment complexes, banks. Having all of the parties at the table that would be involved in a mall attack was powerful in terms of relationship building and a sense of understanding about how this type of scenario may evolve and barriers to successful resolution.

In Portland, Oregon, joint training between local law enforcement and mall personnel paid off during an active-shooter event at the Clackamas Town Center in December 2012. Responding officers knew the mall layout from the training session and were able quickly to corner and stop the shooter, who had already killed two shoppers and seriously wounded a third in a random act of violence. The training initiative is one of many positive developments driven by the International Council of Shopping Centers (ICSC), which, in conjunction with the Department of Homeland Security, Federal Bureau of Investigation, and police, dramatically improved readiness throughout the mall and shopping center industry. Mall security, formerly ridiculed and scoffed at in pop culture, is now a highly trained, professional force (Bradley 2013). They are faced with a rising number of violent incidences ranging from assault to gang violence and mass shootings and are learning and sharing best practices globally. Mall security is also concerned about parents "dumping" their children at the facility to spend the day on weekends, in this case they turn into babysitters. Gang activity at malls is also on the rise, meaning mall security may have violent confrontations.

A new study examined the infrastructure of the Westgate Mall and how it allowed for a successful asymmetric attack by a small group of men against a large group of first responders and military personnel and apparatus. For instance, the open atrium allowed the shooters to get a high position on top floors and shoot down at fleeing customers and arriving police and military. However, the atrium also provided an advantage for store owners on top floors, some of whom could see the carnage below and were able to lower their security doors and barricade themselves in the store, but they were then trapped for the three-day siege. Enclosed areas, such as the casino and the cinema, were used by terrorists as holding areas for hostages (Butime 2014). Studying the Westgate Mall attack from the perspective of the element of surprise achieved by the attackers, the vulnerability of shoppers, the physical layout of the mall, and the poorly coordinated response is critical for all who operate, secure, and visit malls.

SPORTS AND RECREATIONAL VENUES

As discussed in Chapter 6, sports and recreational venues are targeted by terrorist groups who appreciate the large, dense crowds and televised coverage that will ensure a ripple effect of fear across the populace. Current security procedures include limiting entrance points, limiting the size of bags and thoroughly searching them, and using CCTV and facial recognition technology. I was fortunate to work with a group of security professionals protecting our Major League Baseball venues in the US. Concerns included an increase of violent behavior from fans (fights, throwing hard objects on the field at players, belligerent behavior) and a disrespect for responding security personnel.

Although the resident security manager at each professional sporting stadium in the US has law enforcement or military background, most venues rely on part-time, low-paid security guards to fill the ranks. They are both the first line of defense and possibly the weakest link in the sports venue security infrastructure. In 2013, California revoked 154 security guard licenses, often due to criminal convictions discovered after the license was issued, and Florida revokes an average of more than 350 security licenses annually for criminal records. Compounding the problem, there is a "county option" approach to licensing and training of part-time security guards. States vary wildly in their procedures and nine require no security guard licensing at all: Colorado, Idaho, Kansas, Kentucky, Mississippi, Missouri, Nebraska, South Dakota, and Wyoming (Bergal 2015). Among those states that do, several, including Massachusetts, do not require training. In Florida and California, perhaps the strictest states, forty hours of training are required, including a course on terrorism awareness and weapons of mass destruction. Alaska mandates forty-eight hours of training initially, plus another eight hours in firearms training for armed guards; but South Carolina requires just four hours of training and an additional four for those who carry a gun (Bergal 2015). Some companies have even classified employees as "event staff" in security roles at stadiums to avoid training requirements and to increase profits (Schrotenboer 2013). State efforts to increase security are often met with resistance; in Connecticut, a bill requiring security guards to get more training died in the state senate. In Washington state, a measure to mandate FBI criminal background checks for all applicants never made it to the floor.

Also, in the quest to increase profits, sports venues often award security guard contracts to companies that are the lowest bidders. We need to remember part-time staff and volunteers provide a vulnerability in terms of facility access and the ability to stockpile supplies. They can also glean an intuitive understanding of the infrastructure and its vulnerabilities.

According to an Israeli security consultant, there is another inherent problem with security in the United States: Security personnel "don't watch the race, they watch the crowd. That's what they didn't do [at the finish line of the Boston Marathon]" (Schrotenboer 2013). The same consultant explains how, in Israel, unattended packages and backpacks are given about ten seconds before a security official engages. The next time you attend a sporting event, look at the security guards. Are they looking up into the stadium and scrutinizing people walking by? Or are they watching the game, concert, or event? A quick Internet search yields many pictures from major sporting events such as football and baseball games where professional and volunteer security team members are facing in the wrong direction—the most distressing at the Boston Marathon finish line, seen as the first bomb exploded (Figure 9.7).

FIGURE 9.7   CCTV Capture: First Bomb Explodes at Finish Line of the Boston Marathon

In January 2005, the Department of Homeland Security launched the first online vulnerability self-assessment tool (ViSAT) for public venues such as large stadiums. The online tool incorporates industry safety and security best practices for critical infrastructure to aid in establishing a security baseline for each facility. Modules focus on key areas such as information security, physical assets, communication security, and personnel security. As part of the National Infrastructure Protection Plan, DHS also offers site visits and other helpful assistance to collaborate with owners, operators, and security at commercial venues (DHS 2018). There is a delicate balance between providing security and an enjoyable experience for participants in and spectators of sports and recreational events; with technology, training, and practice, this goal is attainable.

HOTELS

Due to a recent history of attacks, hotels in the Middle East are extremely secure. In the fall of 2013, I was fortunate to spend five days on the ground (and off the radar) in Jordan. We first stayed at the Days Inn in Amman, the site of a horrific terrorist attack in 2005. The hotel is now a fortress. Security officers and vehicles are visible outside the facility; inside, they are undercover, but "present." No vehicles may stop in front of the hotel; the former "pull through" area is now filled with decorative concrete planters and other barricades. All property visitors enter an external building for luggage and handbag screening. Individuals may be wanded (wands are handheld detectors), and visitors are questioned about country of origin and travel plans inside Jordan and/or neighboring countries. At check-in, passports are shown, and the numbers are recorded in the registry. Yes, this type of security is inconvenient, but what better place to stay in Jordan than a hotel previously hit that now has blast-proof windows, standoff protection, and its own small police detachment? Any would-be attacker will certainly drive by this property in search of an easier target. Dining in the lobby—steps from the scene of the attack eight years prior—was not even the least bit nerve wracking.

Driving southwest from Amman, we were stopped at several checkpoints and asked for our passports and itinerary. The travel agency provided a copy of the itinerary and told me repeatedly not to lose it, and after showing it for the fourth time in a day's travels, I understood. The concept of internal checkpoints is hard to get used to, but in Jordan, home to millions of refugees from Syria, Lebanon, Iraq, and Egypt, it is easy to understand why they need to know who is moving about the country. The Jordanians are a warm, open people, influenced by the ancient European trade in the southern port city of Aqaba, and they love Americans. We were greeted with handshakes and even hugs; however, not exempted from the security checks. Approaching our next destination, the Holiday Inn at the Dead Sea, we had a taste of resort security in the Middle East. As discussed in Chapter 6, nearby luxurious beachfront resorts were the sites of horrific radical Islamist attacks against vacationers. As a result, the Jordanian Dead Sea resorts just a few hours away are extremely secure. The Holiday Inn had several layers of security, and entering the property was like driving on a very secure military installation. Approaching on the road, we were asked to provide documents verifying our reservation. The vehicle was searched—pop the trunk and hood, mirrors run underneath to look for stowaways or bombs. Our palms were swabbed for chemical residue. We proceeded through the gate to the parking lot. We carried our luggage to the hotel entrance vestibule and every went through scanners, including us. However, as with most fortified places in the Middle East, the grounds inside were luxurious and the atmosphere extremely relaxed. Traveling in the region, I witnessed firsthand the possibilities of achieving the desired security/convenience/aesthetics balance. A little inconvenience up front is surely worth the feeling of absolute security.

Another technique of US hotels in certain Middle Eastern countries is using no signage and flying the flag of the host country at the entrance so the property more resembles an office building. I took the picture in Figure 9.8 of the property of a well-known US chain in a major Middle Eastern city; see the multiple concrete barriers in front of the hotel and the addition of blast-resistant glass. I took the photo from the parking lot, where all guests must park and walk through a gate, clear security, and then enter the lobby. At the center is the flag of the host country. No signage appears on the building.

Naturally, a terrorist can find a specific hotel if it is the primary target; however, it certainly does not hurt to lower the "heat" and profile of the building for opportunists. Since most travelers nowadays book hotels online and not by line of sight, properties in major cities and resorts might not be adversely affected by less signage. A few hints received from security professionals when staying in hotels in Middle East hot spots were to stay above the second floor, where blast damage would be less than on the ground floor, but not on the top floors, from which it would be difficult to evacuate. Also, I have learned the importance of asking for a room in the back of the building, away from the front lobby area, the typical scene of an attack. Furthermore, it is prudent not to have a room facing an enclosed courtyard because rescue vehicles and ladders cannot access the area. As in any situation, individual preparedness when staying at high-profile hotels is important. For example, counting the doors to the stairwell so it can be found in the dark and/or thick smoke,

FIGURE 9.8   US Hotel in a Middle Eastern City

and testing emergency stairwells to ensure doors at the bottom are not locked. Also, travelers may want to reduce their time in public spaces; in the Mumbai attack and others, most casualties occurred in hotel restaurants and bars. Finally, consider staying in a smaller or boutique hotel, because these do not attract terrorists looking for high casualty counts.

   Staff training is a key part of the hotel security framework. Recognizing the importance, the Department of Homeland Security produced an outstanding film in 2010 called "No Reservations: Suspicious Behavior in Hotels" (www.youtube.com/watch?v=ZLCCvjJJZ4w). Going one step further, Safehotels (https://safehotels.com/), a company based in

Sweden, is the first global organization certifying hotel properties based on standard criteria which measures security training and equipment, crisis management response, and fire and evacuation procedures. The certification benefits property owners and travelers alike. US chains with properties certified by Safehotels include the Courtyard by Marriott, Radisson, and Clarion Hotels.

A company in Africa studied recent terrorist attacks on hotels and designed a new type of secure hotel. The Southern Sunshine Hotel factors the issue of terrorist attack into its design; for example, all of the rooms directly "communicate" with the outside through large openings, making escape and rescue operations easy in case of terror attacks or fire outbreak. The staircase area and the corridor access to all rooms are also open to the outside so there is no cover for terrorists to hide and conduct a siege of the building. The hotel will have its own water and power source for emergencies. Finally, the hotel will only have thirty-three rooms, making them lower profile and less inviting to terrorist attack (Gichuhi 2014).

BUSINESSES

After all, a festive gathering of county health workers in San Bernardino would not seem likely to make the top million of a list of shooting targets. It was not an iconic symbol of American freedom or American muscle. It was not a target draped in ideological conflict.
—*The New York Times*, covering the San Bernardino Terrorist Attack (Kleinfeld 2015)

Case Study: Recent Attacks in the Workplace

On December 2, 2015, employees of the San Bernardino Office of Public Health were scheduled for a day of training and afterwards, a holiday party, both held at the Inland Regional Center officer building in San Bernardino, California. Instead the day would be remembered for a violent attack in which fourteen people were killed and another twenty-two wounded by co-worker and ISIS-inspired terrorist, US-born Syed Rizwan Farook and his wife, Pakistani national Tashfeen Malik.

Farook was a food inspector with the San Bernardino Office of Public Health and part of the training and after party. As an insider, Farook had details regarding the day's events, amplifying the impact of his attack. Farook left the building halfway through the training session and returned as it was transitioning into the party event. He and his wife Tashfeen Malik were dressed in black and were wearing black tactical gear, armed with AR15 type semiautomatic rifles, 9 millimeter handguns, and Improvised Explosive Devices (IEDs).

The first shots were fired at 10:58 a.m. and at approximately 11:03 a.m., there were reports of "three" masked suspects seen leaving the premises in a black SUV. In that five-minute span, more than 100 rounds of ammunition were expended. As law enforcement agencies, fire, and EMS from across the area converged on the scene, Farook and Malik were long gone.

The main break in the case came shortly after law enforcement arrived. During an initial interview, one of the witnesses mentioned identified the shooter as Farook. Another lead was that multiple witnesses saw a black SUV with Utah plates leaving the IRC in the moments after the shooting ended.

At approximately 3:00 p.m. San Bernardino County narcotics officers went to an address identified with Farook, and spotted the black SUV leaving the address. The officers made contact with Redlands police and they along with units from Redlands Police Department attempted to conduct a vehicle stop. At that time, according to the timeline from the San Bernardino County Sheriff's Department, the suspects started shooting at the officers. The gun fight that ensued could only be classified as total chaos. With Farook driving, Malik was firing at officers out of the back window of the SUV, with multiple rounds fired at the pursuing officers before the vehicle even stopped. After stopping, the firefight between the officers and Malik and Farook continued, until neutralized. Two police officers were wounded in the shootout.

During the initial attack and the shootout, at least twelve different law enforcement agencies worked together, ranging from federal to local and every step in between. Their flawless coordination proved how exercising with fellow agencies and having established lines of communication will pay off in these types of incidents. Remember the exercises should not only include law enforcement but also fire, EMS, and hospitals that will surely be assisting in the event of a mass casualty incident.

We can compare elements of this attack to the November 2009 Fort Hood attack perpetrated by Nidal Hassan, al-Qaeda sympathizer who killed thirteen army personnel at the base deployment facility and Aaron Alexis, a government contractor who killed twelve people in his former office building at the Washington Navy Yard in September 2013. These three incidents could very well be categorized as "insider attacks." Farook, Hassan, and Alexis had legitimate access to the attack location. They intimately knew the location of their attack and chose the perfect time and place to ambush unsuspecting co-workers. They knew the strengths and weaknesses of the location and personnel, exploiting them for their gain.

Also, due to the location of the massacres, these incidents could be classified as "workplace violence" attacks. They illustrate why it is important to have an organizational workplace violence plan in place. See Appendix I for an example of a workplace violence prevention survey that managers can use in the workplace to gather information on harassment-related behaviors, physical security concerns, the effectiveness of training, and to make a general climate assessment on their organization.

The attackers were either under some form of prior investigation by federal authorities or were thought suspicious by supervisors and co-workers. In addition to a workplace violence plan, it is important that you take all threats seriously, and don't condone harassment or abuse toward anyone regardless of any factor. If employers and co-workers previously raised concerns they later expressed about the killers, and the organization had a confidential reporting system in place, the attack may have been thwarted. Often, workers are hesitant to report on each other for fear of retaliation by the subject, or other types of retribution in the workplace.

(Source: Fisk 2018. Mr. Ralph R. Fisk Jr., ATO, PCP-1, MEMS. Instructor/trainer, subject matter expert, and thought leader in the areas of emergency management, contemporary risk and threat assessment.)

SURROUNDED BY CRISES—WHAT ABOUT SPILLOVER?

Often, soft targets are in the area or even on the grounds of a hard target; they may not be part of the scenario but get pulled into the disaster by virtue of location or services provided, such as shelter, religious comfort, or medical care. In October 1997, LTTE terrorists arrived on the scene at the newly inaugurated World Trade Center in Colombo, Sri Lanka, with its twin thirty-nine-story towers as the target. However, the attackers could not get their truck bomb into the building's parking lot as planned. Instead, they parked next door, at the Galadari Hotel, and detonated the device by firing rocket-propelled grenades into the vehicle. The Murrah Federal Building in Oklahoma City had child daycare on-site, which unfortunately was on the bottom floor of the building and took the brunt of the blast from the 1995 domestic terrorist attack. On 9/11 there was a large daycare center located just a few hundred yards from the Pentagon. As previously discussed, there were a number of schools located near the Twin Towers, and nearby churches were pulled into the attack by being blanketed by toxic dust and used as mortuaries and sanctuaries for weary and devastated citizens and first responders. During the 2012 unrest in Libya, US government officials identified a hotel and ordered all Americans to use it as an evacuation rally point even though the hotel was not consulted, putting its employees and guests directly in the line of fire. Even natural disasters can quickly turn into a period of unrest and violent crime, impacting our facilities. For example, during Hurricane Katrina in August 2005, the Louisiana Superdome was used as a mass shelter of "last resort," becoming a cesspool of sewage, vandalism, a suicide, possible murders, and reported rapes and gang activity.

Several scenarios are ripe for discussion: What if there is a terrorist attack unfolding in your town or city during the school day or a church service? How do you shelter in place and protect your building occupants? Do you open your doors to those fleeing the event, possibly bringing the attacks to your property? Do you share your supplies? What if the event lasts three days? During Hurricane Katrina, Keesler Air Force Base in Biloxi, Mississippi, was the only location in the area with electricity (thanks to emergency generators and fuel) as well as water and food. After the crisis, people came to the base gates to see if they could get help. On 9/11, confused and upset people were congregating at churches and schools, which naturally opened their doors. These are difficult scenarios, but thinking through them is critical to response during crises. In the event of a criminal- or terrorist-related emergency in the community, you may want to turn off lit signage, decrease interior lighting, and lower your profile. Also, investigate "contingency contracts" with local water and food delivery companies in case you are sheltering a group of people and the crisis goes on for an extended period of time. Similar to preparations for natural disasters, your organization may want to have a significant amount of cash on hand to purchase water, ice, and other necessities from stores if the electricity and ATMs are out.

PROTECTING AGAINST VEHICLE TERRORISM

"Stopping the 5,000 Pound Bullet" (DuFour 2017) gives prescriptive advice for how to prepare and respond to terrorist attacks with vehicles. First is to understand the trend, as we discussed in Chapter 7, low-tech, no training and possibility of high-impact and mass casualties, based on size of the vehicle, the compactness of the crowd, ability to gain speed and follow on use of bombs, guns, and knives to inflict more injuries on pedestrians. The best way to protect a crowd is by using barricades, preventing vehicular access to pedestrians. The vehicle operator could be a terrorist, drunk driver, heart attack victim, or individual acting in anger—a barricade stops them all.

Remember, a large truck will defeat simple pedestrian barricades, as seen in the Nice attack. Although heavy and difficult to place and remove for temporary protection, barricades should be heavy duty and concrete to prevent vehicle access, as illustrated in Figure 9.9. Sand- or water-filled plastic barricades are a second alternative. If your venue does not have barricades, use what you can—perhaps school buses, fire trucks, or dump trucks. For long-term solutions, consider cable barriers such as

FIGURE 9.9   Example of Flower Pot Barricades From Genoa, Italy

those used along highways and on military installations—they are more cost effective, longer lasting, and more attractive. Also, there are bollards that venue owners can put up and down at will, to let in delivery trucks, etc. These could be used during peak hours of activity to protect pedestrians, diners, children playing, etc.

Law enforcement should note theft of large commercial vehicles in the days leading up to a public gathering or event, and educated rental companies on any indications of untoward use from their customers (perhaps not being concerned with turn in procedures). For instance, the presentation of an altered or questionable driver's license, proof of insurance, credit cards, or other required documents when purchasing or renting vehicles must be reported to authorities. Nervous behavior, profuse sweating, lack of familiarity with how to operate a large truck, request for unusual modifications, and other atypical customer requests are all signposts of potential nefarious use.

Understandably, it is difficult to protect every street corner and open space, but towns and cities should identify promenades where a vehicle could mount the curb and get to a high rate of speed. Also, I made a recommendation to New York City neighborhoods following the Hudson River Greenway attack simply to ask common area users like pedestrians and bikers for their input. They often see spaces through different eyes than the people who design or protect them (Garofalo 2017).

Finally, although law enforcement in many cities have procedures against shooting at moving vehicles, they should consider the further the vehicle travels, the more casualties, and there is a strong likelihood of follow on attacks by the driver, or his escape into the community, as witnessed in previous attacks. Best to engage and stop the attack at the earliest possible opportunity.

RED TEAMING SOFT TARGETS

As mentioned in Chapter 2, a healthy dose of imagination will help expose your vulnerabilities, especially to asymmetric tactics. According to the 9/11 Commission report: "It is therefore crucial to find a way of routinizing, even bureaucratizing, the exercise of imagination. Doing so requires more than finding an expert who can imagine that aircraft could be used as weapons" (National Commission on Terrorist Attacks upon the United States 2004).

Every security measure has the opportunity to work, but if it fails, it works for the offender. Unfortunately, you, as the facility manager, operator, or security professional, may not see the flaws in your security plan, or may be too close to imagine how your techniques could be defeated. To have the best plan and make sure your methods work, you truly need to think like the bad guy. Red teaming may be an answer. The term "red team" comes from American military war gaming, where the blue team was traditionally the United States, and, during the Cold War, the red team was the Soviet Union. Defined loosely, red teaming is the practice of viewing a problem from an adversary's or competitor's perspective. The goal of most red teams is to enhance decision making, either by specifying the adversary's preferences and strategies or by simply acting as a devil's advocate. Red teaming may be more or less structured, and a wide range of approaches exists. In the past several years, red teaming has been applied increasingly to issues of security, although the practice is potentially much broader (Mateski 2014).

Superior red teams tend to (Mateski 2014):

View the problem of interest from a systems perspective.
Shed the cultural biases of the decision maker and, as appropriate, adopt the cultural perspective of the adversary or competitor.
Employ a multidisciplinary range of skills, talents, and methods.
Understand how things work in the real world.

Avoid absolute and objective explanations of behaviors, preferences, and events.

Question everything (to include both their clients and themselves). Break the "rules."

A red team can undermine a decision maker's preferred strategies or call into question his or her choices, policies, and intentions. As this might be uncomfortable, it is important to put the security of the innocent people who occupy your facility ahead of any ego, sunk cost, or group think about the security of your facilities and organization.

In particular, the Homeland Security Act requires DHS to apply red team analysis to terrorist use of nuclear weapons and biological agents. As terrorists seek to exploit new vulnerabilities, it is imperative that we apply the appropriate tools to meet those threats. Therefore, most red teaming effort currently lies in the WMD spectrum, with professional teams trying to penetrate nuclear facilities, chemical and biological weapons labs, and even military installations that own or operate these sensitive activities. A red team is a group of subject matter experts (SMEs) with various appropriate backgrounds providing an independent peer review of your processes, acting as a devil's advocate, and knowledgeably role playing the potential enemy. Red teaming can be passive and serve to help you understand the threat and expose your biases and assumptions. Or, activity can be active as the red team attempts to probe and test your security to expose your strengths and flaws. Training is another aspect of red teaming.

Although red teaming for soft targets does not exist today, I believe there can be some cross-application of methodology, currently employed by the US government to soft targets including schools, churches, and hospitals. You could begin with the "cross-inspection" of security procedures by trusted colleagues from other facilities and the cross-pollination of ideas. Or, you may ask them to test your security by sending someone in to test your system. One red teaming exercise recently shared by a colleague included the "perpetrators" wearing a shirt bearing the symbol and name of a famous soft drink company. Holding a clipboard and stating the purpose was to check the soda machines, the red teamer had unlimited access to a school.

For more about the red teaming concept, please see the homepage of the *Red Team Journal*, http://redteamjournal.com/, started in 1997 by my colleague, Dr. Mark Mateski, the industry expert on the topic.

STATE DEPARTMENT ENGAGEMENT

All of us want to be able to say truthfully, "I did my very best" when looking into the eyes of grieving survivors and family members.

—Ambassador Prudence Bushnell
(US House of Representatives 2005)

Prudence Bushnell made this statement in a congressional hearing on May 10, 2005. She was the ambassador to Kenya during the al-Qaeda attack on the embassy in Nairobi on August 7, 1998, and was knocked unconscious by the bomb blast and cut by flying glass. After receiving basic treatment at a nearby hotel, she oversaw rescue operations. She attended the funerals of twelve embassy staff personnel killed in the bombing, a task no government leader, school principal, or church or business leader ever wants. She was also present at memorial services for the 201 local nationals killed in the blast, who were also her embassy employees.

Embassies around the world were fortified in light of the twin bombings that day. At nearly the exact time the vehicle bomb exploded in Nairobi, the embassy in Dar es Salaam, Tanzania, was similarly attacked, killing eleven. However, in 2005, the State Department realized the growing threat to the families of their personnel stationed abroad, stating in a congressional hearing:

> But as embassy and consulate compounds are fortified, US government personnel and their families living and working outside those walls draw the aim of criminals and terrorists looking for the next tier of targets. So hardening official buildings is not enough. The security of soft targets hinges on the harder tasks of building personal awareness and sustaining institutional vigilance. Adding cement to the physical plant is an easy part. Precious lives depend on strengthening protections for America's human capital abroad.
>
> (US House of Representatives 2005)

The State Department now has a budget to protect the family members of those serving abroad. Although a specific number is hard to pin down, the State Department receives roughly $15 million a year, including $10 million to increase security at American and international schools abroad. All State Department employees now receive basic security training, including crisis response and self-aid and "buddy care" through programs like Simple Triage and Rapid Treatment. Those stationed overseas receive enhanced training on the local threat through the Security Overseas Seminar (SOS) Program. The Security Overseas Seminar, which concentrates on life in overseas environments, is mandatory for all federal employees and recommended for eligible family members. A similar, age-appropriate program, Young SOS, is offered to young family members in grades 2 through 12.

Under the Soft Targets Program, the State Department is spending $27 million to improve the protection of US officials and their families at department-assisted schools from terrorist threats. This multiphase program provides basic security hardware such as shatter-resistant window film, alarms, radios, and additional protective measures designed based on the threat levels in the country. Also, security walls, bollards, and gate systems were funded for the schools. As a parent of a high school student who attended one such institution in the Middle East, I am eternally gratefully for the funding my government expended to keep her safe while we served in our military assignment.

Ambassador Bushnell also recognized the culture must change along with the shift to protect the State Department's soft targets. She made three prescient recommendations which are applicable to all sectors:

1. Finding the right balance between living vigilantly and normally. People do not stay on high alert for long periods of time. Scare tactics are ultimately self-defeating, and administrative mandates such as checklists risk becoming rote exercises. To use a metaphor, our challenge is to ensure people are looking both ways before they cross the street, becoming neither paralyzed nor indifferent to the oncoming traffic.

2. Maintaining a consistency of funding and attention to security issues.

3. Changing the ethos, perception and the image of the job. Employees can count on experiencing evacuation, civil unrest, kidnapping, natural disasters, assassination, terrorist attacks, biochemical attacks, and other crises.

Certainly, the State Department's mission overseas is far more vulnerable to terrorist attack than a school in the US heartland. However, the ambassador's insight as someone who lived through an unexpected and unanticipated terrorist event against a hard target is thought provoking and a departure for further discussion. She ended her testimony with this statement: "My colleagues are fiercely patriotic, willing to put themselves and their families at risk in order to make a difference on behalf of the American people. At the very least, they deserve our best efforts to keep them safe" (US House of Representatives 2005).

UNITED NATIONS AND SOFT TARGETS

The United Nations has also entered the soft target hardening realm around the world. The organization's preferred manner of engagement is through a program called Public–Private Partnerships (PPPs) for the Protection of Critical Infrastructure including Vulnerable Targets, Internet and Tourism Security (UN 2018). Through its Counterterrorism Implementation Task Force (CTITF: www.un.org/counterterrorism/ctitf/en/ctitf-office), the UN's PPP task force harvests best practices, leveraging the connections and insights of INTERPOL about threat and response. INTERPOL also ensures timely dissemination of threat and attack information through the PPP construct. The UN also runs a Major Events International Academy aimed at those responsible for managing and securing high-attendance events such as the FIFA World Cup, Wimbledon, and multiday stadium concert events, which are popular in Europe. Recognizing that event owners must ultimately decide how to secure their venues, the academy provides a good model for staying engaged and being a conduit for information and training, without imposing its will. Because the United Nations must respond during attacks such as the Boko Haram kidnapping of female students in Nigeria and the Westgate Mall massacre, they are investing money and time up front to help prevent soft target attacks around the world.

The State Department's Overseas Security Advisory Council (OSAC) is a PPP to promote security concepts and enhance cooperation between the state and US organizations operating worldwide. OSAC focuses in particular on soft, vulnerable targets and provides a forum for the exchange of best practices and a platform for the regular and timely interchange of information between the private sector and the Department of State. At the city level, one very successful PPP is Project Griffin in London, a joint venture between the City of London and the London Metropolitan Police forces. Its charter is to advise and update the managers, security officers, and employees of large public- and private-sector organizations across the capital on security, counterterrorism, and crime prevention issues. The initiative focuses on protecting the city and the public from terrorist attacks. It brings together and coordinates the resources of the police, emergency services, local authorities, business, and the private-sector security industry, and helps with implementation of counterterrorism and crime prevention policies and procedures. Awareness and reporting of hostile reconnaissance and other suspicious activity have been dramatically increased across London since the implementation of Project Griffin, and this initiative could surely be replicated in our cities.

The Department of Justice (DOJ) has an Office of Community Oriented Policing Services which hosts PPP initiatives called "Building Private Security/Public Policing Partnerships to Prevent and Respond to Terrorism and Public Disorder." Community-oriented policing can help control crime. The private sector and community members are encouraged to participate actively in the development of prevention strategies including those designed to counter terrorism. The DOJ is helping with the development of knowledge resource products (CDs, guidance documents, and videos) as well as training individuals from the public and private sectors.

The UN's PPP initiative is powerful because it enforces a critical concept related to soft target protection: the role of the private sector should not be limited to involvement in crisis situations. A proactive approach to partner and develop measures to prevent terrorism and enhance overall security can prevent and/or deter attacks. Of course, the type of threat information the government can share with the private sector is an issue and the sector must understand the importance of safeguarding such information. Also, law enforcement should not merely share threat information, but also assist with identifying and mitigating vulnerability. A trusting relationship is the key to successful PPP partnering.

There is much to harvest from soft target hardening efforts around the world, especially through the sharing of best practices. Now, with knowledge of worldwide response efforts, we can more effectively address hardening planning and tactics here at home.

CONCLUSION

Unfortunately, the world has changed drastically since 9/11 and the places we should feel the safest are in the terrorist's target book. Armed with the information about the vulnerability, threat, and response provided in this book, you can confidently move forward to prepare your facility, staff, homes, and families for the unthinkable.

REFERENCES

American Red Cross. "Ready Rating Program." www.readyrating.org/ (2014).

Bergal, Jenni. "In Many States, Security Guards Get Scant Training, Oversight." *Pew Charitable Trusts*, November 10, 2015.

Bradley, Bud. "State of U.S. Mall Security Post 9–11." *Allied Universal*, December 17, 2013.

Butime, Herman R. "The Lay-Out of Westgate Mall and Its Significance in the Westgate Mall Attack in Kenya." *Small Wars Journal* (May 10, 2014).

Canfield, Amy. "Hospital Loading Docks Rival ERs for Security Concerns." *Security Director News*, November 25, 2013.

Carpenter, Mike. "Evolving to Effects Based Operations." www.dodccrp.org/events/9th_ICCRTS/CD/presentations/8/092.pdf (March 2004).

CBS News. "Pulse Nightclub Shooter Intended to Attack Disney, Prosecutors Say." www.cbsnews.com/news/orlando-pulse-nightclub-shooter-omar-mateen-intended-to-attack-disney-shopping-complex-prosecutors-say/ (March 28, 2018).

DHS (Department of Homeland Security). "Options for Consideration Active Shooter Preparedness." www.dhs.gov/options-consideration-active-shooter-preparedness-video (2017).

————. "National Infrastructure Protection Plan: Commercial Facilities Sector." www.dhs.gov/xlibrary/assets/nipp_commerc.pdf (2018).

————. "Security of Soft Targets and Crowded Places: Resource Guide." www.dhs.gov/sites/default/files/publications/Soft_Targets_Crowded%20Places_Resource_Guide_042018_508.pdf (2018).

————. "Soft Targets and Crowded Places Security Plan Overview." www.dhs.gov/sites/default/files/publications/DHS-Soft-Target-Crowded-Place-Security-Plan-Overview-052018-508_0.pdf (2018).

DuFour, Scott. "Stopping the 5,000-Lb: Bullet How to Prepare & Respond to the Trend of Terrorist Attacks with Vehicles." *Calibre Press*, April 20, 2017.

FBI (Federal Bureau of Investigation). "Higher Education and National Security: The Targeting of Sensitive, Proprietary, and Classified Information on Campuses of Higher Education." www.fbi.gov/file-repository/higher-education-national-security.pdf/view (2011).

FEMA (Federal Emergency Management Agency). "FY 2017 Urban Areas Security Initiative and Nonprofit Security Grant Program." www.fema.gov/fiscal-year-2017-nonprofit-security-grant-program (2017).

Fischbacher-Smith, Denis and Moira Fischbacher-Smith. "The Vulnerability of Public Spaces: Challenges for UK Hospitals under the 'New' Terrorist Threat." *Public Management Review* 15, no. 3 (March 27, 2013): 330–343.

Garofalo, Michael. "Hard Lessons of Vehicle Attack." *The Spirit*, November 7, 2017.

Gerkin, Don. "Capabilities Based Preparedness." Case Study, *Soft Target Hardening: Protecting People from Attack*, 2nd ed., Boca Raton, FL: Taylor & Francis, 2019.

Gichuhi, Francis. "Terrorism in Hotels and How to Prevent Attacks through Design." *A4architect*, May 14, 2014.

Headquarters US Army, Washington, DC. *Battlefield Deception*, www.globalsecurity.org/intell/library/policy/army/fm/90-2/index.html (October 3, 1988).

Joint Publication 3–13.4. "Military Deception." https://public intelligence.net/jcs-mildec/ (January 26, 2012).

Kleinfeld, N. R. "Fear in the Air, Americans Look Over Their Shoulders." *The New York Times*, December 4, 2015.

Kuhns, Joseph. "Understanding Decisions to Burglarize from the Offender's Perspective." Charlotte, NC: *The University of North Carolina at Charlotte Department of Criminal Justice & Criminology*, www.researchgate.net/publication/268444817_Understanding_Decisions_to_Burglarize_from_the_Offender's_Perspective (2013).

Lysiak, Matthew. *Newtown: An American Tragedy*. New York: Gallery Books, Simon and Schuster, 2013.

Marion, Steve. "Mock School Attack Tests Readiness." *The Standard Banner*, May 20, 2014.

Mateski, Mark. "Red Team Journal: Understand, Anticipate, Adapt." http://redteamjournal.com/ (2014).

Moses, Manfred. "Synagogue Security: The Basics." http://src.uscj.org/contentpages/pdf/SEC.02.PDF (2014).

"National Commission on Terrorist Attacks upon the United States." Washington, DC: The National Commission on Terrorist Attacks Upon the United States. http://govinfo.library.unt.edu/911/report/index.htm (2004): 344.

Newman, Oscar. "Creating Defensible Space." *Center for Urban Policy Research, Rutgers University*. www.huduser.gov/publications/pdf/def.pdf (April 1996).

Office of the State's Attorney Judicial District of Danbury. "Report of the State's Attorney for the Judicial District of Danbury on the Shootings at Sandy Hook Elementary School and 36 Yogananda Street, Newtown, Connecticut." Danbury, CT: Office Of The State's Attorney. www.ct.gov/csao/lib/csao/sandy_hook_final_report.pdf (2013).

Rose, Roger M., A. Vangura, Jr., and M. Levin. "Wrongful Death, Failure to Deter Crime on the Premises." *Zanin's Jury Verdict Review & Analysis*. www.jvra.com/verdict_trak/article.aspx?id=187168 (2009).

Sant Sipahi Advisory Team. "Security and Risk Assessment." www.harisingh.com/SantSipahiAdvisoryTeam.htm (2018).

Schrotenboer, Brent. "Holes in Stadium Security." *USA Today Sports*, May 2, 2013.

Spencer, Terry. "Investigators: School Design Contributed to Massacre." *Stars and Stripes*, April 24, 2018.

Spicer, Brad. "Bomb Threats and a Tale of Two Cities." Case Study, *Soft Target Hardening: Protecting People from Attack*, 2nd ed., Boca Raton, FL: Taylor & Francis, 2019.

Toppo, Greg. "Nerves Fray as Anniversaries of April Attacks Arrive." *USA Today*, April 19, 2014.

UN (United Nations). "Counter-Terrorism Implementation Task Force." *Counter-Terrorism Implementation Task Force*. www.un.org/counterterrorism/ctitf/en/protection-critical-infrastructure-including-vulnerable-targets-internet-and-tourism-security (2018).

United States Bomb Data Center. "Explosives Incident Report." www.atf.gov/resource-center/docs/report/2017-explosives-incident-report-eir/download (2017).

US House of Representatives. "Overseas Security: Hardening Soft Targets." Washington, DC: US Government Printing Office. www.gpo.gov/fdsys/pkg/CHRG-109hhrg22704/html/CHRG-109hhrg22704.htm (May 10, 2005).

CHAPTER 10

Twenty Takeaways About Soft Target Hardening

> Private-sector preparedness is not a luxury; it is a cost of doing business in the post-9/11 world. It is ignored at a tremendous potential cost in lives, money and national security.
>
> —The 9/11 Commission Report

This book was not meant to cause panic or alarm. The purpose was to provide a compelling, data-based argument that soft targets in our country are at increased risk for attack, not only by violent criminals but also by domestic and international terrorists. The intent was to inform about the case studies, training, education, and tools available to help you identify vulnerabilities and mitigate risk. My hope is there will be a renewed determination to take an active role in securing civilian-centric facilities and venues by community and business leaders, security sector and law enforcement personnel, and citizens—our force multipliers. And that we will not rush to put attacks behind us and quickly move on, but will "marinate" in the lessons learned, and then take corrective action to prevent and mitigate future attacks. Together, we can make a difference and, I believe, save lives.

There are twenty main takeaways for you to continually revisit.

1. We all have a psychological blind eye to soft targeting. We cannot help it: our cultural instinct is to protect, not target, civilians and noncombatants. We have trouble believing bad actors will hit our soft spot and engage where we are most vulnerable, but they will. Modern terrorism has no moral restraints.
2. Understand that soft targets are hit every day around the world. International terrorist groups are actively planning operations in the United States, but a homegrown soft target attack is more likely.
3. Know the threat in your world and in your community. Ask questions of local law enforcement; join groups such as the FBI's

Infraguard or ASIS and attend chapter meetings. There may be "no evidence of a threat," but that is different from "evidence of no threat." Remember, in the "black swan" realm, what we don't know is more important than what we know.

4. Intuitively understand your vulnerabilities and how much risk you are assuming. Identify your Achilles heel as the one vulnerability exposing you to the greatest risk and mitigate it.

5. Before investing in or relying too heavily on technology, recall a popular military axiom: "The human is the best weapon system." By honing your intuition, understanding behavioral detection tactics, and unapologetically engaging people in situations that just "don't feel right," you are taking a significant step to protect your property and its occupants. Technology should complement your other efforts, not be the central focus of your security plan.

6. Practice good steady-state leadership for outstanding crisis leadership when it is required. Frontloaded planning, training, and exercising efforts will pay dividends in an emergency situation.

7. Take steps today to harden your facility. Consider lowering the "heat" of your building by decreasing its profile, removing unnecessary signage and symbols which may be inflammatory or give away too much information (like "kindergarten"). Installing fences and raising the height on current fencing are the easiest and fastest ways to protect your property from intruders and present a fortified appearance and "psychological boundary."

8. Consider the deterrent effect of security officers and vehicles on your property.

9. Remember, as we harden facilities, the insider threat will grow. Someone in your organization may be a threat.

10. Fight the five emotional states increasing your vulnerability: hopelessness (there is not much we can do to prevent or mitigate the threat), infallibility (it will never happen here), inescapability (it is destiny or unavoidable, so why even try), invulnerability (it cannot happen to me), and the most dangerous, inevitability (if it is going to happen, there is nothing I can do about it anyway).

11. When faced with a budgeting dilemma, consider this question: "What is the cost of not protecting our people?"

12. Focus on vulnerability, not probability.

13. Invest in preparedness, not prediction.

14. Understand that we can paint an accurate picture of the consequences of an attack, even if we cannot predict how likely it is to occur.

15. Security isn't a program, it's a culture. Shape the environment.

16. Citizens now expect/demand security at soft targets. They will decide whether to visit your facility based on whether it feels

safe. Therefore, in this age, security will not scare them away, but pull them in!

17. Language and signage are two ways to broadcast your facility's hardened posture.
18. The goal of hardening is to stop the fight before it starts; look hard so the bad actor passes you by.
19. You can strike a balance between normalcy and vigilance.
20. You may never know lives you've saved through vigilance and proactive security measures.

Understandably, making changes for the sake of security sometimes feels like we are conceding our way of life to adversaries. Sadly, the world has changed, and so must we. Thank you for caring about and protecting our citizens from a battle they did not choose to fight.

Now is the time to convert knowledge to action.

REFERENCE

National Commission on Terrorist Attacks upon the United States. "The 9/11 Commission Report: Final Report of the National Commission On Terrorist Attacks Upon the United States." New York: Norton, www.9-11commission.gov/report/911Report.pdf (2004).

Glossary

ALF: Animal Liberation Front is a domestic terror group with extremist views regarding the ethical treatment of animals.

Al-Shabaab: Al-Shabaab is an Islamist extremist organization founded in 2006 that seeks to establish an austere version of Islam in Somalia and also operates in Kenya, Ethiopia, Tanzania, and Uganda.

Anarchist: A person who rebels against any authority, established order, or ruling power and may use violent tactics.

Anarchist extremists: Anarchist extremists advocate violence in furtherance of movements such as anti-racism, anti-capitalism, anti-globalism, anti-fascism, and environmental extremism.

AQ: Al-Qaeda is an Islamist extremist organization founded in 1988 by Osama bin Laden and other Arab foreign fighters who fought against the Soviet Union in Afghanistan in the 1980s. It provides religious authority and strategic guidance to its followers and affiliated groups.

AQAP: Al-Qaeda in the Arabian Peninsula, AQAP is an Islamist extremist organization based in Yemen. It is al-Qaeda's most active global affiliate.

AQI: Al-Qaeda in Iraq, now known as the Islamic State of Iraq and the Levant (ISIL or ISIS) (took advantage of instability in Syria to expand across their shared border).

AQIM: Al-Qaeda in the lands of the Islamic Maghreb AQIM was formed in 2007 and is al-Qaeda's North African affiliate that aims to overthrow regional governments to institute an Islamic state. In March 2017, AQIM merged with several other regional groups to form Jamaat Nasr al-Islam Wal Muslim.

AQIS: Al-Qa'ida in the Indian Subcontinent is an Islamist extremist group that aims to fight the governments of Pakistan, India, Burma, Bangladesh, and to establish an Islamic state.

AQRO: Al-Qaeda-related offense.

Asymmetric operations tactic: Using the element of surprise to attack; also, using an adversary's strength against him while exploiting his weaknesses.

CBRNE: Chemical, biological, radiological, nuclear, and explosive weapons.

CEP: Counter Extremism Project.

CERT: Community emergency response team concept, from FEMA.

CJNG: Jalisco Cartel New Generation is a drug trafficking organization from Mexico; group evolved as a result of killings, captures, and rifts in older cartels like Sinaloa Cartel.

CPTED: Crime prevention through environmental design is a multi-disciplinary approach to deterring criminal behavior through environmental design.

CTITF: Counterterrorism Implementation Task Force.

DFI: Deadly force incident.

DHS: Department of Homeland Security.

DoD: Department of Defense.

DOJ: Department of Justice.

Domestic terrorism: Domestic terrorism involving groups or individuals who are based and operate entirely within the United States and US territories and whose acts are directed at elements of the US government or population. FBI domestic terrorism is violence committed by individuals or groups including race-based, single-issue, anti-government, and religious extremist ideologies.

DTEC: Domestic Terrorism Executive Committee.

DTO: Drug trafficking organization.

EAP: Emergency action planning.

EBH: Effects-based hardening is a system for visualizing violent scenarios in an unemotional, data-driven way. EBH is a way to harmonize, synchronize, and prioritize hardening activities.

ELF: Earth Liberation Front, environmental extremists view man-made threats to the environment as so severe that violence and property damage are justified to prevent further destruction.

ERT: Emergency Response Team.

FBI: Federal Bureau of Investigation.

FDA: Federal Drug Administration.

FEMA: Federal Emergency Management Agency.

FTO: Foreign terrorist organization, officially designated by the State Department.

HAMAS: HAMAS, an acronym for Harakat al-Muqawama al-Islamiyya, or the Islamic Resistance Movement, founded in 1987, is an off-shoot of the Palestinian Muslim Brotherhood that aims to end the Israeli occupation of Palestinian territory and establish a Palestinian state.

Hezbollah: An Islamist militant group based in Lebanon and allied with Iran.

Homegrown violent extremists: HVEs are individuals inspired as opposed to directed by foreign terrorist organizations and radicalized in the countries in which they are born, raised, or reside.

ICCT: International Centre for Counter-terrorism—The Hague.

ICS: Incident Command System.

ICT: Incident Command Team.

Ideology: Visionary theorizing; a systematic body of concepts, especially about human life or culture; the manner or the content of thinking characteristic of an individual, group, or culture; the integrated assertions, theories, and aims that constitute a sociopolitical program.

IED: Improvised explosive device.

International terrorism: Terrorism involving citizens or the territory of more than one country (per 22 U.S.C. § 2656f).

INTERPOL: The organization's official name is ICPO–INTERPOL and the official abbreviation ICPO stands for International Criminal Police Organization. INTERPOL is shorthand for international police.

ISIS: ISIS, also referred to as the Islamic State of Iraq and the Levant, the Islamic State, or Daesh, is a Salafi-jihadist militant group that split from al-Qaeda in 2014 and established its self-proclaimed "caliphate," claiming authority over all Muslims.

LE: Law enforcement.

LeT: Lashkar-e-Tayyiba is an Islamist extremist organization focused on attacking and expelling Indians from Kashmir, a northern state in India that borders Pakistan and is home to a Muslim-majority population.

LEO: Law enforcement officer.

LTTE: Liberation Tigers of Tamil Eelam—a terrorist group mostly defeated in Sri Lanka in 2009.

Militia extremists: Militia extremists view the federal government as a threat to the rights and freedoms of Americans. They judge armed resistance to be necessary to preserve these rights.

NCTC: National Counterterrorism Center.

OSAC: Overseas Security Advisory Council.

PPP: Public–private partnership.

PVI: Place vulnerability index.

SAR: Suspicious activity reports.

Shelter in place: To stay where one is in the event of an emergency: requires people stay inside a building away from windows. If due to a biological, chemical, or radiation event, all windows and air intake systems should be closed and, if possible, covered with sheets of plastic and taped down. Wet towels may be used to seal cracks. If sheltering due to an active shooter, lock and block the door with heavy furniture. Turn off lights and silence cell phones and beepers. Text your location to someone who is outside, but insist the person not call. Get behind a turned-over desk or furniture item in the farthest corner of the room. If sheltering due to a bomb, you must turn off all electronic devices, as many bombs are triggered by cell phones. Stay away from the windows to protect yourself from flying glass.

Single-issue extremists: Single-issue extremists participate in violence stemming from domestic political or economic issues. This includes animal rights extremists, environmental extremists, and anti-abortion extremists.

Sovereign citizen extremists: Sovereign citizen extremists throughout the United States view federal, state, and local governments as illegitimate, justifying their violence and other criminal activity.

SSE: Sensitive site exploitation—the recovery of documents, electronic data, or other information at a sensitive location such as a war crimes site, classified facility, or the operational building or living quarters of an enemy combatant; accomplished by a specially trained team.

ST-CP: Soft Targets and Crowded Places are locations that are easily accessible to large numbers of people and that have limited security or protective measures in place making them vulnerable to attack.

Tactical deception: Tactical deception is a disruptive tool regularly used by the military to gain the advantage; military deception as measures taken to deliberately mislead adversary decision makers about friendly capabilities, intentions, or operations in ways which may be exploited by friendly forces. They include denial and deception, concealment, camouflage, and perception management.

TATP: Triacetone triperoxide, used in explosive devices

TTP: Tehrik-e-Taliban Pakistan is a loose alliance of militant groups in Pakistan, affiliated with the Afghani Taliban. TTP is an Islamist extremist organization seeking to overthrow Pakistan's government and expel US forces from Afghanistan.

Terrorism: Premeditated, politically or religiously motivated violence perpetrated against noncombatant targets by subnational groups or clandestine agents; the unlawful use of force or violence against persons or property to intimidate or coerce a government, the civilian population, or any segment thereof in furtherance of political or social objectives.

TME: Terror multiplier effect—the careful selection of targets that can reap high gains for the attacks whether through casualty counts or tactics employed.

USA PATRIOT Act: Uniting and Strengthening America by Providing Appropriate Tools Required to Intercept and Obstruct Terrorism Act.

USSS: United States Secret Service.

VBIED: Vehicle-based improvised explosive device.

White supremacist extremists: White supremacist extremists believe in the inherent superiority of the white race. They seek to establish dominance over non-whites through violence and other criminal activity.

WMD: Weapon of mass destruction—any explosive, incendiary, or poison gas (chemical); bomb, grenade, rocket having a propellant charge of more than 4 ounces; missile having an explosive incendiary charge of more than 0.25 ounce; mine or device similar to the above; weapon involving a disease organism (biological); or weapon that is designed to release radiation or radioactivity at a level dangerous to human life (nuclear) (Source: 18 U.S.C. § 2332a as referenced in 18 U.S.C. § 921).

Appendix A: List of Foreign Terrorist Organizations

United States Department of State, Bureau of Counterterrorism, May 1, 2018

Foreign terrorist organizations (FTOs) are foreign organizations designated by the Secretary of State in accordance with section 219 of the Immigration and Nationality Act (INA), as amended. FTO designations play a critical role in our fight against terrorism and are an effective means of curtailing support for terrorist activities and pressuring groups to get out of the terrorism business.

(The State Department started FTO designations October 8, 1997.)

CURRENT LIST OF DESIGNATED FOREIGN TERRORIST ORGANIZATIONS

The list is presented in chronological order by designation; groups 1–18 were all designated on October 8, 1997.

1. Abu Sayyaf Group (ASG)
2. Aum Shinrikyo (AUM)
3. Basque Fatherland and Liberty (ETA)
4. Gama'a al-Islamiyya (Islamic Group) (IG)
5. HAMAS
6. Harakat ul-Mujahidin (HUM)
7. Hezbollah
8. Kahane Chai (Kach)
9. Kurdistan Workers Party (PKK) (Kongra-Gel)
10. Liberation Tigers of Tamil Eelam (LTTE)
11. National Liberation Army (ELN)
12. Palestine Liberation Front (PLF)

13. Palestinian Islamic Jihad (PIJ)
14. Popular Front for the Liberation of Palestine (PFLF)
15. PFLP-General Command (PFLP-GC)
16. Revolutionary Armed Forces of Colombia (FARC)
17. Revolutionary People's Liberation Party/Front (DHKP/C)
18. Shining Path (SL)
19. Al-Qa'ida (AQ)
20. Islamic Movement of Uzbekistan (IMU)
21. Real Irish Republican Army (RIRA)
22. Jaish-e-Mohammed (JEM)
23. Lashkar-e Tayyiba (LeT)
24. Al-Aqsa Martyrs Brigade (AAMB)
25. Asbat al-Ansar (AAA)
26. Al- Qa'ida in the Islamic Maghreb (AQIM)
27. Communist Party of the Philippines/New People's Army (CPP/NPA)
28. Jemaah Islamiya (JI)
29. Lashkar i Jhangvi (LJ)
30. Ansar al-Islam (AAI)
31. Continuity Irish Republican Army (CIRA)
32. Islamic State of Iraq and the Levant (formerly al-Qa'ida in Iraq)
33. Islamic Jihad Union (IJU)
34. Harakat ul-Jihad-i-Islami/Bangladesh (HUJI-B)
35. Al-Shabaab
36. Revolutionary Struggle (RS)
37. Kata'ib Hizballah (KH)
38. Al-Qa'ida in the Arabian Peninsula (AQAP)
39. Harakat ul-Jihad-i-Islami (HUJI)
40. Tehrik-e Taliban Pakistan (TTP)
41. Jundallah
42. Army of Islam (AOI)
43. Indian Mujahedeen (IM)
44. Jemaah Anshorut Tauhid (JAT)
45. Abdallah Azzam Brigades (AAB)
46. Haqqani Network (HQN)
47. Ansar al-Dine (AAD)
48. Boko Haram
49. Ansaru
50. Al-Mulathamun Battalion
51. Ansar al-Shari'a in Benghazi
52. Ansar al-Shari'a in Darnah
53. Ansar al-Shari'a in Tunisia
54. ISIL Sinai Province (formally Ansar Bayt al-Maqdis)

55. Al-Nusrah Front
56. Mujahidin Shura Council in the Environs of Jerusalem (MSC)
57. Jaysh Rijal al-Tariq al Naqshabandi (JRTN)
58. ISIL-Khorasan (ISIL-K)
59. Islamic State of Iraq and the Levant's Branch in Libya (ISIL-Libya)
60. Al-Qa'ida in the Indian Subcontinent
61. Hizbul Mujahideen (Kashmir)
62. ISIS-Bangladesh
63. ISIS-Philippines
64. ISIS-West Africa
65. ISIS-Greater Sahara
66. al-Ashtar Brigades (AAB)
67. Jama'at Nusrat al-Islam wal-Muslimin (JNIM)

Identification

The Bureau of Counterterrorism in the State Department (CT) continually monitors the activities of terrorist groups active around the world to identify potential targets for designation. When reviewing potential targets, CT looks not only at the actual terrorist attacks that a group has carried out, but also at whether the group has engaged in planning and preparations for possible future acts of terrorism or retains the capability and intent to carry out such acts.

Designation

Once a target is identified, CT prepares a detailed "administrative record," which is a compilation of information, typically including both classified and open sources information, demonstrating that the statutory criteria for designation have been satisfied. If the Secretary of State, in consultation with the Attorney General and the Secretary of the Treasury, decides to make the designation, Congress is notified of the Secretary's intent to designate the organization and given seven days to review the designation, as the INA requires. Upon the expiration of the seven-day waiting period and in the absence of Congressional action to block the designation, notice of the designation is published in the Federal Register, at which point the designation takes effect. By law an organization designated as an FTO may seek judicial review of the designation in the United States Court of Appeals for the District of Columbia Circuit not later than thirty days after the designation is published in the Federal Register.

Until recently the INA provided that FTOs must be re-designated every two years or the designation would lapse. Under the Intelligence Reform and Terrorism Prevention Act of 2004 (IRTPA), however, the re-designation requirement was replaced by certain review and revocation procedures. IRTPA provides that an FTO may file a petition for revocation two years after its designation date (or in the case of re-designated FTOs, its most recent re-designation date) or two years after the determination date on its most recent petition for revocation. In order to provide a basis for revocation, the petitioning FTO must provide evidence that the circumstances forming the basis for the designation are sufficiently different as to warrant revocation. If no such review has been conducted during a five-year period with respect to a designation, then the Secretary of State is required to review the designation to determine whether revocation would be appropriate. In addition, the Secretary of State may at any time revoke a designation upon a finding that the circumstances forming the basis for the designation have changed in such a manner as to warrant revocation, or that the national security of the United States warrants a revocation. The same procedural requirements apply to revocations made by the Secretary of State as apply to designations. A designation may be revoked by an act of Congress or set aside by a court order.

Legal Criteria for Designation Under Section 219 of the INA as Amended

1. It must be a foreign organization.
2. The organization must engage in terrorist activity, as defined in section 212 (a)(3)(B) of the INA (8 U.S.C. § 1182(a)(3)(B)), or terrorism, as defined in section 140(d)(2) of the Foreign Relations Authorization Act, Fiscal Years 1988 and 1989 (22 U.S.C. § 2656f(d)(2)), or retain the capability and intent to engage in terrorist activity or terrorism.
3. The organization's terrorist activity or terrorism must threaten the security of US nationals or the national security (national defense, foreign relations, or the economic interests) of the United States.

Legal Ramifications of Designation

1. It is unlawful for a person in the United States or subject to the jurisdiction of the United States to knowingly provide "material support or resources" to a designated FTO. The term "material support or resources" is defined in 18 U.S.C. § 2339A(b)(1) as "any property, tangible or intangible, or service, including currency or monetary instruments or financial securities, financial services, lodging, training, expert advice or assistance, safehouses, false documentation or identification,

communications equipment, facilities, weapons, lethal substances, explosives, personnel (1 or more individuals who may be or include oneself), and transportation, except medicine or religious materials." 18 U.S.C. § 2339A(b)(2) provides that for these purposes "the term 'training' means instruction or teaching designed to impart a specific skill, as opposed to general knowledge." 18 U.S.C. § 2339A(b)(3) further provides that for these purposes the term "'expert advice or assistance' means advice or assistance derived from scientific, technical or other specialized knowledge."

2. Representatives and members of a designated FTO, if they are aliens, are inadmissible to and, in certain circumstances, removable from the United States (see 8 U.S.C. § 1182 (a)(3)(b)(i)(IV)–(V), § 1227 (a)(1)(A)).

3. Any US financial institution that becomes aware that it has possession of or control over funds in which a designated FTO or its agent has an interest must retain possession of or control over the funds and report the funds to the Office of Foreign Assets Control of the US Department of the Treasury.

Other Effects of Designation

1. Supports our efforts to curb terrorism financing and to encourage other nations to do the same.
2. Stigmatizes and isolates designated terrorist organizations internationally.
3. Deters donations or contributions to and economic transactions with named organizations.
4. Heightens public awareness and knowledge of terrorist organizations.
5. Signals to other governments our concern about named organizations.

Revocations of Foreign Terrorist Organizations

The Immigration and Nationality Act sets out three possible basis [sic] for revoking a Foreign Terrorist Organization designation:

1. The Secretary of State must revoke a designation if the Secretary finds that the circumstances that were the basis of the designation have changed in such a manner as to warrant a revocation;

2. The Secretary of State must revoke a designation if the Secretary finds that the national security of the United States warrants a revocation;

3. The Secretary of State may revoke a designation at any time.

Any revocation shall take effect on the date specified in the revocation or upon publication in the Federal Register if no effective date is specified. The revocation of a designation shall not affect any action or proceeding based on conduct committed prior to the effective date of such revocation.

From US State Department, "Foreign Terrorist Organizations." (http://www.state.gov/j/ct/rls/other/des/123085.htm)

Appendix B: NIMS, the ICS, and FEMA Courses

Understanding the National Incident Management System (NIMS) is critical for leaders of soft target venues. NIMS identifies concepts and principles that answer how to manage emergencies from preparedness to recovery regardless of their cause, size, location, or complexity. NIMS provides a consistent, nationwide approach and vocabulary for multiple agencies or jurisdictions to work together to build, sustain, and deliver the core capabilities needed to achieve a secure and resilient nation. The Incident Command System (ICS) is a systematic, all-hazards tool used for the command, control, and coordination of emergency response. A terrorist attack of any kind will bring the federal government to the scene and you must understand how its representatives will operate, what they expect from you, and how you both can partner to bring the situation under control.

The following courses provide the basis for understanding NIMS and the ICS as well as recommended FEMA online courses, available to all free of charge.

Course Code	Course Title
IS-100.b	Introduction to Incident Command System, ICS-100
IS-100.FDA	Introduction to Incident Command System (ICS100) for Food and Drug Administration
IS-100.FWa	Introduction to Incident Command System (ICS100) for Federal Workers
IS-100.HCb	Introduction to the Incident Command System (ICS100) for Healthcare/Hospitals
IS-100.HE	Introduction to the Incident Command System for Higher Education
IS-100.LEb	Introduction to the Incident Command System (ICS100) for Law Enforcement
IS-100.PWb	Introduction to the Incident Command System (ICS100) for Public Works
IS-100.SCa	Introduction to the Incident Command System for Schools
IS-200.b	ICS for Single Resources and Initial Action Incidents

Course Code	Course Title
IS-200.HCa	Applying ICS to Healthcare Organizations
IS-700.a	National Incident Management System (NIMS)—An Introduction
IS-701.a	NIMS Multiagency Coordination System (MACS) Course
IS-702.a	National Incident Management System (NIMS) Public Information Systems
IS-703.a	NIMS Resource Management
IS-704	NIMS Communications and Information Management
IS-706	NIMS Intrastate Mutual Aid—An Introduction
IS-800.b	National Response Framework—An Introduction

The Professional Development Series includes seven Emergency Management Institute independent study courses that provide a well-rounded set of fundamentals for those in the emergency management profession.

The Professional Development Series includes seven Emergency Management Institute independent study courses that provide a well-rounded set of fundamentals for those in the emergency management profession. Many students build on this foundation to develop their careers.

After successfully completing all seven required PDS courses through the Independent Study program, a PDS certificate is automatically issued via email to the email address provided on your last exam submission.

Revisions are complete for IS-230.b Fundamentals of Emergency Management to include new policy and guidance. The revised course will be interactive rather than self-study and is numbered IS-230.c Fundamentals of Emergency Management.

Revisions are also complete for IS-244.a Developing and Managing Volunteers to update the information and change to an interactive format. It is numbered IS-244.b Developing and Managing Volunteers.

Course Code	Course Title
IS-120.a	An Introduction to Exercises
IS-230.d	Fundamentals of Emergency Management
IS-235.b	Emergency Planning
IS-240.a	Leadership and Influence
IS-241.b	Decision Making and Problem Solving
IS-242.b	Effective Communication
IS-244.b	Developing and Managing Volunteers

Other courses by FEMA serve to educate and prepare facility leaders, operators, and security and emergency personnel on the myriad threats facing the organization. In some cases, courses may count as college credits.

Course Code	Course Title
IS-3	Radiological Emergency Management
IS-5.a	An Introduction to Hazardous Materials
IS-15.b	Special Events Contingency Planning for Public Safety Agencies
IS-36	Multihazard Planning for Childcare
IS-37.18	Managerial Safety and Health
IS-42	Social Media in Emergency Management
IS-55.a	Household Hazardous Materials—A Guide for Citizens
IS-75	Military Resources in Emergency Management
IS-101.c	Preparing for Federal Disaster Operations: FEMA
IS-102.c	Preparing for Federal Disaster Operations: FEMA Response Partners
IS-106.18	Workplace Violence Awareness Training 2018
IS-201	Forms Used for the Development of the Incident Action Plan
IS-208.a	State Disaster Management
IS-247.a	Integrated Public Alert and Warning System (IPAWS)
IS-248	Integrated Public Alert and Warning System (IPAWS) for the American Public
IS-271.a	Anticipating Hazardous Weather and Community Risk, 2nd edition
IS-288	The Role of Voluntary Agencies in Emergency Management
IS-301	Radiological Emergency Response
IS-315	CERT Supplemental Training: The Incident Command System
IS-317	Introduction to Community Response Teams
IS-318	Mitigation Planning for Local and Tribal Communities
IS-328	Plan Review for Local Mitigation Plans
IS-331	Introduction to Radiological Emergency Preparedness (REP) Exercise Evaluation
IS-340	Hazardous Materials Prevention
IS-346	An Orientation to Hazardous Materials for Medical Personnel
IS-360	Preparing for Mass Casualty Incidents: A Guide for Schools, Higher Education, and Houses of Worship
IS-362.a	Multihazard Emergency Planning for Schools
IS-366.a	Planning for the Needs of Children in Disasters
IS-368	Including People with Disabilities and Others with Access and Functional Needs in Disaster Operations
IS-393.a	Introduction to Hazard Mitigation
IS-394.a	Protecting Your Home or Small Business from Disaster
IS-405	Overview of Mass Care/Emergency Assistance
IS-453	Introduction to Homeland Security Planning
IS-454	Fundamentals of Risk Management
IS-546.a	Continuity of Operations Awareness Course
IS-547.a	Introduction to Continuity of Operations

Course Code	Course Title
IS-548	Continuity of Operations (COOP) Program Manager
IS-559	Local Damage Assessment
IS-660	Introduction to Public–Private Partnerships
IS-662	Improving Preparedness and Resilience through Public–Private Partnerships
IS-775	EOC Management and Operations
IS-800.b	National Response Framework, An Introduction
IS-836	Nuclear/Radiological Incident Annex
IS-860.b	National Infrastructure Protection Plan (NIPP)
IS-906	Workplace Security Awareness
IS-907	Active Shooter: What You Can Do
IS-908	Emergency Management for Senior Officials
IS-909	Community Preparedness: Implementing Simple Activities for Everyone
IS-912	Retail Security Awareness: Understanding the Hidden Hazards
IS-913.a	Critical Infrastructure Security and Resilience: Achieving Results through Partnership and Collaboration
IS-914	Surveillance Awareness: What You Can Do
IS-915	Protecting Critical Infrastructure against Insider Threats
IS-921.a	Implementing Critical Infrastructure Security and Resilience
IS-2001	Threat and Hazard Identification and Risk Assessment (THIRA)
IS-2900	National Disaster Recovery Framework (NDRF) Overview

From Federal Emergency Management Agency, http://training.fema.gov

Appendix C: Federal Bureau of Investigation (FBI) Terrorism Vulnerability Self-Assessment Checklist

*** WARNING: Completed Document Must be Safeguarded ***

This vulnerability self-assessment is intended to help an organization determine its vulnerability to terrorism and to assist local law enforcement in assessing the overall vulnerability of the community. It provides a worksheet that can be customized to the specific organization. The worksheet is intended to be a general guide. It may not include all issues that would be considered in every specific operation. Therefore, it is imperative to consider the unique character of the organization: its functions, its general public image, and its overall public visibility. Consider both who may work in the organization and what the organization does. Assess the symbolic value of the organization to the public. Each worksheet section is ranked on a twenty-point scale. Answering this self-assessment is a subjective process. The person who best knows the physical security and community value of the organization should complete the worksheet. There are no firm guidelines on how to score a category. Because the questions are subjective, give a best estimate when scoring each question.

It is important to remember that the most important threat reduction measure is vigilance on the part of the organization's staff, their awareness of anything out of the ordinary, and their prompt communication of that information to the organization's security team or management. This assessment follows exactly the same format as the community assessment performed by local law enforcement to assist in preventing criminal acts committed by terrorists. Based on the results of this assessment, the organization may wish to share a copy with law enforcement, or to include their representative in the assessment process, to support their understanding of the transportation function and its role in the community.

This assessment should be conducted at least annually, and within the year if there is an increased threat of a terrorist event or whenever there is a significant change to the organization's facilities or activities.

Upon receipt of a high-risk assessment, each law enforcement agency sheriff, chief of police, head, or his or her designated representative may forward that assessment, or other threat report, to the state emergency management agency (or equivalent), to state law enforcement, or to the local FBI office.

Vulnerability self-assessments completed by or provided to state or local governments will be used to prevent crime and may be exempt from disclosure under the public records law; check with your local law enforcement office for clarification. Threat vulnerability self-assessments in the possession of private organizations are not public records. Completed terrorism vulnerability self-assessments should be provided to local law enforcement in hard copy or on digital media. They should not be emailed.

Facility name:
Facility type:
Facility owner—name/cell #:
Facility point of contact for emergency response—name/cell#:

Please provide the latitude, longitude, and elevation of the main entrance to your facility. If you do not have access to a GPS unit, please contact your local law enforcement office for assistance.

_____Lat/Long/Elevation

THE ASSESSMENT

This assessment checklist is broken down into seventeen different categories as follows:

1. Potential terrorist intensions
2. Specific targeting
3. Visibility of your facility or system within the community
4. On-site hazards
5. Population of sites, facility, or activity
6. Potential for mass casualties
7. Security environment and overall vulnerability to an attack
8. Critical products or services
9. High-risk personnel
10. Organization communication systems
11. Security and response

12. Policies, procedures, and plans
13. Security equipment
14. Computer securities, cyber crime, and cyber terrorism
15. Suspicious mail and packages
16. Telephone, bomb, and other types of threats
17. Employee health and the potential for bioterrorism

To complete the assessment, circle the evaluated score on each scale for each question. Then total the scores and enter the total on the last page. Based on the total, use the score guide to assign an overall ranking to the transportation organization.

1. Potential Terrorist Intentions

Low Vulnerability									High Vulnerability										
1	2	3	4	5	6	7	8	9	10	11	12	13	14	15	16	17	18	19	20

The following are issues to be considered in selecting your score.

Are you aware of any terrorist threat to your organization?
Are you aware of a history of terrorist activity in your area or your specialty?
Are you aware of the level of capability of any suspected terrorist that you believe poses a threat to your organization?

2. Specific Targeting

Low Vulnerability									High Vulnerability										
1	2	3	4	5	6	7	8	9	10	11	12	13	14	15	16	17	18	19	20

The following are issues to be considered in selecting your score.

Have you obtained current information from law enforcement or other sources that terrorists have targeted your organization?
What is the reliability of these information sources?
What is your organization's public visibility?
Does the nature of your organization's activity lead you to think it may be targeted?
Are there activities that indicate possible terrorist preparations in your area or specialty?

3. Visibility of Your Facility or Activity Within the Community

Low Vulnerability									High Vulnerability										
1	2	3	4	5	6	7	8	9	10	11	12	13	14	15	16	17	18	19	20

The following are issues to be considered in selecting your score.

Is your organization well known in the community?
Do you regularly receive media attention?
Is your organization nationally prominent in your field or industry?
Are your location and the nature of your activity known generally to the public?
Have you ever had an event or accident with potential health risks that attracted public attention to your facility?

4. On-Site Hazards

Low Vulnerability									High Vulnerability										
1	2	3	4	5	6	7	8	9	10	11	12	13	14	15	16	17	18	19	20

The following are issues to be considered in selecting your score.

Are hazardous materials, explosives, or other dangerous items on your site?
Do you store or use biologic or chemical materials that have the potential to be used as a threat or weapon?
Do you store or use radioactive material at your site?
Do you have a system to control access to hazardous materials, explosives, or any other dangerous materials at your site?
Can any products stored or used on your site be used as or in the manufacture of a mass casualty weapon?
Can any products stored or used on your site cause extensive environmental damage?

5. Population of Site, Facility, or Activity

Low Vulnerability									High Vulnerability										
1	2	3	4	5	6	7	8	9	10	11	12	13	14	15	16	17	18	19	20

The following are issues to be considered in selecting your score.

Do you have more than 250 people normally present at your site?
Do you have more than 1,000 people normally present at your site?
Do you have more than 5,000 people normally present at your site?
Do you hold events at your site that attract large crowds?

6. Potential for Mass Casualties

Low Vulnerability									High Vulnerability										
1	2	3	4	5	6	7	8	9	10	11	12	13	14	15	16	17	18	19	20

The following are issues to be considered in selecting your score.

Do materials stored or used at your site have the potential to create mass casualties on-site?
Do materials stored or used at your site have the potential to create mass casualties within one mile of your site?
How many people live or work within one mile of your site? 500? 1,000? 2,000? 5,000? More than 5,000?

7. Security Environments and Overall Vulnerability to an Attack

Low Vulnerability	High Vulnerability
1 2 3 4 5 6 7 8 9 10	11 12 13 14 15 16 17 18 19 20

The following are issues to be considered in selecting your score.

Does your organization have effective internal security procedures?
What is the law enforcement presence in your area?
What is the hardness, level of blast protection, etc., of your facilities?
How accessible (security presence, access control, id badges, metal detection buffer zones, fences, etc.) is your facility?
Are your assets and/or their potential recognized as a symbol?
What level of public access is necessary for you to function?
Can you control high-speed vehicle approaches to your facility?
Do you have access control to your parking area?
Do you conduct vehicle searches when entering facility grounds or parking areas?
Do you employ detection/monitoring systems (video surveillance, intrusion detection systems, etc.)?
Is your parking delivery area adjacent to or near your facility?
Is your delivery area supervised during hours of normal business?
Is your delivery area access blocked during hours that your business is closed?
Do you have an on-site food service facility for employees and visitors?
Is access to the water supply for your facility protected?
Is access to the ventilation system for your facility protected?
Do you have a way to shut down the water supply or ventilation system for your facility quickly?

8. Critical Products or Services

Low Vulnerability	High Vulnerability
1 2 3 4 5 6 7 8 9 10	11 12 13 14 15 16 17 18 19 20

The following are issues to be considered in selecting your score.

What is the importance of your organization to the community?
Is your organization critical to the local population, economy, or government?
Is your organization critical to the continuity of basic services?
Is your organization critical to state or national commerce?
What would be the social, economic, or psychological ramifications of a terrorist attack against your organization?
What is the nature of your assets: hazardous materials, uniqueness, potential danger to others, etc.?
How long would it take to restore your critical services/functions?

9. High-Risk Personnel

Low Vulnerability									High Vulnerability										
1	2	3	4	5	6	7	8	9	10	11	12	13	14	15	16	17	18	19	20

The following are issues to be considered in selecting your score.

Do you have personnel that are critical to the continuing function of state or local government, basic services, utilities infrastructure, the community, the economy, or of inherent value to your business or agency?
Do you have personnel that are critical for responding to a terrorist act?
What would be the effect of a terrorist act against these high-risk personnel?

10. Organization Communications

Low Vulnerability									High Vulnerability										
1	2	3	4	5	6	7	8	9	10	11	12	13	14	15	16	17	18	19	20

The following are issues to be considered in selecting your score.

Do you have a mass notification system (public address system, intercoms, and alarms)?
Do you have a secure communications network that can be relied upon during a crisis?
Do you have a crisis response team?
Is your crisis response team trained?
Do you conduct regular exercises?

Do local/regional emergency responders participate in your exercises?

Does your crisis response team have its own portable communications system?

Can your crisis response team communicate directly with emergency responders?

Do you have an emergency law enforcement notification system such as a hotline, panic button, or something similar?

Is your alarm system tied into the local law enforcement department or do you have an alarm service?

Are your systems tested regularly?

11. Securities and Response

Low Vulnerability									High Vulnerability										
1	2	3	4	5	6	7	8	9	10	11	12	13	14	15	16	17	18	19	20

The following are issues to be considered in selecting your score.

Are your security forces' staffing and training levels adequate?

Do you have the capability to maintain a security presence in a high-threat situation?

Are additional security personnel available if requested?

Are there affiliated agency/industry/organization support services available?

Do you have trained disaster response teams within the organization?

Do you have necessary specialty detection, monitoring, hazard assessment devices on hand? And are they functional?

Are local/regional law enforcement forces adequate and can they respond rapidly?

Are local emergency responders familiar with your facility and its contents?

Do you keep records on who visits your facility and where they go within the facility?

12. Policies, Procedures, and Plans

Low Vulnerability									High Vulnerability										
1	2	3	4	5	6	7	8	9	10	11	12	13	14	15	16	17	18	19	20

The following are issues to be considered in selecting your score.

Do you have a current crisis response/disaster plan?

Does your plan include the types of crises you are most likely to encounter (e.g., fire, explosion, chemical release)?
Are your employees familiar with the plan?
Have you conducted crisis response and disaster drills and were they effective?
Have you identified the critical functions of your workplace and do you have a plan for continuation of operation during an emergency?

13. Security Equipment

Low Vulnerability									High Vulnerability										
1	2	3	4	5	6	7	8	9	10	11	12	13	14	15	16	17	18	19	20

The following are issues to be considered in selecting your score.

Do you have a security system and is it current technology?
Do you have an intrusion monitoring motion detector or an alarm system?
Do your systems have backup if power is cut or fails?
Do you have security equipment that would detect leaks or ruptures of potentially hazardous materials?
Do you have personnel protective equipment for your emergency response team appropriate for the hazardous materials at your facility?
Is such equipment in working order and has it been inspected recently?

14. Computer Securities, Cyber-Crime, and Cyber-Terrorism

Low Vulnerability									High Vulnerability										
1	2	3	4	5	6	7	8	9	10	11	12	13	14	15	16	17	18	19	20

The following are issues to be considered in selecting your score.

Is your site dependent on information technology such as computers and networks to accomplish its daily business activities?
Is the information stored in your computer systems valuable?
Do you have backup power available for your computer systems?
Do you make backup copies of your data?
Is your backup data securely stored?
Does your site have computers or networks connected to the Internet?

Have you experienced problems with computer security incidents, such as computer viruses, worms, website defacements, and/or denial of service attacks in the past?

Do you have staff in place who are adequately trained and are available to monitor security warnings and take protective measures, such as loading system patches?

Do you have technology security tools in place such as firewalls, intrusion detection systems, or antivirus software to protect your computer systems?

Do you have a computer security policy, plan, and procedure that include a computer security incident response team?

15. Suspicious Mail and Packages

Low Vulnerability										High Vulnerability									
1	2	3	4	5	6	7	8	9	10	11	12	13	14	15	16	17	18	19	20

The following are issues to be considered in selecting your score.

Is the mail for your facility opened in a secured area or an area isolated from the majority of personnel?

Have the personnel who open mail received training on the recognition of suspicious mail and/or packages?

Do you have specific procedures on how to handle suspicious mail and/or packages, including possible facility evacuation?

Do you have a secure and contained location where any unusual or suspect deliveries or mail can be stored until proper authorities can evaluate the suspect items?

16. Telephone, Bomb, and Other Types of Threats

Low Vulnerability										High Vulnerability									
1	2	3	4	5	6	7	8	9	10	11	12	13	14	15	16	17	18	19	20

The following are issues to be considered in selecting your score.

Has your staff received training on how to handle bomb and other threat calls?

Does your staff have a checklist of questions to ask the caller in case of a bomb or other threatening call?

Does your facility have a plan on how to handle bomb and other threatening calls?

Does your bomb threat plan include a system whereby your personnel would search your facility to identify suspicious objects to point out to emergency response personnel?

Does your plan include a decision-making process on whether to evacuate the facility?

Are personnel familiar with the plan? Have evacuation drills been conducted?

Is your plan coordinated with local law enforcement and the local phone company?

17. Employee Health and the Potential for Bioterrorism

Low Vulnerability									High Vulnerability										
1	2	3	4	5	6	7	8	9	10	11	12	13	14	15	16	17	18	19	20

The following are issues to be considered in selecting your score.

Do you have an occupational health safety program in place?

Do you have a health professional working at your facility?

Do you have a procedure in place to track the health of each employee and know if more than one employee has the same symptoms?

Do you monitor the health status of employees on sick status or absent otherwise?

Are employees encouraged to keep supervisors informed on any unusual health-related event or condition?

Are employees required to report any unusual conditions or substances encountered in the course of their normal duties, such as strange substances or odors from packaging or mail?

Do employees know the proper procedures for emergency operation or shut-off of air handler, air-circulating, or ventilation systems?

Do you keep a current list of employees and their home addresses and emergency contact information?

Do you have an emergency notification plan for employees (e.g., calling tree)?

Total score: _____
Self-Assessment Evaluation
(20–85)   Low risk
(86–170)   Low caution
(171–225)   High caution
(256–340)   High risk

If the total score for the organization exceeds 256 and if local law enforcement has not been involved in the assessment, notify them at once. Again, hand carry and do not email or mail the document.

Remarks and Unusual or Significant Issues

Please list any important remarks that should be made concerning the self-assessment. Also, please list any unusual or significant findings that developed during your self-assessment. List significant hazardous materials that might be used as a terrorist weapon or any significant impact a terrorist act against your site may cause to the community.

Notes

*** WARNING: Completed Document Must Be Safeguarded ***

Appendix D:
Bomb Threat Checklist

(For placement next to every telephone in the organization.)

FBI BOMB PROGRAM EBCC-X

Bomb Threat Call Checklist

Fill out during the bomb threat.

Questions to Ask Caller	Exact Wording of the Threat
1. When is bomb going to explode?	_____
2. Where is it right now?	_____
3. What does it look like?	_____
4. What kind of bomb is it?	_____
5. What will cause it to explode?	_____
6. Did you place the bomb?	_____
7. Why?	_____
8. What is your address?	_____
9. What is your name?	_____

Bomb Threat Questionnaire

Fill out completely, immediately after bomb threat.

Caller's Voice: (Circle All That Apply)

Calm	Laughing	Lisp	Disguised
Angry	Crying	Raspy	Accent
Excited	Normal	Deep	Nasal
Slow	Distinct	Ragged	Soft
Stutter	Rapid	Slurred	Loud
Clearing throat	Deep breathing	Cracking voice	

Familiar
If voice is familiar, who did it sound like?

_____

Background Sounds: (Circle All That Apply)

Street noises	House noises	Factory	Local
Kitchen noises	Motor	Heavy Machines	Long distance
Voices	Music	Office Machines	PA System
Clear	Static	Animal	Noises
Other			

_____

Threat Language: (Circle all That Apply)

Well spoken (educated)   Foul   Incoherent
Irrational   Taped   Message read by caller

Report call immediately to:
Name: Phone number:
Today's Date and Time: Your Phone number:
Name_____   Position _____

EBCC-X Bomb Threat Call Checklist

Appendix E: National Counterterrorism Center Bomb Threat Standoff Charts

(Map your property and the surrounding area with these evacuation distances.)

	Explosives Capacity[1] (TNT Equivalent)	Mandatory Evacuation Distance[2]	Preferred Evacuation Distance[3]
Pipe bomb	5 LBS/2.3 KG	70 FT/21 M	1,200 FT/366 M
Suicide vest	20 LBS/9.2 KG	110 FT/34 M	1,750 FT/518 M
Briefcase/suitcase bomb	50 LBS/23 KG	150 FT/46 M	1,850 FT/564 M
Sedan	500 LBS/227 KG	320 FT/98 M	1,900 FT/580 M
SUV/van	1,000 LBS/454 KG	400 FT/122 M	2,400 FT/732 M
Small delivery truck	4,000 LBS/1,814 KG	640 FT/195 M	3,800 FT/1159 M
Container/water truck	10,000 LBS/4,536 KG	860 FT/263 M	5,100 FT/1,555 M
Semi-trailer	60,000 LBS/27,216 KG	1,570 FT/479 M	9,300 FT/2,835 M

FIGURE E1   National Counterterrorism Center Bomb Threat Standoff Chart

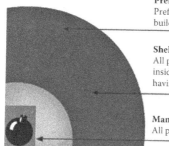

Preferred Evacuation Distance
Preferred area (beyond this line) for evacuation of people in buildings and mandatory for people outdoors.

Shelter-in-Place Zone
All personnel in this area should seek shelter immediately inside a building away from windows and exterior walls. Avoid having anyone outside—including those evacuating—in this area.[4]

Mandatory Evacuation Distance
All personnel must evacuate (both inside of buildings and out).

FIGURE E2   National Counterterrorism Center Bomb Shelter in Place and Evacuation Chart

1. Based on maximum volume or weight of explosive (TNT equivalent) that could reasonably fit in a suitcase or vehicle.
2. Governed by the ability of typical US commercial construction to resist severe damage or collapse following a blast. Performances can vary significantly, however, and buildings should be analyzed by qualified parties when possible.
3. Governed by the greater of fragment throw distance or glass breakage/falling glass hazard distance. Note that pipe and briefcase bombs assume cased charges that throw fragments farther than vehicle bombs.
4. A known terrorist tactic is to attract bystanders to windows, doorways, and the outside with gunfire, small bombs, or other methods and then detonate a larger, more destructive device, significantly increasing human casualties.

Appendix F: Planning and Emergency Smartphone Applications

During the violent earthquake in Haiti, a victim trapped in the rubble used his iPhone app to save his life. Trapped for sixty-five hours in the lobby of his Port-au-Prince hotel, Dan Woolley used information from an iPhone first-aid app to make a tourniquet for his fractured leg and stanch the bleeding from his head wound. He also used his camera to take pictures of his wounds so that he could zoom in and assess the extent of the injuries (Katz 2010). At the very least, there is a psychological aspect to victims participating in self-care and taking control instead of feeling panic or loss of determination, especially for those who are trapped alone and isolated.

The following list of applications is not all inclusive, but rather a few of the apps recommended for the book by law enforcement, first responders, and emergency response experts:

311 App for your city
5–0 Police Scanner
911 toolkit
Accuweather
Bomb threat standoff
Broadcastify
Bugle
CDC blast injury
CitizenAid
Close call
Compass
CPR and choking
Disaster Alert
Echolink
Emergency radio (scanner)
Emergency response guidebook
Emergency survival handbook

Facebook (to mark yourself "safe" in an emergency)
FEMA
FieldFacts
First aid by American Red Cross
Flashlight with SOS and beacons
GasBuddy
Go-ToAid
GPS
GuardlyMobile
HazMat reference
IceBlueButton
iPhone tracking
iStethoscope
iTriage
iWrecked
KiteString
KnowYourPlan
Life360
ManDown
Mobile REMM
MyRadar
NextDoor
NOAA
Notepad
OffLine Survival Manual
palmEM emergency medicine
Pet First Aid (Red Cross)
Pocket first aid
Police siren (scare away intruders, signal for help)
PulsePoint
Radar scope—weather app
RedPanicButton
Red Cross Emergency
Reunite
Responder Self-Care
SafeTrec
Shelterview
Shotspotter
Smart911
Social Alert
StormRadar
Twiage
Twitter
Waze Traffic

WeatherUnderground
Weather Channel
WikiHow
Wiser—HazMat
Zello

Red Cross mobile apps page: www.redcross.org/get-help/how-to-
prepare-for-emergencies/mobile-apps
National Institutes of Health, Health & Human Services apps page:
https://sis.nlm.nih.gov/dimrc/disasterapps.html

The CitizenAID app was developed by military and civilian medics in the UK following the Paris attack to teach people about how to provide potentially lifesaving treatment before the arrival of emergency services in the event of an incident. If the user is in an emergency, clicking on the "I'm in a Live Incident" button provides a host of services including what to do in specific incidents—active shooter, knife attacker, bombs, and vehicles as a weapon. Medical advice includes stopping bleeding, tourniquets, CPR, and opening airways. See www.citizenaid.us for more information.

In case of a communication outage, keep a note on your phone that lists everything you need to know in case of emergency—names, phone numbers, addresses. If you are traveling, screenshot a map with the location of the closet US Embassy in case you need to go there on foot.

Companies are also developing apps users can purchase to access password-protected information and secretly communicate. For example, Spot-on Response provides vital information to emergency responders including blueprints and building evacuation plans. The app also allows for silent, two-way communication; for instance, teachers can use the app to discreetly send a message to notify first responders of their location and also send pictures of the scene to assist in recovery operations.

REFERENCE

Katz, Leslie. "iPhone App Helped U.S. Man Survive Haiti Quake." www.cnet.com/news/iphone-app-helped-u-s-man-survive-haiti-quake (January 10, 2010).

Appendix G: Primary and Secondary School Threat Assessment and Response Checklist

Although the size and scope of an attack on our education system on the scale of Beslan seems unlikely, it is not improbable. We are still very susceptible to international or domestic terrorist activity, therefore should not dismiss the possibility. If you prepare for mass casualty events, your school can handle simpler issues far more effectively. Planning, training, and exercising are all hardening activities.

There are several considerations for the possibility of a school attack. The school may be co-located with a hard target, such as a military installation, or be caught up in a large-scale attack, such as the schools in Manhattan on 9/11 as well as several others mentioned in the book. The School District must take a leadership role and clearly state its goals along with outcome-based, measurable objectives for the program that reflect the intent of the program and address the major aspects of its purpose. The following checklist is not meant to be all inclusive but serves as a basis for planning; your checklist should be tailored to your unique organization and situation.

THREAT ASSESSMENT

With any emergency action planning (EAP) or Emergency Response Plan (ERP) activity, response to a terrorist event should be an annex added to existing plans. For example, a terrorist attack differs from the active-shooter scenario in many ways, so do not cover both events with the same checklist. An active shooter is defined as

> an individual actively engaged in killing or attempting to kill people in a confined and populated area; in most cases, active shooters use

firearms(s) and there is no pattern or method to their selection of victims. Active shooter situations are unpredictable and evolve quickly. Typically, the immediate deployment of law enforcement is required to stop the shooting and mitigate harm to victims. Because active shooter situations are often over within 10 to 15 minutes, before law enforcement arrives on the scene, individuals must be prepared both mentally and physically to deal with an active shooter situation.

(DHS 2017)

Whereas most active-shooter incidents evolve and resolve themselves relatively quickly, terrorists typically seek the prolonged spectacle of media, first responder, and public response, thereby gaining exposure for their cause and legitimacy. Where active-shooter incidents are not as well planned, terror actions could be planned for weeks, months, or even years before the actual incident unfolds. Furthermore, active-shooter incidents are typically perpetrated by either disgruntled employees or students who usually have minimal weapons training and bring rudimentary explosives to the scene. However, terrorists have characteristically received some form of paramilitary/insurgency training, may have a greater depth of understanding in explosives and construction of improvised explosive devices, and have access to larger financial support networks to acquire superior materials.

Although you may certainly use another organization's EAP/ERP as a model for yours, tailor the response plan to your unique situation and challenges. Each individual school campus, should, as a minimum, have a separate annex on the overall district plan, if not their own plan.

Planning should include areas outside the school that could affect your operations. A good rule of thumb is to use a two-mile radius around the school. Examples could be factories, banks, or anything that could possibly "bleed over" to your school.

PLANNING THE ANTI- OR COUNTERTERRORISM ANNEX TO YOUR SCHOOL EMERGENCY RESPONSE PLAN

The Threat Assessment and Planning Team should consist of, at a minimum:

The district superintendent
Respective district principals
District resource officer, local police departments or, in the case of
larger districts, the district police chief
Administration director
Transportation director

Facilities director
Other local law enforcement liaisons (county and state)
Local fire department liaison
Local emergency medical liaison
Local "first care hospital" liaison
District Public Information Officer (PIO)
Other school members to consider as part of the threat assessment
    and planning team
School nurse
School cafeteria manager

When planning your terror threat assessment, the team must consider all terrorist attack scenarios that might affect the school. A good question to consider is: Are other potential terror targets near the school?

Military facility (including recruiting stations)
Federal, state, or local governmental offices (include any and all, no
    matter how small the operation)
Nuclear power plant
Airport, train station, bus station
Mall or outdoor shopping area
Location in an area known for militia, sovereign citizen, or other
    anti-government activities
What is the demographic constitution of your student body and
    how could it be the target of a racial, religious, or other attack?

As discussed in Chapter 8, employee screening is critical, because the insider threat is significant and rising. A few suggestions include:

Review employment screening policy and procedure (administration officials).
    Does your screening process include volunteers, cafeteria workers, mechanics, bus drivers, and security, in addition to educational staff?
    Does your procedure allow for actual courthouse document searches, rather than online Internet database searches, which are usually not as accurate?
    Do your searchers run social security number traces to identify any out-of-state issues that should be checked?
    Do your outside contractors and their potential subcontractors use due diligence screening procedures to check the backgrounds of their workers who regularly visit your school, and do you have a list of those people on file that are authorized to work there?

Review the physical security of bus yards and garages; review transportation security in general (security, bus garage manager, and administration officials).

Are vehicle garages alarmed, and are the alarms in working order?

Are buses stored in fenced-in areas that are gated, locked, and adequately illuminated at night?

If not stored in a gated area, what security protocols are in place to minimize tampering or other nefarious acts?

Do drivers accomplish "pilot inspections" of their vehicles before placing them into service each day?

Perform rear to front inspections, both left and right sides, under the vehicle, and on board the bus itself, looking for signs of tampering, hanging wires, or other suspect conditions. These checks should be mandatory at a minimum if the bus is exposed to the public, such as on field trips or sporting events away for the parent school.

Are bus drivers equipped with two-way radios or cell phones?

Are drivers trained to be aware of and report suspicious vehicles that appear to be following their buses during their routes?

Do drivers keep a student roster for each bus route, and is that roster updated at regular and as needed intervals? Review the physical security of campus buildings and grounds. Security should be "layered." An example of layered security would be from the road/street to the sidewalk, from the sidewalk to the door, and from the door to inside the school itself. Once inside, controlled access points should be established.

Review the procedures for guests. What are the requirements for visitors? Examples include sign-in or issuance of visitors passes or other forms that identify the person as a visitor.

Do they require escorts to and from their destination?

Are they required to report back to the sign-in point to log out?

What is the procedure if they do not log out, for purposes of positive control?

Are alarm systems working and are they tested on a regular basis? This should include main campus buildings as well as maintenance and storage facilities.

Do you control keys, key cards, fobs, or access codes to campus and administration buildings?

Are alarm pass codes changed when an employee leaves the school? Also, make sure that codes are not widely shared and not a typical sequence (e.g., 1-2-3-4). Best preference would be individual codes, as to have a positive knowledge of who accessed these areas.

Is exterior lighting working and is illumination adequate?

Is interior lighting (night lighting) working and is illumination adequate?

Is there a procedure in place to "walk" the school both inside and out prior to the start of the day? Is the same procedure in place at the end of the school day? Looking for signs of unauthorized entry, vandalism, suspicious items or packages.

Review access control procedures and heighten employee awareness (security and administration officials).

Are doors that should remain locked from the outside during the day kept locked, and are those doors checked periodically to make sure that they are secure?

Train all employees to check these doors, but also consider assigning someone the duty.

Are staff members trained to approach and to assist/screen strangers of any age who are observed in and on school property? Immediately report those who have difficulty explaining their presence.

Are staff trained on how to identify a legitimate visitor's badge? Train everyone to recognize and report suspicious activities on campuses (all staff and students, security, and administration officials)

Are observers who are taking pictures or filming campus activities questioned about their authorization to do so?

Be alert for suspicious vehicles that seem to have no apparent purpose for being on campus or that come, go, and then reappear.

Are specific individuals assigned to inspect the outside of campus buildings throughout the day and to report unattended packages or suspicious vehicles near building perimeters?

Have you developed a plan to handle reports of suspicious activity?

Is everyone trained to report unattended or otherwise suspicious packages found inside campus buildings? Is this specific issue placed on routine checklists for maintenance and janitorial personnel?

Do personnel know what to do if a suspicious package is found?

Have you considered a policy that requires staff and students to identify backpacks, book bags, briefcases, and gym bags visibly with luggage-style ID tags?

During a bomb threat, or other incident that may require building evacuation, are there those assigned to scan the perimeter, from the door to the side walk and the side walk to the street, looking for those watching the activity? Some of us call this "watching the watchers." There are instances when evacuations are hoaxes for the reason of collecting intelligence relating to the evacuation procedures, actions of the school staff, and first responder deployment in order to better plan an attack.

Do you conduct enhanced threat assessments on anniversaries of terror attacks and massacres?
February 14, Marjory Stoneman Douglas school shooting
February 28, start of the Waco Branch Davidian siege
March 19, US Invasion of Iraq
April 19, Oklahoma City bombing
April 19, end of the Branch Davidian siege
April 20, Columbine school shooting
May 2, Death of Osama Bin Laden
September 1, Beslan school siege
September 11, Attacks on the World Trade Center and Pentagon
October 7, US invasion of Afghanistan

These are just a few examples of international and domestic terror/ US military combat events that could trigger an attack. Take into consideration your own local anniversaries that could represent a "day of remembrance" to local groups.

Consider a daily risk and threat assessment, encompassing all possible risks and threats—not just violent threats. Conduct these all-hazard assessments prior to field trips, sporting events, etc. The best way to make this an effective tool is to ensure all staff members have a copy of the risk/threat assessment, in hard copy and even electronically on their mobile devices.

Implement a "tip line" program that allows students, teachers, parents, staff, and other members of the school community to report security-related concerns anonymously, if they choose.
Do you have a zero tolerance for verbal/physical threats of any kind?
Do all members of the school community know that any threat or information about a potential threat must be reported?
Do students and staff know that they are responsible for informing the building principal or other pertinent persons (i.e., school security or RSO) about any information or knowledge of a possible or actual terrorist threat or violent criminal act?
Have you communicated a hard stance on hoaxes intended to mimic terrorist acts?
Do students understand that these hoaxes are crimes?

Is a system implemented to identify students, former students, or others that may not be allowed on school property; and is this system used at all levels, including transportation?

Train staff on identifying and handling suspicious packages and letters (security and administration officials).
Look for any of the following:
If delivered by carrier, check balance to see if parcel is lop-sided or heavy sided.
Handwritten addresses or labels from companies are improper; contact the company and, if it exists, see if it sent a package or letter.
Packages wrapped in string are automatically suspicious, as they cannot go through the mail system.
Excess postage on small packages or letters indicates that the object was not weighed by a post office.
Be aware of no postage or non-canceled postage.
Be aware of any foreign writing, addresses, or postage.
Watch for handwritten notes, such as "To Be Opened in the Privacy of . . . ," "CONFIDENTIAL," etc.
Note improper spelling of common names, places, or titles.
Look for generic or incorrect titles.
Be aware of leaks, stains, powder, or protruding wires, string, tape.
Watch for hand-delivered or "dropped off for a friend" packages or letters.
Look for no return address or nonsensical return address.
Note any letters or packages arriving before or after a phone call from an unknown person asking if you received an item.

Remember: most package bombs are delivered and set up by the attacker.

Train staff on identifying and handling bomb threats (security and administration officials).
Does every phone have the bomb threat checklist (see Appendix D) located nearby?
Do staff members handling phone calls understand its use and importance?
Are staff members trained on bomb threat procedures? If a suspected package is found:
Do not use cell phones or two-way radios.
Do not move or touch a suspected package.
Do not activate the fire alarm.
Are there designated search teams?

In some cases local police bomb squads may require that staff members assist in the search, as they have intimate knowledge of the building and its contents.
Are the staff trained to conduct search patterns in rooms?
Search with at least two people per room.
Divide the room into equal parts, preferably down the middle.
First, search from floor to waist level.
Second, search waist level to top of the head.
Third, search head to ceiling.
Fourth, look into the false ceilings.
Search points:

> HVAC ducting
> Rooftops
> Window ledges
> Bushes
> Garbage cans
> Flower arrangements
> Air conditioner units
> Automobiles

Is an emergency response team (ERT) designated and trained? Training consistent with FEMA's community emergency response team (CERT) concept is recommended (FEMA 2018). Depending on your student population, the size of this team should be between seven and twelve individuals per campus location.
Is the ERT trained on the use of the incident command system (ICS) and adapted its principles for use in an education setting?
FEMA offers free online training including an ICS training program for schools, Course Code IS-100.SCA: Introduction to the Incident Command System for Schools—https://training.fema.gov/is/courseoverview.aspx?code=is-100.sca.
ICS is also a great tool to use during other school activities not related to emergency situations.
Have you contacted local offices of emergency management to have a Community Emergency Response Team (CERT) course presented to those assigned and alternates of the Emergency Response Team?
Has an incident command team been designated, comprised of the following positions (at a minimum):
The incident commander has overall command and control responsibility for the incident.
The operations leader leads the ERT.
The public information officer works closely with the incident commander, the building principal, and the district

superintendent to keep media and parents informed as the incident situation develops.

The liaison officer works closely with the incident commander and the local first responders in the relay of information regarding operations and response.

The safety officer works closely with the incident commander, operations leader, and the liaison officer in ensuring safe conduct of any and all responses.

At some point during the incident the local first responders will assume control; however, do not disband your incident command team until after the incident has concluded. The incident command team should stay activated even during the recovery phase of the operation.

EXERCISE THE PLAN

Have staff trained with local first responders?

Evaluate and exercise your plan; this includes down to the lowest possible levels.

Do you conduct full-scale exercises with staff and first responders at least once a year?

Do you conduct tabletop exercises quarterly?

Do you consider conducting full-scale exercises with students and staff present to add to realism of response and challenges?

Do you administer threat briefings to staff on a regular basis? Base your briefings on changes in threat levels. Also consider a daily threat assessment—not just focused on violent threats but also natural disasters.

EVALUATE THE PLAN WITH EXERCISES

Once the planning process is complete and all staff is trained on the plan, exercises need to be conducted. Some forms of exercises that can be conducted are Drills, Tabletop, and Full-Scale just to name a few. Conduct an after-action review to discuss areas of strengths and weakness, such as:

What was effective with your communication laydown and what were the challenges?

Does the plan allow for flexibility of initiative at the scene?

Is the plan "built to fit the situation" or does the situation drive the plan?

Did first responders and school officials understand their roles and responsibilities?

Was an outside or an in-house evaluator used? How did this impact the assessment?

If changes to the plan are necessary, have you established deadlines for their completion?

FINAL THOUGHTS

Leadership is key to all emergency planning and response actions. If you are not the top decision maker in your organization, you must have your leadership's buy-in; without it, your plan is nothing more than words on paper and will likely fail. You also must be a strong advocate for security in your organization, even if others call you a maverick or approach the topic with a sense of infallibility: it has never happened before; therefore, it will not happen. Certainly the Beslan school never saw what was coming, nor did any of the schools involved in violent crimes in our country. At the very least, preparing for a prolonged, intense terrorist attack will enable you and your staff to handle smaller-scale issues with ease.

The world has changed over the last decade—more than any one of us could have imagined. Thirty years ago, the only emergency-related issue we had to worry about at school was the surprise annual fire drill. The escalating violence in our world and attacks on soft targets such as schools, churches, and hospitals have taught us that we are no longer safe in those places we once considered protected sanctuaries. We must strive to provide a safe environment for our innocent citizens, especially our nation's children and those who wake every day to perform one of the most noble of professions, teaching.

(With thanks to Mr. Ralph R. Fisk Jr., ATO, PCP-1, MEMS. Instructor/trainer, subject matter expert, and thought leader in the areas of emergency management, contemporary risk, and threat assessment [Fisk 2018].)

REFERENCES

DHS (Department of Homeland Security). www.dhs.gov/sites/default/files/publications/active-shooter-how-to-respond-2017-508.pdf (2017).

FEMA (Federal Emergency Management Agency). "Community Emergency Response Teams." www.fema.gov/community-emergency-response-teams (2018).

Fisk, Ralph R., Jr. "Fisk Consulting Blog." https://fiskconsultants.wordpress.com/ (2018).

Appendix H: All Hazards Methodology

RISK ASSESSMENT IMPACT MATRIX

Color code the sections as Green for Unlikely/Minimal Risk, Yellow for Occasional/Severe Risk, Orange for Likely, and Red for Highly Likely/Massive Risk.

Term	Probability of Impact	Remarks
Unlikely	0–25%	No real chance of event happening (However environmental and local considerations may dictate a local action plan.)
Occasional	25–50%	There is a medium chance of event happening and should be covered at least in basic plan.
Likely	50–75%	There is a better than average chance for this event occurring and should be covered in basic and annex plans. Activate emergency action plan in the case of an event. Possible casualties Possible operational compromise Possible property compromise
Highly Likely	75–100%	This event may happen at some course during the life cycle of the program. Activate emergency action plan in the case of an event Likely/highly likely casualties Likely/highly likely operational compromise Likely/highly likely property compromise
Minimal	0–50%	Minimal impact to H/S and minimal impact on property (Normal operations can resume after event has been responded to and recovered from or can be ongoing, during the event.)

Term	Probability of Impact	Remarks
Severe	50–75%	Impact may hamper normal operations for a time during and after the event. Conduct event-based risk assessment after conclusion of event. Resumption of normal operations may resume after consultation with emergency action team and organization senior leadership.
Massive	75–100%	Impact will hamper normal operations for a time during and after the event. Conduct event-based risk assessment after conclusion of event. Resumption of normal operations will be after consultation with emergency action team and organization senior leadership.

Threat Assessment

Company: _____

Date:_____

Hazard Type:	Likelihood of Occurrence*	Estimated Impact on Health & Safety	Estimated Impact on Property
Geological Hazards			
Landslide/Mudslide			
Earthquake			
Tsunami			
Volcano			
Glacier/Iceberg			
Meteorological Hazards			
Drought/Heat Wave			
Lightning Strikes/Thunderstorms			
Tornado			
Flash Flooding/Flooding			
Wildfire			
Hurricane			
Winter Storm/Ice			
Health Hazards			
Pandemic Disease			
Accidental Hazards			
Financial Issues (Depression, Inflation, Financial System Collapse)			

	Likelihood of Occurrence*	Estimated Impact on Health & Safety	Estimated Impact on Property
Transportation Accident			
Hazmat Situation			
Structural Fire			
Electrical/Utility Outages			
Building/Structure Collapse			
Computer Systems Failure			
Water System Failure (Dams, Levees)			
Protection Issues			
Active Shooter			
Physical or Information Security Breach			
Workplace/School/University Violence			
Criminal Activity (Vandalism, Arson, Theft, Fraud, Embezzlement, Data Theft)			
Civil Disturbance, Public Unrest, Mass Hysteria, Riot			
Enemy Attack, War			
Insurrection			
Strike or Labor Dispute			
Product Defect or Contamination			
Harassment			
Discrimination			
Terrorism (Explosive, Chemical, Biological, Radiological, Nuclear, Cyber)			
Sabotage			
Communication Hazards			
Computer System Failure			
Misinformation Disinformation			
Telecommunications Failure			

Likelihood of Occurrence:
Unlikely
Occasional
Likely
Highly Likely
See Risk Assessment Impact Matrix

Hazard Threat Analysis (Part Two)
Health, Safety, Protection Issues

Company:_____

Date:_____

	On-Site	Purchase	Needs/ Recommended
Health/Safety/Protection Issues			
First Aid and Fire Safety			
First Aid Kit(s) On-site (AED)			
Fire Extinguisher(s) On-site (TYPE)			
Bags of Sand			
Light Rescue/Emergency Repair Kits			
Access to Emergency Building Repair Kit (2×4s, Plywood, Plastic Sheeting, Duct Tape, Hammer/nails)			
Emergency Cribbing (2×4, 4×4s cut to 1–2 Feet)			
Tool Kit Pliers, Wrenches, Water and Gas Shut off Tools, Screw Drivers			
Lifting Bar (Tankers/Pry Bar)			
A Backup Power Source			
Health/Life Sustainment			
Extra Water and Rations			
Emergency Lighting			
Flashlights			
Secondary Means of Communications			
Shelter in Place Kit			
Card Games/Board Games			
Administrative			
Bomb Threat Worksheet			
Weather Radio/Television			

Emergency Event Reporting Matrix

What Happened	Who Was Involved
When (Date and Time)	Location
How the Event Happened	Actions Taken by Staff
Property Damage	Nature of Injuries/Illnesses

Emergency Event Detailed Reporting Format

Page 1

Confidential When Complete
Remember to fill out as completely and accurately as possible

Name and Position of Person Making Report:
Date/Time of Report:
Nature of Report: (First Report/Supplemental # _____)
Actions Taken
Time of Notification of Emergency Services (If Applicable):
Fire:

Police:
EMS:
Time of Notification of Executive Management:
What Happened (Be Specific):
When and Where Did It Happen (Exact Date/Time/Place):
Name of Staff Involved (Include Phone Numbers/Addresses):

Emergency Event Reporting Format

Page 2

Confidential When Complete
Remember to fill out as completely and accurately as possible

Names/Ages/Addresses of Participants. Attach Participants List:
Witnesses (Obtain Names/Addresses/Phone Numbers). Attach Additional Sheets if Needed:
Actions Taken by Staff:
Ongoing Actions:

Incident/Disaster Form

(Maintain at Command Center)

Upon notification of an incident/disaster situation the on-duty personnel will make the initial entries into this form, then forward to the ECC, where it will be continually updated. This document will be the running log until the incident/disaster ends and "normal business" resumes.

TIME AND DATE

_____

TYPE OF EVENT

_____

_____

_____

_____

_____

LOCATION

_____

_____

_____

BUILDING ACCESS ISSUES

_____

_____

_____

_____

PROJECTED IMPACT TO OPERATIONS

_____

_____

_____

_____

_____

RUNNING LOG (ONGOING EVENTS)

Item Number	Time	Messages/Incidents	Actions Taken	INT

Item Number	Time	Messages/Incidents	Actions Taken	INT
Person Making Report			Date	Time

(With thanks to Mr. Ralph R. Fisk Jr., ATO, PCP-1, MEMS. Instructor/ trainer, subject matter expert, and thought leader in the areas of emergency management, contemporary risk, and threat assessment.)

Appendix I: Workplace Violence Prevention and Security and Safety Awareness Assessment

WORKPLACE VIOLENCE PREVENTION SURVEY
(EMPLOYEE)

Please take time to review this three-part survey on workplace violence prevention and workplace security awareness. This survey will help us evaluate and analyze the effectiveness of our workplace violence prevention strategies and/or help us shape our approach to the implementation of such strategies. If you have been selected to participate in this survey, please review your awareness and understanding of our workplace violence prevention policy and program as it relates to your personal experiences whether reported or not. Your assistance will help our company/organization assess our ability to determine how effective we are in preventing and responding to incidents that can lead to more serious acts of workplace violence. Please answer each question appropriately. **Part 1** involves **thirty-five YES or NO questions.** You may choose to answer **Not Applicable** or **I don't know** for any response. **Part 2** ask an **additional supporting seven questions,** and **Part 3** asks an **additional twelve questions** to rate your particular workplace setting. Please complete this survey as thoroughly as possible and return it to

Mr./Mrs./Ms._____ (Date)_____

Your Name and Department _____ Shift: 1 2 3

Tell us what you know about your specific workplace relative to your workplace safety and security.

PART 1

(Check the appropriate box.)

		Yes	No	Not Applicable	I don't know
1.	I am familiar with the Workplace Violence Prevention Policy.				
2.	I have received formal training (minimum of three hours) in the area of workplace violence prevention.				
3.	I know what constitutes incidents of workplace violence.				
4.	I am aware of the workplace violence reporting protocols.				
5.	I know that contributing factors can lead to misunderstanding and conflicts.				
6.	I know how to recognize warning signs and risk indicators in reporting potential at risk situations.				
7.	I know the actions that can be taken against me if I am involved in a workplace violence incident.				
8.	I have noticed situations that could (or did) lead to violence *between employees*.				
9.	I have noticed situations that could (or did) lead to violence between *supervisors and managers and/or staff*.				
10.	I have noticed situations that could (or did) lead to violence *between non-employees*.				
11.	I have been harassed *by a non-employee*.				
12.	I have been harassed *by a supervisor or staff member*.				
13.	I have been verbally abused *by an employee*.				
14.	A supervisor or manager or staff member has verbally abused me.				
15.	I have been physically assaulted *by a non-employee*.				

		Yes	No	Not Applicable	I don't know
16.	I have been physically assaulted *by an employee, supervisor, or staff member.*				
17.	I have missed work on at least one occasion because I felt threatened or bullied by an *employee, supervisor, staff, or non-employee* during the course of my employment. *(Please explain)*				
18.	Over the past twleve months I have seen an increase in violent behavior at my worksite.				
19.	I have reported my observations to supervisors but have not noticed any follow up or changes.				
20.	I have requested assistance *from co-workers* in dealing with potential workplace violence incidents.				
21.	After a report is filed there does not seem to be a formal system to track and monitor employee complaints.				
22.	Reported incidents are not taken seriously.				
23.	Following a reported incident there is no feedback.				
24.	When I request assistance there is no follow up or investigation.				
25.	During the past twelve months, I have requested assistance *from management* several times.				
26.	During the past twelve months, I have requested assistance *from the police.*				
27.	In the past twelve months I have witnessed and/or reported an incident that occurred in my workplace.				
28.	I travel between workplaces alone.				
29.	I have a personal safety alarm and/or a panic security system to alert police.				
30.	There is inadequate lighting in the parking lot.				

		Yes	No	Not Applicable	I don't know
31.	I am bothered or worrisome about an existing unresolved workplace situation.				
32.	I am concerned about workplace violence.				
33.	I have received training in active-shooter situations to enhance my personal security.				
34.	I have received training in conflict management and de-escalation techniques.				
35.	I am concerned about safety/security in the areas noted below.				

PART 2

Additional Supporting Questions (Leave blank any question not pertaining to your situation.)

36. In the last twelve months, have you witnessed or been a victim of a workplace violence related incident?
    (Circle answer)　Yes　No　(Briefly describe incident below)
    If yes to above, did you report the incident? (Circle answer)
    Yes　No　(If yes, what was the outcome?)
37. Who did you report the incident to? (Circle answer)
    Supervisor　Safety　Coordinator　Security　Senior Management　Police
    Other (please specify) _____
38. In the last twelve months, following a reported incident was an official investigation conducted?
    (Circle answer)　Yes　No　(Briefly describe incident below)
39. In the last twelve months, following a reported incident were you ever interviewed?
    (Circle answer)　Yes　No　(Briefly describe incident below)
40. In the last twelve months, following a reported incident were you ever informed of the outcome?
    (Circle answer)　Yes　No　(Briefly describe incident below)
41. In the last twelve months, following a reported incident was there an increased emphasis on conflict resolution?
    (Circle answer)　Yes　No　(Briefly describe incident below)

42. In the last twelve months, prior to a reported incident was there a formal workplace violence prevention program instituted? **(Circle answer)**   Yes   No   (Briefly describe incident below)
43. In the last twelve months, following a reported incident did your supervisor inform you of the proper reporting procedures? **(Circle answer)**   Yes   No   (Briefly describe incident below)

PART 3

Rating Section (circle the answer that best expresses your own opinion)

44. The managers at my workplace support the workplace safety and workplace violence prevention—security program. **(Circle one)**
Strongly agree   Agree   No opinion   Disagree Strongly   There is no program
45. My supervisor/manager makes workplace safety and security a priority in our work unit. **(Circle one)**
Strongly agree   Agree   No opinion   Disagree   Strongly
46. I feel comfortable talking to my supervisor/manager about a workplace safety or security issue. **(Circle one)**
Strongly agree   Agree   No opinion   Disagree   Strongly
47. Our workplace safety and security program clearly defines what constitutes workplace violence. **(Circle one)**
Strongly agree   Agree   No opinion   Disagree   Strongly
48. Our workplace violence prevention policy emphasizes reporting all incidents. **(Circle one)**
Strongly agree   Agree   No opinion   Disagree   Strongly
49. My supervisor or manager has reinforced the company's workplace violence prevention policy and program. **(Circle one)**
Strongly agree   Agree   No opinion   Disagree   Strongly
50. I know that what my workplace is as defined under the OSHA regulation is both my permanent and temporary location. **(Circle one)**
Strongly agree   Agree   No opinion   Disagree   Strongly
51. My workplace provides annual refresher training on workplace violence prevention. **(Circle one)**
Strongly agree   Agree   No opinion   Disagree   Strongly
52. My workplace provides new employee safety and security training as part of my new employee orientation. **(Circle one)**
Strongly agree   Agree   No opinion   Disagree   Strongly
53. My workplace provides adequate physical security protective measures. **(Circle one)**

Strongly agree   Agree   No opinion   Disagree   Strongly
54. My workplace has a formal visitor management control policy. (Circle one)
Strongly agree   Agree   No opinion   Disagree   Strongly
55. My workplace provides formal training on domestic/relationship violence. (Circle one)
Strongly agree   Agree   No opinion   Disagree   Strongly
56. My workplace provides formal training on a Hostile Intruder Potential Threat/Disgruntled Person (Active Shooter). (Circle one)
Strongly agree   Agree   No opinion   Disagree   Strongly
57. I feel that my employer offers adequate workplace security and provides for a safe and secure workplace. (Circle one)
Strongly agree   Agree   No opinion   Disagree   Strongly

Please use this space below to provide any additional comments regarding this survey or personal issues that might contribute to at-risk situations affecting your workplace safety and security. Please include current or existing situations as well as past incidents you feel had an adverse impact on employee safety and security. You may include attachments.

This assessment generously contributed by Mr. Felix Nater, president of Nater Associates, Ltd and the foremost violence interdiction expert in the US. Please visit his website at www.naterassociates.com for more information on this important topic.

Appendix J: Syllabus for Soft Target Hardening Course

COURSE DESCRIPTION

In this course, attendees will learn about the vulnerabilities of soft targets, understand the motivation and capabilities of the actors most likely to strike soft targets, critically review case studies of soft target attacks and lessons learned, assess the current threat against soft targets, study hardening tactics and understand their proper application, assess a soft target in their community, and develop a tailored action plan for hardening the facility.

Week 1

Read *Soft Target Hardening: Protecting People from Attack*, 2nd edition, Chapters 1 and 2.

- Define soft targets.
- Explain the difference between threat, vulnerability and risk.
- Define terrorism and identify its goals.
- Understand terrorist motivation to attack soft targets and behaviors.
- Explain black swan theory and discuss how soft target attacks are a black swan.
- Describe our unique vulnerability as Westerners to soft target attacks.
- Summarize the psychology of soft targeting.

Week 2

Read *Soft Target Hardening: Protecting People from Attack*, 2nd edition, Chapter 3.

- Explain the roots of modern terrorism.
- Identify the major international terror groups designated by the State Department and threatening the United States.

- Understand the history of al-Qaeda and the rise of its affiliates.
- Discuss the rise of ISIS.
- Explain Hezbollah's group structure, tactical methodology, proficiency and Western Hemisphere operations.
- Explore Hamas activity in the Western Hemisphere.
- Summarize threat of international terrorist groups to the United States and their propensity to attack soft targets.

Week 3

Read *Soft Target Hardening: Protecting People from Attack*, 2nd edition, Chapter 4.

- Explain the history of domestic terrorism in the United States.
- Define extremism.
- Explore the rise of domestic extremism in the twenty-first century.
- Define right-wing extremism and identify the major actors.
- Summarize left-wing extremism and identify the major actors.
- Understand single-issue or special-interest terrorism.
- Explore homegrown violent extremism including Jihadism and counter radicalization efforts
- Discuss the major Drug Trafficking organizations impacting the United States and their nexus with gangs.
- Summarize threat of domestic terrorist groups to the United States and their propensity to attack soft targets.

Week 4

Read *Soft Target Hardening: Protecting People from Attack*, 2nd edition, Chapters 5 and 6.

- Assess the soft target threat against schools, churches and hospitals.
- Assess the soft target threat against malls, sporting events, and recreational venues.
- Review case studies of soft target attacks on these venues from the last five years.

Week 5

Read *Soft Target Hardening: Protecting People from Attack*, 2nd edition, Chapters 7 and 8.

- Understand emergent issues such as the use of vehicles to attack pedestrians, the growing insider threat, increase of kidnapping

and use of hostages as human shields, the targeting of first responders, exploration of use of WMD, and using drones as a weapons delivery platform.
- Describe steady-state and crisis leadership.
- Explain the importance of intuition.
- Discuss the insider threat as a "fifth column;" summarize the importance of good hiring practices, including background checks; explain the "No Dark Corners" methodology.
- Understand the SIRA method, elements of suicide terrorism, and the face of rage.

Week 6

Read *Soft Target Hardening: Protecting People from Attack*, 2nd edition, Chapters 9, 10, and Appendices.

- Study hardening tactics at global hotspots and best practices we can apply in the United States.
- Learn how to deter and mitigate attack.
- Explain the use of deception in hardening.
- Understand the effects-based hardening methodology.
- Explore physical security tactics.
- Understand the unique challenge of emergency preparedness at soft target locales.
- Explore emergency preparations such as a hold room, command center, and crisis communication through social media and the press.
- Consider hardening challenges at various venues.
- Summarize the twenty takeaways about soft target hardening.
- Study the appendices.

Culminating Project

- Identify a soft target in your community.
- Approach the site manager or leader and discuss what you've learned in the course.
- Together, using the FBI checklist, assess the unique vulnerabilities of the target.
- Identify the Achilles heel, the most pressing vulnerability.
- Thinking about case studies and hardening tactics learned in the course, explore ways to eliminate or reduce the primary vulnerability.
- Using effects-based hardening methodology, develop a time-phased plan to address and mitigate other identified vulnerabilities.

Index

Note: Page numbers in *italic* indicate a figure and page numbers in **bold** indicate a table on the corresponding page.